DATE DUE

GAYLORD			PRINTED IN U.S.A.

PROPERTY

NOMOS

XXII

NOMOS

Lieber-Atherton, Publishers

I	Authority 1958
II	Community 1959
III	Responsibility 1960
IV	Liberty 1962
V	The Public Interest 1962
VI	Justice 1963, reissued in 1974
VII	Rational Decision 1964
VIII	Revolution 1966
IX	Equality 1967
X	Representation 1968
XI	Voluntary Associations 1969
XII	Political and Legal Obligation 1970
XIII	Privacy 1971
XIV	Coercion 1972
XV	The Limits of Law 1974
XVI	Participation in Politics 1975

New York University Press

XVII	Human Nature in Politics 1977
XVIII	Due Process 1977
XIX	Anarchism 1978
XX	Constitutionalism 1979
XXI	Compromise in Ethics, Law, and Politics 1979
XXII	Property 1980
XXIII	Human Rights *(in preparation)*
XXIV	Ethics, Economics, and the Law *(in preparation)*

NOMOS XXII

Yearbook of the American Society for Political and Legal Philosophy

PROPERTY

Edited by

J. Roland Pennock, *Swarthmore College*

and

John W. Chapman, *University of Pittsburgh*

New York: New York University Press • 1980

Property: Nomos XXII
edited by J. Roland Pennock and John W. Chapman
Copyright © 1980 by New York University

Library of Congress Cataloging in Publication Data
Main entry under title:

Property.

   (Nomos ; 22)
   Includes papers presented at the American Society
for Political and Legal Philosophy meetings held in
New York, Dec. 1977.
   Bibliography: p.
   Includes index.
   1. Right of property—Addresses, essays, lectures.
2. Property—Addresses, essays, lectures.
I. Pennock, James Roland.   II. Chapman, John
William, 1923-   III. American Society for Political
and Legal Philosophy.   IV. Series.
JC605.P76   323.4'6   79-55007
ISBN 0-8147-6576-9

Printed in the United States of America

PREFACE

Nomos XXII, Property, derives from the meetings of the American Society for Political and Legal Philosophy held in New York, December 1977, in conjunction with those of the American Philosophical Association, Eastern Division. The topic of those meetings was "The Concept of Property and Its Contemporary Significance." The contributors to this volume, seven of whom particiated in the meetings of the Society, deal both historically and analytically with the concept of property and the right to property, including its relation to other rights, and also with certain aspects of the law of property as it is related to legal theory and to the Constitution. The issues that arise out of the distribution of wealth in modern societies are not discussed in any systematic and empirical manner; and the same is true of Marxist-inspired critiques of capitalism. Each of these subjects would call for independent book-length treatment. Some important lines for future investigations are laid out in Gerald Gaus's bibliography on "Property and Justice," which is included in this volume.

Part I comprises three chapters of an introductory nature. Kenneth R. Minogue leads off with a wide-ranging essay that wrestles with a number of problems. In a key sentence, he declares that "the concept of property became, from the seventeenth century onward, the institutional symbol of that element of federalism which had previously been implicit in the concept of citizenship and political participation." He finds the struggle between society and individual will, or between justice, on the one hand, and liberty, individuality, and human nature, on the other hand, one that gives form and substance to the history of the concept of property. The two following chapters are concerned, in more step-by-step fashion, with the development of this concept. Charles Donahue, Jr., focuses especially on the gradual evolution of a monistic theory of property as the various rights it comprises became agglomerated; and then upon the recent developments in the opposite direction — what might be called the "de-thingification" of property. Thomas C. Grey is especially concerned with this last phenomenon. He argues that the breakdown of the "thing-ownership" conception arises from causes *internal* to the capitalist market system and, moreover, that a consequence of this process is the erosion of the moral basis of capitalism. He concludes that property is no longer an important category in legal and political theory.

Part II is concerned with the ideas of some of our great political theorists. Christopher J. Berry argues that both Hume and Hegel, though in differing ways, see property in some sense as essentially a social matter, in contrast to Locke's theory of property, which Berry regards as thoroughly individualistic. In a similar vein, Frederick G. Whelan takes Blackstone — often considered an ardent advocate of natural rights — as providing a perspective from which one can measure the development of thinking about private property from Locke's era. The idea of property as grounded on natural law evolves in a direction that admits more readily of state regulation. Finally, Peter G. Stillman elaborates Hegel's theory of property at some length, arguing that it provides the very foundation of his political theory and that it is, at least in one proper sense of the word, an individualistic concept as well as a social one. He goes on to show that Marx's views on property are by no means the complete contrary of Hegel's, and he proceeds to discuss the quite intricate relations between the two theories.

The four chapters in Part III consider justification of the institutions of property, not for the most part in terms of past thinkers, but as a problem of contemporary political philosophy. In a rather general consideration of some standard arguments, and some not so standard, and emphasizing their interrelations, J. Roland Pennock comments on the problem of justification. His introductory essay is followed by Lawrence C. Becker's contribution, in which Becker moves on from the position set forth in his *Property Rights: Philosophic Foundations* (London: Routledge & Kegan Paul, 1977). Here Becker deals directly with the moral *basis* of property rights, that is, facts about human nature and the human condition that lend support to moral arguments for property rights. In the following chapter, Richard E. Flathman takes a more skeptical view of the solidity of property rights as they have been asserted in our civilization. By way of conclusion to this part, Hillel Steiner grounds the case for property (equally distributed) on the proposition, which he elaborates, that property provides the only basis on which slavery can be *categorically* condemned.

In Part IV, two papers take up the relation of property rights to other rights, in particular, rights to liberty, equality, and justice. Jean Baechler combines an analysis of the relation of property rights to liberty and equality with vigorous defense of the former. He bases his argument on the theorem that "a political regime can guarantee its members security, prosperity, and freedom only on the condition that each member or coalition of members constitute *autonomous centers of decision.*" Next John W. Chapman, in a discussion of the implications of social justice for freedom and private property, deals with eight particular positions along the "moral gradient" from libertarianism to egalitarianism. He concludes that justice, liberty, and property must stand or fall together.

In the concluding part of the volume, the first three papers depart from our usual procedure in that the first two comment on an already published book; the third is a response to these comments by the author of the book, in the course of which he enlarges upon his own ideas. The book in question is Bruce A. Ackerman's *Private Property and the Constitution.* Duncan MacRae criticizes it from the standpoint of a political scientist and sociologist concerned especially with public policy. He believes Ackerman would accord the legal profession and the courts too much authority and not enough to the political process itself, in which assistance would come from the work of policy-oriented social scientists. T.M. Scanlon, a philosopher and hence committed to taking a comprehensive view, finds Ackerman's contrast between the positions of the "Ordinary Observer" and that of the "Scientific Policymaker" (which involves a "Comprehensive View") rather overdrawn. "Comprehensive Views," he holds, often originate from arguments about some "Ordinary Observation" and, in any case, may involve analysis that begins with the same question as does the "Ordinary Observer" — and may lead to similar results.

These critiques move Ackerman to further reflections on his original application of Wittgensteinian methods to the problem of the relation between law and the larger society. In a general way, subject to nuances and exceptions, he thinks that an "activist" political theory tends to lead to use of the "Scientific Policymaking" technique, whereas political theory that conceives the state in a more neutral role goes with the "Ordinary Observer" style of jurisprudence.

The fourth and final chapter of this Part, and of the volume as a whole, evaluates an often-heard argument to the effect that the Constitution was drawn up with an eye to the interests of the propertied classes and that it continues today to offer special protection to those interests. Lawrence Sager considers arguments that have been and might be made in support of the second part of this proposition and finds them without substance either in the text or the practical operation of our constitutional machinery.

So much by way of guidelines and invitations to the reader. It remains to express our deep thanks to our contributors, whose composition is gratifyingly international in scope; to Kenneth Winston, who chaired the Program Committee for the Society's meetings; and to the ever watchful Eleanor Greitzer, who does far more than serve as a prod to contributors and liaison between them and wandering editors, not to mention our patient publisher.

It is also our pleasure to express again, on behalf of the Society, our indebtedness to the John Dewey Foundation and to the Ritter Foundation for generous benefactions.

J.R.P.
J.W.C.

CONTENTS

Preface   vii
Contributors   xiii
Part I: Historical Trends   1
      1.   The Concept of Property and Its Contemporary
             Significance   3
             KENNETH R. MINOGUE
      2.   The Future of the Concept of Property Predicted from
             Its Past   28
             CHARLES DONAHUE, JR.
      3.   The Disintegration of Property   69
             THOMAS C. GREY

Part II: Some Philosophers on Property   87
      4.   Property and Possession: Two Replies to Locke — Hume
             and Hegel   89
             CHRISTOPHER J. BERRY
      5.   Property as Artifice: Hume and Blackstone   101
             FREDERICK G. WHELAN
      6.   Property, Freedom and Individuality in Hegel's and
             Marx's Political Thought   130
             PETER G. STILLMAN

Part III: The Right to Property   169
      7.   Thoughts on the Right to Private Property   171
             J. ROLAND PENNOCK
      8.   The Moral Basis of Property Rights   187
             LAWRENCE C. BECKER
      9.   On the Alleged Impossibility of an Unqualified
             Disjustificatory Theory of Property Rights   221
             RICHARD E. FLATHMAN
     10.   Slavery, Socialism, and Private Property   244
             HILLEL STEINER

xi

Part IV: Property and Other Rights   267
         11. Liberty, Property, and Equality   269
             JEAN BAECHLER
         12. Justice, Freedom and Property   289
             JOHN W. CHAPMAN

Part V: Legal Theory, Property, and the Constitution   325
         13. Scientific Policymaking and Compensation for the
             Taking of Property   327
             DUNCAN MACRAE, JR.
         14. Comments on Ackerman's *Private Property and the
             Constitution*   341
             T.M. SCANLON
         15. Four Questions for Legal Theory   351
             BRUCE A. ACKERMAN
         16. Property Rights and the Constitution   376
             LAWRENCE G. SAGER
Property and Justice: A Select Bibliography   385
             GERALD F. GAUS

Index   407

CONTRIBUTORS

BRUCE A. ACKERMAN
Law, Yale University

JEAN BAECHLER
*Political Science and Sociology, Centre Nationale de la
Recherche Scientifique, Paris*

LAWRENCE C. BECKER
Philosophy, Hollins College

CHRISTOPHER J. BERRY
Political Science, University of Glasgow

JOHN W. CHAPMAN
Political Science, University of Pittsburgh

CHARLES DONAHUE, JR.
Law, Harvard University

RICHARD E. FLATHMAN
Political Science, The John Hopkins University

GERALD F. GAUS
Political Science, Australian National University

THOMAS C. GREY
> *Law, Stanford University*

DUNCAN MACRAE, JR.
> *Political Science, University of North Carolina at Chapel Hill*

KENNETH R. MINOGUE
> *Political Science, London School of Economics and Political Science*

J. ROLAND PENNOCK
> *Political Science, Swarthmore College*

LAWRENCE G. SAGER
> *Law, New York University*

T. M. SCANLON
> *Philosophy, Princeton University*

HILLEL STEINER
> *Political Science, University of Manchester*

PETER G. STILLMAN
> *Political Science, Vassar College*

FREDERICK G. WHELAN
> *Political Science, University of Pittsburgh*

PART I

HISTORICAL TRENDS

1

THE CONCEPT OF PROPERTY AND ITS
CONTEMPORARY SIGNIFICANCE

KENNETH R. MINOGUE

The problem of property, as it occurs in contemporary political theory, is a problem of justification. At the level of political polemic, socialist writers have attacked the right of private property, whereas liberals and others defended it. But at a philosophical level, the same fundamental question: How ought property to be distributed in a just society? has been no less insistent, and the great success of John Rawls[1] in focusing political philosophy around the concept of justice has, in a sense, put the normative issues raised by property at the very center of political philosophy. In earlier times, however, the topic of property arose as part of a practical inquiry into the relation between social conditions (such as the distribution of property) and the constitution of the state. James Harrington, for example, merely revived a long-standing classical tradition of thought in arguing that the balance of landholding tends to determine the constitutional superstructure.[2] A constitutional state would be possible only if land were widely distributed, and the conjunction of a single landowner in a society with a single ruler of the state could only result in despotism.

The tradition of political thought yields, then, not one but two problems of property, one arising from the value of justice, the other from the value of liberty. But they are largely different *kinds* of theory, one being largely normative, the other being largely empirical. Normative inquiries into the just distribution of property are seldom concerned with constitutional possibility, whereas those interested in empirical generalizations about the relation between distribution of property, on the one hand, and constitutional structures, on the other, have paid virtually no attention to the justification of property titles. The concern of this essay is to bring these two questions into the same focus, and the best way to bring out the significance of the issue is to broach the apparently innocuous question: Is property a central topic in political philosophy?

Remembering modern thinkers from Locke onward, we would be likely to decide that property is of the essence of political philosophy. "Necessity begat property," wrote Blackstone in a typical view of the period, "and, in order to insure that property, recourse was had to civil society, which brought along with it a train of inseparable concomitants; states, government, laws, punishments, and the public exercise of religious duties."[3] The state arose, that is to say, for the regulation and security of individual property rights. Marx takes exactly the same view and transposes all questions of liberty into questions about the effects of the institution of private property. And although the term "property" hardly appears in Rawls's index (there is a short entry covering "private property economy"), *A Theory of Justice*, in dealing with the distribution of goods, cannot help but give property a central place. It would seem from these considerations that political philosophy cannot avoid treating the subject. But it is alternatively possible to argue that property is fundamentally peripheral to politics, because it belongs to the private world of households and business dealings and is consequently of only indirect concern to the res publica. Aristotle believed that the polis was an association of households, and the head of a household was a proprietor whose business it was to manage the household's property (including slaves) for the benefit of its members. The household was in the sphere of economics, or household management, and was quite distinct from politics, which concerned deciding what was best for the city. Aristotle does indeed discuss[4] the question of how property (in effect, land) ought to be distributed, but he does so not in a context of justice but in a context of how civil discord may be prevented. The distribution of land is, as it were, a condition of social life to be settled prior to the question of justice, which is about how social and political structure is reflected in the constitution. Phaleas of Chalcedon appears in this discussion as a kind of proto-socialist, since he believed that all the citizens of a polis should have equal amounts of property, but he did this merely because he though it would prevent civil discord. The institution of agrarian laws in Greece and Rome shows (rather like our own antimonopoly legislation) a recognition that certain distributions of property may be hostile to certain desirable constitutions. Property has thus always been recognized as having an important place, like climate and the fertility or otherwise of the environment, in politics, but not necessarily a central one.

No one would doubt that justice is a central problem for political philosophy, nor that disputes about property may often raise questions of justice. But the relation between property and justice is contingent, and does not imply the centrality of property. Indeed how, we may ask, could property ever be a central issue, given that it is nothing else but one term of the relationship of owning and consequently can never be what the Hegelians call a "concrete whole"? We shall indeed find that the attempt to grasp the concept of property is beset with mirage effects. The best way to approach it is by indirection, and I propose to do so by linking it to the idea of citizenship as Europeans have understood that idea at various points in their history. The Greek and Roman citizen was the head of a household containing women, children, slaves, and perhaps clients. So too was a medieval magnate. Modern citizenship, by contrast, includes every member of the community provided that he or she has reached the age of eighteen and is neither criminal nor insane. We commonly interpret this change as an extension, or democratization, of the right of citizenship, but we are wrong. Citizenship has been transformed. In the polis, the Roman Republic, and in the medieval world, a citizen was in effect a magnate or power in his own right, deliberating along with other magnates about what ought to be done in the public interest. Now, it was precisely this element of independent power possessed by the citizen in his relations with the sovereign element of the state that constituted citizenship, and thus distinguished a civil society from the kind of despotism that has always haunted and repelled the minds of Europeans from at least the time of Aristotle onward. An Oriental despot was defined as the owner, not only of the land, but of all the subjects within his realm. The grand signor of the Ottomans, wrote the Venetian ambassador to the Porte in an entirely typical letter of 1585, can "of course seize whatever he wants from his subjects when he pleases."[5] The subject of such a total, arbitrary, and capricious power was helpless against his ruler and, having no secure property rights himself, was in effect the property of his ruler. We may sum up this point by saying that in earlier times the conception of the state was implicity federal, an association of people each of whom exercised a degree of independent power; the basis of that independent power might well be seen as primarily residing in the right of property.

The modern citizen is, of course, quite different. *Every* subject is now a citizen and he is thus a member of a different *sort* of association from the civil societies of earlier times. One of the main differences is that the modern state is a source of direct and substantial benefits to its members. It is true that this is not entirely new. Aristotle tells us that "there was once a time when two obols were a sufficient allowance [for ceremonial attendances], but now that this has become the tradition men are always wanting something more, and are never contented until they get to infinity."[6] In a discussion of the changes in the Roman Republic attempted by the Gracchi, we learn that "In the larger cities of the Greek East it had become a generally accepted doctrine that the state was responsible for the welfare of the poor. . . ."[7] In medieval times civil rulers generally left the arrangement of benefits to the needy to the church, but from Tudor times onward, poor laws arranged for some help for those in need. But none of this prepares us for a radical change in the European conception of the state that can be seen as beginning to emerge already in the seventeenth century. The state, now coming to be recognized by that name, and constituted by the concentration of powers previously held by such disparate authorities as church, Parliament, and nobility, began to conceive of itself as the organizer of the energies of its subjects. It was, to be sure, some centuries before states turned into what Daniel Bell has called "public households,"[8] both managing and disposing directly of a large proportion of the resources of the entire community. Even in the seventeenth century, the actual property of the state in most parts of Europe was limited to what military and administrative necessity required. But by the nineteenth century the outline of the modern welfare state could already be seen.

Now, although there has been an immense amount written on this subject, there does not seem to me to be much in the way of terminology that quite suits my purpose.[9] The institution that concerns me is the modern state, but I wish to emphasize the difference between the kind of civil association in which the (limited class of) citizens consisted of independent powers with their own purposes, on the one hand, and the kind of modern community in which everyone is a "citizen" and also something like a shareholder and beneficiary in benefits accruing from resources managed, or at least acquired in various ways, by the government. Let us employ the traditional term "civil society" for the first, and let us term the second "civil community." The adjective "civil" here is to indicate that the members are people with rights to participate in the public business; the word "community" is meant to pick up the densely interconnected relations between the members of this human aggregate. The word "community" is also designed to pick up associations with the ideal of *Gemeinschaft,* in which term much of this development has been discussed and pondered.

Historically, the civil community emerged from the civil society by way of disputes about property as a qualification for political participation. In Great Britain, the history of these disputes stretches from the Levellers in the 1640s to at least the Third Reform Act of 1884. In the United States, manhood suffrage was achieved rather earlier. How has this change come about? It has resulted from the spread of a generalized, and often passionate, hostility to the very idea of private property. The most violent statement of this hostility was, of course, Proudhon's paradox that property was theft. Property was thought to constitute an unjust form of power exercised by one man over another, and hence a property qualification was nothing more than a monopolization of the power of the state in the hands of the already privileged so that they could arrange things to suit themselves. We shall presently consider some of the thoughts consequent upon this idea, but we may note here that even in the middle of a severely formal book on the logic of justifying property claims, the effect of this hostility is such that one modern writer can write, as if it were the most uncontentious of truisms: "The history of property acquisition is a sordid one."[10] It must be counted exceedingly curious that the very idea of property should have become derided in direct proportion to the spread of prosperity.

In view of this almost automatic denigration, it becomes important to see what those who supported a property qualification for the suffrage were concerned with. Property came to be, in fact, the conversion of a tradition into a principle. A limited set of people had traditionally taken part in English politics; most people did not. As political arrangements became clarified and formalized in early modern times, property was the obvious test allowing a clear demarcation between the political and the nonpolitical classes. Property signified three things: independence, responsibility, and liberty.

It signified *independence* because a man of property was less likely to be dependent upon another man's goodwill than someone with nothing to sell but his labor. This criterion meant that personal servants, who long constituted a very large proportion of the population, could not be citizens, and it is on this very point of independent judgment that the Levellers rested their argument for making all free and independent men capable of exercising the suffrage.[11] In effect, ownership of property made it likely that a man was a householder; lack of it indicated the likelihood that he had the status of a client. Second, property signified *responsible judgment* for reasons most persuasively advanced in various passages of the writings of Edmund Burke. Most property was inherited and therefore gave a man a sense of the past; the present owner, usually being keen to hand it on to his descendants, could be relied upon to think responsibly about the future. Property was thus the material link constituting the state's partnership between the living, the dead, and those yet to be born.[12]

Finally, property was, as we have seen, the condition of a state in which liberty was possible. The man of property was preeminently someone charged with the maintenance of conditions of liberty and opposition to capricious and absolute government. And although the liberty of everyone was important and indivisible, those with great aggregations of property were charged with the responsibility of maintaining a state in which liberty was possible at all. Such men were the great oaks under which the browsing cattle of a population could happily rest.[13]

My argument is, then, that the concept of property became, from the seventeenth century onward, the institutional symbol of that element of federalism that had previously been implicit in the concept of citizenship and political participation. Both the attack on property and its defense signified, no doubt, many things. At times, the cry of property may well have sustained self-seeking magnates opposed to all change, although in fact the history of Great Britain suggests that this must have been a relatively rare phenomenon. We need not doubt that property and selfishness were sometimes conjoined, but what we must above all avoid is falling—as Karl Marx notably does—into the error of identifying a type of motive, namely egoism, with a social institution, namely private property.[14] Greed and selfishness are extremely frequent occurrences in human life, and they do not need an institutional structure to sustain them; rather, they invade all institutional structures. The simple idea that it needs only a change in some external thing (such as the structure of property rights) to transform the human condition is superstition lurking behind many treatments of the subject. Property comes to be the outward, visible sign of an inward and invisible disgrace. But although the defense of property was no doubt tainted with the usual partiality of human nature, it was also the defense of a certain sort of responsible participation in politics by a limited class of solid and responsible men. Correspondingly, the attack on property *also* signified an attack upon what I have called civil society and an espousal of the idea of civil community. In time, the most popular version of the civil community by far came to be called socialism, but what concerns me is really an idea much more fundamental than the various (and highly miscellaneous) proposals that have been advanced under that name. Although that idea has usually focused upon the idea of property, it is actually much broader in scope and is concerned with nothing less than the question of how we ought to live. It is in this context that we may judge Locke's fatal justification of the idea of private property.

That justification involved the issues we have raised, but it transposed them into a different key by seeking, in the manner of the time, a rational origin to explain the idea of property. Locke is often said to be a bourgeois writer seeking to defend bourgeois property rights, but to the extent that this is true and relevant to anything specific, it will appear that he chose exactly the wrong way to serve this cause.

He employed the familiar Old Testament materials as a justification of property, but it is not entirely clear what his justification was directed against. Every Christian knew from the Book of Genesis that God had given man dominion over the fruits of the earth and that as a result of the fall of man, labor was necessary to convert those fruits into things useful for man. Locke's own solution in section XXVIII of the *Second Treatise* to the problem of how to convert common property to individual use smacks of a certain impatience, as if he recognized it as in part a bogus problem. He rejects the consent theory of property by parodying it as requiring the consent of all mankind to each and every immediate appropriation from nature. Labor, we are told, put the difference of value on everything. It is difficult, however, to justify the origin of private property in terms of labor without seeming to justify (much more plausibly, and also more disruptively) the present possession of property in the same terms, whatever array of qualifications is assembled to prevent such an inference being made. Out of this somewhat obscure intellectual project, a host of questions emerge.

Some come immediately to mind. One of them is the paradox on which the appeal of socialism was to rest a century later: in the world as it now is, those who labor have little property and those with property seem to do little labor. This observation is no doubt misleading. It is complicated by an equivocation about the idea of labor, which is dominated by the metaphor of sweat on the brow. Hence it is that the least imaginative work counts most securely as labor. The squires and merchants of the seventeenth century were far from idle men, but administration and entrepreneurship do not so obviously qualify for the title of labor as the felling of trees and the planting of corn.

A more serious problem is that Locke does not greatly concern himself with analyzing the concept of property into what have in later times come to seem its constituent parts. Acorns, water in pitchers, landed estates, and the property each of us has in his own person are all run together with a fine insouciance. Writers after Locke have sharpened considerably a distinction between personal property (sometimes extended into the rather different idea of what caters to immediate human needs) and productive property or capital.[15] My toothbrush and my farm are certainly both my own property, but we are now very well aware that a justification of my right to own my toothbrush raises different considerations from a justification of my right to own my farm. An argument vindicating the right of an isolated forest dweller to own the acorns he picks up for his supper does not go far to establish the right to great landed estates; and the moves by which Locke extends his justification of property past its supposed beginnings are, as many commentators have pointed out, less convincing than those beginnings themselves.[16] In addition to these problems, there remains the fact that we are on shaky ground in criticizing Locke because it is hard to discover what weight ought to be given to his arguments. It is clear that what interested him is not precisely the same as what interests us; and that the theological question is central to what he had to say: given that God gave the earth and its fruits to men in common, how is it that any man can exclude any other man from some part of the earth?[17] Before clarifying Locke's significance as it appears in this argument, it is necessary to consider the idea of property in more general terms.

II

The idea of property is rather like an iceberg. It is more complicated than it looks, and much of its significance is submerged. As a normative problem, it might seem that its general outline is simple:

How are we to discover the right set of rules governing a situation in which persons manage things? For it does at least seem obvious that ownership is a relation involving a person at one end and a thing (of some sort) at the other. We might well congratulate ourselves that this excellent bit of simplification is the result of modern moral enlightenment. In the past, persons could own persons, if the latter were slaves. The modern world has institutionally and conceptually smoothed out at least that complication. Again, modern practices would seem to contrast with those of the Middle Ages in that ownership is an exclusive right to enjoy limited only by law, by contrast with the various forms of feudal duty that could at times engulf the inheritor of a fief.[18] We are accustomed to the truism that the modern world is getting much more complicated all the time, and it is perhaps salutary to observe that in some respects it has been simplified. Yet there are significant complications with which Locke did not adequately deal, although some of them were inevitably present as the background to his thought.

Consider, for one thing, the fact that property is the concept by which we find order in things. The world is a bundle of things, and things are recognized in terms of their attributes or properties. This works both at the social and the epistemological levels. The etymological root of the term (*proprius*-one's own) gives us the sense of the connection between a property and what possesses it. Whiteness is a property of snow, and leafiness of trees in summer, and it is appropriate that it should be so. We extend this ordering into social situations to discover ways of behaving that are *appropriate* to situations. Respect is a *proper* response to the elderly and to dignitaries. When in a recent film *La Cecilia* an anarchist spits out: "Organization? Property!" he is making a profound connection, and it runs both ways. The word "property," like the word "law," belongs both to civil and to scientific life. It is well known that we can break some laws (like laws against theft) but merely illustrate others (as when we illustrate the law of gravity by falling off a cliff). Similarly, I can alienate some property (such as swapping my penknife for something else) but can only exercise other properties (such as exercising my capacity to run fast). It might seem that these considerations relate only to a remote and irrelevant sense of the word "property," but we shall, I think, discover that etymological blood is thicker than logical water.

Consider also the fact that almost everything in the world may be identified as someone's property. This extends to the most remarkable things. The air we breathe, it might be thought, belongs to no

one; but I can object if the pure and wholesome air around my house
is polluted by a neighboring factory or a newly established fish-and-
chips shop. The clouds above would seem to be free from such *appropriation* but in times of drought one American state has brought
another to court on a charge of "cloud-rustling."[19] Lord Byron once
apostrophized the sea with the words:

Man marks the earth with ruin — his control
Stops with the shore.[20]

No longer. The law of the sea and modern technology have con-
jointly seen to that. The history of human endeavor, from man's first
hesitant scramblings upon this planet up to his present dizzy emi-
nence is a history of progressive appropriation, and indeed also of the
continuing invention of new things (such as copyrights) that might be
appropriated. And at the same time, it has been to create an orderly
understanding of things in terms of their properties.

Hence the term "property" cannot but conjure up for us a spectrum of types of property, ranging, as it were, from the girl with
green eyes to the lady with the little dog and then to the tenant of
Wildfell Hall. Now, in each of these cases, the property cited is a
means of identification and, to put the matter around the other way,
people and things cannot even be identified except in terms of their
properties. Further, much of the criticism of the general idea of
property amounts to saying that people should be identified and
judged in terms of properties like being green eyed and golden
hearted rather than in terms of properties like being the heiress to a
bundle of 5 percent bonds. For it seems to us that "personal properties" (like being green eyed) are part of nature and the person,
whereas claims to land or shares in industry are merely the contingent excrescences of a mismanaged and inegalitarian system of production. The ownership of Wildfell Hall, it often seems, is a form of
power that allows us to exploit other people, whereas (we might say,
though we could hardly say it with much conviction) the possession of
green eyes is natural, and not capable of being exploited.

There is, then, a significant continuity between property understood as the ownership of productive capital and property understood as personal characteristics, a point that haunts the literature
and is recognized in Locke's famous remark that "Every man has a
property in his own person."[21] Most political discussion, however,
assumes that property can be satisfactorily divided at some point between obviously productive capital and personal characteristics. Between the two lies the no-man's-land of personal property, and many

attempts have been made to determine just what forms of personal property escape the charge of being forms of exploitative power. Our problem is: How can we clarify the structure of thought underlying these issues?

The first step in such a clarification is to be clear about the terms of ownership. In what capacity does one own property? We have taken it for granted that it is persons that own property, and indeed it is this assumption that allows us to assimilate personal characteristics like green eyes to the possession of capital assets like landed estates. But in what capacity does a person own a property? Persons are clearly centers of consciousness, and locations of desires, and are also animated bodies, and in each of these aspects they clearly possess properties; but they own properties only insofar as they are *wills*. It is in their activity of willing that individuals seek to appropriate things and use what they have in order to bring about such changes in the world as may satisfy their desires.

The second step in such a clarification is to distinguish between properties lying dormant, as it were, and properties in active use. The ownership of agricultural land leads to the active management of property, and this is very likely to affect the lives of others. A strawberry birthmark on my leg is, except in very odd circumstances, a "property" only in the sense of an attribute; it plays no part in my relations with other people. A distinction of this sort, between an active and a passive sense of property would seem to underlie most proposals for a radical change in the distribution of goods of this world. Communist states, for example, vest the management of productive property in some form of communal will, but allow individuals some sort of property rights in their toothbrushes and the clothes on their backs. But where should this line be drawn? It might well be possible to equalize the number of toothbrushes possessed, but equalizing strawberry birthmarks would be difficult, and the principle of such equalization would soon lead to logical impossibilities. Indeed, it might seem that it would be pointless, rather like demanding that every stone in the world ought to be the same size. But it would not, of course, be pointless if these personal properties were being actively managed and thus gave power over other people. Green eyes are, from one point of view, merely identifying properties like strawberry birthmarks; but when flashed to charm or to express anger, they become sources of power by which one person may be able to exploit others.

These distinction have profound implications for the understand-

ing of human societies. They involve the bifurcation of the practical
problem of property into two radically different possibilities. The
first of these is that people's property should be equalized. This is a
pragmatic principle that in one version or another has always had a
great deal of support, and policies derived from it may well make
perfectly good political sense even if the logic of the principle itself
should prove to be defective. And defective it evidently is. For a great
number of familiar reasons, it is virtually impossible to equalize the
goods with which each person (or should it be families? or com-
munes?) is endowed. But even if one could, such equalization would
in fact be unequal. What one person can do with two acres and a
cow, or even a chicken in the pot, is vastly different from what
another can do. Beyond these obvious considerations lies a
horizonless space of problems arising from the active deployment of
personal properties in the game of life. Marlene Dietrich's legs are
not merely part of the standard human equipment; they are ex-
ploitable capital and recognized as such by insurance companies.
Only one bold thinker has ever faced up to these problems in a
serious way—the novelist Kurt Vonnegut. In a short story called
"Harrison Bergeron,"[22] he has envisaged a society in which an official
called the Handicapper-General put small noisy devices into the
heads of intelligent men so as to reduce their wits to an average level,
and he forces graceful ballerinas to wear lead-ballasted shoes so that
their gracefulness does not exceed that of the clumsy of the world.[23]

The second possibility is one to which we shall return. Let us first,
however, summarize what we have said about property by saying that
it involves two sets of distinctions. Active properties are anything the
will can use to produce an effect in the world and include everything
from productive capital to personal characteristics. Passive properties are simply attributes or possessions not of a will, but of a person;
they may serve to identify and constitute that person but are not used
to produce effects in the world. The impossibility of the equalization
principle arises from the fact that this distinction is clearly not one
between actual things in the world, but merely between different human attitudes, or uses of things. There is virtually nothing in the
world that cannot become active property.

Besides this distinction, we have invoked another and more
familiar distinction between types of property, but it is a distinction
that has the character of a spectrum. Some property is, as it were,
natural and consists of personal attributes like green eyes, quick wits,

strong hands, and so on. Some property is personal, such as the clothes on our back and the food on the plate before us. Possibly the little dog owned by the woman in Chekhov's story might come into this class, but the exponents of animal rights might wish on that point to issue a demurrer. And some property is productive, such as farms, factories, lathes, or anything that will allow us to hire a work-man and set him to work. Money, as being the power to acquire many kinds of property, must be classed with this third type.[24]

Now, it is important to recognize that we are here dealing with a spectrum of types of property, not only because the attempt to establish watertight classes of property has proved to be theoretically impossible, but also because attempts at practical implementation of it in communist states have produced endlessly unstable results. Some have tried to make a clear line of distinction but are haunted by the fact that the distinction, though plausible, is arbitrary. One might almost say that "a spectrum is haunting Europe — the spectrum of property." It can cease to haunt, like all specters, only when it has been recognized for what it is. On the face of it, it is plausible to think that some forms of property are preeminently likely to be exploited in attaining power over men (such as land and factories) and that other properties are merely part of human individuality. But in an important sense, the magnetism of a dictator or the glib tongue of a confidence trickster are no less properties that may be used to exploit others than is capital itself. This is one more of the ways in which the problem of property in political philosophy dissolves into another question; in this case, it dissolves into questions of the will and the way in which we use the things of this world.

We have seen that one solution to the practical problem of unequal powers of enjoyment of property (sometimes described in terms of self-realization or self-fulfillment) is the principle of equalizing the goods of this world. We also saw that that principle is essentially incapable of achieving the equal powers of self-realization it seeks. In the actual activity of politics, however, it is in practice perfectly possible to take property away from some people and give it to others; and hence the principle of equality has a kind of prominence in theory, resulting from its practical uses, that is not theoretically warranted. But another and more profound way of dealing with the problem, whatever its practical disadvantages, does give the promise of greater coherence. Instead of equalizing property, one might destroy its correlate, the will.

Space permits mention of but three of the ways in which this might be done. A casual and common way of doing it is to transpose the things we most commonly seek out of the idiom of wants and desires into the idiom of needs. Needs are the necessary conditions for the equilibrium of an organism, and it is possible by concentrating on abstract features of behavior to ignore the element of free will in human actions. Men are treated, instead, as complicated physiological systems. The will disappears and material things lose their aspect of property. A variety of ancillary theorizing supports this dissolving of the concept of the will, most of it having to do with a denial of the freedom of human action and a determined attempt to interpret what people do as being the result of a set of conditioning factors. The second way in which the individual will may be destroyed is often associated with the first: it consists in allowing individuals to possess personal property but to vest all productive property in some form of collective will. In socialist thought, there is much discussion about whether the collective will should be one or many, whether it should be the state, the party, the commune, collective, or some other organ that will perfect the translation of what the members want directly into the policies of the organ. But quite apart from socialist thought, modern states have shown a strong tendency to evolve from what we have called civil societies into what we have called civil communities, and this means increasingly that the management of productive resources is at a minimum supervised by, and at a maximum totally managed by, the state. Nor is this the result of grand struggles to wrest the control of property away from individual property holders. Our moral dispositions are changing, and we all tend these days to think even of such things as trained talent as a national resource (and hence we talk of "brain drains"). When it was discovered that Lady Churchill had destroyed a painting of her husband by the notable painter Graham Sutherland, many people were shocked that an individual should exercise such power over her property without consideration for the national interest in such an object.[25]

We live then in a half world between an inherited tradition, allowing individual ownership of most kinds of property, and a growing tendency to restrict and abolish individual willing insofar as it deploys capital resources. But it will be clear even from this very brief discussion that this halfway house is conceptually unstable. It is probably none the worse for that; the conditions of life never completely make sense, and we should not expect them to do so. If they did, reality would freeze and time would have a stop. But the theoretical point is clear: there is no fundamental distinction between the three kinds of property we have discussed, and the property that is merely a passive attribute can at any time become an active resource we may use in getting our way or fulfilling our will. The only real solution is the total abolition of property, which requires the abolition of the will and of any sense of mine and thine. In practice, it is hard to see how this could be achieved, but it has certainly been conceived, most notably perhaps in Plato's *Laws*. One can at least imagine a situation in which men see through the eyes of the community and hear with the ears of the community. Such a transformed human nature has long been one of the great human dreams.

The problem of property turns, then, into a problem of individuality and what beckons to us is the project of devising a community that will defeat the untidiness by which men lead lives that vary greatly in happiness, fulfillment, and value. But any such project would require a mighty power capable of remaking human nature itself. The conceptual instability of the idea of property thus brings us back to the traditional preoccupations with *liberty* and *property* — and back also to Locke.

III

Locke is a curious figure in political philosophy. Generally regarded as a cautious and prudent bourgeois, he was the promoter of one revolution, and his work has never failed to inspire radical and revolutionary tendencies in subsequent generations. He is a Janus figure, whose explicit arguments look back to Aquinas and Hooker, but who contains germs of radicalisms he himself could hardly have imagined — germs found growing luxuriantly in the writings of Condillac, Paine, and the Ideologues. Locke's arguments on property are of just this character, and the reason is that he attempted something very odd: a comprehensive justification of property as originating in the state of nature.

Earlier writers sought nothing so ambitious as a justificatory origin of the right of property; they emphasized that it was a consequence of human laws. Private property, Aquinas tells us, is not opposed to natural law, but is an addition to it, devised by the human reason.[26]

And Hobbes insists that there is no property in the state of nature, but that property strictly arises only as the result of the laws made by the sovereign. "Seeing therefore the introduction of *propriety* is an effect of commonwealth," he tells us in Chapter 24, "which can do nothing but by the person that represents it, it is the act only of the sovereign; and consisteth in the laws, which none can make that have not the sovereign power. And this they well knew of old, who called that *Nomos*, that is to say, *distribution*, which we call law; and defined justice, by *distributing* to every man *his own*." Hobbes is perfectly aware that labor often transforms what is found in nature into commodities useful to man, but he makes no attempt at suggesting a labor theory of value. Nor would he have wished to have done so, because it would have caused him more problems that it would have solved.

So far as Hobbes was concerned, some notional right to a piece of property carried over from the state of nature would have been so much divisive lumber likely to cause quarreling in the civil society and in any case incapable of being juxtaposed against the power of the sovereign without reducing Hobbes's thought to absurdity. Hobbes accepts the consequence, which is that the sovereign has an initial and overriding right of distribution. The constitution of *mine*, and *thine*, and *his*, he tells us, "belongeth in all kinds of commonwealth to the sovereign power," and in this case he has the common law of England on his side and he goes on to tell us that a people coming into possession of a land by war (which is, so far as Europe is concerned, the universal situation) may leave to many, or most, or all of them their estates—by contrast with the Jews, who, he remarks exterminated the ancient inhabitants. After such a conquest, "they hold them afterwards, as of the victor's distribution; as the people of England held all theirs of William the Conqueror."[27]

But if the right to property is created by nothing else but the laws made by the sovereign, who is taken by Hobbes to have a fundamental right to all property in the kingdom, then how is a civil sovereign to be distinguished from an Oriental despot? The risk that this absolute sovereign is a despot is clearly present if we juxtapose the traditional view of the despot as the owner, and therefore manager, of everything in his realm (including his subjects), with Hobbes definition of "propriety" as consisting in "a right to exclude all other subjects from the use of them; and not to exclude their sovereign, be it an assembly, or a monarch."[28] It is in fact clear from Chapter 24 of *Leviathan* that Hobbes thinks it vain for the sovereign to manage land in a public, rather than merely in a natural, capacity. The absolute centrality in Hobbes's thought of this distinction between a public and a natural capacity, along with his consistent assumption that the sovereign will act in a regular and law-governed manner, clearly distinguishes his conception of absolute sovereignty from the notion of an Oriental despotism. But as we have seen, the minds of many seventeenth-century Europeans were haunted by the possibility of a sovereign turning into a despot. Locke's characteristically Whiggish solution to all problems of this kind was to attempt to entrench whatever he thought valuable in a moral realm beyond the tampering of sovereigns and positive law. This is clearly why he elevates the common opinion that there "needeth no more but the labour and industry"[29] of men to enjoy the fruit of nature as given to them by God into a supposedly natural justification of an original right to private property.

The problem we face with Locke's argument about property is the same problem that confronts us in judging many arguments in the *Second Treatise*; namely: What is Locke arguing against, and at what level is the argument to be taken? Just as Locke was long taken to have been arguing against Hobbes rather than against Filmer, so also he has often been taken as a defender of the institution of private property. But to interpret him in this way is implicitly to set up a protosocialist belief in communal property, which Locke was trying to refute. It is true that the seventeenth century had indeed thrown up a few odd sects like the Diggers who did affirm such views, but it is in the highest degree unlikely that Locke was particularly bothered about such people. Nor were they likely to be found among those who would buy the *Two Treatises of Government*. What we do know for sure is that Locke's main enemy was monarchial absolutism in the form of James II, with whom he had no quarrel whatever about the validity of the institution of private property. But he certainly did have a quarrel with James about the limits of the power of sovereigns, and it is in that context that the issue of property arose.

This view is strengthened if we remember the distinction between personal and productive property. Even in a work as spectacularly casual as the *Two Treatises of Government*, it would seem extremely odd to produce a defense of productive property—in fact a defense of large-scale landholding—in terms of a charming pastoral fantasy about a chap satisfying his hunger by picking up some acorns and boiling them. The chapter on property in the *Second Treatise* rests fundamentally on the basis of personal property and the satisfaction of need. With every step by which Locke moves from this case toward justifying the complex property structure of modern Europe, the argument becomes more vulnerable as a justification; but it does serve the main purpose of removing some fundamental basis of property rights out of the jurisdiction of sovereigns and the civil law.

Our conclusion, then, is that in pursuit of one aim — namely establishing a justification of the origin of property independent of positive law — Locke raised a problem of the distribution of property that is categorically unsolvable. If we take the labor theory of property justification seriously, and if we abandon hungry noble savages collecting acorns, we shall very soon find ourselves in very serious difficulties. Most working upon the fruits of nature is cooperative; and the more complex an economy becomes, the more difficult it becomes to work out the relative contribution of different kinds of labor and skill to the fabrication of a particular product. Apart from the operation of the market, the relative assessment of inputs and outputs is so complex as to be beyond the powers of any principled disentanglement. In addition, the labor theory of value encourages us to see property, not as a legal right, but as part of a productive process. It belongs more to the history of economic thought than to that of jurisprudence. We are driven inexorably toward a view of the community as a single productive unit, and of the government as the initial beneficiary of all this production, which is charged with the difficult business of distributing it in a just manner. In other words, the moment one switches the question away from the legal right to property toward the question of how property may be justified in terms of a process of production (which is implied by moving labor into the center of the problem), one can find no real stopping place short of a completely socialized manner of living, a fully elaborated version of what we have called in this essay a civil community. The irony is that such a community, when fully developed, is exactly what Locke would have regarded as a despotic government. The irony has not been lost on some of those who have read Locke. Thus, Lawrence Becker is clearly aware that Locke's argument cannot easily be extended from personal to productive property, and far from continuing the Macphersonite picture of Locke as merely a "bourgeois apologist," he concludes from the fact that in competitive situations, ownership of productive property must be extended, that "Locke's argument then becomes a foundation for socialism rather than 'possessive individualism.' "[30]

Our conclusion about Locke illustrates well the general character of the problem of property: it is extraordinarily volatile. Locke raised a problem about property that not only cannot be solved in its own terms but that leads logically toward exactly the very conception of political life (as the union of political power and economic management) he wished to oppose. In this small context of the great broad history of discussions of property, Locke is the bridge by which the earlier problem of property as the basis of the constitution passed over into the normative problem of a just distribution of the goods of this world. Both problems have continued to provoke discussion, but they have led largely separate lives.

The concern with property and the constitution goes back as far as Solon and Lycurgus and focused for many centuries around the issues of agrarian laws and sumptuary laws. Its central idea, however, lay in the belief that the union of the power to rule and the power to manage the resources of a community in one single man was a special form of government called despotism, that it was inferior to a civil society, and desperately unfree. This strand of thought arising from property has generated some of the most characteristic preoccupations of European thinkers, especially since the days of Harrington and Montesquieu. De Tocqueville's analysis of the modern idea of equality, John Stuart Mill's distinction between the active and the passive characters in politics, Marx on the Asiatic mode of production, and more recently Karl Wittfogel's theory of Oriental despotism arise directly from it. While it is no doubt the value of freedom that vibrates through a great deal of this literature, much of which belongs to the arena of practical discussion, its intellectual value lies in its attempt to generalize about human nature and the conditions of politics.

The second problem of property has largely been the preserve of socialist writers. It has usually concerned distribution rather than production, and it has in large measure ignored the danger of despotism. It is instructive to ask why. Part of the answer is that many exponents of this view — the socialists from compassion, as it were, by contrast with the socialists from efficiency — took property to be a form of power exercised by the rich over the poor, and hence they conceived of government as a liberator rather than as an oppressor. The work of government was often conceived to be that of a continuous equalizer and redistributer of the goods that piled up so unequally as a result of market processes. Such, indeed, is the business of a government of a civil community.

Second, the danger of despotism has been obscured in this tradition, partly by a belief in democracy, and partly by the development of a collection of institutional rules that might substitute for the independence property might give. So far as democracy was concerned, the general argument tended to be that the danger of governmental oppression feared by earlier writers resulted, not from the essential features of any state, but from the contingent fact that most states had hitherto been ruled by hereditary monarchs in the interest of a small privileged group. A democratic state, it was believed, would present no such dangers. In any case, written constitutions could be constructed in which were declared the rights of every citizen, who would thus be given a constitutional guarantee against oppression. In earlier times, it was often conceded, the rights of citizens had no doubt been protected by the independence that possession of property allowed, but such protection was no use to the poor, and was, in any case, the direct source of inegalitarian oppression as a by-product of whatever protection it gave against the state.

Faith in democracy led, then, to a belief that a fully representative or (in some versions) fully participatory state could take on the formal characteristics of despotism, such as were thought to be necessitated by the growth of modern industry, without succumbing to despotism's deadly defect: total loss of freedom. The plausibility of this hope was buttressed by the steady development in modern times of what we might well call "property substitutes." It was widely recognized that to own spacious acres, to come from a family celebrated for distinction over many generations, to have abundant friends and dependents gave a man an admirable independence in his relations with the state. To oppose threats to liberty requires more time, energy, and money than the majority of men possess, and hence the defense of liberty has sometimes fallen to the rich by a kind of political noblesse oblige. The problem thus becomes how to engineer the conditions for the defense of liberty while abolishing the very classes of people hitherto so closely associated with its defense. The most popular of these property substitutes has been the declaration of rights, themselves summaries of the conditions achieved over many centuries by the upper classes of Western Europe. Such declarations have, it is well known, been of varying practical effect, but they have been supplemented by such institutional innovations as the ombudsman, and by such social developments as the growth in already free societies of pressure groups whose resources, pooled in resistance to a grievance, gave them the equivalence of individual wealth.

In very crude terms, the problem of property reduces to an empirical theory of liberty and a normative theory of property, and seldom the twain have met. It is true that in such major accounts of the normative theory of justice as that produced by John Rawls, these two principles are formally reconciled.[31] But this has been done only in the hothouse of normative theory rather than on the windswept fields of actual politics, subject as they are to remarkable meteorological effects. It is also true that the empirical theory of liberty can generate normative rules of constitution building, such as the doctrine of the separation of powers. But in general political philosophers have inclined strongly to an interest in the one type of theory or the other.

One exception to this is perhaps Marx. He grasped the nettle of combining these two theories by the bold assertion that the modern European state was in fact a despotism and most of its subjects were in fact slaves. His argument was that the government was the executive committee of the bourgeoisie, which implies precisely the union between the political, lawmaking power, and the economic power of management in which despotism consists. He is thus the inventor of an ingenious hybrid concept in European political thought: class despotism. This hybrid concept is, it is true, strengthened by a theory of development that would make it more plausible and that arises from what we may call the Monopoly problem. One of the boldest and simplest images of a modern economy is given in the well-known game of Monopoly, in which a collection of players equipped with money and properties throw dice and manage their properties until the point when all but one have gone bankrupt. The last player is the monopolist and wins the game. Now why, one might wonder, does this not actually happen in the real world, since money and property give the power to continue accumulating money and property. The answer is, perhaps, that the resources of a community consist in much more than merely productive capital. But it has certainly seemed to many people in the modern world that too few people have at times acquired too much power, and hence various steps, from death duties and progressive taxation to antitrust legislation have been taken to prevent excessive concentration of wealth. But Marx, of course, did in fact argue that modern capitalism would generate a few people as monopolists and that all the human skills and other properties of the community would unite to expropriate them. Marx may then be said to have had a clear and vibrant sense of the idea of despotism and in part to have diagnosed the modern state as a form of it. At the same time, however, he recognized Oriental despotisms as being a different form of political life in his theory of the Asiatic mode of production. In such a mode of production the state was the expropriator of surplus value, and no real classes existed. Given this sensitivity to the idea, why did Marx not fear that a socialist state, combining the functions of ruling and managing, would not also be despotic? He had complicated responses to this problem, but his main point was that in a socialist state (as he imagined it) persons would all be in the position of rulers, and only things would be subject to human power.

In the widest sense of the word, property neither can be justified nor needs to be justified, because it is inextricably part of the way we understand the world. In the narrow sense, the problem of property is so unstable that it dissolves into other questions as soon as it is pressed upon by argument. In the contemporary world, the problem resolves itself into a clash between the value of liberty, which in our civilization means a space for individuality, and the value of justice, which for us has a strong component of equality. Within these terms, the rewards and the burdens of individuality, which cannot but express itself in terms of property, are ceaselessly debated. Liberty and justice cannot, of course, be separated; they are part of each other. But each of them involves pains and disadvantages that imply that the human situation is imperfect, and hence it is at least possible to conceive of a world in which this whoe issue has been transcended. Often when the problem of property is being discussed, some hint of this dream of transcending all the problems associated with property may be discerned. The clearest statement of this dream can be found close to the beginnings of political philosophy in the words of the Athenian Stranger;

> The first-best society, then, that with the best constitution and code of law, is one where the old saying is most universally true of the whole society. I mean the saying that "friends' property is indeed common property." If there is now on earth, or ever should be such a society — a community in women-folk, in children, in all possessions whatsoever, if all means have been taken to eliminate everything we mean by the word *ownership* from life; if all possible means have been taken to make even what nature has made our *own* in some sense common property, I mean, if our eyes, ears, and hands seem to see, hear, act, in the common service; if, moreover, we all approve and condemn in perfect unison and derive pleasure and pain from the same sources — in a word, when the institutions of a society make it

most utterly one, that is a criterion of their excellence than which no truer or better will ever be found.[32]

NOTES

1. John Rawls, *A Theory of Justice* (Oxford 1972).
2. "An equal agrarian is a perpetual law establishing and preserving the balance of dominion, by such a distribution that no man or number of men within the compass of the few or aristocracy can come to overpower the whole people by their possession in lands." *The Political Works of James Harrington,* ed. John Pocock (Cambridge, 1977), p. 18.
3. Sir William Blackstone, *The Sovereignty of the Law* (Selections from the *Commentaries on the Laws of England),* ed. Gareth Jones (London, 1973), pp. 123–124. *Commentaries,* Book II, chap. I.
4. *Politics,* II, vii, 1266aff.
5. *The Purusit of Power: Venetian Ambassador's Report on Spain, Turkey and France in the age of Phillip II, 1650–1700,* ed. James C. Davis (New York, 1970), p. 143. Cf. a quite different characterization of despotism originally used to abuse the Tories of 1679: "They are so certain that monarchy is *jure divino,* that they look upon all people living under Aristocracys or Democracys to be in a state of damnation; and fancy that the Grand Seignor, the Czar of Muscovy and the French King dropt down from Heaven with crowns on their heads, and that all their subjects were born with saddles on their backs." *Somers Tracts,* cited in David Ogg, *England in the Reign of Charles II* (Oxford, 1956) vol 2, p. 610.
6. *Politics,* II, chap. 7, 1267b. One might note in reading this section that, by the criterion of "bourgeois" laid out in C. B. Macpherson's *The Political Theory of Possessive Individualism* (London, 1962), Aristotle must be a bourgeois apologist, since he goes on to say: "It is of the nature of desire to be infinite, and the mass of men live for the satisfaction of desires."
7. Arthur E. R. Boak and William G. Sinninger, *A History of Rome to A.D. 565,* 5th ed. (New York, 1964), p. 182.
8. Daniel Bell, *The Cultural Contradictions of Capitalism* (London, 1976), pp. 220ff.
9. The most thorough exploration known to me of the whole question is in the second essay of Michael Oakeshott's *On Human Conduct* (Oxford, 1974.)
10. Lawrence Becker, *Property Rights: Philosophic Foundations* (London, 1977), p.2. The history of virtually everything in this sense of history meaning "the moral record" is pretty sordid. The essential point, is, I suppose, that "property acquisition" is an abstract concept and therefore does not have a history.

11. See the discussion of this issue by Macpherson in op. cit., pp. 279ff.
12. Burke tells us in the *Reflections on the Revolution in France* (London: Everyman Edition, 1951), pp. 48–49 that "The characteristic essence of property, formed out of the combined principle of its acquisition and conservation, is to be *unequal* [italics in text]. The power of perpetuating our property in our families is one of the most valuable and interesting circumstances belonging to it, and that which tends the most to the perpetuation of society itself."
13. A point Burke makes particularly in *Letter to a Noble Lord*.
14. Thus in a passage typical of the early writings he interprets the French Declaration of Rights: "Hence man was not freed from religion, he received religious freedom. He was not freed from property, he received freedom to own property. He was not freed from the egotism of business, he received freedom to engage in business." Karl Marx, Friedrich Engel, *Collected Works* (London, 1975), p. 167.
15. This distinction underlies, of course, the Marxist view of property. Thus, Jerzy Wroblecoski writes: "According to historical materialisation, property of the means of production ('productive property') is the factor determining the basic structures and power relations of a society, and, hence, determines essential characteristics of state and law." "Property: Typology, Axiology and Policy in Socialist Framework," in *Beiheft Neue Folge* No. 10 Archives for Philosophy of Law and Social Philosophy, p. 117.
16. Macpherson, op. cit., chap. 5, pp. 194ff, criticizes the development of the argument, remarking that "Locke somewhat confused matters by sometimes defining that property whose preservation is the reasons [sic] for entering civil society in unusually wide terms" (p. 198). Becker, op.cit., chap. 4, pp. 32ff., is concerned both with the actual labor theory itself and the steps by which it is used to justify all property.
17. This is entirely explicit in the *Second Treatise*, V. sec. 25. Hobbes raises the same question in the "Epistle Dedicatory" of De Cive: "What nature at first laid forth in comon, men did afterwards distribute into several in propriations." Hobbes's short answer to the problem raised was in terms of consent; but the real solution is to be found in his entire political philosophy.
18. A. M. Honoré in "Ownership" in *Oxford Essays in Jurisprudence*, ed. A.G. Guest (Oxford, 1961), discusses the duties imposed by the state upon those who own farms in Great Britain. Owning property has never, as the famous case of Rylands v. Fletcher reminds us, been devoid of duties, but it is perhaps true that the incidence of duties has greatly increased in the nineteenth and twentieth centuries. Property is normally assumed to be an unambiguous advantage, but there have always been a few who have preferred to renounce any form of power, including the power involved in owning large quantities or property.
19. Washington State seeded the clouds to the displeasure of Idaho. *Guardian*, February 3, 1977.
20. *Childe Harolde's Pilgrimage*, 4, 179.
21. *Second Treatise*, V, sec. 27.

22. Published in the collection *Welcome to the Monkey House* (London, 1968).

23. Quite apart from the difficulty of fair shares for all, a whole moral and religious dimension opens up. Most discussions of equality operate with a single scale of advantages — the assumption that allows us to talk — idiotically — of people being "deprived" or "disadvantaged" or "over-privileged." But in Christian terms, all things are the work of Providence and inscrutably wise. And Plato provides the complementary principle: "I affirm with confidence that so-called evils are evil for the just, and so-called goods, though really good for a good man, evil for a bad one." *Laws,* II, 661.

24. Cf. Hobbes in *Leviathan,* chap. 24, where he distinguishes "propriety in a portion of land, or in some few commodities, or a natural property in some useful art."

25. "Is it not sad," wrote a correspondent to the *Times* of January 17, 1978, "that Lady Spencer Churchill . . . should have deprived posterity of Mr. Sutherland's vision of her late illustrious husband."

26. *Summa Theologica,* qu. 66, art. 2.

27. *Leviathan,* chap. XXIX, p. 162.

28. Ibid.

29. Ibid.

30. Becker, op. cit. p.43.

31. Thus, Rawls's first principle in its revised form reads: 'Each person is to have an equal right to the most extensive total system of equal basis liberties compatible with a similar system of liberties for all." Rawls, op. cit., part I, chap. 4, sec. 39, p. 250.

32. *Laws,* V, 739.

2

THE FUTURE OF THE CONCEPT OF PROPERTY PREDICTED FROM ITS PAST

CHARLES DONAHUE, JR.*

INTRODUCTION

American lawyers, even academic lawyers, rarely think seriously about broad concepts like "property." They are dimly aware that there is some speculation on the concept of property in writings on philosophy, politics, and economics and to a lesser extent in those on psychology, sociology, and anthropology. But American lawyers avoid such speculation, perhaps on the ground that it brings them too close to Jhering's heaven of pure juridical concepts.[1] Nonetheless, even in the narrow, pragmatic, and anti-intellectual world of the American lawyer, there are a number of indications that the concept of property itself is in trouble.

A series of cases in the 1960s starkly posed a conflict between property rights and civil rights and suggested, if they did not quite hold,

*I would like to acknowledge with thanks the assistance of George Spera, who made the tedious computer searches that form the basis of the penultimate section of this essay and who helped in preparing the footnotes for the whole. Howard Abrams did his best to see to it that I got the statistical concepts right; any errors are of course solely my responsibility. I have benefited much from the writings both published and unpublished of, and discussions with, Daniel Coquillette, Morton Horwitz, and Duncan Kennedy, although I am sure they will be surprised to learn it and will probably repudiate most of what is said here.

that a humane society could hardly prefer the former to the latter.[2] At approximately the same time, a revolution took place in landlord and tenant law, a revolution characterized by many judges and commentators as a triumph of contract over property concepts.[3] More on the academic side, a number of writers have suggested that property rules interfere with the achievement of allocational efficiency and should be replaced by liability rules.[4] The only recent development that suggests anything other than a dim future for the concept of property is a bold attempt by Charles Reich in the early 1960s to apply the concept to a citizen's expectations that he would continue to be the recipient of government largesse.[5] For a while, the idea found favor with the courts but then seemed to be lost from view.[6]

Other developments suggest that the institution if not the concept of property is in trouble. A whole new body of regulatory law designed to protect the environment has further restricted the traditional privileges of owners of resources to use them to their advantage.[7] While the concept of property is usully not directly involved in the debate over these regulations, their existence suggests a further weakening of the practical powers of the property holder. Further, and perhaps in the long run most significantly, the continuing debasement of the currency suggests a declining significance of property in American life.

Before we announce, however, that property, like contract, is dead,[8] let us examine the various uses of the term in the different situations which seem to indicate its demise. The property rights versus civil rights controversies usually concern the right of a corporate property owner to exclude others from its land. In the landlord- tenant situation, on the other hand, property is not being equated with the right to exclude, but with the power to convey; and the issue is not whether the landlord has the power to convey but whether its exercise should be accompanied by a series of implied obligations on the part of the landlord. The property rules versus liability rules controversy involves both the right to exclude and the privilege of use, but neither is being restricted in the abstract. The issue is what remedy should be granted when the right or privilege is concededly interfered with, and the label "property" is being applied to the remedy of an injunction, while "liability" is being applied to the remedy of damages. The new property involves none of the traditional rights, powers, and privileges, but rather the notions that the state may not deprive a person of property without due process or take his property without payment of just compensation. In the case of environmental legislation, neither the privilege of use nor the power of the state to regulate that privilege is normally questioned. What is feared is that the quantum of state regulation may ultimately reduce the privilege of use to meaninglessness. In the case of inflation, none of the traditional rights, privileges, or powers is directly affected; rather, the notion is that the property owner will no longer have any incentive to make use of the elaborate provisions for the future the law allows him, because inflation has raised the discount rate so that present benefits will regularly be preferred to future ones.

The question thus becomes: What is property? Is it one or a combination of the property rights, privileges, and powers involved in the examples? Is it the value the possession of those rights, privileges, and powers gives to the holder? Or is it the use to which the holder puts those rights, powers and privileges? Obviously, any examination of the future of the concept of property must begin by defining the term "property."

THE DEFINITION OF PROPERTY

Property is frequently defined as the rights of a person with respect to a thing.[9] The difficulties with this definition were forcefully pointed out by Hohfeld over half a century ago.[10] The law does not deal with rights and duties in the abstract; the law deals with relationships. Although the relationship of a person to a thing may have meaning in philosophical discourse, it does not in legal discourse, because a thing cannot bring or defend a lawsuit.[11] Thus, we are forced back to Hohfeld's familiar pairings of jural relations: right, duty; privilege, no right; power, liability; disability, immunity. The law of property deals with the complex of those jural relationships with respect to things, those things being normally tangible things, although in some legal systems, including our own, those intangibles that the law somewhat arbitrarily classifies as property are also included.[12]

The Hohfeldian definition of property is descriptive. If Jean Valjean may take the loaf of bread, indeed if the baker must give it to him, those are as much rules of property as the rule that says that Valjean must go to the galleys for having taken it. And the bishop's notion that Valjean was entitled to the plate and the candlesticks is as much a concept of property as that of the gendarmerie, who insisted on seeing evidence that the bishop had conveyed them.

I know of no legal system that does not have a concept of property so defined, and indeed it is hard to conceive of one that did not. Obviously, there must be something more, something that leads detractors from property to define it in a way which suggests that there is a property view of a problem of the legal relationships between people with respect to a thing and a nonproperty view of that same problem. If we glance even briefly at the property systems of non-Western societies, their extraordinary diversity will lead us to the conclusion that any concept of property other than the definitional one is dependent upon the culture in which it is found.[13] Even in the West the concept has varied remarkably over time. Our effort, then, will be to determine if there is any core concept or concepts to which the word "property" has been applied in the West that might lead us to understand why it is that the varying controversies we have mentioned have been characterized as a conflict of property as against something else.

Our word "property" comes either directly or through French *propriété* from Latin *proprietas* which means "the peculiar nature or quality of thing" and (in post-Augustan writing) "ownership."[14] *Proprietas* is itself derived from *proprius,* an adjective, equally applicable to physical things or qualities meaning, "own" or "peculiar," as opposed to *communis*, "common," or *alienus,* "another's." *Proprius* itself is of uncertain etymology but is probably related to the Indo-European root that appears in Latin *pro, prae,* and *prope;* Greek πρό and πρίν; Sanskrit *pra* — the meanings of all of which point to a core meaning within the notions of "in front of," "before," "close to," and "on behalf of."[15] We would not be far wrong if we suggested that even before it comes to be a legal term "property" is an abstraction of the idea of what distinguishes an individual or a thing from a group or from another. It is the face of one to other(s), what separates me from thee and ye, what lies in a person's view, what has priority in time.

When the word "property" first comes into English it is regularly used in either of the two senses of the Latin *proprietas,* or one easily derivable from them.[16] Before the seventeenth century it is rare to find the word in its modern sense of an object of legal rights, or possessions or wealth collectively, and even where it is so found, the context almost always suggests a thing or group of things owned by an individual.[17] It is thus a quite modern usage of the word that allowed us to abstract from the idea of property as the object of legal rights a

definition of property as a branch of law which did not require that
the word "property" connote individual ownership.

Whether that branch of law has had any core concept that might
be defined as the Western concept of property is the topic to which
we now must turn, but in doing so we encounter a number of methodological problems. A legal system may be defined as (1) a body of
ideas and rules that are applied to (2) various social situations
through the medium of (3) legal institutions. The way the three
elements interact is the fundamental topic of legal history. Unfortunately, the theory of this interaction is only in its infancy.[18] Certainly
it has been developed with nothing like the precision that would
allow us confidently to determine what one of the elements is,
granted that we know what the others are.[19] For this reason, any attempt to trace the history of the legal concept of property, even in the
West, will be full of unknowns. Further, recent work with some of the
critical points of development in Western property law suggests that
previous generations of legal historians may have profoundly misun-
derstood what was at stake in these developments.[20] That in turn suggest that any survey that rests, as this one must, largely on secondary
accounts, some of which are quite old, must be regarded as tentative
and subject to revision in the light of further work with the original
materials.[21]

Despite these methodological difficulties, however, one tendency
seems to characterize the legal concept of property in the definitional
sense in the West: a tendency to agglomerate in a single legal person,
preferably the one currently possessed of the thing that is the object
of inquiry, the exclusive right to possess, privilege to use, and power
to convey the thing. In Hohfeldian terms, Western law tends to ascribe to the possessor of a thing: the right to possess the thing with a
duty in everyone else to stay off, the privilege of using the thing with
no right in anyone else to prevent him (coupled with a right in the
possessor to prevent others from using the thing), a power to transfer
any and all of his rights, privileges, and powers with a liability in anyone to be the object of that conveyance (coupled with a disability in
everyone else to change and an immunity in the possessor from
change of those same rights, privileges, and powers).

The tendency has never been more than that for reasons which we
shall examine shortly, but it has been aided by devices of categorization. Where the complex of rights, privileges, and powers with respect to a thing could not be ascribed to one legal person, the tend-

ency has dictated that one legal person have "the property" and that the other interests be called something else, such as "equities" in our own law or "obligations" on the Continent. Similarly, the law of persons has aided the tendency: in older law by denying legal personality or property-holding capacity to, for example, slaves, serfs, children, or married women; in our own law by freely allowing the creation of fictitious legal persons, corporations, and to some extent partnerships, in whom "the property" may rest. Thus, if actual possession of the thing rests in one to whom the full panoply of rights, powers, and privileges could not be ascribed or is shared by some who could hold the full panoply and some who could not or is shared by a group any of whom could hold the full panoply but who are not single, the law of persons frequently allows us to ignore these complexities and focus on a single legal person who is "constructively possessed."

Even if the actual possessor is a single legal person, we hesitate to ascribe to him this great bundle of exclusive rights, privileges, and powers if he came by that possession by violating the right to possession of another. Our sources will treat this problem in various ways: sometimes they will say that possession must be "rightful" before it is protected, that is, before the agglomerative tendency comes into operation; sometimes they will manipulate the category "possession" so that it remains in him in whose benefit the tendency has operated, even though he is no longer actually possessed; sometimes they will assert that "ownership and possession have nothing in common."[22] The problem of wrongful possession remains, however, a primal problem in Western law, and as in the case of the person–actual possession problem we must normally look to another category, this time the law of actions, to see the whole picture. But there is a difference: the law of persons is normally used to preserve the conceptual integrity of the agglomerative tendency, whereas the law of actions frequently masks its operation.

Once the appropriate possessor has been identified, the tendency to agglomerate in him all rights, privileges, and powers concerning the thing carries with it two inherent contradictions. The exercise of the power to convey by any individual cannot begin to be full unless he can limit the power to convey of the individual to whom he conveys. The earl of Arundel knows that his heir is insane and likely to be childless. He wishes to give the barony of Grostok to his second son, but to give the barony to his third son if his second son should become earl. If the earl cannot do this, his power to convey the barony is severely hampered. If he can do this, the power of his second son to convey the barony is severely hampered.[23] The second contradiction is similar to the first. My privilege of use of any thing, if exercised to the fullest, is likely to interfere with your privilege of use of your things. Two absolute privileges of use cannot coexist within even reasonable proximity.[24]

Both contradictions tend to arise in situations in which the current possessor of the thing is being sued. The Grostok case will normally arise after both the earl and the heir are dead and the third son seeks possession from the second. The agglomerative tendency will favor the current possessor and may even operate to mask the contradiction, that is, obscure the fact that a ruling for the current possessor will diminish the power to convey of all property holders. Similarly, cases of incompatible land uses will normally result in the passive land user suing the active. Because the plaintiff in Western law generally has the burden of proof, the burden will be on him to justify a limitation on the privilege of use of the defendant. If the issue is framed in these terms, the agglomerative tendency will favor the defendant as current possessor and may even mask the fact that the privilege of use of the plaintiff as current possessor is equally at stake.[25]

The notion that the law has a tendency to agglomerate rights, privileges, and powers over a thing in a single individual is a commonplace on the Continent where it has long been believed that the tendency was inherent in Roman law. That it is also a tendency in Anglo-American law is more controversial, because Anglo-American law recognizes more types of interests in things than does continental. Indeed, one might question any statement that ascribes to English law even a tendency to absolute property rights prior to the philosophical support of possessive individualism and liberalism,[26] that is, any time much before Blackstone. Nonetheless, the tendency does exist in Anglo-American law, if perhaps not to quite the extent that it does in continental, and it long antedates Blackstone. The two laws differ in the extent to which and the ways in which they use the law of persons, obligations, and actions to preserve the tendency to agglomerate: and they differ in the ways in which they resolve the two inherent contradictions, but the tendency is there in both systems. Our first effort, then, will be to show that the tendency does exist, that it antedates the philosophy that might be thought to have given rise to it, and that there is no obvious social explanation of its existence.

THE TENDENCY BEFORE POSSESSIVE
INDIVIDUALISM: ROME

In classical Roman law the sum of rights, powers, and privileges a legal person could have in a thing was called *dominium,* "ownership," less frequently *proprietas,* but frequently enough that it is clear that the two were synonymous.[27] The classical Roman authors do not say that their law tends to ascribe *proprietas* to the current possessor, but that they did is clear enough from a large body of rules that deny the label "possession" to the one in fact possessed in order to keep it in the *proprietarius.*[28] That the person legally possessed is presumed to be the *proprietarius* is clear enough from a complex body of procedural rules that essentially require that one who is not peaceably possessed of a thing affirmatively establish that his title is better than that of the peaceable possessor.[29] Once the system had found the *proprietarius,* it was loath to let him convey anything less than the full bundle. Full use rights divorced from ownership could be given only to a living person, and that person could not convey those rights to another.[30] The number of restrictions on his privilege of use to which the owner could agree was sharply limited.[31] Anyone who found himself owning a thing jointly with others could petition for a division.[32]

We might argue that the tendency toward absolute individual property rights in Roman law was more apparent than real. The classical Roman law never developed a remedy whereby an individual could, upon proof of ownership, specifically recover the thing. The court would declare his right to the thing, but the defendant could always choose to respond in damages.[33] The Roman law of persons put extraordinary power over things in the hands of the head of the household, the pater familias, so extraordinary that it had to develop an elaborate system whereby individuals could make binding legal transactions with things that were in fact but not in law their own.[34] The tendency of the Roman law not to allow division of ownership led to its treating landlord and tenant law as a branch of obligation rather than of property, but the final results were not far different from those of our own legal system.[35] Indeed, the results were somewhat more favorable to the tenant than those, until very recently, of our legal system. The Romans' univocal concept of ownership greatly limited the types of rights one might have in the land of another. But it would seem that the Romans sometimes used devices categorized as part of the law of obligations to achieve ends that in other laws would be achieved by devices categorized as part of the law of property.[36] Finally, and perhaps most important, the sharp cleavage in Roman law between public law and private law prevented them from ever developing a legal notion of protection of property as against the state. Thus, many of the conflicts in land use that in our system were until quite recently the subject of private tort suits or private agreements enforced by the courts were probably dealt with in Roman law as legislative or administrative matters.[37]

We may question, therefore, how different the sum of property rules in the definitional sense of the term was in the Roman legal system from that of legal systems that have a less univocal concept of property. Further, the great differences between the Roman economy and society and the economies and societies of recent Western experience should make us hesitate to create, in the manner of modern comparativists, certain simple hypothetical situations to compare the results under the Roman and any other system.[38] To my knowledge, a more sophisticated comparison has never been done; perhaps it cannot be done, granting the state of our sources. We must content ourselves, then, with two observations. First, the intellectual tendency that we stated was generally characteristic of legal thinking about property in the West existed to a marked extent in Roman legal thinking. Indeed, the Roman division of property from obligation may be the single most important determinant of the Western concept of property. Second, this tendency is one that has no obvious explanation in Roman political or philosophical thinking, other than the broadest of connections with general philosophical ideas of individual worth.[39]

The state of our knowledge of the relationship of Roman law to Roman society makes hazardous any attempt to explain the existence of the agglomerative tendency on the basis of social causes. That the tendency, coupled with the Roman law of persons, favored the property-holding classes, seems obvious, perhaps too obvious. That it was a product of their power, particularly in the Republican period, cannot be disproved.[40] A number of its manifestations, however, cannot easily be ascribed to class interest. Among the most notable of these are the law's refusal to allow settlements of any but the most short-lived variety, the paucity of land-use control devices, and the failure of the law to develop any notion of protection of property against the state.

THE TENDENCY BEFORE POSSESSIVE INDIVIDUALISM: THE ENGLISH MIDDLE AGES

When we turn to England, we turn to a legal system in which the structure of the law of actions prevented any sharp cleavage between property and obligation. The action that today forms the basis of the right to own land is a type of trespass action originally given to a lessee wrongfully dispossessed of his property who would otherwise not have had a remedy because he was not a freeholder.[41] The availability of an injunction, now thought to be so characteristic of property rules, derives, at least in part, from the moral judgment of the chancellor that a given individual had brought too many of those trespass-based actions to recover a piece of land and must be ordered to desist on the penalty of going to jail if he contemned the order.[42] It is, therefore, even more remarkable that English law shows the same tendency at critical points to move in directions similar to the Roman, to agglomerate property rights in a single individual.

The mechanisms by which a notion of property emerged at the end of the twelfth century from a mass of discretionary feudal rights and obligations were extraordinarily complex.[43] Suffice it to say here that what began as essentially an appellate jurisdiction, offered by the king in his court to insure that a feudal lord did right by his men, ended up with the free tenant as the owner of the land, in a quite modern sense, with the lord's rights limited to receipt of money payments. Ideas derived from the same process led to a rule that the conveyor of land could not limit its descent to the direct descendants of the conveyee but could only claim it back if the conveyee died without himself leaving direct decendants. This latter result was reversed by legislation at the end of the thirteenth century; and in one of the few deviations from the principle of consolidating the power to convey in the present holder, the courts extended the scope of this legislation in the fourteenth century.[44] The trend was, however, again reversed, probably in the late fifteenth century.[45]

In the sixteenth century the process that had operated to consolidate ownership rights in the free tenant in the thirteenth was replicated for the copyholder.[46] Once again, the royal courts opened appellate jurisdiction to copyholders wronged by what they deemed to be unjust behavior of their lords' courts, and the end result was that the copyholder became the owner of what had theretofore been, in the eyes of the king's law, the lord's land.

Other developments of the late medieval and Tudor periods illustrate the same tendency of the law to consolidate property rights in a
single person. The sixteenth century development of the doctrine of
destructibility of contingent remainders permitted the cutting off of
contingent rights in land held by someone other than the current
possessor. The ladening of the doctrine of covenants that run with
the land with requirements that made them impossible, in many instances, to enforce limited the landowner's power to convey in the interests of a fuller use right in the current possessor. The rule in
Shelley's Case, the requirement of the Statute of Uses that legal title
follow the use, and, of course, the nascent doctrine invalidating perpetuities, all had the effect or could be used to achieve the effect of
giving the current possessor a cleaner title than he would otherwise
have had.[47]

The history of land-use law in this period has not been well explored, although material exists for an adequate history of the ways
in which the English law resolved the problem of conflicting land
uses.[48] It may be that a more static society produced fewer land-use
conflicts than our own. It may also be that most conflicts were resolved at a level below that of the king's courts.[49] Be that as it may,
the cases in the king's courts suggest, somewhat surprisingly, that the
agglomerative tendency was working on behalf of the plaintiff and
not the defendant in nuisance cases.[50]

So far, we have dealt only with the emergence of the tendency in
areas that today would be called private law. If we ask what protection the citizen's property received against the state in the Middle
Ages, we are asking a question that requires considerable translation
for a world that knew citizens only as privileged residents of a city
and that knew the state, in the modern sense, not at all. There are,
however, some intimations of a notion that property ought to receive
some legal protection against the king. It may even be an idea that
underlies the Magna Carta. One of the justifications for the deposi-
tion of Richard II in 1399 was that while Richard was king no man's
property was safe.[51] It is hard to know whether the early statutes dat-
ing from the reign of Henry VIII, which take private property for public works, are more important for their recognition of the eminent
domain power of the state or for their provision for compensation to
the owner whose property is taken.[52] The theoretical elaborations of
the eminent domain power in the continental legal writers of the seventeenth century already show the familiar requirements of public

purpose and compensation as prerequisites of a lawful taking.[53]

The developments discussed above all antedate the rise of the philosophy of possessive individualism at the end of the seventeenth century and certainly antedate any of the liberal notions of property that we associate with the late eighteenth century and the nineteenth century. Maitland was guilty of one of his few anachronisms when he suggested that the promotion of the free alienability of land could have been a conscious policy of the courts in the time before the reign of Edward I.[54] His perception of the tendency was clearly correct, but the body of ideas available to the judges of Henry III's time makes it highly unlikely that free alienability was a policy whose virtues they could have perceived. Nonetheless, painting with a broad brush, that was the effect of most of the significant developments in English property law from the thirteenth through the seventeenth centuries.

In the Roman legal system we noted that the word "property" existed and that it was ascribed to the product of the agglomerative tendency. Property and ownership were categories with which Roman legal authors dealt. In medieval and early modern English law the category property was far less important because the dominant categories were those of the actions. English legal writers occasionally do use the word property however. Glanvill and Bracton both use it in a way that reveals that they are attempting to apply a Roman category to what the demandant is seeking in the writs of right or entry.[55] As a technical matter this usage is incorrect. Roman *dominium* and English "right" are not the same thing. But if we are correct that the agglomerative tendency was already manifesting itself in the operations of English writ system in the late twelfth century, then Glanvill and Bracton's use of the word may point to a profounder reality—the existence of the tendency in both systems. Further, if our chronology is correct, the tendency existed in English law before English legal thinkers had much exposure to Roman legal ideas, although it does not antedate what some have seen as a revival of ideas of individualism in the twelfth century.[56]

The earliest manifestations of the agglomerative tendency in thirteenth century England seem to have announced a virtual revolution in the English social system. The man who was seized of a freehold emerged as not far different from what we would call the owner of the property, and the rights of lords of freeholders became more like those of taxing authorities and the rights of the non-freeholders who held of the free tenant became obscured by the fact that they were not protected in the king's court. An earlier generation saw a clear political purpose in this development: The king was allying himself with the middling men of the kingdom against the great lords.[57] But our understanding both of the purpose and the effect of the development is obscured by the fact that we cannot date with precision when the changes either in law or in society took place. It may be that the relationship between lord and free man had already become largely a fiscal one by the end of the twelfth century, in which case the developments of the law simply reflected what had already happened in society. It may be the developments in the law either precipitated or aided these developments of society, in which case we must ask to what extent they indicate a purpose to change society. It may be, as has recently been suggested, that the purpose of the intervention of the king's courts was to shore up a system that was weakening and that the intervention, by shifting jurisdiction from the lord's courts to the kings' courts, had the unintended effect of destroying the system.[58]

The developments in the later Middle Ages, which we noted tended to have the effect of giving a more absolute power to convey to the present holder of the land at the expense of his power to convey in such a way as to deprive future generations of that same power, have often been seen as the product of what was left of the conflict between landholder and lord.[59] At first glance, the king and his courts would seem to be most interested in protecting feudal revenues because as the lord who has no lord the king has the most to gain and nothing to lose by such protection. But that analysis is too simplistic. The king also has a family and to the extent that he is bound by the same rules as the great landowners feels the same tension between his interests as a head of a family and his interests as a lord.[60] Further, although feudal revenues are critically important to the understanding of such developments as the abolition of subinfeudation in 1290 and the passage of the Statute of Uses in 1535, they tell us little about why the courts first extended and then restricted the power of the landowner to entail his land.[61]

THE TENDENCY IN MODERN HISTORY

The importance of property as a key concept in the development of the theory of possessive individualism at the end of the seventeenth century is well known.[62] Our question here is the extent to which that theory manifested itself in the development of property law in the late seventeenth and eighteenth centuries. Unfortunately, it is a question we can only raise, not answer. Despite some admirable recent beginnings, eighteenth-century legal history remains a relatively poorly explored field.[63] The towering figure of Blackstone has too often been assumed to have restated what the law was, whereas it is equally plausible that he put his own mold upon a divergent and much more complex reality. Blackstone's concept of property is curiously bifurcated. In a famous passage he lists it along with life and liberty as one of the absolute rights of Englishmen, but when he comes to restating the rules derived from his absolute private right, the tendency to absolutism is far less manifest.[64]

The nineteenth century, the high-water mark of political liberalism, was also the period in which the agglomerative tendency of Western European property law was most manifest. On the Continent the pandectists took the tendency inherent in the Roman conception of property and developed it to a point that most modern scholars find goes far beyond what the Roman sources themselves suggest.[65] The tendency is also remarkable in common law jurisprudence on both sides of the Atlantic. The closing of the classification of easements in the early nineteenth century; the turning of the rule against perpetuities into a rigid device that could be used to strike down many forms of family settlement; the development in this country of a law of waste that gave far more power to the current landholder; and the development, again in this country, of a water law that favored commerical development may all be seen as illustrations of the same fundamental tendency.[66] Legislation went even further. New York's notorious "two-lives" rule against perpetuities that struck down even more settlements in the name of the power of the present hoder to convey; the English Settled Land Acts, which gave considerably more power to the present holder of settled land than the common law had given him; and the Married Women's Property Acts in both countries, which divided property within the marital unit by assigning it to one or the other spouse, are notable examples.[67]

As in the case of Roman law, so too in the case of the nineteenth-century common law, focusing on the law of property so called may obscure the reality of the total law with respect to the possession, use, and conveyance of things. In the face of a restrictive law concerning the creation of easements, English equity in the middle of the nineteenth century developed a new form of obligation, the equitable servitude, which has had an increasing tendency to take over the field of private land-use arrangements, so much so that few courts today would not call the beneficiary of an equitable servitude the holder of a "property" right.[68] While the agglomerative tendency affected the law of trusts, the express trust resisted any attempt to defeat its basic division of legal from beneficial title. It came to be used increasingly to avoid the strictures of the law of settlements and as a form of holding increasingly important aggregations of personal property in order to avoid the rule of the older law that no division between present and future estates in personal property was permissible.[69] The spread of the idea of the spendthrift trust in the late nineteenth century again checked the agglomerative tendency.[70] Similarly, the increasing complexity of land-use questions and conflicts led to an ever growing body of local land-use regulations, and the first comprehensive zoning and planning act was passed in England at the beginning of the twentieth century.[71]

The social situation against which the law was operating changed markedly in the sixteenth and seventeenth centuries. The demise of fiscal feudalism relegated the tension between the free landowner and his lord to the background, and a new tension emerged between the established country landowner seeking to perpetuate his family and the newly wealthy man of commerce seeking to buy country land.[72] By the nineteenth century this conflict will become a conflict between commerical and agricultural land uses, and the key issue will not be the power to alienate land but the privilege to use it.[73] It seems fairly clear that the restrictions on the power to tie up land for long periods of time, which the law either adopted from the later Middle Ages and continued to enforce, or which, as in the case of the doctrine against perpetuities, it invented in this period, favored commercial interests. That the law stopped short of abolishing all restrictions on the power of the conveyee himself to convey is a product not only of a recognition of the contradiction inherent in the fundamental tendency to agglomerate but also of the countrymen and their conveyancers to influence the course of legal development.[74] Similarly, although the nineteenth-century courts gave broad scope to industrial development of land at the expense of adjoining agricultural uses, the fact that the courts at no time recognized an absolute privilege of use of land is the product both of the inherent contradiction in the fundamental tendency and of the fact that the agricultural classes retained some social power.[75]

Perhaps because the category "property" told little of the real extent of the property holder's rights, powers, and privileges, the Anglo-American analytic jurists of the late nineteenth and early twentieth centuries were not nearly so successful at constructing a system of a "scientific" property law as they were in the area of contract and perhaps of tort. The analytic jurists could note the tendency to agglomerate, but the tendency itself was inherently contradictory and the whole of property law carried with it a more extensive baggage from previous centuries than did contract and tort. Analytical jurisprudence thus tended to focus on particular aspects of property to which its technique was peculiarly adapted.[76] Common law estates in land and future interests became the *system* of estates and future interests; the doctrine of perpetuties became the *rule* against perpetuities; systematic categories developed around the three bodies of law dealing with private land-use controls, easements, covenants, and equitable servitudes. Not surprisingly, the first Restatement of Property limits itself to the two broad areas of estates and private land-use controls.[77] Notably missing from the restaters efforts was any attempt to restate conveyancing law, except to the extent that it was included in estates and future interests. Nuisance, and to a large extent waste, were relegated to tort; landlord-tenant was missing entirely; no attempt at all was made to deal with public control of land use or with the law of natural resources.

We saw in the Middle Ages intimations of a notion that property should be protected against the king. In the seventeenth century this idea became converted into the idea that the citizen's property should be protected against the state. Blackstone's economium of property reflects much that gone before in the philosophy of possessive individualism[78]. Nonetheless, it is in the Fourth and Fifth Amendments to the U.S. Constitution that these ideas find their embodiment as specific legal principles; and it is not until the second half of the nineteenth century, until after the passage of the Fourteenth Amendment, that these ideas received any substantial elaboration in federal jurisprudence.[79] But when they were elaborated, the elaboration was extreme. Economic regulation, taxation, and land-use regulation of various kinds were all struck down as interfering with the citizen's property rights.[80]

The early part of the twentieth century saw an extended debate over the extent of permissible state interference with property rights. Both the content and the outcome of the debate are well known. By the middle of the 1930s income taxation had been established by constitutional amendment; federal and state regulation of the economy could no longer be challenged on the ground that it constituted a deprivation of property rights without substantive due process of law (unless it could be shown that the legislative scheme failed to meet a minimum test of rationality); and direct restrictions on the use of property in the form of comprehensive zoning and planning ordinances had been sustained even if they involved considerable loss of value to the property owner, so long as they could be denominated a "regulation" rather than a "taking."[81] Thus, the trend seemed clearly away from use of the property clauses of the Constitution to protect the citizen against the state. There remained, of course, the protections against unreasonable searches and seizures afforded by the Fourth Amendment and that against uncompensated takings by the Fifth. The former was to take on great significance in the 1960s, but as a personal, not a "property" right.[82]

REASONS FOR THE TENDENCY EXAMINED

So far we have treated the development of the concept of property in Anglo-American law and to a lesser extent in continental law with some regard to the intellectual and social contexts in which the development occurred. We have identified a tendency that has been followed with sufficient frequency that it is worthy of being described as a fundamental tendency of property law in the West. How are we to account for this fundamental tendency? We have seen that it antedates the philosphy of possessive individualism, that it long antedates nineteenth century liberalism, although it may not antedate certain general individualistic trends in Western thought. Possessive individualism and liberalism may have had considerable influence in furthering the tendency in the law, but any explanation of the tendency must seek its origins outside those ideas. Social factors may partially account for the tendency in Roman law, but if the *dominus* of Republican Rome was the most important element in that political system, the same can hardly be said to have been true of the ordinary freeholder of thirteenth century or even less of the copyholder of sixteenth century England.

I am inclined to think that to explain the tendency something more fundamental is required than the influence of a particular philosophical idea or the product of a balancing of social interests or of the dominance of one social interest over another. Both the Roman legal system and our own begin as disputes-resolution mechanisms. Both the Roman legal system and our own begin with possession of a resource by an individual. The intellectual convenience of assuming that that possessor has all the other rights, powers, and privileges that one may have in a resource may go a long way to account for the presence of the tendency in both legal systems. The tendency begins as an allocation, as it were, of a burden of producing evidence: a dispute arises over a thing; we begin by determining who is the possessor; we presume that he has all the rights, powers, and privileges that go along with property until someone can show us differently.

Now it must be admitted that the Western legal system is not unique in beginning as a disputes-resolution mechanism; many, if not most, legal systems do. But the Western concept of property is, if not unique, certainly unusual. We may speculate that what makes this disputes-resolution device operate in favor of the individual property holder in the West is an accident of chronology; the coincidence of the emergence of systematic legal thinking (associated with professionalization) and a state of society that saw one individual's connection with a thing more clearly that it saw any group's connection with the thing.[83] What caused that state of society and how much it was necessary that there be general notions of individual autonomy and worth before the idea developed I cannot say. Our history tells of more of what happened to the tendency after it started that it does of how it started.

As the need for a category arose to describe the sum of the rights, powers, and privileges that an individual could have with respect to a thing, we chose the noun derived from the adjective that means "own." The category at once described the concept and also the tendency. As time went on, the tendency took on an independent life. We excluded from the category property certain rights, powers and privileges with respect to a thing because they existed in someone else other than the property holder. In modern legal systems, though not in the Roman, property came to represent one of the rights of the individual against the state, perhaps originally because property had come to rest in the freeholder and not in his lord, and the king was the lord of all. The tendency became reinforced with philosophical ideas; social forces attached themselves to it but also arranged themselves around contradictions within it.

In the classical Roman law and in the late 19th and early 20th centuries when the agglomerative tendency was at its strongest, we noted that the sum of rules pertaining to things in fact undercut the tendency, but if one looked solely to the rules labeled "property," the system of categorization obscured this fact. We even raised the question with regard to Roman law whether the strength of the tendency made any difference. I suspect, although I cannot prove, that it did. In nineteenth century America the categorization process itself clearly left the tendency to work in a more unfettered fashion that it would have if more conflicting interests had had to be reconciled under one category.

THE RECENT HISTORY OF THE LEGAL CONCEPT OF PROPERTY

The reaction in the early twentieth century came on two fronts. In public law the tendency fell before greater political force, marshaled on the side of increasing government regulation. In both public and private law the legal realists attacked the categorization process itself, and they found an easy mark in property, if only because the systematizers had been less successful there than they had been in the case of contract.[84] Thus, when we come to reexamine the controversies with which we began this essay, we should bear in mind that property is in somewhat of a shambles. The fundamental tendency has received a major setback in the public law field, and the whole process of categorization with which the tendency has been associated is discredited.

If we define the Western concept of property as an agglomerative tendency with two inherent contradictions, we can begin to see how it is involved in some of the modern controversies about property. One of these contradictions is directly at issue in the environmental controversy. Perhaps the only reason it is not always perceived as simply a variant on the old nuisance problem is that environmental effects are sufficiently diffused that we find it difficult to see that it is the property of those who feel the effect that is at stake. To a certain extent, the property rules versus liability rules controversy involves the same contradiction inherent in the notion of absolute privileges of use. Once the law has chosen one land use in preference to another, should it compromise with the nonfavored land use by giving the favored use less than full remedies? In another sense, the agglomerative tendency itself is at stake here. Once the law has decided that a given land use is privileged, should it not give the holder of that privilege all possible remedies? In the landlord-tenant controversy, that agglomerative tendency can also be seen to be at stake. The landlord is the owner; all that the lease purports to do is convey possession to the tenant for a term. The agglomerative tendency (at least in the nineteenth century) led to the assumption that nothing else had been conveyed and, somewhat inconsistently, that no promises had been made. The agglomerative tendency is also involved in the property rights versus civil rights controversy to the extent that that tendency would lead us to define the right to exclude broadly and require that it be protected even where it is being used discriminatorily.[85]

Thus, although nothing concerning the definitional concept of property is at stake in the controversies with which we began the essay, those who have identified these controversies as controversies about property rights as opposed to something else have, at least to some extent, touched on something that is fundamental to the concept to property in the West. Coming as these cases do, at the time of the decay of liberalism, a period in which the agglomerative tendency reached its pinnacle, we may fairly ask not only whether these controversies indicate a change from the extremes to which the agglomerative tendency was brought during the nineteenth and early twentieth centuries but also whether they indicate a reversal of the fundamental tendency itself.

THE FUTURE OF THE TENDENCY

Now, it is by no means clear that all of these tensions in our legal thinking will be resolved in favor of the antiproperty forces, probably even less clear that they ought to be so resolved. Even if we assume, however, an affirmative answer to both these questions, a large body of law covering a large variety of human interactions would not necessarily be affected. Our study of the tendency, however, has shown that it took on a life of its own, that it came to apply to more and more areas. The reversal of the tendency in a few important areas might lead to a countertendency if no social forces resisted it, perhaps even if they did.[86] But in order to see whether a countertendency is now at work and to speculate as to what social forces might resist it, we need some idea of the uses to which the concept of property is being put in areas outside the spectacular controversies with which this essay began.

Many of the ways in which the concept of property is used are difficult if not impossible to discover. We know that people regularly convey both land and chattels, but the records of those conveyances are widely scattered and the attitudes of the parties and their conveyancers to the concept of property are frequently not conscious and, if conscious, frequently not revealed in the records. The protection that the criminal law affords property gives rise to numerous transactions in our society; but again the records are scattered, the attitudes of the property owners, the police, and the criminals hard to discover. One relatively accessible source, however, makes frequent use of the concept of property—the opinions of appellate courts. By examining the use that the appellate courts have made of the concept over the last twenty years, we may be able to perceive trends that tell as much or more of what the future of property is likely to be than do the articulated controversies with which we began the paper.

The full text of the appellate opinions of sixteen of the fifty states, including the ten most populous states, is in a computer data bank.[87] Every region of the country is represented, but there is a bias in favor of the more populous states. The bank contains all the reported opinions for the past ten years; some jurisdictions' opinions are missing if we go back twenty years.

We first asked the computer to count all the opinions in which the word "property" was used in three test years 1957, 1967, and 1977, and we compared that number with the total number of opinions rendered. There has, of course, been a great increase in the number of reported state appellate opinions, but the proportion of them that use the word property has remained quite constant: 29 percent in 1957 and 1967 and 26 percent in 1977. When we separated intermediate appellate courts from state supreme courts, however, the latter showed a marked decline in the use of the word: 38 percent in 1957, 31 percent in 1967, and 25 percent in 1977.[88] These raw statistics, however, told us nothing about how the word was being used. The concept could be changing radically, even if the incidence of its use remained relatively constant.

We decided to focus on the opinions of the highest courts of five states: California, Illinois, New Jersey, New York, and Pennsylvania. These states were chosen because all of the highest court opinions for each of the test years were in the data bank in an accessible form,[89] and each state in at least two out of the three years varied from the national average by more than 10 percentage points in the proportion of cases that used the word "property."[90] Taken together, however, they mirrored the national trend.[91] The selection was, of course, biased in favor of populous states of the industrial Northeast, and we attempted to correct this bias by drawing another sample with which we shall deal later.

For each of the states we drew a sample of thirty property cases for each of the test years and asked the computer to print out five lines of text of the opinion where the word property occurred. By examining the use of the word in its context we hoped to determine whether the use of the word gave us some clue as to: (1) why it was that these states varied from the national average; (2) why the use of the word had declined over time; and (3) any changes in the use of the concept over the twenty-year period.

As we poured over our print-outs from 450 cases, a few things were immediately apparent about the way the courts use the word "property." By far the most common use of the word is to describe the object, either individual or collective, of a person's rights, powers, or privileges: "the property was located at 304 Linda Vista"; "he left all the residue of his property to his wife." The next most common use indicated the legal context more directly: "property is protected by the U.S. Constitution"; "are pension rights 'property' within the meaning of the statute?" Fortunately, the word is rarely used outside a legal context: "one of the properties of this drug is that . . ." In the overwhelming majority of cases it turns out that even if the word is used simply to describe an object, a property right, power, or privilege is involved in the case. It may not be the key issue in the case. It may be assumed that the location of the property at 304 Linda Vista gives the plaintiff the privilege of objecting to changes in zoning of a nearby parcel, and the issue is whether the change was authorized under the statute; but property law in the definitional sense is involved in one way or another in most of the cases that use the word.

Ten categories will rought describe 85 percent of the contexts in which the word property is used. Criminal: "the defendant was arrested for possession of stolen property"; damage to or from property: "in a suit for personal injury and property damage" or "noxious fumes escaping from defendant's property"; property tax: "the city evaluated the property for tax purposes"; constitutional: "charges

that the ordinance deprives her of property without due process";
conveyancing: "defendant contracted to sell (or mortgaged) his property to plaintiff"; trusts and estates: "the executor distributed the
property"; zoning and public land use regulation: "plaintiffs' property was reclassifiedin Zone R-2-B"; condemnation: "the state filed a
declaration of taking of the property"; marital property: "incident to
the divorce they entered into a property settlement agreement"; and
creditor's rights: "alleging that the property had a mechanic's lien at-

Table 2.1
Percent of Types of Contexts in Which "Property" Is Used in Five State Supreme Courts

	57	67	77	3-year avg	change 57–77	* ±
Property tax	11.8	11.2	11.2	11.4	– .6	
Trusts and estates	14.4	11.2	7.7	11.1	–6.7	7.1
Criminal	2.8	13.4	16.2	10.8	+ 13.4	6.5
Damage	10.6	9.4	12.1	10.7	+ 1.5	
Conveyancing	12.7	7.9	10.5	10.4	–2.2	
Zoning	9.9	11.9	7.7	9.8	–2.2	
Constitution	4.9	4.7	11.2	6.9	+ 6.3	6.1
Condemnation	3.6	7.6	4.2	5.1	+ .6	
Creditor	7.7	4.0	2.4	4.7	–5.3	5.5
Marital	4.8	1.9	3.3	3.3	–1.5	
Total	83.2	83.2	86.5	84.3	+ 3.3	

*The statistic in this column gives the confidence interval at the 95
percent level for difference between the 1957 and 1977 proportions.
See Thoman H. Wonnacott & Ronald J. Wonnacott, *Introductory
Statistics for Business and Economics*, 2d ed. (Santa Barbara: John
Wiley, 1977), p.227. The sign of the difference in the case of the
criminal and constitutional categories is significant, that is, a
random sample from the same underlying populations will not
produce this amount of difference more than one out of twenty
times. In the case of the trusts and estates and creditor categories the
sign is not significant at the 95 percent level but is at the 90 percent
level; that is, a random sample from the same underlying
populations will not produce this amount of difference more than
one out of ten times.

tached to it." The categories are not mutually exclusive, and where the usage smacked of more than one category we classified it on the basis of which seemed more important for the key issue in the case.[92]

Our analysis of the legal contexts in which the word was used told us relatively little about why some states had a higher proportion of cases using the word than others. New Jersey has a larger proportion of property tax cases than the others — not surprising for a state that had until recently no income tax.[93] Illinois used to allow appeal as of right to its supreme court in cases in which a freehold was at stake,. and this may explain why Illinois had the highest percentage of conveyancing cases in 1957 and perhaps in 1967.[94] The principal reason for the variation in the overall proportion among the five states, however, seems to be that New York for all three years and Pennsylvania in 1967 and 1977 each had as many cases as the other three combined. Many of these cases were one-line dismissals, affirmances, or denials of review. These cases normally did not contain the word "property," or any other word indicating the legal context of the case.[95]

When we weighted our samples for the overall proportion of that state's property cases to the five-state total and summed up the categories over the five states, some interesting patterns began to appear (see Table 2.1).

Most of the categories appear relatively stable over the twenty-year period. In four, however, there has been a marked change: the proportion of criminal cases has increased sixfold over the period, the category moving from tenth in rank order in 1957 to first in 1967 and 1977. The proportion of constitutional cases has more than doubled (seventh in 1957, eighth in 1967, and fourth in 1977). There were only half as many trust and estates case in 1977 as there were in 1957 (first, third, sixth) and one third as many creditor cases (sixth, ninth, tenth).[96]

How should we interpret these numbers in the light of our initial questions? All five courts have considerable control over their dockets.[97] Most of the cases in the sample reached the court because the court decided that it wanted to hear them. On the other hand, the court cannot manufacture cases. The parties and their lawyers must decide whether they are going to litigate at all and, if so, whether they are going to try to get the highest court in the state to hear the case. Thus, we are looking at the product of two judgments, both of which must be affirmative, that of the court that the case is worth hearing and that of the losing party below that it is worth pursuing to the highest level. In the case of the criminal cases, the ready availability of legal aid has greatly reduced the cost to many defendants of pursuing the case to the next higher level. Rapid change in constitutional procedural doctrines have led many courts to exercise what discretion they have in favor of taking criminal appeals. The great increase in appellate criminal cases is well known, and I suspect that except for the search-and-seizure area the increase in criminal property cases tell us relatively little about changes in the concept of property. This great increase in criminal appeals may, however, go some of the way toward explaining the decline in the overall proportion of property cases. Since we did not sample the non-property cases, we can rely only on judgment, but I suspect that more civil appeals involve property concepts, and hence the word, than do criminal. Indeed, criminal cases that raise essentially procedural issues may not use the word even if the underlying crime is a "property crime": "The defendant was convicted of robbery. The question raised by this appeal is whether his confession was properly admitted into evidence."

Having disposed of the most dramatic change over the last twenty years and having decided that the overall decline probably cannot be explained by the uses of the word "property," the question remains whether the other three changes tell us anything about changes in the use of the concept. I think they do, but to show this we need one more set of statistics. In 1957 roughly 42 percent of the property cases involved a governmental entity as one of the parties; in 1967 it was 56 percent; in 1977, 65 percent. Part of this increase is attributable to the increase in criminal cases, but not all. In 1957, 40 percent of the civil property cases involved a governmental party; in 1967, 49 percent; in 1977, 58 percent. Some of the causes of this increase can be seen in Table 2.1. The proportion of zoning and condemnation cases increased 6 percentage points between 1957 and 1967. While they declined between 1967 and 1977, the decline was more than compensated for by the increase in constitutional cases. Some of the causes of the increase lie below the surface of the table. There are more cases involving damage to or by property involving governmental entities and more government cases in the large category of miscellaneous cases that makes up the difference between the ten categories listed above and the total. Accompanying this increase in cases with a governmental party has been a decline in the proportion of cases involving trusts or decedents' estates, creditors' rights, and conveyancing.

Many issues, of course, are involved in these civil cases with governmental parties. Sometimes one governmental body is suing another over property that both claim; sometimes the government has intervened to protect one citizen's property against another (e.g., disbarment on the grounds of misuse of client's property); sometimes a citizen qua citizen is claiming that a governmental body has misused its property (e.g., sold parkland in violation of a statute); but the vast majority of these cases involves a claim by a citizen that his property rights have been infringed by governmental action. If we add the search-and-seizure cases from the criminal sphere, the picture becomes even clearer. Increasingly citizens are claiming, either as plaintiff or as defendant, that the government is violating some interest of theirs in property: it is taking it when it shouldn't or without paying adequate compensation; it is taxing it when it shouldn't or at too high a rate; it is preventing them from using their property in its most profitable way; it is removing regulatory protection on which they have relied; it is searching or seizing it without probable cause; it is using its property in a way that interferes with their use of theirs. Most of these cases do not involve novel principles. Little in our 1977 sample would surprise a well-trained lawyer of 1957. What has changed is the emphasis: certain old ideas are appearing more frequently, others less.

Although we can only speculate about the causes of this trend, the most obvious hypothesis would seem to be that property is increasingly being viewed by litigants as a bastion against an ever encroaching state. It is not property rights versus civil rights or property rules versus liability rules or property versus contract but rather the property holder versus the state that is at stake in these cases. Sometimes the environmental controversy seems to have precipitated the conflict; sometimes it is the claim of "new property"; sometimes the assertion of a property right succeeds, and sometimes it fails, but the significant thing would seem to be who is asserting the claim and the fact that it is being done with greater frequency.

We should not exaggerate this trend. The proportion of cases in our sample that mention property at all has declined by 14 points over twenty years.[98] In the face of this decline, criminal property cases and constitutional property cases are the only ones that have increased in proportion to the total; the proportion of governmental property cases to the total has remained roughly constant. Thus it is a bit hard to tell whether the phenomenon we need to explain is an increase in the proportion of governmental property cases or a decline in the proportion of private ones.

In order to obtain some points of comparison, we drew another sample, this time from the supreme courts of four states in the "Sunbelt": Georgia, Florida, Kansas, and Arizona. All of these states are reputed to have booming economies; none is heavily industrial; several of them still have large amounts of sparsely settled land.[99] We would expect the judicial style to be more conservative in these states and the government less a factor in litigation. Table 2.2 breaks down the property cases in the four jurisdictions by category.

Table 2.2
Percent of Types of Contexts in Which "Property"
is Used in Four State Supreme Courts

	67	77	avg.
Conveyancing	26.6	20.1	23.4
Criminal	11.3	11.4	11.4
Marital	11.6	10.7	11.1
Trusts and estates	11.7	6.4	9.1
Damage	12.3	5.2	8.8
Property tax	5.6	3.9	4.8
Creditor	1.7	5.3	3.5
Constitution	2.5	3.5	3.0
Zoning	1.2	2.3	1.8
Condemnation	1.9	.5	1.2
Total	86.4	69.3	78.1

The table hardly needs explaining. For 1977 there is about twice the percentage of conveyancing cases as in the industrial states, three times the percentage of marital property cases. Property tax, constitutional, zoning, and condemnation cases are seventh, eighth, ninth, and tenth in the rank order as opposed to third, fourth, seventh, and eighth. Even more remarkable is the proportion of cases involving governmental parties: 28 percent of the cases (17 percent if the criminal cases are excluded) as opposed to 65 percent (58 percent in the northern states). In fact, the pattern for 1977 in these states looks far more like the pattern for 1957 in the northern states than it does that in 1977.[100]

Thus, if state supreme court litigation is any measure,[101] the concept of property remains far more important in the relationships between citizen and citizen in the Sunbelt states than it does in the more populous northern states. In the North, on the other hand, the concept of property is becoming increasingly important; at least it is not losing its importance in relationships between the citizen and the state, perhaps because property is seen as increasingly attacked by the state. Citizens of states with large and concentrated populations, industry, and declining or slow-growth economies seem to have different concerns about property than do those in states with sparser populations, greater amounts of agriculture, and more rapidly growing economies. Whether the Sunbelt states will gradually become more like those in our other sample is hard to know. But if they do, we would predict the same shift in property concerns.

CONCLUSION

In conclusion, let me suggest another way of looking both at the history of the legal concept of property and at its modern uses that may enable us better to predict its future. When we looked at the social context within which property was used, our primary focus was on which social groups the concept served, and looking at it in this way we were unable to explain the persistence of the agglomerative tendency on the basis of the interests of a given social class. Our failure to do so was partly due to the imperfect state of our knowledge; partly due to the fact that in some cases we found it difficult to explain why it was that the courts should favor the group, such as copyholders, for whose benefit the tendency worked; partly because the group interests seemed in many periods to arrange themselves around one of the inherent contradictions in the tendency. Thus, we sought an explanation for the tendency elsewhere.

Taking the tendency as a given, however, perhaps we can return to the social history and see how the function of the concept of property changed over time as the nature of the things to which it was applied changed.

Prescinding the Roman development on the ground that the social history is too problematical for this kind of inquiry and turning directly to the English high Middle Ages, the original beneficiary of the agglomerative tendency was the freeholder who was seised in

demesne as of fee.[102] His property was land, worked either by himself
or by others, but if by others, these others were not persons so far as
property law was concerned. For the property holder the land was
normally both a production and consumption unit. This last characteristic remained throughout the sixteenth and seventeenth centuries. Despite the great increase in commercial activity in these centuries, manufacturing and commercial uses of property are not the
main foci of property law. What Karl Polanyi called "the great
transformation" of the eighteenth and nineteenth centuries wrought
a radical change in the object of property law.[103] Family farms, of
course, continued, reflecting the older pattern; but increasingly
property for consumption and property for the family became disas-
sociated from property for production, which fell into the hands of
corporations. The agglomerative tendency followed both kinds of
property, even as property for power became increasingly separated
from property for security.[104]

In the regulatory state of the early twentieth century, property
came to lose its power to protect the regulated from the regulator.
This was a major development. The agglomerative tendency suffered
a setback. It seems likely that it will do so again in the face of the environmental movement. The question facing us today is whether the
tendency will also be reversed in the area of property that the great
transformation left behind, property for consumption, for the
family, for security. Property for these purposes has been increasingly held in the form of intangibles.[105] The value of intangibles can
be destroyed by inflation. The decline of the proportion of trust and
estates cases in our samples may reflect an increasing perception of
the lack of significance of the traditional trust and estate devices for
preserving property intact from generation to generation in the face
of persistent inflation. The persistence or even increase of property
cases with a governmental party, on the other hand, may reflect an
increasing desire on the part of litigants to protect what they regard
as the source of their security against government encroachment.[106]

The history suggests that the agglomerative tendency has remained remarkably powerful even when the social groups whose interests it served have changed and even when the types of property
holding in the society have changed. On the other hand, the recent
setback is in just that area (property versus the state) that is also at
stake in the current cases, despite the fact that there may be a difference in the type of property involved. The future of the concept of

property in America may well depend on whether the courts find a way to draw a distinction between property for power and property for security, [107] on whether they feel, in the oblique way that courts do, the political forces that favor the drawing of the distinction, and on whether they are convinced that it ought to be drawn. The last question is addressed in a number of the succeeding essays; a closing word may be in order about the first two.

The history of the Western concept of property suggests that the agglomerative tendency has been more a matter of intellectual convenience than of profound philosophical commitment. Its emergence in both the Roman and the Anglo-American systems has been traced to what was probably an accident of chronology coupled, in the case of the latter, with some influence from the former. As society changed from what it had been at the time the concept emerged, the concept came to be applied to other social institutions with different substantive if not formal results.

If it is true, as our samples suggest, that another change is occurring in the social reality to which the concept of property is applied, the law will not be the same as it has been in the past, whether the courts apply the basic tendency or the newer countertendency to the new phenomena. In the past the courts have either not perceived this type of social change and have simply bluntly applied the old categories to the new phenomena, or if they have perceived the change, they have manipulated the categories, consciously or unconsciously, to accomodate the change. In this way, whether the courts perceived the change or not, the categories remained formally unimpaired while the reality of the law, the product of the rules and the social phenomena to which they were applied, changed, because one of the factors in the equation had changed. [108]

If today's courts cannot differentiate between the property claims being made against the government now and those rejected in the 1930s, then the countertendency will prevail; and although the law will remain formally unimpaired, the importance of the concept of property will decline to the extent that property claims against the government come to represent more and more of the social reality of property in the definitional sense. But today's courts are probably more sensitive to social change than those of the past. Even if the courts do perceive, however, that litigants are increasingly raising property claims against the government in order to insure their security rather than to preserve their power over others, they may still be reluctant to invoke the concept of property to support them, whatever the ultimate result of the cases. Not only is property associated with rejected constitutional doctrines, but it is also associated with the discredited categorization process. The need to preserve formal continuity with past concepts is not felt so strongly today as it was in the past. This means that today's courts would not necessarily feel bound to follow the countertendency, but it also means that they would not feel much need to state their decisions in terms of the categories of the older agglomerative tendency.

All of this suggests an uncertain future for the Western concept of property. If nothing more than a burden of producing evidence were at stake, there might be a little cause for concern. But maybe there is something more, something that is not the cause of the Western legal concept of property but of which it may be an expression. We have noted how the Western legal concept of property has always been associated with various forms of individualism. The individualism of some forms of classical philosophy may lie behind the Roman concept of property. The individualism of the twelfth century may lie in the background of the emergence of property in English law. The philosophy of possessive individualism and the individualism of nineteenth century liberalism are surely related to nineteenth century developments of the concept. Individualism has always had an opposite. There is a tension between individualism and communalism, the individual and society, self-protection and self-giving. The concept of property in the West, however, has normally been associated with one side of this basic dichotomy. Both sides, of course, embody fundamental values, and the legal system must resolve the tensions between them. The issue posed by this essay is whether it continues to be useful to have a legal concept that expresses what lies on one side of the dichotomy. For those who still believe that something may be said for the Western conception of individualism, I suspect the answer is yes.

NOTES

1. Rudolf von Jhering, *Scherz und Ernst in der Jurisprudenz* (Leipzig: Breitkopf and Hartel, 1892) pp. 249–50.
2. E.g., Bell v. Maryland, 378 U.S. 226 (1964); State v. Schack, 58 N.J. 297, 277 A. 2d 369 (1971). See Charles Donahue, Thomas Kauper, and Peter Martin, *Cases and Materials on Property* (St. Paul: West, 1974), pp. 194–97, 209–34.
3. See Samuel B. Abbott, "Housing Policy, Housing Codes and Tenant

Remedies: An Integration," 56 *Boston University Law Review* 1 (January 1976); Charles Donahue, "Change in the American Law of Landlord and Tenant," 37 *Modern Law Review* 242 (May 1974); Javins v. First National Realty Corp., 428 F. 2d 1071 (D.C. Cir.), *cert. denied,* 400 U.S. 925 (1970).

4. See Guido Calabresi and A. Douglas Melamed, "Property Rules, Liability Rules, and Inalienability: One View of the Cathedral," 85 *Harvard Law Review* 1089 (April 1972); Richard A. Posner, *Economic Analysis of Law* (Boston: Little, Brown, 1977) §§ 3.4–3.7.

5. Charles Reich, "The New Property," 73 *Yale Law Journal* 733 (April 1964).

6. The article was cited nineteen times in printed judicial opinions rendered between 1967 and 1970, nineteen times between 1971 and 1974, and only seven times between 1975 and 1978. *Shepard's Law Review Citations,* 2d ed. (Colorado Springs: Shepard's, 1974), p. 846; id. (March 1979 Supp.), pp. 583–4. For one view of what happened, see William van Alstyne, "Cracks in 'the New Property,' " 62 *Cornell Law Review* 445 (March 1977).

7. See generally William H. Rogers, *Environmental Law* (St. Paul: West, 1977).

8. Cf. Grant Gilmore, *The Death of Contract* (Columbus: Ohio State, 1974).

9. E.g., Frederick H. Lawson, *Introduction to the Law of Property* (Oxford: Clarendon, 1958), p. 1; but cf. id. at 1–2.

10. Wesley N. Hohfeld, "Some Fundamental Legal Conceptions as Applied in Judicial Reasoning," 23 *Yale Law Journal* 16 (November 1913), reprinted in Wesley N. Hohfeld, *Fundamental Legal Conceptions* (New Haven: Yale Univ. Press, 1923), p. 23; Wesley N. Hohfeld, "Fundamental Legal Conceptions as Applied in Judicial Reasoning," 26 *Yale Law Journal* 710 (June 1917), reprinted in Hohfeld, op. cit., p. 65

11. This, of course, assumes that "the law" encompasses only those situations in which the coercive power of the community may be brought to bear. Cf. Christopher D. Stone, "Should Trees Have Standing?— Toward Legal Rights for Natural Objects," 45 no. 2 *Southern California Law Review* 450 (1972).

12. See Lawson, op. cit., pp. 3, 5–6, 15–31. I have avoided any use of the word "real" (in the sense of "good as against the whole world") in my definition. Although "real" may describe some kinds of property rights, powers, and privileges in some legal systems, including our own, it has never seemed to me to be a very useful concept in *defining* property. Cf. Felix N. Cohen, "Dialogue on Private Property," 9 *Rutgers Law Review* 374 (Winter 1954).

13. See, e.g., Max Gluckman, *The Ideas in Barotse Jurisprudence* (New York: Humanities, 1972) pp. 75–140; Paul Bohanan, *Justice and Judgment Among the Tiv* (London: Oxford Univ. Press, 1968), pp. 102–12; Robert H. Lowie, "Incorporeal Property in Primitive Society," 37 *Yale Law Journal* 551 (March 1928).

14. "Property, sb.," *The Oxford English Dictionary* (Oxford: Clarendon, 1933), § P, p. 1471; "proprietas," Charlton T. Lewis and Charles Short, *A Latin Dictionary* (Oxford: Clarendon, 1966), p. 1472.

15. "Proprius," "prae," *A Latin Dictionary,* op. cit., pp. 1472, 1410.

16. "Property, sb.," definitions nos. 1 and 5, *The Oxford English Dictionary,* op. cit. Until the sixteenth century, of course, the uses were all in nonlegal writing. The lawyers wrote in Latin or Law French.

17. "Property, sb.," definition no. 2, *The Oxford English Dictionary,* op. cit.

18. For some beginnings, see Roberto M. Unger, *Law in Modern Society* (New York: The Free Press, 1977); Alan Watson, "Comparative Law and Legal Change," 37 *Cambridge Law Journal* 313 (November 1978).

19. See Alan Watson, *Legal Transplants* (Charlottesville: Univ. Press of Virginia, 1974), pp. 12–15; Alan Watson, *Rome of the XII Tables* (Princeton: Princeton Univ. Press, 1975), pp. 7–8.

20. E.g., Stroud F. C. Milsom, *The Legal Framework of English Feudalism* (Cambridge: Cambridge Univ. Press, 1976), which has revolutionized our view of the English twelfth and thirteenth centuries.

21. One further qualification: I teach modern property law and Roman and medieval legal history. The weakness of my knowledge of what lies between will be painfully apparent.

22. *Digest* 41.2.12.1.

23. These are basically the facts of The Duke of Norfolk's Case, 3 Ch. Cas. 1, 22 Eng. Rep. 931 (1682).

24. For a witty and trenchant statement of this point, see Louisiana Leasing Co. v. Sokolow, 48 Misc. 2d 1014, 1015–16, 266 N.Y.S. 2d 447, 449 (N.Y. City Civ. Ct. 1966).

25. Logically the problem of conflicting land use is one of joint causation. It makes no more sense to say that the smoking factory causes a nuisance in a residential area than it does to say that the residents do. Take one or the other away and the problem goes away. The realization of this fact, however, was long in coming. See Ronald H. Coase, "The Problem of Social Cost," 3 *Journal of Law and Economics* 1 (October 1960); Joseph L. Sax, "Takings, Private Property and Public Rights," 81 *Yale Law Journal* 149 (December 1971). Perhaps the reason why it was so long in coming is that problems of conflicting land use are rarely problems of mutual incompatability. The factory can frequently exist quite well even if the residents are there, but the converse is not the case. This characteristic of the problem means that we can almost always identify who is going to sue whom. In the language of the text, the passive user will sue the active. How the agglomerative tendency will work in this situation has varied over time. The statements in the text are generally true for nineteenth- and early-twentieth-century Anglo-American law and probably for Roman (but cf. Alan Rodger, *Owners and Neighbours in Roman Law* [Oxford: Clarendon, 1972]). It does not seem to be true of medieval and Tudor

English law, where the tendency seems to have attached itself to the plaintiff's privilege of use. See below at nn. 48–50.

26. On possessive individualism, see especially Crawford B. Macpherson, *The Political Theory of Possessive Individualism: Hobbes to Locke* (Oxford: Clarendon, 1969). On liberalism, see generally Harold J. Laski, *The Rise of European Liberalism* (London: George Allen & Unwin, 1962); Harry K. Girvetz, *The Evolution of Liberalism* (New York: Collier, 1963).

27. "Proprietas," Hermann G. Heumann, *Handlexikon zu den Quellen des römischen Rechts,* 7th ed., rev. A. Thon (Jena: Gustav Fischer, 1891), pp. 430–1.

28. See Fritz Schulz, *Classical Roman Law* (Oxford: Clarendon, 1951), p. 431.

29. Id., pp. 444–54, 368–74.

30. Id. pp. 386–90; William W. Buckland, *A Textbook of Roman Law,* 3d ed., rev. Peter Stein (Cambridge: Cambridge Univ. Press, 1963), pp. 269–73.

31. Schulz, op. cit., pp. 392–96.

32. Id., pp. 336, 47–48.

33. Id., pp. 370–71.

34. Buckland, op. cit., pp. 65, 280–81, 533–34.

35. See now Bruce W. Frier, *Landlords and Tenants in Imperial Rome* (Princeton: Princeton Univ. Press, forthcoming 1980).

36. William W. Buckland and Arnold D. McNair, *Roman Law and Common Law,* 2d ed., rev. F. H. Lawson (Cambridge: Cambridge Univ. Press, 1952), pp. 115–17.

37. Fritz Schulz, *Principles of Roman Law* (Oxford: Clarendon, 1936), pp. 29–30; Biondo Biondi, *La Categoria romana delle "servitutes,"* (Milan: Univ. of the Sacred Heart, 1938), pp. 557–625.

38. Perhaps the most successful work in this genre is Buckland and MacNair, op. cit.

39. See Gregory Vlastos, "The Individual as an Object of Love in Plato," in *Platonic Studies* (Princeton: Princeton Univ. Press, 1973), p. 3; Harry V. Jaffa, "Aristotle," in *History of Political Philosophy,* ed. Leo Strauss and Joseph Cropsey (Chicago: Rand McNally, 1963), p. 64. On the possible influence of Stoic thinking on the Roman law, see Richard Schlatter, *Private Property: The History of an Idea* (New Brunswick, N.J.: Rutgers Univ. Press, 1951), pp. 21–30.

40. See generally John A. Crook, *Law and Life of Rome* (Ithaca, N.Y.: Cornell Univ. Press, 1967), pp. 139–78.

41. Alfred W. B. Simpson, *An Introduction to the History of the Land Law* (Oxford: Oxford Univ. Press, 1961) pp. 135–41.

42. Id., p. 139

43. See generally Milsom, op. cit.

44. Theodore F. T. Plucknett, *Legislation of Edward I* (Oxford: Clarendon, 1949), pp. 110–35.

45. Theodore F. T. Plucknett, *A Concise History of the Common Law,* 5th ed. (Boston: Little, Brown, 1956), pp. 552–54, 620–23.

46. Charles M. Gray, *Copyhold, Equity, and the Common Law* (Cambridge: Harvard Univ. Press, 1963); Simpson, op. cit., pp. 145–62.

47. On these developments see id., pp. 198–201 (destructibility); pp. 109–11, 131–32, 237–38 (covenants); pp. 90–96 (Shelley's Case); pp. 173–76 (Statute of Uses); pp. 195–218 (perpetuities).

48. For the beginnings, see Janet Loengard, "The Assize of Nuisance: Origins of an Action at Common Law," 37 *Cambridge Law Journal* 144 (April 1978). For the later history I have relied on Daniel R. Coquillette, "Mosses from a Very Old Manse: Another Look at Some Historic Property Cases about the Environment," 64 *Cornell Law Review* 761 (June 1979).

49. E.g., Helena M. Chew and William Kellaway, eds., *London Assize of Nuisance 1301–1431* (London: London Record Society Publications No. 10, 1973).

50. Coquillette, op.cit., pp. 765-81.

51. *Rotuli Parliamentorum* (London: House of Lords, 1767 X 1783), vol. III, par. 43, p. 420.

52. Stat. 6 Hen. 8, c.17 (1514–1515) (authorizing the city of Canterbury to improve a river, provided that anyone whose mill, bridge or dam was removed should be "reasonably satisfied"); Stat. 31 Hen. 8, c.4 (1539) (granting power to the Mayor and Baliffs of Exeter to clear the River Exe: "They shall pay to the owners and farmers of so much ground as they shall dreg, the rate of twenty years purchase, or so much as shall be adjudged by the justices of assise in the county of Devon.") See William Stoebuck, "A General Theory of Eminent Domain," 47 *Washington Law Review* 553, 565–66 (August 1972).

53. See, e.g., Hugo Grotius, *De Jure Belli ac Pacis*, 1646 ed., trans. Francis W. Kelsey (New York: Oceana, 1925), pp. 219, 385, 796–97, 807.

54. Frederick Pollock and Frederic W. Maitland, *The History of English Law Before the Time of Edward I*, 2d ed., reissue (Cambridge: Cambridge Univ. Press, 1968), vol. 2, pp. 18–19. For Continental precursors of the philosophy of possessive individualism, see Paolo Grossi, "La proprieta nel sistemo privatistico della seconda scolastica," in Paolo Grossi, ed., *La seconda scolastica nella formazione del diritto privato moderno* (Milan: Giuffre, 1973), pp. 117–222. The influence of these ideas, even in sixteenth and seventeenth century England, strikes me as unlikely, however.

55. George D. G. Hall, ed., *The Treatise on the Laws and Customs of England, Commonly Called Glanvill* (London: Nelson, 1965), § 11.1, p. 132; ed. George E. Woodbine, trans. Samuel E. Thorne, *Bracton on the Laws and Customs of England* (Cambridge: Harvard Univ. Press, 1977), vol 4, fol. 317b, p. 21; fol. 373, p. 170

56. See, e.g. Colin Morris, *The Discovery of the Individual, 1050–1200* (London: Church Historical Society, 1972).

57. A useful summary of the debate with references may be found in Loengard, op. cit., p. 145, n. 1. See also Frederic Joüon des Longrais,

Henry II and His Justiciars: Had They a Political Plan in Their Reforms About Seisin (Limoges: A. Bontemps, 1962) (Lecture delivered at Gonville and Caius College, Cambridge, September 19, 1961).

58. Milsom, op. cit., esp. pp. 183–86.

59. Plucknett, *Legislation,* op. cit.

60. I hope to develop this point in a forthcoming article on marital property in England and France in the thirteenth century.

61. On the Statute of 1290 (Quia Emptores), see Plucknett, *Legislation,* op. cit., pp. 77–108; on the Statute of Uses, see Eric W. Ives, "The Genesis of the Statute of Uses," 82 *English Historical Review* 673 (October 1967).

62. See Macpherson, op. cit.

63. A notable exception is Edward P. Thompson, *Whigs and Hunters: The Origin of the Black Act* (London: Lane, 1975).

64. Compare William Blackstone, *Commentaries on the Laws of England* (London: Dawsons, 1966) (reprint of 1768 edition), vol. II, p. 1, with id., vol. III, pp. 216–22 (on nuisance).

65. Schulz, op. cit., p. 338; Rodgers, op. cit., pp. 1–4.

66. Simpson, op. cit., pp. 243–51 (easements); John H. C. Morris and Walter B. Leach, *The Rule Against Perpetuities,* 2d ed. (London: Stevens, 1962), pp. 8–13; Morton J. Horwitz, *The Transformation of American Law* (Cambridge: Harvard Univ. Press, 1977), pp. 31–62 (water law and waste).

67. For the New York "two lives" rule, see Richard R. Powell, *The Law of Real Property* ed. Patrick J. Rohan (New York: Matthew Bender, 1977) , ¶¶. 791–807B. For the English Settled Land Acts, see Settled Land Act, 1882, 45 & 46 Vict., c. 38; Simpson, op. cit., pp. 258–59. For married women's property, see Married Women's Property Act, 1870, 33 & 34 Vict., c.93; Married Women's Property Act, 1882, 45 & 46 Vict., c.75; 1839 Miss. Laws, c.46; 1844 Mich. Acts, No. 66; 1844 Me. Acts, c.117; 1848 N.Y. Laws, c.200; Elizabeth G. Brown, "Husband and Wife—Memorandum on the Mississippi Woman's Law of 1839," 42 *Michigan Law Review* 1110 (April 1944).

68. Russell Reno, "The Enforcement of Equitable Servitudes in Land: Part I," 28 *Virginia Law Review* 951, 975–78 (May 1942).

69. Austin W. Scott, *The Law of Trusts,* 3d ed. (Boston: Little, Brown, 1967) § 1.7.

70. Erwin N. Griswold, *Spendthrift Trusts,* 2d ed. (New York: Prentice Hall, 1947), § 555.

71. See National Commission on Urban Problems, *Building the American City* (Washington, D.C.: Government Printing Office, 1968), pp. 199–201; Housing, Town Planning, etc., Act of 1909, 9 Edw. 7, c.44. For a history of the town planning movement in Great Britain, see William Ashworth, *The Genesis of Modern British Town Planning* (London: Routledge & Kegan Paul, 1954).

72. George L. Haskins, "Extending the Grasp of the Dead Hand: Reflections on the Origins of the Rule Against Perpetuities," 126 *University of Pennsylvania Law Review* 19 (November 1977).

73. Horwitz, op, cit.; Lawson, op. cit., pp. 177–86.
74. Haskins, op. cit.
75. Horwitz, op. cit.
76. E.g. John C. Gray, *The Rule Against Perpetuities* (Boston: Little, Brown, 1886).
77. The topics treated by the American Law Institute's *Restatement of the Law of Property* are *Freehold Estates,* vol. 1 (1936), *Future Interests,* vol. 2 (1936) for vol 3 (1940), *Perpetuities and Other Social Restrictions,* vol. 4 (1944), and *Servitudes,* vol. 5 (1944).
78. Blackstone, op. cit., vol. II, p. 1.
79. E.g., Pumpelly v. Green Bay Co., 80 U.S. (13 Wall.) 166 (1871); Munn v. Illinois, 94 U.S. 113 (1877); Mugler v. Kansas, 123 U.S. 623 (1887); Chicago, B. & Q. R.R. Co. v. City of Chicago, 166 U.S. 226 (1897); for the state law background see Harry N. Scheiber, "Road to Munn: Eminent Domain and the Concept of Public Purpose in the State Courts," 5 *Perspectives in American History* 329 (1971).
80. Truax v. Corrigan, 257 U.S. 312 (1921); New State Ice Co. v. Liebman, 285 U.S. 262 (1932) (labor and economic regulation); Pollock v. Farmer's Loan & Trust Co., 157 U.S. 429 (1895) (striking down income tax on the ground that taxes on income from real estate are direct taxes which must be apportioned under the U.S. Constitution); Note, "The Constitutionality of Zoning Laws," 72 *University of Pennsylvania Law Review* 421 (May 1924), discusses early cases in which land use regulation was struck down.
81. Village of Euclid v. Ambler Realty Co., 272 U.S. 365 (1926) (upholding zoning ordinance) (loss in value of 75%); Hadachek v. Sebastian, 239 U.S. 394 (1915) (88%); cf. Pennsylvania Coal Co. v. Mahon, 260 U.S. 393 (1922) ("taking" occurs when government's control over a person's use of his property is so great that the value to the owner has been virtually destroyed). The Sixteenth Amendment (1913) legitimized the income tax by eliminating the requirement that taxes on income be apportioned among the states. West Coast Hotel Co. v. Parrish, 300 U.S. 379, 191 (1937) (minimum wage law upheld on rational relation test); Nebbia v. New York, 291 U.S. 502 (1934) (the same for price regulation).
82. Katz v. United States, 389 U.S. 347, 353 (1967) ("Fourth Amendment protects people . . . not simply 'areas' "); Silverman v. United States, 365 U.S. 505, 511 (1961) (Fourth Amendment guards against recording of oral statements accomplished without property law trespass).
83. This needs considerably more expansion than I have either space or competence to give here. It seems, however, that it must be more than chance that the notion of individual property emerges in English law and Roman at a time when family ties to property are weakening *and* legal professionalization is occurring. In the Rome of the early jurists (roughly 100 B.C.), the *gens* is ceasing to have the power over family property it once had. In the England of the late twelfth century, the heir is losing his power to control his ancestor's alienation. (Compare Glanvill and Bracton on this point.) At the same time, neither society

was prepared to see others' connections with the property, e.g., slaves and those in power in Rome, serfs in England.

84. For a realist approach to property law, see Myres S. McDougal and David Haber, *Property, Wealth, Land: Allocation, Planning and Development* (Charlottesville: Michie, 1948); cf. Walter B. Leach, *Property Law Indicated!* (Lawrence: Univ. Press of Kansas, 1967).

85. The possible relevance of the agglomerative tendency to the inflation and "new property" problems is discussed in the concluding section.

86. For some of the theory underlying these statements, see Charles Donahue, "Comparative Reflections on the 'New Matrimonial Jurisprudence' of the Roman Catholic Church," 75 *Michigan Law Review* 1010–19 (April–May 1977).

87. The computer system, known as LEXIS, contains appellate opinions from the following states (with population rank for the first ten as given in U.S. Department of Commerce, Bureau of the Census, *Statistical Abstract of the United States 1978* (Washington, D.C.: Government Printing Office, 1979) p. 14: Arizona, California (1); Connecticut, Florida (8); Georgia, Illinois (5); Kansas, Kentucky, Massachusetts (10); Michigan (7); Minnesota, Missouri, New Jersey (9); New York (2); Ohio (6); Pennsylvania (4); Texas (3); Virginia; and Washington; but the jurisdictions are not equally represented. For instance, whereas the LEXIS file contains all appellate cases decided by Ohio courts after 1939, no case decided by the Michigan Supreme Court after 1965 is available to the LEXIS researcher. The computer file also includes opinions from all levels of the federal court system, and various other legal documents (e.g., state constitutions and rules of procedure).

   A LEXIS research project begins when the researcher supplies the computer with words or phrases likely to occur in cases or statutory material that the researcher believes may be of help to him. The computer then searches that portion of its file in which the researcher is interested. (A research request may be limited by jurisdiction (e.g., the Supreme Court of Pennsylvania), by time (e.g., all cases decided between 1965 and 1968), or by some combination of these elements.) The computer then supplies the researcher with a list of all sources in which the suggested words and phrases occur. LEXIS terminals are also supplied with a display screen on which the sources discovered by the computer may be examined by the researcher, in whole or in part.

   For a description of the LEXIS system and an introduction to its use, see *LEXIS: A Primer* (Mead Data Central, Inc., 1975).

88. 2,452 of the 8,330 appellate court opinions in the LEXIS file for 1957, use the word "property"; for 1967, 3,834 of 13,017; and for 1977, 5,954 of 23,112. When only state supreme court decisions are considered, 945 of 2,478 opinions reported for 1957 mention "property," 1,195 of 3,809 reported for 1967, and 1,043 of 4, 197 reported for 1977. These figures are incomplete in several respects. At the time the research for this paper was done (January 1979), three of the states listed in n. 87 (Connecticut, Minnesota, and Washington) were not

represented in the LEXIS file. In addition, there were no 1957 opinions from Arizona, Florida, Georgia, Kansas, or Michigan, nor did the file contain Florida's 1967 opinions. (The file included the latter when the search discussed below at 99–100 was made.) Finally, opinions from certain of the states were arranged in the file in a manner that made it impossible to differentiate opinions from courts of last resort from those of intermediate appellate courts. This was true of Kansas for 1977, Texas for 1977 and 1967, and Missouri for all three sample years. Thus our supreme court figures do not include these states for these years.

89. The computer file was complete with regard to each of the five states for each of the sample years. The five states sampled are among the nine most populous in the nation. See n. 87 above. Two of the nine largest states, Texas and Michigan, could not be sampled because of the inadequacies in the LEXIS file. See n. 87, above. Florida, another of the nine largest, was not included in this sample, but was examined in connection with another sample discussed below at nn. 99–100, below. Ohio was excluded in favor of the smaller New Jersey because of the latter's unusually high percentage of "property" cases. See n. 90, below.

90. For California, the percentage of high court opinions mentioning property was 34 in 1957, 38 in 1967, and 59 in 1977. For Illinois, the percentages were 54, 27, and 36; for New Jersey, 46, 33, and 48; for New York, 21, 18, and 15; and for Pennsylvania, 47, 30, and 16.

91. Taking the five states together, 36% of the high court opinions mentioned property in 1957, 26% in 1967, and 22% in 1977. The decline of 14 percentage points over twenty years is almost identical to the decline of 13 points over the same period in the sample consisting of all states in the LEXIS system.

92. Where, however, the case involved a zoning regulation we classified it as a zoning case even if the key issue seemed to be constitutional. On the other hand, only those cases where the power of eminent domain was formally invoked were classified as condemnation cases; cases in which informal or regulatory "takings" were claimed were classified as constitutional.

93. The New Jersey legislature enacted the state's first income tax statute in 1976. See Gross Income Tax Act, 54 N.J.S. §§1–1 to 9–28 (1978).

94. The Illinois freehold rule, formerly 110 Rev. Stat. §75, allowed direct appeal from the trial court to the state supreme court in cases involving a freehold. Adopted in 1872, the rule was repealed in 1964.

95. The statement in the text is truer of New York that it is of Pennsylvania. The Pennsylvania Supreme Court does, however, have a very high case load and disposes of many of its cases in short, though normally not one-line opinions.

96. We are less confident of this last change than we are of the others because it is almost entirely the result of a decline in the New York creditor cases that affects the overall weighted proportions markedly because of the large number of New York cases.

97. The Illinois statute is typical: it provides that except in cases where

there is appeal as of right, the granting of for leave to appeal to the supreme court is a matter of "sound judicial discretion." 110A Ill. Rev. Stat. §315 (a) (1978). See also Cal. Rules of Court 28, 29 (1978); New Jersey Court Rules, 2:12–4 (1978); 7B N.Y. Stat. Ann. §5602 (McKinney 1978); 17 Pa. Stat. Ann. §211.204 (Purdon 1978).

State supreme courts do not have total control over their dockets, however. Some states provide for appeal as of right in certain types of cases; for example, New York allows appeals to its highest court whenever there is a dissent in the court below that favors the party seeking to appeal, 7B N.Y. Stat. Ann. §5601 (a) (i). And even when permission to appeal is required, some states have decided that at least in certain cases, leave to appeal can be granted by the court from which the appeal is taken. See, e.g., 37 Ill. Rev. Stat. §32.3 (b) (1978); 7B N.Y. Stat. Ann. §5602 (a), (b) (McKinney 1978).

98.   See n. 91, above.

99.   Of the residents of Kansas, 54.1%, and 43.2% of those of Georgia live in areas which the Bureau of the Census classifies as "nonmetropolitan." Nationwide, only 27.1% of the citizenry lives in such areas. The other two states in the sample are closer to the national average: 25.5% of Arizona's residents live in nonmetropolitan areas; in urbanized Florida, 14%. Each state in our first sample is more urban than the nation as a whole. In California, only 7.2% of the population lives outside metropolitan areas; in New Jersey, 7.8%; in New York, 11.5%; in Illinois, 18.7%; and in Pennsylvania, 19.5%. U.S. Department of Commerce, Bureau of the Census, *Statistical Abstract of the United States,* 1978, p. 19.

100.   Unfortunately, the pattern for 1957 for the Sunbelt states could not be calculated because the data was not in the computer file. See n. 87, above.

101.   This is, of course, a big "if." As we noted above (nn. 86–87), the legal concept of property is used in many ways that have nothing to do with litigation. Supreme court litigation may be a fairly good measure, however, of what both the litigants and the courts think are the important issues. See text at note 97 above.

102.   See above text at n. 57.

103.   Karl Polanyi, *The Great Transformation* (New York: Farrar and Rinehart, 1944).

104.   See Morris R. Cohen, "Property and Sovereignty," in id., *Law and the Social Order* (New York: Harcourt, Brace, 1937), pp. 46–49. The distinction I am drawing here is not the traditional one between property for production and that for consumption, nor quite Cohen's distinction between property for power and that for use. It shares with the other two distinctions the difficulty that some objects will fall into both categories and has the added difficulty that the feeling of security that property gives the property holder may come from the fact that his property gives him power over others. Nonetheless, I think it is possible in many instances to distinguish objectively between offensive and defensive use of property, between property as a sword and property as a shield, and to protect in law the latter when the former

would not be protected. For what seems to me to be a successful effort to draw this distinction in the context of case involving access to a migrant labor camp, see State v. Shack, 58 N.J. 297, 277 A.2d 369 (1971).

105.   See Thurmon W. Arnold, *The Folklore of Capitalism* (New Haven: Yale Univ. Press, 1937), pp. 121–27; David T. Bazelon, *The Paper Economy* (New York: Random House, 1963) pp. 45–67; Charles Reich, op. cit. n. 5, pp. 738–39.

106.   In both the trusts and estates and the governmental party case we should bear in mind that we are drawing inferences from a sample of litigated cases. See n. 101, above. Hence we cannot conclude that traditional trusts and estates devices *are* less important today than they were twenty years ago or that government *is* increasingly encroaching on citizens' property. I have the impression that the former is not the case and that the latter is, but my evidence for both propositions is anecdotal. What the evidence does suggest is a change in what litigants regard as important and/or a change in what the courts regard as important. What the text offers is some speculation as to why their views might have changed.

107.   For the difficulty of drawing this distinction, see n. 104 above.

108.   For a remarkable statement of this point from another era, see Karl Renner, *The Institutions of Private Law and Their Social Functions* (London: Routledge & Kegan Paul, 1949) (first published in 1929).

3

THE DISINTEGRATION OF PROPERTY

THOMAS C. GREY

I

In the English-speaking countries today, the conception of property held by the specialist (the lawyer or economist) is quite different from that held by the ordinary person. Most people, including most specialists in their unprofessional moments, conceive of property as *things* that are *owned* by *persons*. To own property is to have exclusive control of something—to be able to use it as one wishes, to sell it, give it away, leave it idle, or destroy it. Legal restraints on the free use of one's property are conceived as departures from an ideal conception of full ownership.[1]

By contrast, the theory of property rights held by the modern specialist tends both to dissolve the notion of ownership and to eliminate any necessary connection between property rights and things. Consider ownership first. The specialist fragments the robust unitary conception of ownership into a more shadowy "bundle of rights." Thus, a thing can be owned by more than one person, in which case it becomes necessary to focus on the particular limited rights each of the co-owners has with respect to the thing. Further, the notion that full ownership includes rights to do as you wish with what you own suggests that you might sell off *particular aspects* of your control— rights to certain uses, to profits from the thing, and so on. Finally, rights of use, profit, and the like can be parceled out along a temporal dimension as well—you might sell your control over your property for tomorrow to one person, for the next day to another, and so on.

Not only can ownership rights be subdivided, they can even be made to disappear as if by magic, if we postulate full freedom of disposition in the owner. Consider the convenient legal institution of the trust. Yesterday A owned Blackacre; among his rights of ownership was the legal power to leave the land idle, even though developing it would bring a good income. Today A puts Blackacre in trust, conveying it to B (the trustee) for the benefit of C (the beneficiary). Now no one any longer has the legal power to use the land uneconomically or to leave it idle—that part of the rights of ownership is neither in A nor B nor C, but has disappeared. As between B and C, who owns Blackacre? Lawyers say B has the legal and C the equitable ownership, but upon reflection the question seems meaningless: what is important is that we be able to specify what B and C can legally do with respect to the land.

The same point can be made with respect to fragmentation of ownership generally. When a full owner of a thing begins to sell off various of his rights over it—the right to use it for this purpose tomorrow, for that purpose next year, and so on—at what point does he cease to be the owner, and who then owns the thing? You can say that each one of many right holders owns it to the extent of the right, or you can say that no one owns it. Or you can say, as we still tend to do, in vestigial deference to the lay conception of property, that some conventionally designated rights constitute "ownership." The issue is seen as one of terminology; nothing significant turns on it. [2]

What, then, of the idea that property rights must be rights in things? Perhaps we no longer need a notion of ownership, but surely property rights are a distinct category from other legal rights, in that they pertain to things. But this suggestion cannot withstand analysis either; most property in a modern capitalist economy is intangible. Consider the common forms of wealth: shares of stock in corporations, bonds, various kinds of commercial paper, bank accounts, insurance policies—not to mention more arcane intangibles such as trademarks, patents, copyrights, franchises, and business goodwill.

In our everyday language, we tend to speak of these rights as if they attached to things. Thus we "deposit our money in the bank", as if we were putting a thing in a place; but really we are creating a complex set of abstract claims against an abstract legal institution. We are told that as insurance policy holders we "own a piece of the rock"; but we really have other abstract claims against another abstract institution. We think of our share of stock in Megabucks Corporation as part ownership in the Megabucks factory outside town; but really the Megabucks board of directors could sell the factory and go into another line of business and we would still have the same claims on the same abstract corporation.

Property rights cannot any longer be characterized as "rights of ownership" or as "rights in things" by specialists in property. What, then, *is* their special characteristic? How do property rights differ from rights generally—from human rights or personal rights or rights to life or liberty, say? Our specialists and theoreticians have no answer; or rather, they have a multiplicity of widely differing answers, related only in that they bear some association or analogy, more or less remote, to the common notion of property as ownership of things.

Let me briefly list a number of present usages of the term property in law, legal theory, and economics.

1. The law of property for law teachers and law students typically is the whole body of law concerned with the use of land: the doctrines of estates in land, title registration and transfer, the financing of real estate transactions, the law of landlord and tenant, public regulation of land use (including zoning and environmental regulation), and public subsidy and provision of low-income housing. The only thing these doctrines have in common with each other is that they concern real estate as distinguished from other aspects of the economy.[3]

2. Lawyers (and some economists) identify property rights with rights *in rem* (rights good against the world), as distinguished from rights *in personam* (rights good against determinate persons). This distinction does not fit closely with popular notions of property; for example, the rights to life, bodily security, and personal liberty protected by criminal laws against murder, assault, and kidnapping are on this account "property rights." Neither the application of the distinction nor its purpose is very clear; for example, *in personam* contract rights shade into property rights as they become freely assignable, and assumable, and as "interference with contractual relations" is recognized as a tort.[4]

3. Some economists seem to adopt, implicitly, a purposive account of property, including among property rights all and only those entitlements whose purpose (in some sense) is to advance allocative efficiency by allowing individuals to reap the benefits and requiring them to bear the costs generated by their activities. Again, on this account rights to life, liberty, and personal security are included within the field of property. On the other hand, legal entitlements to transfer payments, such as are conferred by welfare and social security laws, are presumably excluded.[5]

4. By contrast, some modern legal theorists have stressed that a traditional purpose of private property has been to protect security and independence, and that public law entitlements to social minima serve this purpose in the modern economy, and hence should be considered a "new property."[6] This view has been embodied in the construction the courts have given to the constitutional requirement that persons not be "deprived of . . . property without due process of law." Protections offered to property have been extended to entitlements conferred by, for example, welfare and public education law.[7]

5. Another contrasting view of property is suggested by the prevailing interpretation of another constitutional provision, the prohibition against "taking" private property except for a public purpose and upon the payment of just compensation. Here, the kind of property that can be taken is confined to those conglomerations of rights that, in the popular mind, have been reified into "things" or "pieces of property." Thus, the Supreme Court recently held that designation of Grand Central Station as a historic monument, and the consequent prohibition of construction of a skyscraper over the station, did not "take" any property of the landowners—the right to use the airspace over the building, an economically valuable entitlement, was not sufficiently thing-like to be subject to the just compensation requirement.[8] (This body of "takings" law, which most nearly corresponds to popular conceptions of property as thing ownership, is difficult to rationalize in the terms of modern legal and economic theory.)[9]

6. Another specialized usage distinguishes between "property" and "liability" rules according to the nature of the sanctions imposed upon their violation. Property rules are enforceable by injunction or criminal sanctions or both—sanctions designed to prevent violation even when it would be cost justified in terms of market valuation. Liability rules are enforced only by the award of money damages, measured by the market valuation of the resources lost to the victim. This conception departs widely from popular usage; thus, a person's ownership of his car, for example, is protected by both liability rules (tort doctrines of conversion and liability for negligent damage to property) and property rules (criminal laws against theft).[10]

The conclusion of all this is that discourse about property has fragmented into a set of discontinuous usages. The more fruitful and useful of these usages are those stipulated by theorists; but these depart drastically from each other and from common speech. Conversely, meanings of "property" in law that cling to their origin in the thing-ownership conception are integrated least successfully into the general doctrinal framework of law, legal theory, and economics. It seems fair to conclude from a glance at the range of current usages that the specialists who design and manipulate the legal structures of the advanced capitalist economies could easily do without using the term "property" at all.

II

It was not always so. At the high point of classical liberal thought, around the end of the eighteenth century, the idea of private property stood at the center of the conceptual scheme of lawyers and political theorists. Thus, Blackstone wrote: "There is nothing which so generally strikes the imagination, and engages the affections of mankind, as the right of property."[11] And the French Civil Code had as its "grand and principal object" (in the words of one of its authors) "to regulate the principles and the rights of property."[12] Kant began his discussion of law in the *Metaphysics of Morals* with an analysis and justification of property rights.[13] The earliest American state constitutions proclaimed property as one of the natural rights of man.[14]

The conception of property held by the legal and political theorists of classical liberalism coincided precisely with the present popular idea, the notion of thing-ownership. Thus, Blackstone described property as "that sole and despotic dominion which one man claims and exercises over the external things of the world, in total exclusion of the right of any other individual in the universe.[15] And, in perfect concord, the French Civil Code defined property as "the right of enjoying and disposing of things in the most absolute manner."[16]

It is not difficult to see how the idea of simple ownership came to dominate classical liberal legal and political thought. First, this conception of property mirrored economic reality to a much greater extent than it did before or has since. Much of the wealth of the preindustrial capitalist economy consisted of the houses and lots of freeholders, the land of peasant proprietors or small farmers, and the shops and tools of artisans.[17]

Second, the concept of property as thing-ownership served important ideological functions. Liberalism was the ideology of the attack on feudalism. A central feature of feudalism was its complex and hierarchical system of land tenure. To the rising bourgeoisie, property conceived as a web of relations among persons meant the system of

lord, vassal, and serf from which they were struggling to free themselves. On the other hand, property conceived as the control of a
piece of the material world by a single individual meant freedom and
equality of status. Thus Blackstone denounced the archaisms of
feudal tenure.[18] The French Civil Code marked the culmination of a
revolution that abolished feudal property.[19] Hegel wrote that the abolition of feudal property in favor of individual ownership was as
great a triumph of freedom as the abolition of slavery.[20] Jefferson
contrasted the free allodial system of land titles in America with the
servile English system of feudal tenure.[21]

Third, ownership of things by individuals fitted the principal justifications for treating property as a natural right. In England and
America, the dominant theory was Locke's; rightful property resulted from the mixing of an individual's labor with nature.[22] The
main rival to Locke's theory within liberal thought was the German
Idealist conception of Kant and Hegel, who saw original property resulting from the subjective act of appropriation, the exercise of the
individual will over a piece of unclaimed nature. On this view, property was an extension of personality. Ownership expanded the natural sphere of freedom for the individual beyond his body to part of
the material world.[23]

III

We have gone, then, in less than two centuries, from a world in
which property was a central idea mirroring a clearly understood institution, to one in which it is no longer a coherent or crucial category in our conceptual scheme. The concept of property and the institution of property have disintegrated. I want to offer first a partial
explanation of this phenomenon, and then some suggestions about
its political significance.

My explanatory point is that the collapse of the idea of property
can best be understood as a process internal to the development of
capitalism itself. It is, on this view, not a result of the attack on capitalism by socialists, and not a result of the modifications of laissez-
faire that we associate with the coming of a mixed economy or a welfare state. Rather, it is intrinsic to the development of a free-market
economy into an industrial phase. Indeed, it is a factor contributing
to the declining prestige, the decaying cultural hegemony, of
capitalism. To say this is not to deny that the causation may run the

other way as well. The decline of capitalism may also contribute to the breakdown of the idea of private property, so that the two phenomena mutually reinforce each other; but my purpose is to isolate a sense in which the disintegration of property follows from the workings of an idealized market economy.

The development from an economy of small property owners to an industrial economy proceeds by the progressive exploitation of the *division of labor or function* and the *economies of scale*. This development can be pictured as taking place through a series of free economic transactions, with the state playing only its classically liberal, neutral, facilitative role. Proprietors subdivide and recombine the bundles of rights that make up their original ownership, creating by private agreement the complex of elaborate and abstract economic institutions and claims characteristic of industrial capitalism, particularly the financial institutions and the industrial corporations. With very few exceptions, all of the private law institutions of mature capitalism can be imagined as arising from the voluntary decompositions and recombination of elements of simple ownership, under a regime in which owners are allowed to divide and transfer their interests as they wish.[24]

The few aspects of the modern private economy that require state action beyond the enforcement of private agreements are the newer forms of originally acquired intangible entitlements, such as patents, copyrights, and trademarks on the one hand, and on the other hand the privilege of corporate limited liability against tort claims. (Limited liability against claims by employees and creditors could be created by contract, as could the rest of the structure of the modern corporation.)[25] The intangible entitlements are of nontrivial but relatively peripheral significance to the functioning of mature capitalism. And although the corporation is the central institution of the modern economy, it is not likely that the corporate economy would collapse without limited liability in tort.

The transformation of a preindustrial economy of private proprietors into an industrial economy by the process suggested here presupposes that the entrepreneurs, financiers, and lawyers who carry the process through have the imagination to liberate themselves from the imprisoning concept of property as the simple ownership of a thing by an individual person. They must be able to design new forms of finance and control for enterprise, which can take maximum advantage of the efficiencies of scale and division of function, forms that fractionate traditional ownership and that create claims remote from tangible objects. Similarly, if the process is to go forward smoothly, the courts will have to free themselves from stereotypes about the appropriate forms of control over the economic resources of the community, stereotypes founded on an economy of artisans, tradesmen, and family farms.[26]

The creation of new forms of enterprise and new structures of entitlement would require doctrinal formulation, at least by lawyers and courts. And where law, business, and finance are subjects of theoretical study, these new legal structures of economic organization would eventually become the focus of examination by commentators and scholars, particularly as they come to replace older forms of property as the chief economic institutions of the society. Leaving ideological considerations aside for the moment, it would not be surprising if the replacement of thing-ownership by abstract claim structures in the real world should eventually lead some theorists to the kind of analysis of the concept of property I sketched in the first section. Even if the analysis did not go that far, the basic need to teach lawyers the technical tools of their trade would suggest if not require some movement toward a bundle-of-rights formulation of property, as against the historical and popular thing-ownership conception. The main point is that all of these developments — the new economic structures, the legal forms through which they are organized, and the theooretical analysis of property that they suggest — can be plausibly seen as entirely *internal* to the capitalist market system; entirely consistent with full loyalty to that system; in no way fueled by the ethics, politics, or interests of socialism, collectivism, paternalism, or redistributive egalitarianism.

I must repeat that this account is not offered as an accurate narrative of historical events. (No society has practiced as pure an economic liberalism as this; industrial development has been subsidized, retarded, and actively shaped by government throughout.) But this account is intended to abstract out a plausible *partial* explanation, based on simplified assumptions, of the collapse of the idea of property between 1800 and today. I now want to turn to the ideological factors this simplified account has left out. If the internal logic of the market tends to fragment the concept of property in the ways I have suggested, what does a recognition of this development mean in political terms?

IV

The dissolution of the traditional conception of property erodes the moral basis of capitalism. Capitalism has commonly been conceived, by friends and enemies alike, as a system based on the existence and protection of private property rights. Given this conception, the view that property rights have intrinsic worth must strengthen the case for capitalism—at least so long as "property rights" are viewed as a single coherent category. But the phenomenon of the "death of property" breaks the connection between simple thing-ownership and the legal entitlements that make up the framework of the capitalist organization of the economy. And it is simple thing-ownership that has been justified in classical liberal theory, and I think in popular consciousness, as having intrinsic worth.

The theories that support an intrinsic moral right to property can be roughly divided into the labor and personality justifications for private ownership. The labor theory expresses the intuition that the individual owns as a matter of natural right the valued objects he has made or wrested from nature. Thus, the farmer naturally owns the land he has cleared and the crops he has grown; the artisan owns the tools he has fashioned, the raw materials he has gathered, and the products he has made.[27] The idealist "personality" theory rests on the different but no less powerful idea that human beings naturally come to regard some objects as extensions of themselves in some important sense. This idea gains its intuitive force from the way most people regard their homes, their immediate personal effects, and other material things that play a double role as part of their most immediate environment in daily life and at the same time as expressions of their personalities.[28]

Insofar as capitalism connotes a general regime of protection of private property, it enlists these still potent justifications on its side. Conversely , attacks on capitalism engender the sense of outrage that most people feel at a threat to their simple possessions and the immediate fruits of their labor. Marx and Engels realized this well when they sought to dissociate the socialist case for abolition of private property from any threat to the security of ordinary possessions:

We communists have been reproached with the desire of abolishing the right of personally acquiring property as the fruit of a man's own labor. . . . Hard-won, self-acquired, self-earned property! Do you mean the property of the petty artisan and of the small peasant, a form of property that preceded the bourgeois form? There is no need to abolish that; the development of industry has to a great extent already destroyed it, and is destroying it daily.[29]

I have argued in this essay that we no longer have any coherent concept of property encompassing both simple thing-ownership, on the one hand, and the variety of legal entitlements that are generally called property rights on the other. If correct, this argument means that the forceful intuitions behind the moral arguments for simple thing-ownership can no longer be as readily transferred to the legal institutions of the capitalist economy, as they could when private property was a clearly comprehended unitary concept.[30]

Of course, the legitimacy of capitalism does not rest solely, or perhaps even predominantly anymore, on the notion of intrinsic moral rights to private property. Especially among the professionals and intellectuals for whom the breakdown of the concept of property is most likely to be apparent, the moral basis of capitalist institutions is likely to be found in other, more instrumental, values. Thus, capitalism is more commonly defended today on the basis of its capacity to produce material well-being and its tendency to protect personal liberty.

However, the belief that capitalist economic organization is especially protective of personal liberty is itself linked in a subtle way to the traditional conception of property. The connection is suggested by the theory of capitalist private law offered by the Austrian legal sociologist Karl Renner.[31] Renner described the fundamental structure of the capitalist legal order as made up of two basic elements: the right of ownership and the right of personal liberty. Ownership defines the relationship between man and nature, which consists of the control by separate individuals of separate parcels of the material world. The right of personal liberty defines the relations between persons—a relation of independent equality, in which each person is free to do as he likes, consistent with respect for the rights of others. The interaction of the two rights creates a structure in which atomistic individuals stand, on the one hand, in a vertical relation of domination to the things they own, and on the other hand, in a horizontal relation of mutual independence to all other individuals. The only legal relations among the individuals, then, are those created by their voluntary agreements.[32]

The ideological significance of this simple and compelling picture of civil society is that it masks the existence of private economic power. The only relation of domination it recognizes is the relation of *dominium* or ownership over things. The danger of domination over persons — infringement of liberty — arises only when the state and public law are introduced, creating the power of sovereignty, or *imperium*. Thus, liberty can be threatened only by the sate, and by the state only in its public law role, not in its role as neutral enforcer of the private law relations of ownership and contract.

This structure depends for its plausibility upon the obsolete thing-ownership conception of property. Acceptance of the bundle-of-rights conception breaks the main institutions of capitalist private law free from the metaphor of ownership as control over things by individuals. Mature capitalist property must be seen as a web of state-enforced relations of entitlement and duty *between persons*, some assumed voluntarily and some not.

Given this conceptual shift, the neutrality of the state as enforcer of private law evaporates; state protection of property rights is more easily seen as the use of collective force on behalf of the haves against the have-nots. It then becomes a matter for debate whether the private power centers of the unregulated capitalist economy, on the one hand, or the augmented state machinery of a socialist or mixed system, on the other, pose the more serious threat to personal liberty. The conflict between capitalism and socialism can no longer be articulated as a clash between liberty on the one side and equality on the other; both systems must be seen as protective against different threats to human freedom.

V

The breakdown of the traditional conception of property serves at the same time to undermine traditional Marxism, and to suggest that the natural development of industrial capitalism is toward a mixed economy. To put the point briefly: private property need not be *abolished* by revolution if it tends to *dissolve* with the development of mature capitalism.

Marxists have tended to view the transition from capitalism to socialism as necessarily a convulsive, qualitative transfer of ownership of the means of production from the bourgeoisie to the proletariat — a revolution. This revolution might under certain historical circumstances take place peacefully,[33] but the end of capitalism cannot, on a Marxist view, be gradual or partial.[34] There can be no compromise or halfway house between forms of social system; people live either under capitalism or under socialism.

This world view is strongly compatible with a thing-ownership conception of property — indeed, perhaps influenced and reinforced by such a conception. Marxist definitions of the forms of social system tend to focus on who owns the means of production.[35] Marxists sometimes note that this does not necessarily mean formal or juridical ownership, but rather real or economic ownership.[36] Nevertheless both real and formal ownership have in common an all-or-nothing character. Something owned is either mine or thine, but not a little bit of each.

The Marxist approach is then substantially undermined by the demonstration that the category of all-or-nothing ownership has become increasingly unimportant as a form of legal thought in modern capitalist economies, where legal control over resources is increasingly fragmented into particularized entitlements. This fragmentation of property is most strikingly evident with respect to the large publicly held corporations that control the chief means of production. I am not speaking here primarily of the much-debated "separation of ownership and control."[37] The growth of power of non-shareholding management is only one aspect of the more general phenomenon of the dispersion of lawful power over the resources involved in a modern corporation. Not only managers and common shareholders, but also other classes of shareholders, directors, bondholders, other creditors, large suppliers and customers (through contractual arrangements), insurers, government regulators, tax authorities, and labor unions — all may have some of the legal powers that would be concentrated in the single ideal thing-owner of classical property theory.

There are clear structural similarities between this multiple institutional control and the mechanisms often suggested for controlling socialist enterprises — workers' councils, hired expert managers, central planners, suppliers, and buyers, each with influence, none with anything that might be called total power. Once the perspective of ownership is abandoned and the focus of inquiry shifts to particular legal rights and duties, on the one hand, and actual practical control, on the other, it seems natural to suppose that under any social system a variety of individuals, institutions, and interests are likely to share both the legal and the actual power over anything so complex as a major productive enterprise.[38]

On this view, capitalism and socialism become, not mutually exclusive forms of social organization, but tendencies that can be blended in various proportions.[39] Important differences between profit-oriented market exchange and political collective decision as methods of organizing and operating enterprises remain. But the idea that natural necessity somehow imposes a stark choice between organizing an economy according to one or the other mode becomes less plausible, once the single-owner presupposition is dropped.

I do not want to overstate the extent to which the breakdown of classical property theory undercuts Marxist socialism. The central theoretical feature of Marxism remains the view that capitalist society is fundamentally divided into two sharply distinct and irreconcilably opposed classes, the bourgeoisie and the proletariat. Once this picture of society is accepted, it becomes a matter of detail that economic resources are controlled through complex and overlapping legal forms. As long as all rights of ownership are held within a compact and identifiable bourgeois class, it makes sense to characterize capitalism as ownership of the means of production by the bourgeois class as a whole. What analysis of the disintegration of property does is to indicate how totally Marxism depends upon the dubious reifications of its theory of class division and class struggle.

VI

The substitution of a bundle-of-rights for a thing-ownership conception of property has the ultimate consequence that property ceases to be an important category in legal and political theory. This in turn has political implications, which I have explored in the last two parts of this chapter. I believe that history confirms the centrist political tendency of the attack upon traditional conceptions of property. The legal realists who developed the bundle-of-rights notion were on the whole supporters of the regulatory and welfare state, and in the writings that develop the bundle-of-rights conception, a purpose to remove the sanctity that had traditionally attached to the rights of property can often be discerned.[40]

The same point is illustrated by the most influential recent theoretical work on questions of economic justice, John Rawls's *A Theory of Justice*. The concept of property rights plays only the most minor role in that monumental treatise, which on the whole displays a welfare state liberal orientation toward questions of the organization of economic life.[41]

I would want to deny, however, that the account and explanation of the breakdown of the concept of property offered here is in the last analysis ideological, in the pejorative sense of a mystifying or false apologetic. The development of a largely capitalist market economy toward industrialism objectively demands formulation of its emergent system of economic entitlements in something like the bundle-of-rights form, which in turn must lead to the decline of property as a central category of legal and political thought.

NOTES

1. See the excellent explication of the "ordinary" conception of property in Bruce A. Ackerman, *Private Property and the Constitution* (New Haven and London, 1977), pp. 97–100, 113–67. See also A. M. Honore, "Ownership," in A. G. Guest, ed. *Oxford Essays in Jurisprudence* (London, 1961). [Relevant parts of the latter are summarized in Lawrence Becker's paper in the present volume (eds.).]

2. For modern property vocabulary, see Ackerman, op. cit., pp. 26–28. For the still common vestigial use of the notion of ownership by lawyers, see American Law Institute, *Restatement of the Law of Property* (St. Paul, 1936), vol. 1 pp. 25–27. Compare J. C. Vaines, *Personal Property,* 4th ed. (London, 1967), pp. 39–40.

3. I draw this point from conversations with colleagues who teach law school courses in property. Some of them do deal with a few aspects of the law of "personal property," particularly rules concerning original acquistion.

4. For the *in rem* vs. *in personam* distinction, see, e.g., Felix Cohen, "Dialogue on Private Property," 9 *Rutgers Law Review* 373–74 (Fall 1954).

5. See, e.g., Richard Posner, *Economic Analysis of Law*, 2d ed. (Boston and Toronto, 1977), pp. 27–31; Harold Demsetz, "Toward a Theory of Property Rights," 57 *Am. Econ. Rev. Papers and Proceedings* 347 (1967).

6. See Charles A. Reich, "The New Property," 73 *Yale Law Journal* 733 (April 1964).

7. Goldberg v. Kelly, 397 U.S. 254 (1970); Goss v. Lopez, 419 U.S. 565 (1975).

8. Penn Central Transp. Co. v. New York City, 438 U.S. 104 (1978).

9. See the discussion in Ackerman, op. cit., especially chap. 6. [See also Ackerman's essay in this volume (eds.).]

10. This usage was introduced by Guido Calabresi and A. Douglas Melamed, "Property Rules, Liability Rules, and Inalienability: One View of the Cathedral," 85 *Harvard Law Review* 1089 (1972).

11. Sir William Blackstone, *Commentaries on the Laws of England* 11th ed. (London, 1791), vol. II, p.2.

12. Quoted by Richard Schlatter, *Private Property: The History of an Idea* (New Brunswick, N.J., 1951), p. 232, from J. G. Locre, *La Legislation Civil de la France* (Paris, 1827), vol. 31, p. 169.

13. Kant, *Philosophy of Law,* trans. W. Hastie (Edinburgh, 1887), pp. 81–84.

14. Quoted in Schlatter, op. cit., pp. 188–89.

15. Blackstone, op. cit., p.2.
16. Code Civil, Art. 544, quoted in Schlatter, op. cit., p. 232.
17. See R.H. Tawney, *The Acquisitive Society* (New York, 1920), pp. 55–60.
18. Blackstone, op. cit. p. 77, where he said of the feudal institution of tenure by knight service: "A slavery so complicated, and so extensive as this, called aloud for a remedy in a nation that boasted of its freedom."
19. See Schlatter, op. cit., p.222.
20. Hegel, *Philosophy of Right,* trans. W. W. Dyde (London, 1896), pp. 65–68
21. Jefferson, "A Summary View of the Rights of British America," in Boyd et al., *The Papers Of Thomas Jefferson* (Princeton, 1950–   ), vol. 1, pp. 121–135.
22. Locke, *Second Treatise of Government* (London, 1964), chap. 5, "Of Property."
23. Kant, op. cit., pp. 62–64; Hegel, op. cit., pp. 48–53.
24. The free creation of property interests by proprietors has in fact never been allowed to go this far; the types of property interests that could be carved out has typically been limited, often in the name of facilitating market transactions by prohibiting unduly complex holdings. See the discussion in F. H. Lawson, *The Law of Property* (Oxford, 1958), chap. 6. In the civil law systems of continental Europe, the law has allowed only quite limited formal freedom to create new property interests; this apparently is the outgrowth of a Roman law heritage, combined with a prejudice in favor of simple thing-ownership arising out of the association of complex forms of property with feudalism. See generally, John Merryman, "Ownership and Estate," 48 *Tulane Law Review* 916, 924–29 (June 1974).
25. See the analysis in Posner, op. cit., pp. 292–96.
26. See n. 24, above.
27. This is, roughly, Locke's theory of property. See above, n. 22. It must be noted that Locke did not confine the scope of his natural right to property to objects with which the individual mixed his labor, but argued that the invention of money justified a natural right of unlimited accumulation. See the discussion in C. B. MacPherson, *The Political Theory of Possessive Individualism: Hobbes to Locke* (London, 1962), pp. 197–220.
28. See works cited in n. 23, above; see also the discussion in T. H. Green, *Lectures on the Principles of Political Obligation,* reprinted in C. B. MacPherson, ed, *Property: Mainstream and Critical Positions* (Toronto, 1978), pp. 103–17.
29. Marx and Engels, *The Communist Manifesto,* trans. Moore (Chicago, 1969), pp. 41–42.
30. Compare the interesting passage in Joseph Schumpeter, *Capitalism, Socialism and Democracy,* 3d ed. (New York, 1950), p. 142:

> The capitalist process, by substituting a mere parcel of shares for the walls of and the machines in a factory, takes the life out of the idea of property. It loosens the grip that once was so strong—

the grip in the sense of the legal right and the actual ability to do as one pleases with one's own. . . . Dematerialized, defunctionalized and absentee ownership does not impress and call forth moral allegiance as the vital form of property did.

31. What follows is a quite free interpretation of the argument of Renner's *The Institutions of Private Law and their Social Functions,* ed. O. Kahn-Freund, trans. A. Schwarzschild (London, 1949). Renner's discussion at pp. 81–95 captures the main thrust of his theory.

32. See the interestingly similar interpretation of Locke's *Second Treatise* in Louis Dumont, *From Mandeville to Marx: The Genesis and Triumph of Economic Ideology* (Chicago and London, 1977), chap. 4. C. B. MacPherson, n. 27 above, has argued persuasively that in early liberal theory the category of "equal individuals" was confined to property owners.

33. For a discussion of Marx's view that socialism might be achieved without violence in some advanced capitalist countries, see Shlomo Avineri, *The Social and Political Thought of Karl Marx* (Cambridge, 1968), pp. 211–20.

34. The classic Marxist account of the transition to socialism is the celebrated passaged from *Capital,* vol. 1, trans. Moore and Aveling (London, 1887), pp. 788–89:

> Along with the constantly diminishing number of magnates of capital, who usurp and monopolise all advantages of this process of transformation, grows the mass of misery, oppression, slavery, degradation, exploitation; but with this too grows the revolt of the working-class, a class always increasing in numbers, and disciplined, united, organized by the very mechanism of the process of capitalist production itself. The monopoly of capital becomes a fetter upon the mode of production, which has sprung up and flourished along with, and under it. Centralisation of the means of production and socialisation of labor at last reach a point where they become incompatible with their capitalist integument. This integument is burst asunder. The knell of capitalist private property sounds. The expropriators are expropriated.

35. See, for example, the definition of advanced capitalist countries in Ralph Miliband, *The State in Capitalist Society* (New York, 1969), p.7: "They have in common two crucial characteristics; the first is that they are all highly industrialized countries; and the second is that the largest part of their means of economic activity is under private ownership and control."

36. See, e.g., Nicos Poulantzas, *Political Power and Social Classes,* trans. T. O'Hagan (London, 1973), pp. 26–28.

37. In their classic account, *The Modern Corporation and Private Property,* rev. ed. (New York, 1967), p. 66, Berle and Means do suggest the important fragmenting and disintegrating effect of the recog-

nition that "ownership" has become a formal and largely meaningless conception with respect to the modern corporation: "Control divorced from ownership is not . . . a familiar concept. . . . Like sovereignty, its counterpart in the political field, it is an elusive concept, for power can rarely be sharply segregated or clearly defined."

38. See the argument to this effect in C. A. R. Crosland, *The Future of Socialism* (New York, 1963), pp. 35–42.

39. This approach to questions of economic organization has recently been given perhaps its most impressive and systematic treatment in Charles E. Lindblom, *Politics and Markets: The World's Political-Economic Systems* (New York, 1977).

40. The "bundle-of-rights" conception of property appears in well-articulated form for the first time (insofar as I have discovered) in Wesley Hohfeld, "Some Fundamental Legal Conceptions as Applied in Judicial Reasoning," 23 *Yale Law Journal* 16 (1913). Thereafter, it became part of the conceptual stock-in-trade of the legal realist movement, often with a strong implication that "private" and "public" property were not as different as traditional property theory would suggest. See, e.g., Cohen, op. cit., n. 4 above, pp. 357–59.

41. See John Rawls, *A Theory of Justice* (Cambridge, 1971), pp. 265–74. This is the place for a recantation. Some years ago I criticized Rawls for failing to treat property (in the classic thing-ownership sense) as a fundamental category within his theory of social justice. Thomas Grey, "Property and Need: The Welfare State and Theories of Distributive Justice," 28 *Stanford Law Review* 880–84 (May 1976). I now think that I was wrong, for the reasons implicit in this entire essay.

PART II

SOME PHILOSOPHERS ON PROPERTY

4

PROPERTY AND POSSESSION: TWO REPLIES TO LOCKE — HUME AND HEGEL[1]

CHRISTOPHER J. BERRY

The most distinctive element in Locke's theory of property in his two *Treatises of Government*[2] is his justification of private ownership in purely individual terms. With regard to the prevailing accounts, this distinctiveness is implied by Locke's own explicit endeavor to "shew how Men might come to have a property in several parts of that which God gave to mankind in common, and that without any express Compact of all Commoners" (sec. 25).

As Laslett points out in an attendant note Locke's direct target here (as elsewhere) was Filmer because of his rejection of the natural law account of the emergence and justification of private property; more particularly, Filmer had rejected as self-contradictory the (Grotian[3]) argument that universal consent was needed for private property to be instituted out of an original state where all things were common.[4] Though Pufendorf had circumvented this problem by distinguishing between a positive and negative community of goods,[5] Locke did not utilize this argument; instead, as the quotation above signifies, he rejected as superfluous the necessity to invoke consent at all in a justification of private property. This rejection was a departure from natural law orthodoxy. Pufendorf, for all his criticism of Grotius, explicity agrees with Grotius's view that private ownership was not instituted by "a mere act of will . . . but rather by a kind of agreement"[6] for "the proprietorship of things has resulted immediately from the convention of men, either tacit or express."[7]

Locke's own argument is both sufficiently well known and not as such the subject of this paper that the briefest exposition of his derivation and justification of private property is defensible. Man is

God's creature (men are God's property [sec. 6]) and their property in their own person[8] is not theirs to destroy (secs. 23, 135). Men, accordingly, are duty bound to preserve themselves so that they might be "about his [God's] business" (sec. 6) and to achieve this end God gave to mankind in common the earth and all its fruits. A man now has the right to use, or to appropriate (that is, to make his 'own' or his property), by labor, whatever he requires "to the best advantage of Life and convenience" (sec. 26). This is the "original Law of Nature for the beginning of property" (sec. 30). Property exists for man's enjoyment. That this is the case is evident from the injunction of natural law that proscribes unlimited accumulation, since man is entitled to appropriate only so much as "he can make use of to any advantage of life before it spoils" (sec. 31).[9]

The point of significance, for the current argument, is that in this account and in neither of Locke's definitions of property — in his "own person" and in whatever he "hath mixed his labour" — do other rational agents directly figure (whereas natural law enjoins that enough be left over for others, this injuction does not enter into the definition of property). Both Hume and Hegel reject this individualism. This paper is an examination of these rejections premised on the conviction that their theories of property can fruitfully be explored from the perspective of this shared rejection; a rejection that can be seen to hinge on the difference between property and possession.

To turn first to the Humean reply: the keystone of Hume's social and political philosophy is that justice is an artificial virtue. In outline his argument is that justice is a convention that arises from the inconveniences that ineluctably follow when the "selfishness and confined generosity" of men is coupled with the "scanty provision nature has made of his [man's] wants" (T495). As a convention it means that justice is not the immediate spontaneous product of natural sentiment but is the product of rules — hence the artificiality. These rules arise from the universal experience of the combination of selfishness and scarcity, and their function is to restrain the passions in order to maintain society, since without them society "must immediately dissolve" (T 497).

It is through the convention of justice, a supposed sense of common interest, that any individual acts "in expectation that others are to perform the like" (T 498). Once exceptions are made to the rules, when they are flexible, then justice in the form of such expectations will break down; and if justice breaks down then, to repeat, society breaks down. In this way justice is fundamental to social existence, and accordingly all other conventions depend on its presence. This applies to property relationships.

For Hume the property relation is internal or mental. Pufendorf had used similar language[10], but the premises of Hume's position can be best grasped in the context of a seemingly obscure point, namely, his explicit connection between property and causation.

This connection is referred to on three occasions. The first is found in book II of the Treatise, where Hume, in fact, first mentions property. There he defines property as "such a relation betwixt a person and an object as permits him, but forbids any other, the free use and possession of it, without violating the laws of justice and moral equity" (T 310). This relation is a "particular species of causation" because, regardless of the theory of justice held (natural or artificial) the proprietor has the "liberty" "to operate as he please upon the object" and to reap advantages from it.

The second reference occurs in Book III of the *Treatise*. There a definition of possession as "not only when we immediately touch it [anything] but also when we are so situated with respect to it, as to have it in our power to use it; and may move, alter or destroy it, according to our present pleasure or advantage" is immediately reported to be a relation which is "a species of cause and effect." Whereupon property, designated as "nothing but stable possession," is "to be considered as the same species of relation" (T 506).

The final reference is to be found in the *Dissertation on the Passions* (a re-presentation of Book II of the *Treatise*), which was first published in 1757, although the passage here in question was included only in a note appended to the 1760 edition. Hume there declares that "to be the proprietor of anything is to be the sole person who, by the laws of society, has a right to dispose of it and to enjoy the benefit of it" and such disposal and enjoyment "produces, or may produce, effects on it, and is effected by it. Property therefore is a species of causation" (P 206).

The replication of terminology in these references is sufficient to dispose of any doubts about the deliberateness of Hume's remarks. What, then, does Hume mean by saying that property is a species of causation?

Though the answer to this question can be divined from the *Treatise*, Hume's fullest account of his position occurs in the later *Dissertation* (although its appearance in only later editions of that work

suggests that he was aware of the somewhat cryptic nature of his remarks). Since property is defined as a *relation*, it follows that the answer to the question above hinges on Hume's account of relation or
the association of ideas. Of the three principles of association — resemblance, contiguity, causation — the last is the most extensive. For
Hume, two objects are causally related when one is the cause of the
existence of another, of the action or motions of the other, and also
when one has the power of producing a motion or action in the other
(T 12). It is in this last sense that property is a species of causation,
for "it [property] enables the person to produce alterations on the object and it supposes that his condition is improved and altered by it"
(P 206).

Now, what is of general importance here is that in the *Treatise*
Hume goes on to remark that causation as understood in this last
sense is "the source of all the relations of interest and duty by which
men influence each other in society and are placed in the ties of government and subordination" (T 12). As, for example, when a master
has the power of directing the actions of his servant, that is, the master merely needs to exercise his will to bring about his end. It is this
sense of cause as power, and its explicit application to 'social' relationships, that ties in with property, and moreover, explains Hume's
claim that this relation is "the most interesting of any and occurs
most frequently to the mind" (P 206).

Our property is something that we are able to do with what we
will, is the power of using an object. The importance of 'power' here,
and likewise the importance of defining possession as more than immediate tangibility is that a temporal dimension is built into the notion of property. Hume, in fact, declares that "property being produced by time is not anything real in objects but is the offspring of
sentiments on which time alone is found to have any influence" (T
509) (the reference to property not being 'real' will be taken up
shortly). Time operates "gradually on the *minds* of men" so that indeed "nothing causes any sentiment to have a greater influence upon
us than custom" (T 556; emphasis mine).

Since, as is well known, Hume declares that "the idea of cause and
effect is derived from experience, which informs us that such objects,
in all past instances, have been constantly conjoined with each other"
(T 89–90), property and cause are implicitly related; likewise custom
and cause ("the mind is determined by custom to pass from any cause
to its effect . . . their constant conjunction in past instances has pro-

duced such a habit in the mind") (T 128); and now, also, property and custom. Seeing property in the context of this complex of relations helps to explain why it, for Hume, is an internal relation.

Property is "nothing real in objects" in the same general way that causation is not a "real" relation but "belongs entirely to the soul, which considers the union of two or more objects in all past instances. 'Tis here that the real power of causes is placed along with their connexion and necessity" (T 166). More particularly, in the case of property this is so because the "sensible qualities" of any object continue "invariably the same while the property changes" (T 527). Whereupon it follows that "property must therefore consist in some relation of the object," that is, a relation between objects and "intelligent rational beings," which means that "it is therefore in some internal relation that property consists" (T 527).[11] It is an internal relation because its defining quality of constancy is a habitual mental relation.

Since property is an internal relation, it follows, to Hume, that external relations, such as occupancy do not themselves constitute property. Occupation only "causes" property by having "an influence on the mind, by giving us a sense of duty in abstaining from the object"; in other words, via justice (T 527). Thus, as Hume had commented earlier, a man's property as the relation of an object to him is not "natural" but "moral and founded on justice" (T 491). Hume is explicit that property is incomprehensible without "any reference to morality or the sentiments of the mind" (T 515; cf. T 523). Accordingly, in all Hume's definitions of property, 'possession' is qualified as 'stable' (T 491) or constant (T 491, T 503, T 504n.), and such qualifications are the product of human artifice, the "laws of justice" (T 491). For Hume, possession becomes property only through men establishing conventions.

This account by Hume of the property relation is directed against Locke's theory. Neither of Locke's definitions square with Hume's own relational anaylsis. For Hume the property relation depends on the existence of other rational beings, who have instituted conventions to effect stability. Locke's theory is individualist par excellence. He has merely provided a definition of possession and not property.

It should be acknowledged that Locke believed that his account escaped this censure. It is an injunction of the laws of nature that men preserve themselves, and this law "obliges everyone" (sec. 6). Since appropriation is necessary to the end of preservation, it follows that it is perfectly consonant with the moral axioms of natural law. This means that the act of appropriating is no neutral arbitrary act but engenders a right to what is so appropriated (sec. 31). This right *of itself* imposes duties on others, because given the universal obligatoriness of natural law, and the "one Community of Nature" that all men share, then no man is permitted (without due cause) to "take away or impair the life or what tends to the preservation of life, liberty, health, limb or goods of another" (sec.6). Thus, it is for Locke that without any agreement between men both a man's life and the possessions necessary to maintain that life (and its convenience) are properly denominated his property (sec. 123).

But to return to Hume's reading of Locke: Hume's subsumption of the property relation under that of causation entails (on his analysis of the genus) that the "elements" are separable. This has a number of consequences. It is indeed because men can be separated from their property that instability arises (given scarcity and confined generosity). An implicit critique of Locke can here be discerned. Locke, with his broad definition of property as life, liberty, and estates (sec. 123), has conflated what Hume considers to be "three different species of goods" — internal satisfaction of our minds, external advantages of our body, and enjoyment of acquired possessions (T 487). The first cannot be separated from us, and although the second can it is no use to the perpetrator. However, the third is separable both voluntarily and involuntarily. As we have seen, it is the artificially created stability of such possessions that for Hume truly demarcates what constitutes property. More generally, Hume is also here rejecting, by implication, the meaningfulness of the long-established natural law doctrine that a man enjoyed property in his own person.

Another consequence of this separability is that the property relation, as a species of causation, comprises constant conjunction. Thus the earliest reference to property in the *Treatise* is an example of the "perfect relation of ideas" whereby the "mention of property naturally carries our thought to the proprietor and of the proprietor to the property" (T 310). As the wording here reveals, this is an instance of causation understood as natural relation or association of ideas rather than as a philosophical relation (T 94, T 170). Although it is in this way natural to associate in our minds property and a proprietor, the Humean analysis of causation, of which this is to repeat once more a species, has consequences again critical of Locke. The general point here has been noted by D. D. Raphael, although he approaches the question from a different angle. Raphael has drawn attention to Locke's discussion of the possibility of morality becoming a science "capable of demonstration," wherein he cites, as an example, the relationship between property and justice (*Essay Concerning Human Understanding* [1690, IV, iii, 18]), so that just as Hume's general theory of causation is an attack on rationalist accounts of that relation, his theory of property is here an attack on Locke's rationalist pretensions in this quarter. [12]

Finally, another consequence of the thesis of the separability of property concerns Hume's account of the principles of its distribution. Here Hume implicitly, though obviously, attacks Locke's 'labour theory.' We do not join our labor to a thing, but rather, what we do is make an alteration upon it (T 505–6n.). This alteration is a relation, and this is, as we have seen, central to Hume's definition of property as a species of causation. In addition, Hume's general account of the principles of distribution is that they are "fix'd by the imagination or more frivolous properties of our thought" (T 504n), and this accords with the basic theory of causality as the association of ideas in the imagination (T 12). Thus, Locke's theory here is an example of the acquisition of property by accession, which itself is "nothing but an effect of the relations of ideas and of the smooth transition of the imagination" (T 510n.).

To turn to the second response: Hegel's theory of property can be apprehended only if his account of human nature is first appreciated. Man uniquely is self-conscious because man uniquely qua thinking mind (*denkende Geist*) is free. This means, for Hegel, that man (spirit) and animals (nature) are radically disjoined. All animals as living beings feel hunger and are impelled to assuage it. Men, however, are not merely animals, for, as Kojève remarks, [13] whereas animal desire might be a necessary condition of self-consciousness it is not a sufficient condition. For human desires to be *human* they must have as their object another human being since "self-consciousness attains its satisfaction only in self-consciousness." [14] Self-consciousness proper therefore subsists only by being acknowledged or recognized by another self-consciousness. Men qua spiritual beings (self-conscious universals) need to be recognized; they are irreducibly social beings. Only this can explain why men compete and struggle for more than appetitive satisfaction, mere biological survival. We cannot understand human interaction in terms of the pleasure-pain calculus.

For Hegel it is first of all in his property that the individual achieves recognition in the objective or sociohistoric world. Whereas

the emergent self-conscious belongs, in the Hegelian system, to subjective *Geist,* it enters the sphere of right (objective *Geist*) as personality, that is, as consciousness of oneself as an abstract ego, as free —
for I know I can through thought abstract myself from every concrete
restriction (PR 37). This constitutes man's universality. It is, however, perfectly abstract or empty and needs, therefore, to be objectivized or externalized. In order that this freedom should be more than
potential it must be actualized, for it is only as actualized that man
can enter the objective realm of right, that he can exist as idea or reason (PR 40). Property is the initial agent of this objectification. This
crucially is its function and justification.

How does this objectification take place? That which differentiates
man from things and animals is, as we have seen, his spirituality;
more particularly, with regard to right, it lies in his free will — "the
will is free, so that freedom is both the substance of right and its goal
[Bestimmung], while the system of right is the realm of freedom
made actual" (PR 20). By putting his will into "any and everything"
man thereby makes it his, for things *[Sachen]* possess no will of their
own. This is the right of appropriation *(Zueignungsrecht).* Through
this process of objectification, "I as free will am an object to myself in
what I possess and thereby also for the first time am an actual will,
and this is the aspect which constitutes the category of property" (PR
42). It follows from this that property is necessarily private, for it is
the individual will that is existent *(Dasein)* or objectivized in property. I am only an "object to myself" when I can say of a particular
"thing" that it is mine.

Like Locke, Hegel extends this analysis to the body. For Hegel this
is a corollary of man's ability (though not the unqualified right [PR
242] to kill himself, to withdraw his will from his body [PR 43]). Although the individual can be free in himself while enchained, Hegel
does not subscribe to the Stoic's idea of *apatheia,* where the body belongs to the realm of "things indifferent"; because, as Fichte had earlier also argued,[15] from the point of view of *others* I am my body and
to restrict my body is to curtail my freedom.

Though property bearing occurs at the level of objective *Geist* and
thus presupposes recognition by others, nevertheless that a particular
thing is my property, having been appropriated by my will, is purely
an inward idea, and it is necessary that others recognize *that* particular thing as mine. This is achieved in general terms through occupancy *(Besitzergreifung),* which is an "external activity whereby we

actualize our universal right of appropriating natural objects" (PR 45). This activity takes on various guises, which constitute the modifications in the relationship between the will and the thing.

Hegel specifies three general modifications (PR 46–57). First, there is taking possession (*Besitznahme*). This progresses through mere physicality, to "forming," where possessions have a degree of independence, as in the case of plant cultivation, to possession in idea alone, that is, symbolically through marking *(Bezeichung)*. The second modification is by use *(Gebrauche)*. This involves the change, destruction, or consumption of the thing, whether singly, intermittently, or persistently. The final modification is by alienation *(Ent* or *Veräusserung)*. This entails the withdrawal of the property-defining will, though this by the very definition of property can refer only to externalities. Hegel does, however, remark, in a passage that hindsight imbues with great significance, that the alienation of the whole of my work would mean that "I would be making into another's property the substance of my being, my universal activity and actuality, my personality" (PR 54).

What this last statement indicates, above all, is the basis of Hegel's theory of property. Property as the initial embodiment of freedom is a "substantive end," or end in itself, since freedom is the "substance of right." Property of itself is freedom; it needs no functional justification. To attain freedom, it is necessary that I have property, for in my property I become an "object to myself." Not to have a sphere of property that is one's own is to fail to attain self-conscious knowledge of oneself as free. To have property, therefore, follows necessarily from the very premise of man's spirituality, his free will. To regard property merely as a contingency, as a means to an end, such as the satisfaction of need, is to misapprehend its significance (PR 42).

Here we confront the polemical aspect of Hegel's theory. Part of the general thrust of the entire section devoted to abstract right in the *Philosophie des Rechts* is to criticize partial theories of the state; in particular, to criticize natural law theorists,[16] who endeavor, by using abstract empty notions of an extra social 'person' to elucidate man-in-society. Despite Locke's criticisms of Grotius and Pufendorf, he himself, as his rejection of Filmer testifies, operates with the premises of natural law. This applies to his theory of property, because the Lockean theory, like that of Pufendorf[17] and the other natural lawyers, is effectively instrumentalist.

Hegel takes issue with such an instrumentalist reading. "Use," for

Hegel as we have seen, is one of the *modifications* of property and is, as such, secondary to its basis in the owner's will. It is a weakness of the state-of-nature theorists that, by failing to make this distinction, they look upon any property as derelict when it is not in use (PR 49). Hegel is here preempting the radical theory that if something (especially land) is not being used by the owner, then his title to it is forfeit. Use as a modification of the basic will is an event in time, and so long as the will continues to express itself the "thing" remains my property. This durational element is prescription *(Verjahrung)* (PR 52). The fact that property thus rests internally on will, and not on use or some other externality, seems akin to Hume's theory of property as an internal relation. We can now briefly compare Hume's and Hegel's theories of property from the perspective of their common rejection of Locke.

Both reject Locke's extreme individualism. In Hume the property relation is artificial in that it depends on prior social convention — on the existence of justice and sentiments of morality that give us a "sense of duty" in abstaining from an object. In Hegel the property relation intrinsically depends on mutual recognition. In both Hume and Hegel there is an implicit distinction between possession and property. For Hume, property is "stable possession," but the stability is the result of the convention of justice; for Hegel, possession is property only when it is imbued with my will and when my will therein is recognized by others.[18] But, just as with the social contract[19], though both Hume and Hegel reject Locke, that does not make their positions identical.

This can be succintly and decisively illustrated. Just as Hume's theory of property parallels his theory of causation, so the same parallel can be seen between Hegel's concepts of property and cause. Hegel's account of the causal relation is in fact the *locus classicus* for objections to Hume's own classical analysis; it is at the root of Collingwood's account, for example. Hegel remarks that the cause and the effect are commonly conceived as two independent existences, but this is the typical product of *Verstand*, because when apprehended correctly (dialectically) by *Vernunft*, the two terms though distinct are also identical, as a simple example illustrates: "The rain [the cause] and the wet [the effect] are the self-same existing water. With respect to form the cause [rain] collapses into the effect [wet]: but now the outcome can no longer constitute an effect, since without the cause it is nothing and only the indifferent wet remains."[20]

Implicit in their different theories of causation is the crux of their divergence in their theories of property. Thus, for Hume the relationship between a man and his property is contingent; property is a separable external good constantly conjoined with the "owner." For Hegel, the relationship between a man and his property is necessary; a man's will and its objectification constitute a conceptual whole.[21] In sum, although Hume and Hegel both reject Locke's individualistic explanation of property, their own explanations of this institution fully manifest the basic gulf between their philosophies as a whole.

NOTES

1. The following abbreviations are inserted in parentheses in the text:

    T   Hume *A Treatise of Human Nature* (1739/40), ed. L. A. Selby-Bigge (Oxford: Clarendon, 1946).

    P   Hume *A Dissertation on the Passions* (1757) in *Works*, vol. IV, A. and C. Black (Edinburgh and Boston: Little, Brown, 1854).

    PR Hegel *Philosophy of Right* (1821), trans. T. M. Knox (Oxford: Clarendon, 1942).

    All other Hegel references are to *Sämmtliche Werke*, ed. G. Lasson and F. Meiner (Leipzig, 1921–   ).

2. All references to P. Laslett's edition, rev. (New York: Mentor Books, 1965).

3. H. Grotius, *On the Law of War and Peace*, trans. F. Kelsey (Oxford: Carnegie Classics of International Law, 1925) book II, chap. 2, sec. vi.

4. *Observation upon H. Grotius* in *Patriarcha and Other Works*, ed. P. Laslett (Oxford: Blackwell, 1949) pp. 273–74.

5. *On the Law of Nature and Nations*, trans. C. and W. Oldfather (Oxford: Carnegie Classics of International Law, 1934), book IV, chap. 4, sec. ii.

6. Grotius, op. cit., cited by Pufendorf, op. cit., book IV, chap. 4, sec. ix.

7. Pufendorf, op. cit., book IV, chap. 4, sec. iv.

8. Such a definition is a natural law commonplace. Cf. K. Olivecrona, who argues that Locke's term "property" is a direct translation of Grotius's *suum*. "Appropriation in the State of Nature: Locke on the Origin of Property," *Journal of the History of Ideas* 35 (1974), p. 218.

9. Cf. *First Treatise*, sec. 92: "Property, whose original is from the right a man has to use any of the inferior creatures for the subsistence and comfort of his life, is for the benefit and sole advantage of the proprietor, so that he may even destroy the thing that he has property in by use of it, where need requires."

10. Op. cit., book IV, chap. 4, sec. i.

11. Cf. T 236, where animals are held to be incapable of right and

property and thus the causes of their pride lie solely in the body and "can never be plac'd either in the mind or external objects."

12. "Hume's Critique of Ethical Rationalism" in W. B. Todd, ed., *Hume and the Enlightenment,* (Edinburgh: Edinburgh Univ. Press, 1974). Cf. J. Moore who "suggests" in the light of Hume's early exposure to legal theory as a student that his theory of causation is an attempt to produce a comprehensive response to the theory of power and property outlined in Locke's epistemology and political theory. "Hume's Theory of Justice and Property," *Political Studies* 24 (1976), p. 115.

13. *Introduction a la lecture de Hegel,* 2d ed. (Paris: Gallimard, 1944), p. 11.

14. *Phänomenologie des Geistes* (Lasson), vol. 2, p. 121.

15. *Grundlage des Naturrechts nach Principien der Wissenschaftlehre,* in *Werke,* ed. I. H. Fichte (Berlin, 1845), vol. 3, p. 114.

16. Cf. P. G. Stillman, "Hegel's Critique of Liberal Theories of Rights," *American Political Science Review* 68 (1974) pp. 1086–92.

17 Op. cit., book IV, chap. 4, sec. vi.

18. Hegel had drawn the distinction between possession and property in his early writings, *Jenenser Realphilosophie II* (Lasson), vol 20, p. 206. Fichte had earlier also distinguished between property and possession in terms of recognition *(Grundlage,* vol. 3, p. 130). Kant, too, in his own terms, had argued that external things were property only in civil society, where mutual obligations to restrain from using the objects of others are presupposed — without this there is merely physical possession. *Metaphysical Elements of Justice,* trans. J. Ladd (Indianapolis: Bobbs-Merrill, 1965), pp. 54–67.

19. I have demonstrated this in my "From Hume to Hegel: The Case of the Social Contract," *Journal of the History of Ideas* 38 (1977), pp. 691–703.

20. *Encyclopädie der Philosophischen Wissenschaft,* sec. 153.

21. This is intrinsic to Hegel's conception of Actuality *(Wirklichkeit),* since it is the unity of the inner and outer *(Encyclopädie,* sec. 142), and "genuine actuality is necessity" (PR 283).

5

PROPERTY AS ARTIFICE:
HUME AND BLACKSTONE

FREDERICK G. WHELAN*

I. INTRODUCTION: BEYOND LOCKE

Both the friends and the critics of classical liberalism acknowledge the central role of property in this tradition of political theory. This subject is treated most frequently in connection with Locke, whose doctrine of property is comparatively well known and still influential. It is too often and erroneously assumed, however, that a dogged, Lockean insistence on full and abolute private property as a natural right was the characteristic position of the British liberals of the eighteenth century. This assumption, moreover, carries as a corollary the view that the property theory of this era can be easily summarized and dismissed as an outdated phase in the history of speculation on the subject.

In this chapter I shall consider the views on property of two other important but less often read figures from within the classical liberal consensus: David Hume and Sir William Blackstone. Both the Scottish philosopher and the English legal commentator adhered to a view of property as artifice, as a matter of positive rights established through the existence of an elaborate, conventional system of social rules. "Artifice" is a distinctively Humean term; his treatment of property is central to an abstract moral philosophy. Blackstone's aim is to set forth a concrete, reasoned exposition of the particular artifice represented by the English law of property. Despite the apparent differences of intention and style, Hume and Blackstone are fundamentally similar in their manner of conceptualizing and justifying the institution and the particular rules governing property, and in this they stand in marked contrast to Locke.

In theorizing about property in these terms, neither Hume nor Blackstone advances any serious criticism of the actual property system with which they were most familiar, the same that Locke had earlier sought to justify and secure against arbitrary government. Their guiding insight—that property rights are to be conceived as conventional rather than natural—leads in their cases to no less strong a defense of private property and the other institutions of a commercial society. It does, however, reflect a greater sensitivity to historical change and variability of property than Locke evinces, and the fact that the understanding of property as artifice can accomodate such phenomena renders it more adequate theoretically in modern eyes.

The understanding of property represented by both Hume and Blackstone was probably more widespread among the educated public in England (although perhaps not in eighteenth and nineteenth century America) than that of Locke. This seems especially likely in the case of Blackstone, who purports simply to explicate current law and whose audience was extensive and appreciative. Hume's doctrines were of course not popular in this sense, but I shall try to show that Blackstone for the most part works out what may be seen as a specification of Hume's general principles. From this it seems to me, first, that the classical liberal theory of property was not so unitary as is often supposed, and second, that the Lockean theory has been unduly emphasized as the predominant one for this period.

Looking back from the standpoint of contemporary thought on property, furthermore, I shall argue that the doctrines of Hume and Blackstone are far closer to prevailing views than is that of Locke. Today it is generally agreed that property is to be thought of not naively as "things" but as rights in things, that "property" or "ownership" must be analyzed as a complex "bundle" of various possible specific rights, that such rights are constituted by rules or social practices, and that the sorts of "things" that can become property, as well as the conditions on which they can be owned, are necessarily matters for legal determination.[1] The doctrines of Hume and Blackstone contain or anticipate most of the elements essential to this way of thinking about property, revealing a greater degree of continuity between the thought of their age and ours than could be gathered from a consideration of Locke alone.

Both Hume and Blackstone formulated their views of property in conscious opposition to Locke, evidently believing that his theory contained neither an adequate account of property as an existing social institution nor a satisfactory justification of what it is in a system of property that must be justified. I shall conclude this section with a brief review of three aspects of Locke's theory of property that appear to be points of weakness from a modern perspective, and to which Hume and Blackstone address themselves more satisfactorily.

The natural right to property that Locke defends in the *Second Treatise* is, in the first place, a rather special right to appropriate, through labor and subject to other conditions, unowned goods in the state of nature. The moral plausibility of the root notion that a laborer or creator is entitled to the fruits of his work (so long as no other person's rights or legitimate interests are damaged in the process) has given the theory a continuing attractiveness, but the scope of its applicability within society is arguably too restricted for it to provide the basis for property rights generally that Locke intended. Property in patents and copyrights, where the owner's labor brings a new good into existence (and benefits all indirectly), seems an intuitively clear illustration of the Lockean process within civil society, where there is by and large no "common stock" of unowned things on which to labor. Yet it is positive law that defines exactly what property rights derive from the creative process, and otherwise even more clearly the acquisition of property in society seems possible only under rules generally recognized by the members of that society. Locke may have been acknowledging this point when he speaks (vaguely) of the "regulation" of property by civil society, but it is not clear that anything remains of a natural right unless it be a general right of each person to acquire property, under the laws, on the same terms as everyone else, or a broad moral claim regarding the just deserts of labor that legislation ought to accomodate. That Locke offers virtually no guidance concerning the status of property as "regulated" in civil society left a very large theoretical gap for his eighteenth-century successors to fill.

Locke's illustrations of property acquisition in the state of nature, second, always involve tangible objects such as fruit, game, or land, the last clearly being the most important kind of property in his mind. The labor theory, with its metaphor of mixing labor with an unimproved natural object, seems to work in illuminating the basis of a property that a person may come to have in a pre-existing physical thing; in making such cases the norm Locke exemplifies the naive view that property *is* things or external goods, over which "full" or "absolute" ownership may be exercised, which has been said to typify his age.[2] Increasingly, however, in his time and still more our own, much significant property consists of rights in "things" that are intangible, or whose existence is a matter of legal definition. Such property is inconceivable in a state of nature and thus seems to fall outside the scope of Locke's theory altogether. This insight lawyers, including Blackstone, have long taken for granted.

Locke's theory, finally, is radically incomplete in its almost entire neglect of the issue of the legitimate modes of transfer of property among persons, laterally or between generations. A complete normative theory of property must contain, in Nozick's words, a doctrine of "justice in transfer" as well as "justice in acquisition"; and the rules regulating transfers are at least as significant as those governing what may be owned in giving a functioning system of property its distinctive character. From the perspective of the modern theory of property, the various possible rights of transfer exist side by side with those of use, exclusion, and so forth, as items in the "bundle-of-rights" constituting ownership. Although Locke presumably envisaged a market economy based on readily alienable property, the only transfer right that he explicitly defends is, oddly, that of inheritance (*Two Treatises*, I: 87–91, 93; II: 182–83, 190), which on a strict interpretation is incompatible with market fluidity. Passing references to the bequest and sale of property (II: 72, 120–21, 176) imply that this subject falls under the appropriate "regulation" of property in civil society, but neither natural law nor the labor theory seems to offer prescriptions or guidelines.

Despite the force of Locke's specific argument regarding the appropriation of unowned things, which still find adherents today, his doctrines can scarcely be said to comprise a full or adequate theory of property. This is not a modern discovery, however: Locke's successors within the classical liberal era address themselves, at least implicitly, to these weaknesses, and the theory of property as artifice advanced by Hume and Blackstone is an alternative that in retrospect appears more generally satisfactory.

II. HUME: PROPERTY AND ARTIFICIAL VIRTUE

David Hume's theory of property is to be found in two of his principal philosophical works: in the first six chapters of book III, part II of his *Treatise*, and in chapter III of his *Inquiry Concerning Morals*.[3]

In both of these works property constitutes a major part of discussions of justice, obliging us to consider some of the general features of Hume's moral theory.[4]

Hume's central distinction is between what he labels the natural and the artificial virtues. The former, which include such qualities as benevolence and pity, correspond to natural impulses and arouse spontaneous approval in spectators without regard to anything but the immediate context. The artificial virtues, by contrast, consist in conduct in accordance with, or a disposition to observe, general moral rules or conventions; they achieve their desired effect, and they meet with reflective approval, only when a number of people or society as a whole joins in coordinated observance of the rules. Hume calls the systems of rules constitutive of such virtues "artifices"; unlike the natural virtures, they are social institutions, defining a segment of our moral life that is dependent upon invention, habit, and social learning.

Justice for Hume is a system of artificial virtue that satisfies some of the principal necessities of human society, which can be grasped by imagining the infirmities of men without society. Of the various kinds of goods that men may enjoy, it is the possession of external things that is most uncertain, in consequence of their scarcity and the instability of their possession (THN III.II.2), and it is this "inconvenience" that society, conceived here abstractly as a system of justice, serves to remedy. Justice consists in the observance of a large number of specific rules falling under three general rubrics, rules that together constitute a system of property and define the rights with respect to property and contractual relations that persons may have or acquire within a society.[5] The first set of rules ("stability of possession") defines property rights, as distinguished from mere possession, or the manner in which socially acknowledged titles to property are acquired other than by transfer (THN III.II.3). The second set ("transference by consent") defines the valid modes and forms of deliberate transfer that make possible a system of exchange, division of labor, and commerce (THN III.II.4). Hume's doctrine that the third general rule, promise keeping, is an artificial virtue is well known, serving as it does as the basis of his criticism of the contract theory of political obligation. In the *Treatise* promising is treated as economic contracting, permitting nonimmediate transferences of property, and its artificiality is emphasized through consideration of the elaborate subrules specifying the exact forms and conditions of valid promises or contracts (THN III.II.5.)

As this brief outline makes clear, Hume's theory of justice falls within the main current of classical British liberalism, although in Hume's version the "self-interested commerce of man" (THN III.II.5) on which it is premised is clearly a conscious abstraction from the actual characteristics of human nature and social relations. Hume's theory of property, being an adjunct of his theory of justice, is accordingly formulated with reference to a particular sort of actual property system, although the terms in which it is framed are suitably general to accommodate a wide range of particular variations.

Hume's theory of justice is an abstract one, centering on an analysis of the social benefits derived from the general observance of a set of "rules" that render possessions and promises secure. Occasionally Hume suggests that such rules might have originated as mere conventions (the continuing status of some other such artifices; e.g. "good manners"). Usually, however, the rules of justice exist as laws, specified and enforced by government. For practical purposes justice for Hume is a legal artifice, in which rules have their source in legislation rather than convention (IM 27).

What, then, exactly is property for Hume? We may best approach this question by considering his most explicit passage on the subject. Following the convention that establishes the basic rule of stability of possessions, Hume says,

> there immediately arise the ideas of justice and injustice; as also those of *property*, *right*, and *obligation*. The latter are altogether unintelligible without first understanding the former. Our property is nothing but those goods, whose constant possession is establish'd by the laws of society; that is, by the laws of justice. Those, therefore, who make use of the words *property*, or *right*, or *obligation*, before they have explain'd the origin of justice, or even make use of them in that explication, are guilty of a very gross fallacy. . . . A man's property is some object related to him. This relation is not natural, but moral, and founded on justice. . . . The origin of justice [in the artifice and contrivance of man] explains that of property. (THN III.II.2)

It may be said first of all that although Hume occasionally speaks naively of property as objects or goods, his considered doctrine is that property consists of a "relation" between a person and an external good (cf. THN III.II.3n). Indeed, although Hume rarely speaks of rights, it may be gathered from the juxtaposition of terms in this passage that the property relation consists in rights (and corresponding obligations) with regard to objects. The relation, at any rate, is an artificial moral relation defined by the rules of justice, to which property is conceptually subordinate. Possessions, or things held in a physical or "natural" relation by a person, might exist in a conceivable state of nature, but the moral relation of property ownership is itself an artifice created by social rules. (THN III.II.2).

Hume's insistence that justice is an artificial virtue is directed against those philosophers who argue that there is such a thing as natural justice, whose standards are self-evident and independent of social conventions. Hume is willing to accept the label "laws of nature" for his rules of justice only in the weak sense that rules of this generic sort are universally adopted by human societies, and because, though artificial, they are not arbitrary (THN III.II.1). Likewise, in his insistence that property is a moral and not a natural relation, he rejects theories, including Locke's,[6] which portray property as directly constituted by a naturalistic process such as labor, occupation, or exchange; such processes may serve as the basis for specific rules of justice, but they can establish property rights as a moral relation only when legitimated, by convention or law, as elements in a social artifice.

Hume's argument that justice and property are not natural depends on an understanding of nature at variance with that of his opponents, for whom nature included or indicated a body of moral principles evident to human reason. Nature for Hume is human nature, in which, on his account, the passions and various instinctual and imaginative "propensities," not reason, are the decisive elements, in morals as well as in the operations of the understanding. The natural virtues, such as benevolence, are natural because they correspond to specific, original inclinations, a foundation that is lacking for the recognition of property rights and other practices enjoined by justice. That justice is often at odds with our feelings in particular cases is a point that Hume stresses and that comprises one of his strongest arguments for its artificiality. Vice and virtue, he observes, "run insensibly into each other," determined as they are by our moral feelings of approval and disapproval. But,

> whatever may be the case, with regard to all kinds of vice and
> virtue, 'tis certain, that rights and obligations, and property,

admit of no such insensible gradation, but that a man either has
a full and perfect property, or none at all; and is either entirely
obliged to perform any action, or lies under no manner of obligation. (THN III.II.6).

Hume here is of course not affirming that property ownership is
always "full" or "absolute," but making the point that any rights in a
system of justice, including property rights, must be precisely defined. The rules of justice are more rigid, and the rights they confer
more exact, than our natural moral feelings can ever be. Our moral
life proceeds on two planes, and property falls entirely within the
realm where our private inclinations must yield to the rules, rights,
and specifiable obligations constitutive of a public order.

Having located property and explained its nature as an artifical relation within Hume's analytic moral theory, we may turn to the normative dimension of his theory—the justification of the institution of
property that accompanies his explication of it. Here we may distinguish between the general and the specific, between the outlines of
Hume's mode of justification of justice (and property) in general,
and the justificatory account he gives of certain specific rules that de-
lineate a particular kind of property system.

The decisive move in Hume's ethics is the priority he accords to the
artificial over the natural virtues, of social utility over generous impulse, in cases of conflict. Why do the artificial virtues (and especially justice) have this special importance? A clue may perhaps be
had by considering another problem in Hume's moral theory: Why
must the rules of artificial virtue be inflexible? Hume argues that
these rules are justified entirely by utility and yet that they must be
rigorously applied even when the effect is "contrary to *public
interest*"—as when the property rights of a miser or bigot are upheld
(THN III.II.2).[7] The solution to both of these problems lies in the
value Hume attaches to orderly social life among the possible components of utility or general happiness, and in his analysis of society as
being dependent upon, perhaps even conceptually identified with,
general practices constituted by rules. Circumstances may be imagined, Hume points out—extremes of scarcity or abundance, or alterations in human nature—in which the existence of society itself (in
this sense) would become impossible or unnecessary; in such cases the
artificial virtues would lose their virtuous or obligatory character.
But in the normal course of affairs, the orderly coexistence and inter-

course of people is a great good and the necessary condition of other goods, and Hume's "utility" has reference primarily to the preservation of society itself rather than to the most efficient generation of other goods, such as wealth, within the context of social life. Social order as the principal element in utility as the justifying standard for the artificial virtues includes the minimal (Hobbesian) sense of peace and personal security. More generally, for Hume, it includes the conditions necessary for the rational formation of expectations and pursuit of personal goals, which can be undertaken only when one's own conduct and that of others is guided in certain important respects by general social rules. Most generally, the artificial moral rules may be seen as exemplifying the normal tendency of the human mind to confer stability on its environment— otherwise a flux of ephemeral perceptions and events—through the imposition of rules. The artificial moral rules are the equivalent in the moral realm to the cognitive rules (such as the rule that the future must resemble the past) followed by the imagination in reasoning.

Hume's justification of property, then, is set in the context of a moral theory far more abstract than Locke's; the rules of property are an example of a larger class of moral rules whose justification follows the general form just outlined. In his discussions of justice, however, Hume often argues, in "Lockean" fashion, that stability of property (though not the protection of preexisting property rights) is the principal function of society. The scarcity of external goods, in contrast to the internal satisfactions of the mind and the goods of the body, and their liability to transfer without loss, render their enjoyment precarious, and the source of the most important conflicts or inconveniences of life without society. Hence, justice is treated as the most fundamental of the artificial virtues. Society for Hume requires, minimally, an external order of property, a publicly acknowledged system of rules and rights with respect to external goods whose observance is regarded as a virtue.

Thus far the argument remains at a fairly abstract level: the existence of some rules of property are conceptually connected with the notion of social order and are justified insofar as this order is useful or agreeable to us. But what rules of property, what form of property, is to be desired? Hume's moral theory is no doubt most adequate at the abstract level, and the common charge that when he discusses particular rules he accepts too uncritically the rules of the prevailing property system of his time and country has force. We must also consider the related criticism that he inconsistently fails to apply the same test of utility to the particular rules he invokes for the institution of property in general. I turn now to the more concrete tenets of Hume's doctrine of property, then, with the caution that they do not follow necessarily from the general theory.

Hume holds not only that any society must have some rules of property, but also that these rules display a generic similarity everywhere, regardless of the apparent historical variability of property (IM 33); his three general rules of justice are intended to be formulated broadly enough to encompass all the various actual rules that may be encountered. The first and third of the basic rules of justice appear to meet this criterion, but the second is questionable: it is possible to imagine (and to think of historical cases of) property systems and notions of justice that do not provide for transference of property by consent, or for the sort of clear-cut ownership that seems to be implied in the idea of consent as Hume uses it here. Even at the general level Hume may have committed the error of assuming a specific kind of property system, one in which property is readily alienable.

In any case, the general rules must be specified in order to yield a concrete system of property rights and relations, and at this level it is clear that Hume is discussing (and implicitly defending) a market society based on private property and substantial contractual freedom, or the rules of justice as this virtue is understood in what Hume and his contemporaries identified as the commercial stage of civilization. Hume offers a detailed analysis of four specific rules, or as he puts it, "reasons which modify" the general rule "concerning stability of possession": these are the rules that confer title to property on the basis of occupation, prescription, accession, and succession (THN III.II.3). Occupation of unowned things, which in circumstances that must be specified by further elaborations of this rule creates a valid title, includes Locke's labor theory as a special case; what Hume wishes to emphasize is that, however "natural" (in his sense of psychologically compelling) the association of labor or occupation and ownership, the moral and legal relationship that is the essence of property is established through the application of an artificial rule. Prescription is the acquisition of a right through long possession; accession gives a title to the increase of property ("the offspring of our cattle"); succession refers to inheritance. All of these are common modes of acquiring title to property under various legal or conventional codes; the details of their operation vary considerably and

must be defined by further subrules; all, however "natural" in the
sense of "frequently encountered" or "obviously useful," give no natural right but serve rather as the basis for the recognition of positive
rights. Hume devotes less space to refinements of the other two general rules, simply emphasizing that, however apparently simple and
self-evident, both transference of goods and promising must be conducted according to elaborate conventional forms if they are to serve
the general purpose of justice, public order and the avoidance of disputes over things. Hume discusses all of these rules in abstraction
from any particular legal system, although it has been observed that
they are essentially rules of Roman or the civil law, which was taught
in the Scottish universities of the time.[8] In any case, they are rules
that define the basic characteristics of a definite property system,
and not rules that are conceptually inseparable from the notion of
property or justice as such. In the *Treatise* Hume does not make this
distinction clear, with the result that he sometimes seems to suggest
that the property rules of eighteenth-century Scotland, or perhaps of
modern Europe, are equivalent to the rules of "justice" as such. It is
not difficult for the reader to distinguish among the different levels
of abstraction in Hume's theory, but the effect of the presentation is
that Hume appears to be justifying particular rules of property in the
same terms as the institution of property in general.

The final question we must address concerns the nature of the justification Hume offers for the particular rules of justice which he presents as the only ones worthy of analysis. Here the accusation has
been made that Hume is inconsistently utilitarian: he shows convinc-
ingly in general utilitarian terms why some rules of property are desirable, but he fails to apply the test of utility, perhaps in a critical
fashion, to the actual rules that prevailed in the society with which he
was most familiar; instead, it is complained, he lapses into psychological analysis of the probable origins of these rules, meanwhile conveying the impression that he regards them as being *the* embodiment
of justice.[9] Having already suggested that this criticism has merit,
and that Hume's treatment of particular rules ought to be distinguished from his more adequate analysis of artificial virtue, I shall
now inquire into what may be said on behalf of Hume's treatment of
the former subject.

We may begin with the passage in which Hume seems to grant the
objection—and on questionable grounds. The general rule ordaining
stability of possession, he says, is "not only useful, but even absolutely

necessary to human society"; the general rule, however, must be modified by particular "reasons"; and,

> 'Tis obvious, that those reasons are not deriv'd from any utility or advantage, which either the *particular* person or the public may reap from his enjoyment of any particular goods, beyond what wou'd result from the possession of them by any other person. (THN III.II.3)

From this premise Hume goes on to discuss the various particular rules (occupation, prescription, etc.) in terms that imply indifference to their relative utility, so long as they serve the clearly useful general aim of stability. What Hume appears to have in mind is his often emphasized point that all of the rules and subrules of justice must be general in form and inflexible and cannot take account of the public interest in rendering particular judgments. What he does seem to overlook, however, is that considerations of the public interest (utility) ought to determine the choice of the rules themselves, and serve as a standard for criticizing actual rules. Do the rules of occupation, prescription, and so on, promote the greatest happiness; or might not other rules, equally compatible with the general requirements of order and precision, serve better? The only reason that can be offered for Hume's not explicitly raising this question seems to be his putative (and dubiously true) belief that different degrees of utility achieved by alternative rules are negligible compared with the overriding good of social order served by any of them.

Instead, as the critics charge, Hume turns to a detailed analysis of occupation, prescription, and so on, in terms of his associational psychology. Without going into the details, it can be said that Hume holds these rules to have arisen and to have such widespread currency because they correspond to certain natural inclinations of the human imaginative faculty, whose operations Hume affirms to underlie the workings of the mind generally.

> There are, no doubt, motives of public interest for most of the rules, which determine property; but still I suspect, that these rules are principally fix'd by the imagination, or the more frivolous properties of our thought and conception. (THN III.II.3 n)

To illustrate by the clearest case: the rule of accession, in Hume's view, arises from the propensity of the imagination to join firmly together objects, such as land and its produce, that are related by contiguity and causality. Hume presents this analysis of the existing rules of property as a finding of his science of human nature. The difficulty is that at this point in his moral theory he abstains from any possibly critical employment of his ethical criterion of utility. He can, however, be rescued in part from this lapse by the following line of argument. His argument is that the prevailing rules of property (actual laws) have been adopted principally because they reflect our imaginative dispositions to associate certain kinds of objects. By convention or artifice, right has been conferred on relationships that represent "smooth" or "facile" or "easy" transitions of ideas, more often than on relations that have been calculated to promote public utility. Such correspondence of social rules to imaginative facility, however, would tend to increase the ease with which the rules can be grasped and the habits that assure observance instilled. For this reason it would seem that a utilitarian ought to take such psychological factors into account in assessing the various possible rules, especially given the special problems of motivation that arise, as Hume correctly emphasizes, in the case of the artificial virtues. This would not, of course, be the only thing that a utilitarian would take into account, and therefore Hume's treatment of the rules, insofar as it is merely psychological, is one-sided.

It is, finally, unfair to Hume to suggest that he entirely forgets his ethical standard when he delineates a particular kind of property system as the archetype of justice. The three broad rules of justice, as is the case for all the artificial virtues, are founded on utility; and it will be recalled that the second of these (transfer by consent) seems to indicate a specific form of property system. The third rule (promise keeping) seems more generally necessary, but Hume's discussion makes clear that he is thinking of contracts for the exchange of goods and services in a market economy. With respect to both of these two general rules, then, Hume's sketch of their utility amounts in effect to an outline of a defense of private and readily alienable property on the grounds of the social benefits it brings; only the subrules regarding "delivery" and the forms of words for valid contracts are treated as being due to imaginative factors. With respect to the rules that confer title, too, the charge against Hume has been put too strongly. It is only the rule of accession that Hume asserts is entirely "imaginative"; the others all exhibit evidently useful features, although their utility no doubt does not reflect the conscious intention of their "inventors" (THN III.II.6).[10] Hume offers a few suggestions in particular on the utility of succession, as tending to encourage industry and frugality.

This hint of an economic utilitarian approach to the justification of property is expanded to some extent in the *Inquiry*, which is generally more concerned with emphasizing utility than with psychological analysis. The most important passage is found in connection with Hume's rejection of the proposal for the equal division of goods, where we find the kernels of what remain the two most common arguments for the free-market system: the argument from economic efficiency, which states that a system based on "liberal" property generates more goods (and hence higher average utility) than any other system; and the argument from political liberty, which states that only "the most rigorous inquisition" and "the most severe jurisdiction"— only tyranny, in fact—will suffice to maintain an equal (or any other fixed) distribution of goods in the face of diferences among individuals (IM 25). In contrast, Hume argues, the rules of property he advocates encourage *"useful* habits and accomplishments" that "beget that commerce and intercourse which is so *beneficial* to human society" (IM 26). The overall economic prosperity of the society, over and above mere order, is here clearly assumed to constitute a basic element of "happiness" or utility, although it must be said that Hume is not nearly so interested in attaining precision in the application of this standard to social institutions as have been later utilitarians. But in accordance with his more thoroughgoing orientation to utility, Hume here argues that rules based on "analogy" and other nonutilitarian methods of reasoning are justified only when "the interests of society may require a rule of justice in a particular case, but may not determine any particular rule, among several which are all equally beneficial" (IM 26). The *Inquiry* omits the detailed analyses of particular rules contained in the *Treatise,* but it makes clear that utility is the standard that Hume would see applied to them, as well as to the artificial virtues as general institutions.

III. BLACKSTONE: PROPERTY AND THE COMMON LAW

Sir William Blackstone is more than the mere commentator suggested by the plan of his principal work, ostensibly an exposition of the laws of England as they existed in his time, along with historical sketches of their development from feudal antecedents.[11] His first and most acerbic critic, Bentham, recognized that Blackstone undertook as well to offer reasons for the laws, and since "the very idea of a *reason* betokens approbation," he became in effect a defender of the laws that he purports only to expound.[12] His importance for us lies in the fact that he enunciates the "official" view of property in the classical liberal era—the views, that is, of members of the legal establishment, who had a professional interest in conceptualizing the prevailing property system and (no doubt) justifying it as it actually functioned. His importance also lies in his widespread influence on the educated lay public. Blackstone was the first to lecture on the common law at Oxford, his intention being to make law a branch of liberal education, a subject with which every gentlemen ought to be acquainted (Comm. I, 3–37); and the sales of the *Commentaries* suggest that he succeeded. The views on property expressed by Blackstone are probably more representative of educated public opinion on the subject in the later eighteenth century than those of either Locke or Hume.[13]

Blackstone's theory of property rests on a premise similar to Hume's: that the rules establishing and regulating it constitute an elaborate social artifice that is to be evaluated in the final analysis by its consequences for the happiness of society. There is no question, moreover, with Blackstone, that these rules constitute a legal artifice and that property rights are conferred by positive, or as he often calls it, municipal law. This claim will be documented below; it will be helpful, however, to begin by taking notice of the classification of law and of types of property Blackstone employs. The law of England, insofar as it bears on the "rights of things" or property, falls into two categories: the unwritten common law, which must be inferred from custom and from the records of court decisions; and statutory law, comprised of acts of Parliament. This distinction corresponds roughly, for historical reasons, to the basic distinction between real and personal property. Most of the law pertaining to real property (of which land is the most important example) is common law, simply because the great body of rules and precedents respecting this kind of property survives from the period before Parliament claimed the prerogatives of a sovereign legislature and has not been overridden by parliamentary action. The common laws "receive their binding power, and the force of laws, by long and immemorial usage, and by their universal reception throughout the kingdom" (Comm. I, 64). Their origin is obscure; it may perhaps go back to something like a speculative "convention" in Hume's sense. The authoritative source for the common law, however, is the records of the duly constituted courts in historical times. Common law is subordinate to statutory law in that it must yield to the clearly stated will of Parliament; statutes can and, occasionally in the case of the law of real property, have modified common law. Much of the current law respecting personal or movable property, on the other hand, has its origin in statutes, a fact that reflects the relatively greater importance of this kind of property in modern times, characterized as they have been by the growth of commerce (Comm. II, 384–85). The subordination of common to statute law has its explanation in Blackstone's doctrine of the sovereignty of Parliament, whose "absolute" and "uncontrollable" authority extends to everything "not naturally impossible" and not "manifestly contradictory to common reason" (Comm. I, 89–91, 160–61). The sovereign will of Parliament in any case expresses itself in law, so that law of one sort or the other contains the rules of property. And since Parliament has not, for the most part, chosen to set aside the common law, it is primarily this that Blackstone discusses in those portions of his work that deal with property.

I turn now to the topic of natural law and natural rights and to the relationship between Locke and Blackstone on this matter, on which there has been some misunderstanding. Blackstone clearly believes in a law of nature that human law must not offend (Comm. I, 41). Positive law in part embodies natural law (as in prohibiting murder); otherwise, and for the most part, it creates rights and wrongs with respect to matters that are indifferent under natural law. The important point for our purposes is Blackstone's location of property rights among these "things in themselves indifferent" — things that

> become either right or wrong, just or unjust, duties or misdemeanors, according as the municipal legislator sees proper, for promoting the welfare of the society, and more effectually carrying on the purposes of civil life. (Comm. I, 55).

That property belongs here is indicated by Blackstone's listing of life and liberty, but not property, as natural rights (Comm. I, 54).

What has confused commentators on Blackstone is his doctrine that there is, or would have been, a kind of natural right to property in a state of nature. This doctrine represents Blackstone's effort to give as favorable a reading of Locke's theory as the actuality of English law will permit, although the differences between them are fundamental. The earth, Blackstone says, was originally given to men in common; use, however, is of necessity private; and the natural right of property, such as it is, consists in use rights:

> For, by the law of nature and reason, he, who first began to use it, acquired therein a kind of transient property, that lasted so long as he was using it, and no longer, or, to speak with greater precision, the *right* of possession continued for the same time as the *act* of possession lasted. Thus the ground was in common, and no part of it was the permanent property of any man in particular; yet whoever was in the occupation of any determined spot of it, for rest, for shade, or the like, acquired for the time a sort of ownership, from which it would have been unjust, and contrary to the law of nature, to have driven him by force, but the instant that he quitted the use or occupation of it, another might seize it, without injustice. (Comm. II, 3–4).

The natural right to property thus extends to use during actual occupation. Ownership is of the use, not the substance, of things; it is temporary (during use), not permanent; it does not include any rights of alienation or inheritance.

The natural right of property as Blackstone conceives it provides no foundation for property in civil society and indeed would seem to be incompatible with civil order; on the establishment of civil society it is replaced by a system of positive property rights that differs in important respects from the natural. Civil property rights can be (though they are not always) in the substance of things, and permanent. Rights of alienation and succession, which are entirely creatures of positive law, are added, thus substantially enlarging the notion of property ownership. Possessory rights or title on the basis of mere occupancy, although it remains as a last resort, is restricted as far as possible in the interests of peace.[14] Civil society prescribes rules for property in accordance with the maxim that "everything capable of ownership [have] a legal and determinate owner," a rule again required for peace; only "some few things" such as air and light remain in common, the possible objects of a "usufructuary property" (the right to enjoy during occupancy only) such as obtained for everything in the state of nature (Comm. II, 14–15). Property, finally, becomes an element in a legal system in which possible injuries, the modes of their redress, and the type and amount of restitution due must be precisely defined; the law of England observes the maxim that for every right, including property rights, there is a corresponding remedy by suit or action at law when the right is invaded (Comm. III, 23). Hence property is legally inseparable from, and may even be defined in terms of, the possibility of redress for injury, and hence the vast complex of rules and procedures respecting what Blackstone calls "private wrongs" or civil injuries.

In spite of this analysis Blackstone sometimes speaks of an "absolute right" of property in a way that can be misleading. In considering the question of possible inconsistencies we may begin with the famous definition of property which opens Blackstone's book II:

> There is nothing which so generally strikes the imagination and engages the affections of mankind, as the right of property; or that sole and despotic dominion which one man claims and exercises over the external things of the world, in total exclusion of the right of any other individual in the universe. (Comm. II, 2).

I shall argue that this passage is inconsistent with Blackstone's considered doctrine in several crucial respects; from what has been said already it would seem that property rights amounting to "sole and despotic dominion" are a contingency that might or might not be provided for by law, and one might well wonder how such property as this is compatible with sovereignty. Since this seems to be Blackstone's clearest single statement on property, it is often quoted out of context. Doubts about its correct interpretation immediately arise, however, when one reads on:

> And yet there are very few, but will give themselves the trouble to consider the original and foundation of this right. . . . We think it enough that our title is derived by the grant of the former proprietor, by descent from our ancestors, or by the last will and testament of the dying owner; not caring to reflect that (accurately and strictly speaking) there is no foundation in nature or in natural law, why a set of words upon parchment should convey the dominion of land: why the son should have a right to exclude his fellow-creatures from a determinate spot of ground, because his father had done so before him: or why the occupier of a particular field or of a jewel, when lying on his deathbed, and no longer able to maintain possession, should be

entitled to tell the rest of the world which of them should enjoy it after him. (Comm. II, 2)

This makes it clear that much, at least, of what usually passes for the right of property is mere positive right, and moreover that the "right of property" is a form of shorthand for a complex of different rights not accounted for by the simple notion of "sole and despotic dominion," or a right to exclude others only. In light of what follows, the opening assertion appears almost an ironic allusion to popular or unsophisticated usage.[15]

It is not only the passage just cited that can be misleading, but several others as well in which Blackstone alludes to an "absolute" right to property (Comm. I, 138; III, 138). By this phrase Blackstone does not mean a right which the individual is conceived to bring to and retain against civil society, but rather a right he enjoys under positive law. The Englishman's "absolute right" to property "consists in the free use, enjoyment, and disposal of all his acquisitions, without any control or diminution, save only by the law of the land" (Comm. I, 138). The force of "absolute" appears to be that a property right, once legally conferred, will be strictly protected by law and cannot be forfeited or overridden except by rigorous due process of law. The law here as in other respects in inflexible in its defense of specific rights: that a man is starving, for example, is not a defense against a charge of larceny (Comm. IV, 31–32). Property rights in a given thing, however, are never wholly exclusive or entire: the law of nuisance (Comm. III, chap. 13) imposes limitations on the uses to which an owner can put his property; certain common law exceptions to the law of trespass (e.g., entry onto another's land to glean, or to kill a ravenous beast) also detract from "full" ownership (Comm. III, 212–13). Forfeiture or confiscation of property for serious crimes such as treason is a loss of "advantages which before belonged to him purely as a member of the community" (Comm. IV, 382), a penal consequence of the theory that property rights are a creation of civil society (Comm. I, 299).[16] Apparently favoring an "absolutist" interpretation is Blackstone's statement: "So great, moreover, is the regard of the law for private property, that it will not authorize the least violation of it; no, not even for the general good of the whole community" (Comm. I, 139). But this passage must also be read with the implicit qualification, "save only by the law of the land." An owner may be compelled by law to alienate his property, with just compensation, for public purposes, as Blackstone immediately goes on to point out. All of these qualifications serve to emphasize that the alleged "absoluteness" or inviolability of property rights under the law of England is in reality a tautology, since property consists of rights defined and qualified by law.[17]

Since the only presocial, natural property right that Blackstone acknowledges is a right of occupancy, it follows that all rights of succession, inheritance, and alienation (without which there can be no system of property in the usual sense of the word) are in particular to be understood as legal artifices. Of these rights that of inheritance is probably the oldest and most universal, a fact reflected in the elaboration of common law rules on this matter; hence the common error (as in Locke) of regarding inheritance as a natural right:

> We are apt to conceive at first view that it has nature on its side; yet we often mistake for nature what we find established by long and inveterate custom. It is certainly a wise and effectual, but clearly a political, establishment; since the permanent right of property, vested in the ancestor himself, was no *natural*, but merely a *civil* right. (Comm. II, 11)

The variability of rules of inheritance is an indication of their artificial status: whereas the rule prescribing lineal descent of property is nearly universal, for example, English law differs (for good feudal reasons) from Jewish and Roman law in prohibiting lineal ascent; and objections to this as violating "natural justice" fail to recognize that "all rules of succession" are "creatures of the civil polity" (Comm. II, 210–11). Succession by lineal descent, moreover, seems natural because it follows relations of consanguinity which are themselves natural — or so it seems. In fact, the manner of reckoning degrees of kinship must itself be prescribed by law, and common law as it happens differs in some respects from civil law in this (Comm. II, 202ff.). So even blood relationship, as a basis for enjoying rights of inheritance of property, may be regarded as a legal artifice. On the other hand, all rights to dispose of property by devise, will and testament, sale, and other modes of voluntary alienation are more obviously matters of historical contingency, hence "creature[s] of the civil state" (Comm. II, 491). From his historical study of English and other legal systems Blackstone is aware that Hume's rule of "transference by consent," far from being a universal convention, serves in fact to define a particular type of property system and society.

With the exception just noted, Blackstone may thus far be read as confirming, through an analysis of one actual legal system, Hume's philosophical conclusion that property is a creation of law, a relationship of right between a person and a thing that is established through the existence of rules comprising a social artifice. Although certain natural relationships between persons or between persons and things (such as labor, occupancy, long usage, descent from a previous owner, and so forth) may constitute necessary or sufficient conditions for the recognition of a property right, the fact that they do so is a contingency of a given system of social rules. The property relationship itself — the right — is an artificial moral relationship, inconceivable apart from rules or convention. Although he is concerned mainly with presenting the rules of a particular body of law, Blackstone recognizes even more explicitly than Hume that the conventional status of property rules implies variability and historical change, as in one way or another society adapts and modifies its rules in accordance with changing conditions.

In one important respect, however, Blackstone makes a conceptual advance beyond Hume. While emphasizing that the relationship constitutive of property is an artifical one, Hume nevertheless speaks of it as a relationship obtaining between persons and things that are themselves natural. In particular, although Hume defines a man's property generally as "some object related to him," the context makes it clear that by "objects" Hume is thinking of "external goods," or tangible things (THN III.II.2). As a lawyer, however, Blackstone is inevitably aware not only that the property relation is one of legally defined rights, but that these rights pertain to legally defined things, indeed to things whose existence is in some cases constituted by the rules of property.[18] This insight is developed most explicitly when Blackstone discusses the subject of "incorporeal hereditaments," which form one of the two divisions in the category of real property and which are the object of an elaborate body of common law rules. Incorporeal hereditaments include ten important types of property (advowsons, tithes, commons, rights-of-way, offices, dignities, franchises, pensions, annuities, and rents) that share the peculiarity that the property consists of no "substantial" *thing*, although it may "issue out of" or be "collateral to" a tangible thing. Incorporeal hereditaments are themselves "things invisible," which have "only a mental existence"; an advowson, for example "is an object of neither the sight, nor the touch; and yet it perpetually exists in the mind's eye, and in contemplation of law" (Comm. II, 20–21). Not only is it easy in the case of incorporeal hereditaments to conceive of property as consisting of rights in things; it is necessary also to conceive of the "things" in question as merely legal things, themselves artifices of the law. The doubly artificial quality of such property and the related complexities of law on the subject mean that the common lawyer is professionally attuned to thinking of property in things of this sort—a fact that further belies Blackstone's opening but untenable definition of property quoted above as dominion over the "external things of the world." Property of this type would be amenable to Humean analysis, but not to a Lockean justification as a natural right acquired through labor; it is clearly a creation of, and not simply regulated by, positive law.

While incorporeal hereditaments were a long-standing topic in the common law, Blackstone points to two other forms of property in intangible things that were of more recent origin. The common law with respect to literary property was a matter of uncertainty and growth in Blackstone's time (Comm. II, 406–7); he himself served as an advocate on behalf of property in copyright in an important case.[19] Although in this instance labor seems to provide a plausible moral basis for the right, the absence of a tangible thing as the object of property necessitates that the right must be defined by positive law, and Blackstone points out that legal systems have differed in exactly what they protected. Another kind of property, of recent origin and unknown to the common law, was important and controversial in England in Blackstone's time: this was "funds," or creditors' shares in the principal of the national debt, on which annual interest was paid out of tax revenues. This "new species of property," which had an obvious money value and could be transferred from one person to another like other property, "exists only in name, in paper, in public faith, in parliamentary security" (Comm. I, 327). Blackstone, like many others, regarded the national debt with great distrust, in part because of the mysterious way in which new wealth was apparently being created on a wholly insubstantial foundation. There was no doubt, however, that property and property rights of a new sort had come into existence in consequence of parliamentary acts and public confidence in the government. Funds are only one example of new types of property characteristic of the commercial age; one consequence of the evolution of property is that the old common law concerning "offenses against property" has continually to be amended by statute in order to comprehend the new forms of stealing that accompany newly invented forms of property (Comm. IV, chap. 17).

We may turn now to Blackstone's defense or justification of property. On this matter his doctrine is less abstract and certainly of less philosophical interest that Locke's or Hume's: he is concerned, not to show why human society must have property rules of one kind or another, but to offer reasons for approving the laws of England and the institution of property as it exists under them.

It has been shown that Blackstone's *Commentaries* are artfully arranged so as to present the law as comprising an orderly and rational system such as had not previously been apparent to its students.[20] We are not, however, simply left to infer excellence from order; Blackstone points out to us the perfection of the law with respect to the constitution (Comm. I, 50–51, 154) and to private injuries (Comm. III, 266), and he assures us that the common law as a whole embodies the "perfection of reason" (Comm. I, 70), the consequence of the cumulative exercise of judicial intelligence and the adaptation of rules to circumstances. If we press to discover more precisely what criteria Blackstone applies, we find an eclectic mixture of themes. The common law acknowledges nothing "flatly absurd or unjust," or "repugnant to natural justice" (Comm. I, 70–71); its rules are equitable. The common law guarantees to Englishmen a more extensive set of rights than is enjoyed by other peoples, rights that together constitute that "political or civil liberty," which Montesquieu had taught was the special object of the laws of England (Comm. I, 127ff.). Another aspect of political liberty — government by consent — is realized in the customary origin and evolved character of common law (Comm. I, 74). Finally and most important, the law of England displays "reason" in its evident tendency to promote the public welfare, or utility, the standard that governs the definition of rights, under law, in civil society (Comm. I, 124–25, 139). Modern students may see in these standards the bases of distinct political theories; Blackstone combines them in an eclectic fashion, assuming like many of his contemporaries a harmony or congruence among them.

The most frequent mode of justification of the laws in Blackstone, however, is by reference to public "convenience" or welfare; and it is no doubt most accurate to regard him as sharing in the loose utilitarianism that was widespread in the period, although he no more than Hume uses this term or advances a precise ethical doctrine. If we proceed to inquire into his account of the content of public utility, we find that, as is the case with Hume, peace and order are the primary ingredient. From this follows, for example, the prohibition of forceful recaption or reprisal (the seizure of wrongfully taken property by the injured party without recourse to legal processes): the "public peace" is a "superior consideration," to which the rights of property must yield (Comm. III, 4). The law promotes peace not only by defining rights but also by providing legal means of redress for every conceivable injury.

Beyond this, however, Blackstone occassionally defends particular rules pertaining to property in the law of his time in terms of furtherance of the public good. These particular justifications are often set in the context of discussions of changes in the law corresponding to the evolution from a feudal society, based on military tenure, to the modern commercial type of society, in which the public happiness comes to be equated with the growth of trade and prosperity. The comparatively modern right to devise land, for example, is defended as tending to prevent large accumulations of property—something that "should always be strongly discouraged in a commercial country, where welfare depends on the number of moderate fortunes engaged in the extension of trade" (Comm. II, 374). The law's abhorrence of perpetuities, to take another example, rests on a sensible reason:

> because by perpetuities . . . estates are made incapable of answering those ends, of social commerce, and providing for the sudden contingencies of private life, for which property was at first established. (Comm. II, 174)

Blackstone's infrequent criticisms of the law usually pertain to anachronistic rules whose rationale is feudal and which appear arbitrary in modern times (cf. Comm. II, 230; III, 266, 430). He clearly welcomes the commercial society whose gradual growth out of feudalism he sees reflected in the evolution of the law, in particular the law of property.

Blackstone's main interest as a theorist of property, as might be expected from a legal commentator, lies in his insistence that property is entirely a matter of rights in things as constituted by positive law. Both analytically and in the history of classical liberal speculation on the subject, Blackstone's work may be read as a specification, and in some respects a further development, of the position adopted by Hume, with whom he stands in opposition to Locke and the theory that a natural right of property exists within civil society. Blackstone shares with Hume the view that property is to be thought of as a social artifice, constituted by right-conferring rules (laws), the sum of which form a system appropriately evaluated in terms of its consequences for overall social utility, although within the system the rules must be rigid and the rights inviolate.

The most conspicuous difference between Blackstone's treatment and Hume's is Blackstone's assumption that property is necessarily a matter of *legal* rules subject to the authority of a political sovereign (whose assent to common law, in the case of England, is presumed). Hume's category of "rules of justice" is more general and permits the philosophically interesting assimilation of property to other conventions or moral artifices. On the other hand, Hume's theory of property suffers from the weakness (to modern eyes) of being insufficiently political: it seems to bear traces of the Lockean tenet that a more or less stable property system could be independent of, or prior to, government; nor does Hume explain changes in the rules of property as being normally the product of acts of political authority. Since Hume and Blackstone share the view that property is a "convention" or a matter of "municipal law," is is not surprising that they both take its historical and local variability as an important indication of its nature. Blackstone makes the changes in the law of property from feudal to commercial society an integral feature of his explication of the law; Hume, however, wishes to stress the generic similarities of all systems of justice in his philosophical works, and one must turn to his essays and *History of England* to discover his full awareness of precisely the same historical evolution of property in British society.

Blackstone's more substantial theoretical advances over Hume lie rather in his treatment of certain kinds of intangible things that can acquire a legal existence as the object of property rights, and in his stress on the various modes of transfer of property as a distinct category of rights apart from the more usual notion of a property right as legally protected possession and use. Locke scarcely discusses the topic of transfer; Hume treats "transference by consent" as a general rule of justice, which it is not. Blackstone sees that the historical variance in the rights of devise, bequest, inheritance, and alienation is perhaps the most important feature of a given property system from a broad social and functional perspective.

IV. CONCLUSION

The aim of this chapter has been to call attention to two theories of property in eighteenth-century Britain, Hume's and the more "official" legal theory of Blackstone. I have emphasized the similarities between these two theories, and the differences between them and Locke's better-known doctrine. They both conceive of property rights as founded in positive rather than natural law, or as positive rather than ideal rights, a perspective that is perfectly compatible with a strong defense of such rights. From an analytical point of view, property institutions are the creatures of civil societies, and they in fact vary, reflecting in their rules and the rights they confer the character of different sorts of society. Public recognition and (in principle) enforcement of rights is regarded as essential to the concept of property. [21]

Blackstone adds that forms of property are ultimately a matter for determination by the political sovereign, anticipating the more explicit claims of Austinian jurisprudence in the following century. Blackstone describes with approval the changes in property law that lay at the heart of the transition from feudal to commercial society, although he rests content with current law as by and large in accordance with the requirements of public happiness. It may be said, however, that the theory of property as artifice, and especially the legal version of this theory in connection with a notion of sovereignty, implies a perspective that is both collective and political: property rights and institutions are to be evaluated by reference to social ends, and they may properly be modified, as they were at first invented, by public authority for such purposes.

This kind of analysis of property, along with these political implications, seems close to prevailing (liberal) conceptions at the present time. That the fundamental elements of this theory are present in Hume and Blackstone, however, does not mean that it has been the commonest way of thinking about property since their time. In the perspective that I have sketched in this chapter, the Lockean natural rights theory appears as a brief interlude in the history of speculation on property, preceded (in medieval thought) and succeeded by legalistic and collectivist theories. Practically, however, the Lockean notion of property continued to exercise a great influence through the nineteenth century, especially in American jurisprudence, where the Benthamite theory of legislation never took hold, and where Blackstone was conveniently misread as claiming the common law simply incorporates and guarantees basic natural rights, including the right to private property. [22] This interpretation, however, depended on a consistently Lockean reading of Blackstone's ambiguous passages concerning "absolute" rights, a reading which I have sought to show is not warranted by his overall doctrine. The implicit natural rights assumptions about private property, it may be added, have often been associated with a simple or naive analysis of property as tangible things of the sort whose existence can be conceived independently of positive law, a view obviously untenable to a legal mind in Blackstone's day or our own.

Although the prevailing contemporary notion of property as a "bundle of rights" is not explicit in Hume or Blackstone, the essential insight that property is a rule-governed social artifice is perfectly clear in both. The refinements of modern theory have been made within this tradition of thought, principally by lawyers, and philosophers have relied on jurists (such as Hohfeld) in treating the subject.[23] If the interpretation offered in this chapter is correct, however, it was a philosopher, Hume, who first stated the essential elements of the theory, although the lawyer Blackstone provided a more concrete and detailed treatment. Recent philosophical interest in the subject of property reflects in many cases a continuing synthesis of these two traditions of analysis.

NOTES

*Preparation of this paper was facilitated by a faculty research grant from the Faculty of Arts and Sciences of the University of Pittsburgh during the summer of 1978.

1. See Lawrence C. Becker's essay in this volume. On the development of the modern theory see Richard T. Ely, *Property and Contract in Their Relation to the Distribution of Wealth* (1914) (Port Washington, NY: Kennikat, 1971), 2 vols.; C. Reinhold Noyes, *The Institution of Property* (New York: Longman, Green, 1936); and A. Irving Hallowell, "The Nature and Function of Property as a Social Institution," in his *Culture and Experience* (Philadelphia: Univ. of Pennsylvania Press, 1955).

2. C. B. Macpherson, *Democratic Theory* (Oxford: Clarendon, 1973), pp. 127ff.

3. David Hume, *A Treatise of Human Nature*, ed. L. A. Selby-Bigge (Oxford: Clarendon, 1928); and *An Inquiry Concerning the Principles of Morals*, ed. Charles W. Hendel (New York: LIberal Arts, 1957). References to these works, abbreviated as THN and IM, by section and page, respectively, will be incorporated in the text.

4. I shall not consider Hume's influential economic essays. See Eugene Rotwein's Introduction to his edition of David Hume, *Writings on Economics* (Madison: Univ. of Wisconsin Press, 1955).

5. David Miller takes Hume's "justice" to embrace the distribution, in accordance with legal rules, of all sorts of rights among the members of a society, *Social Justice* (Oxford: Clarendon, 1976), esp. p. 158.

6. Locke is not named in the *Treatise,* although his theory is clearly intended. Locke is also criticized by Hume in "Of the First Principles of Government," in *Essays Moral, Political and Literary* (Oxford: Oxford Univ. Press, 1963), p.30

7. See D. D. Raphael, "Hume and Adam Smith on Justice and Utility," *Proceedings of the Aristotelian Society,* New Series 73 (1972–73), pp. 87–103.

8. James Moore, "Hume's Theory of Justice and Property," *Political Studies* 24 (1976), pp. 112–13.

9. See John Plamenatz, *Man and Society* (London: Longmans, 1963), vol. 1, pp. 308ff.; and *The English Utilitarians* (Oxford: Basil Blackwell, 1958), pp. 29–30. A similar criticism is suggested in John B. Stewart, *The Moral and Political Philosophy of David Hume* (New York: Columbia Univ. Press, 1963), pp. 114–15; and Paschal Larkin, *Property in the Eighteenth Century* (1930) (Port Washington, NY: Kennikat, 1969), p. 100.

10. The notion that the utility of a legal order is a matter of evolution and gradual adaptation rather than of conscious design is the basis of F. A. Hayek's appreciation of Hume; cf. his "The Legal and Political Philosophy of David Hume," in V. C. Chappell, *Hume: A Collection of Critical Essays* (Garden City, NY: Doubleday, 1969); and the references to Hume in *Law, Legislation, and Liberty,* vol. 1, *Rules and Order* (Chicago: The Univ. of Chicago Press, 1973).

11. Sir William Blackstone, *Commentaries on the Laws of England,* with notes by George Sharswood (Philadelphia: Lippincott, 1879), 4 books in 2 vols. The division into four books, and the pagination, are standard in all editions; references will be incorporated into the text.

12. Jeremy Bentham, *A Fragment on Government,* Preface, sec. 15.

13. Richard Schlatter, *Private Property: The History of an Idea* (New Brunswick, N.J.: Rutgers Univ. Press, 1951), p. 162, suggests that by this time Locke's theory seemed a little too radical to the propertied classes, who preferred a solid legal foundation for their rights to an abstract, philosophical one.

14. See Commentaries book III, 168. Abatement, or the seizure of the estate of a deceased person without legal right, is a civil injury for which redress is provided. Blackstone notes that the same action would be permissible and indeed normal in the state of nature, where all right ceases with the death of the occupier and the goods revert to the common stock.

15. Noyes, op. cit., pp. 295–305, suggests that there is confusion in Blackstone arising from a superficial overlay of Roman law usage, which conceived *dominium,* or ownership, as complete, on English common law, where this concept does not work at all. Noyes points out that Blackstone's general treatment accurately reflects common law concepts, where ownership is always qualified by the "law of the land" and the rights of others, amounting in fact simply to the paramount interest from among a "bundle" of different rights in something.

16. The same reasoning applies to escheats; the king "is esteemed in the eye of the law, the originial proprietor of all the lands in the kingdom" (Comm. I, 302). These practices would appear to be unjustifiable by Locke's theory.

17. Daniel J. Boorstin, *The Mysterious Science of the Law* (Gloucester, Mass.: Peter Smith, 1973), pp. 176–78.

18. See Noyes, op. cit., pp. 307ff. A "thing" in a legal theory of property turns out to be anything in which there can be a legal interest, or anything that can be the object of a property right in a legal system.

19. David A. Lockmiller, *Sir William Blackstone* (Chapel Hill, N.C.: Univ. of North Carolina Press, 1938), p. 61.

20. Boorstin, op. cit., chap. 1 and passim.

21. Hallowell emphasizes the conceptual necessity of a public system of sanctions for property rights; op. cit., pp. 244–45.

22. See Roscoe Pound, *The Spirit of the Common Law* (Boston: Marshall Jones, 1921), pp. 150–51.

23. Roscoe Pound, *An Introduction to the Philosophy of Law* (New Haven: Yale Univ. Press, 1964), p. 108. Ethnology as well as law has influenced contemporary thinking about property; see Hallowell, op. cit., pp. 241–43. The *locus classicus* for the anthropological version of the modern theory of property is Bronislaw Malinowski's analysis of the ownership of a canoe among the Trobrianders. *Crime and Custom in Savage Society* (1926) (Totowa, N.J.: Littlefield, Adams, 1976), part I, chap. 2.

6

PROPERTY, FREEDOM, AND INDIVIDUALITY IN HEGEL'S AND MARX'S POLITICAL THOUGHT

PETER G. STILLMAN *

For many nineteenth-century thinkers, much of the argument about property revolves around the relation between forms of property and the development of individuality and of individual freedom. In his attempt to decide between socialism and systems of private property, John Stuart Mill poses the general issue in his own language: "If a conjecture may be hazarded, the decision will probably depend . . . on one consideration, viz. which of the two systems is consistent with the greatest amount of human liberty and spontaneity"[1] or individuality, as Hegel and Marx might think of it. For Hegel, a primary value of private property is its contribution to individuality; for Marx, much of the problem of systems of private property is their limiting or suppressing of individuality.

1. This chapter spells out the major arguments that underlie their disagreements. It treats first Hegel's political philosophy, in which private property assumes great importance in two ways.[2] First, property is the initial concept discussed in Hegel's *Philosophy of Right*,[3] and the right to property the initial right; his complete political thought rests on property as its logical beginning point. More so than most political thinkers, then, Hegel's thought is grounded on property. Second, for Hegel property has far-reaching implications. He conceptualizes property broadly and sees its many dimensions. He sees that property requires individuals to act in determinate ways in the external world; that through property men dominate nature and distinguish themselves from nature; that the right to property is the

basis of the rights to life and liberty; and property forms a basis for intersubjective relations, including contract. All these aspects of property Hegel links to the development and filling out of a rich individuality.

But Hegel, in his sophisticated explanation of the importance of private property, does not omit its flaws. He sees that in a civil society based on private property the few who are very rich and very poor do not work to satisfy the needs of others and are thus only imperfectly and defectively members of civil society (185), and the flourishing of such a civil society inevitably creates a class of propertyless rabble, for whom the myriad benefits of property are not available (243–45). For this second flaw Hegel perceives no solution.

While Marx does see that in an early stage of the development of capitalism property earned by its owner's own labor may have contributed to a limited and stunted individuality, in his analysis of capitalism Marx criticizes capitalist private property as suppressing individuality on each of those central points on which Hegel linked property and individuality. The differences between Hegel and Marx on these points have repercussions throughout their thought. Marx also presents an ideal of socialized property and a social individual; while there are similarities between Hegel's and Marx's ideas of individuality, there are deep differences about how that individuality can be attained.

Ironically, in the twentieth century the self-styled "Marxist" states have not approached Marx's ideal of individuality very closely; and developments in the West have undermined in practice those aspects of property that Hegel saw as essential to individuality, so that individuality as Hegel conceptualized it has been lost and has not been replaced. Whether Marx's version of individuality can be established, whether Hegel's idea of individuality can be reclaimed, whether the West is going to continue to move away from a rich individuality, as in Hegel's conception, without arriving at a new one, or whether out of the decline of Hegel's attempt to comprehend the world as spirit it is possible to create a new world in thought and practice — these questions (though not always in these terms) are at the heart of much contemporary thought.

2. Hegel's discussion of property must be seen within the context of his political philosophy as a whole. For Hegel, the state is the ethical entity, the universal end, the full community, in which individuals find their true purpose and their ultimate goals. The state is the manifestation of reason, giving rational direction and order to secu-

lar life. But Hegel's state is not uniform nor monolithic. Indeed, "the essence of the modern state is that the universal be bound up with the complete freedom of its particular members and with private well-being" (260A). Hegel attaches great importance to the particular: the rights and goals of the individual subjects, their own interests, their "private well-being," and their "right to be satisfied" (260A, 124R). Hegel criticizes Plato's *Republic,* for instance, because it does not allow scope for individual choice (262A).

The principle of particularity — or, as Hegel develops it more fully, "the principle of the self-subsistent inherently infinite personality of the individual, the principle of subjective freedom" (185R) — is an essential "achievement of the modern world" (182A). In the modern world, the main locus for subjective freedom and individual choice is *bürgerliche Gesellschaft* (civil society), which is composed of the system of needs (and their satisfaction), the administration of justice, and the police or public authorities and "corporations" — private organizations similar to Tocqueville's secondary associations (188). Civil society is based in part on the rights of property, contract, and punishment that Hegel discusses in the opening part of the *Philosophy of Right,* entitled "Abstract Right."

In Hegel's discussion of property abstractly in "Abstract Right" and concretely in the section on civil society, he closely links private property with the personality of the individual. Through his property, a human being develops his reason, his will (which is the active, acting moment of his reason [13R]), and his personality or individuality.[4] For Hegel, "man is implicitly rational, but he must also become explicitly so by struggling to create himself, not only by going forth from himself but also by building himself up within" (10A). In claiming things as his property, man goes forth from himself into the external world of nature; through his property, man goes forth to relate to other men and to build social institutions; and, by developing his will in the natural and social world as well as by claiming his own life and liberty as his property, man builds himself up from within.

In other words, property for Hegel is essential for men if they are to lead a full life of reason. In owning property, men act in the external world. They dominate Nature. They create social institutions. In shaping the natural and the social orders according to their intentions and goals, men develop and express their own capabilities; in reflecting on the results of their actions, they educate themselves about the world of actuality and about themselves and thereby prepare themselves for further action in the natural and social worlds.

At the same time, men claim themselves, their minds and bodies, as their own properties; from the right to property derive the rights to life and liberty, so that they are permanent subjects and actors, continuously shaping the natural and social worlds, and themselves.

Property for Hegel is to be seen not merely as an economic category or the result of utilitarian calculus; not only as a result of labor or convention; not solely as a requisite for social stability or diversity. It is more. For Hegel, property is a political and philosophical necessity, essential for the development of men as rational beings.

3. Hegel first discusses property in the opening section of "Abstract Right." Unlike a prepolitical state of nature that is a historical construct, "abstract right" is a logical construct. The human actors in "Abstract Right" are logical abstractions from humans: they are persons, subjects aware of their subjectivity and self-conscious of their free will, with a capacity for rights, natural human characteristics like height, age and impulses, and—at the beginning—little else (35). Similarly, the external world is an abstraction from the full world of institutions and shaped nature: it is a world of natural objects and animals that, lacking free will and incapable of rights, are defined as things (42).

The person confronting this external world, sees that he is limited to being only subjective by this world that, as external, appears different and strange to him. "Personality is that which struggles to lift itself above this restriction and give itself reality, or in other words to claim that external world as its own" (39). To overcome the restriction, the person "has as his substantive end the right of putting his will into any and every thing and thereby making it his" property (44). A property is a thing that contains a person's will.

Inherent in property for Hegel are four further characteristics. First, property results from a mental act; the person decides that he wishes the thing and wills it—"I want it," "this is mine." Hegel's person claims property by willing it; by contrast, Locke's natural man is entitled to property when he mixes his labor with the natural object, Blackstone's prehistorical man when he occupies the object. [5] Second, Hegel sharply distinguishes property from possession: property is based on the will, produces rights, and is thus unique to humans, whereas possession is power over something in order to satisfy a "natural need, impulse, [or] caprice" (45), in other words, possession is physical and naturalistic, based on what man shares with animals. Third, since a person is a single unit, his will is a single will; when *his* will is put into a thing, the thing becomes *his* property; so "property acquires the character of private property" (46). Fourth, "what and how much I possess . . . is a matter of indifference so far as rights are concerned" (49); the distribution of property can be unequal as long as each person has some property (Enc. 486) so that his free will has actuality.

When Hegel discusses property in civil society, the abstractions from "Abstract Right" become actualized, full and concrete: the person becomes a full human being; the external world of things is transformed into the world of actuality, with social institutions and fabricated nature that are actual because they are created and maintained by rational will (157, 258R). Property too becomes concrete: the meaning and implications of abstract property continue in civil society, and new ones emerge. Fully to comprehend Hegel's treatment of property requires examining its dimensions in both "Abstract Right" and civil society.[6]

4. For Hegel, one central dimension of property is that it elicits and requires from the person determinate actions in objectivity that result in the structuring of self, society, and actuality. Hegel stresses the importance of action in externality (or objectivity): when the person puts his will into an external thing and manifests his "right of appropriation" (44), he becomes in his property "for the first time" an actual will (45). To affirm to himself and others that his will is in his property, the person must "occupy" it, by an "external activity" that gives the property "a predicate, 'mine,' which must appear in it in an external form and must not simply remain in my inner will" (51A).

So the person has superseded his original "pure subjectivity of personality" (41A); he now exists in the external world, and the thing stands in the external world as his property, transformed by his will from an "external pure and simple" (42) to an embodiment of a person's will and hence something actual (45). Through property the person attains an "objective mode of existence"[7] and creates an objective, actual world.

What occurs at the level of will is manifested in the person's actions. In appropriating property, the person acts "to destroy [*aufheben*] the thing and transform it into his own" (44A). This creative destruction and transformation of property takes many forms. The person marks, modifies, and labors on his property; he uses it; and he alienates it (53). With property the person's range of activities expands into the objective world, which he shapes and changes.

When the person of "Abstract Right" becomes the man of civil society, he remains a property owner; and his property requires that he act in the world of actuality. His right to property is formalized in the administration of justice, whose laws he must know and obey (208). In the system of needs, he develops and manifests new capabilities: as he transforms nature, he develops new needs (190, 194), his labor becomes more sophisticated (194–98), and he learns through activity in all forms of actuality (187).

In his emphasis on property, Hegel insists that individuals act in the world and have "secular pursuits."[8] For him, holy medieval Roman Catholics who renounced property in their vows of poverty were renoucing a whole realm of human life, the "moral life in the socioeconomic sphere" (Enc. 552R). Similarly, in the *Phenomenology* (chap. IV. B) Hegel describes some forms of consciousness that attempt to get beyond servility by ignoring or denying the world — the stoics and the skeptics, for instance; these attempts fail, and one of their defects is that they do not confront, transform, and learn from external reality.[9] A generation after Hegel, John Stuart Mill asserted that "the appropriate region of human liberty" is in the "inward domain of consciousness";[10] Mill omits what Hegel stresses, namely the important developments and manifestations of self that come from action in objectivity. In addition, since secular action modifies the objective world, the individual shapes the environment in which he must choose, and thus lessens the chance that he will be forced to choose among alternatives each of which is undesirable.[11] Property contributes to freedom and individuality because it allows and requires man to act in and to shape the objective world.

Property also contributes to individuality because acting in the external world by willing to own property requires determinate action, the self-determination of the ego. Rather than holding to the abstract freedom of the will to dissipate and reject every content and possibility, in property the person's will "leaves undifferentiated indeterminancy and proceeds to differentiate itself, to posit a content or object and so to give itself determinacy" (6A) by placing itself in a specific property with specific characteristics (52).

Thus, the person overcomes and rejects the pure abstract negativity that refuses to will anything determinate and consequently either rejects the external world (as do the Hindus [5R] and the "beautiful soul" who eventually pines and wastes away in his rejection of determinate action [13A]) or tries to impose on the objective world an undifferentiated indeterminacy in which all are identical, as happened during the Terror in the French Revolution (5R).

At the same time, the person, in determining his will to own property, knows that it is he who is deciding and thus that his decision is a self-chosen and so a free restriction, a determinacy "which is [his will's] own . . . and in which it is confined only because it has put itself in it" (7). The self-determination in property is a precondition for and a paradigm of self-determination in civil society, which is essential if men are freely to create, act in, and maintain a complex civil society. By their decisions, men determine their places in the class structure, the division of labor, and the system of needs (200, Enc. 527). But in these self-limitations come individual development, education, and differentiation. It is only by choosing a vocation, joining a class, and becoming a corporation member that a man can be recognized by others and by himself as a valuable member of civil society, producing goods for the general wealth of the nation, and working within the structures of civil society for its "conservation and advancement" (Enc. 396A). These choices of vocation, class, and corporation are also an essential part of the education of each individual: these "temporal interests" (Enc. 396A) introduce him to society and concern with what others do, and they—along with the specialization of the division of labor—allow him to penetrate the world by knowing one part of it in depth and detail, and thereby also to understand by analogy other processes and skills as well as to see himself in other kinds of activity.[12] In restriction the individual is liberated from the impossible goal of universal action, that is, of doing everything; in his self-limitation the individual can develop within himself and in society by undertaking specific, recognized, and valued activities.

The person's self-determination of his will in property involves the development of individuality in yet another way. When the person freely determines his will into an external object that he makes his property, he is externalizing or objectifying his will; when he then examines his property, he sees his objectification. This discovery, however, is itself the transcending of self-objectification; as soon as the person sees his will in the thing, he can see that his will is still his and still free (7). His will is not irrevocably placed in the object or lost in it because he can withdraw his will from the property by letting it fall ownerless (65) or by exchanging it in contract for another property (73). More importantly, his will is not subjugated or essentially determined by the object, because his will has transformed the thing into property and he can further shape and use it for his purposes, and because he can learn about himself and his purposes by analyzing his activities with his property.[13]

This self-objectification and its transcending is a recurrent process. Through it, the human will develops the objective world by creating institutions that are the actualizations of will; concurrently, through creating and maintaining those institutions, the human will develops to civilized, social modes and comes to comprehend itself. At the same time, the transcending of objectifications allows the will to return to itself from objectivity. (Indeed, this process of self-objectification and its overcoming is also the path of the world-spirit throughout history, which develops by objectifying itself into the world and then by comprehending and transcending its objectification.) This process appears in the science of objective spirit first with property, which is paradigmatic; it reappears experientially for all men when they work to satisfy needs, and in so doing exchange properties in civil society. For Hegel, to be human inherently involves self-objectification and its overcoming, the shaping of both self and the external world, the creation, discovery, and maintenance of actuality.

Furthermore, as a result of my property, "I as free will am an object to myself" (45); the person is self-conscious. He sees his own will in the object, as the manifestation of himself in objectivity, and thus he recognizes himself, in actuality, as a free will and a person. With this self-consciousness of his actualized personality comes also his recognition of himself as having rights, acting determinately and objectively, and shaping the external world; through these determinations of his properties, he sees himself structuring and shaping himself, and thus both transforms and learns about himself. Self-consciously in his property, the individual uses it to give reality to his conception of his own goals and purposes; in attempting to actualize these goals and purposes, the individual develops himself. In property, a person exists "for himself"; he can see himself, his will, his purposes and dreams in the objective things that are his. "The slave does not know his essence, his infinity, his freedom; . . . and he lacks this knowledge of himself because he does not think himself" (21R); the person in his property recognizes and "apprehends [him]self through thinking" as a free will and a person. In civil society, the property-owning person is transformed into a concrete man who is a permanent subject and actor: a self-conscious being, freely determining himself in action in actuality, shaping the external world and himself in order to realize his goals and wishes.

5. Another central dimension of property that Hegel ties to freedom and individuality is the domination of nature. In property, the person asserts and proves the domination of man over nature, "the

absolute right of appropriation which man has over all 'things'" (44). As Joachim Ritter has argued well, behind the apparent immobility of property as a thing is hidden, for Hegel, the historical activities of work and interaction that have domesticated nature[14] by demystifying it, purging it of its natural gods, proving that natural objects exist not for themselves but only for man, and transforming the natural world into "things" lacking reason or purpose in themselves (42) and thus, as things, into that which can be appropriated by man.

Property is thus a continuing manifestation and willful proof of man's domination, as the individual continuously asserts in property that nature and natural objects exist for man and that man in property maintains and proves his free mastery of nature. In making this assertion, the individual also expands his will's scope of action and influences his surroundings. The properties a person owns are his way of controlling and shaping nature in order to develop, affect, and express his own character and his ways of living and working.

The domination of nature is not, for Hegel, just the technical manipulation of particular natural objects in order to satisfy human desire (Enc. 245A). The modern domestication of nature has led to the insight that nature has laws and structure (Enc. 252) and to the (Hegelian) comprehension that nature and its structure form the prespiritual basis for the existence of human beings as free subjects (Enc. 381A). Thus nature, comprehensible and comprehended, is transformed; human beings have discovered nature's rationality and necessity, and indeed have discovered this rationality and necessity by thinking and positing nature's substantiality, structure and processes (Enc. 384A). So nature "is not something alien and yonder" (Enc. 246A) but is a world in which human beings can feel "at home," free through their active knowledge of nature.[15] As Hegel lectured, "I am at home in the world when I know it, still more so when I have understood [*begriffen*] or conceptually comprehended it (4A).

The domination and comprehension of nature by man's will in his property has direct analogies to Hegel's philosophy as a whole, in which the foreign character and otherness of all objects disappear *(aufheben)* as reason penetrates and comprehends them. Reason literally makes the object its own by grasping it in thought: "in thinking an object, I make it into thought and deprive it of its sensuous aspect; I make it into something which is directly and essentially mine" (4A); likewise, reason maintains the object as its own because the object's apparent autonomy and otherness is seen to be the result of the positing of that autonomy by reason itself. For Hegel, this grasping is complete and total. Nothing is left that might be Kant's "thing-in-it-self": "in the face of the free will, the thing retains no property in it-self" (52R). Nor is a materialistic or "realist" philosophy valid, as the will dominates the thing:

> The free will . . . is the idealism which does not take things as they are to be absolute, while realism pronounces them to be absolute. . . . Even an animal has gone beyond this realist philosophy since it devours things and so proves that they are not absolutely self-sufficient. (44A)

In Hegel's idealist idea of property, man as will transforms a thing that confronts him into a property, that is, an existent that embodies a free will (29); in Hegel's idealist philosophy as a whole, spirit — in its many forms, including human will in objective spirit — transforms everything confronting it into manifestations of its own knowledge and activity (Enc. 577). When Hegel asserts that "to comprehend what is, this is the task of philosophy, because what is, is reason" (Preface, p. 11), he can know that "what is, is reason" because the will and spirit have fully penetrated the world, in property and in other ways, and thus made the world rational, destroyed its foreignness, and made it comprehensible.

Man's domination and comprehension of nature is at the same time the liberation of the human and the spiritual from the natural and the prespiritual; man is clearly differentiated from nature. With this differentiation, there can no longer be slavery because "all historical views of the justice of slavery and lordship . . . depend on regarding man as a natural entity pure and simple" (57R), not free, without rights. Because Greeks saw man and nature in immediate harmony, they directly linked the human and the natural, with the result that some humans were, for the Greeks, by nature slaves. Because the Romans had not yet risen to the full distinction between man and nature, they also had slaves; in Roman law "there could be no definition of 'man,' since 'slave' could not be brought under it — the very status of slave indeed is an outrage on the conception of man" (2R). In Christianity, however, "the individual personality is recognized as infinite, as absolutely self-conscious and free," because "individuals have infinite worth and should be received in grace into absolute spirituality. . . . It is therefore only under Christianity that men become personally free, i.e. capable of owning property in freedom."[16] To actualize Christian freedom on earth in property was a

long, difficult process (62R); but the *Philosophy of Right* celebrates
the culmination of that process: the complete differentiation of man
from nature in a Christian notion of freedom that is realized in property rights in the Western Europe of 1820, in which all humans are
free and permanent subjects liberated from the exclusively natural,
from being natural objects, and from existing merely for others, and
liberated to the rational, spiritual, and free core of their being.

6. Property is directly tied to personality and its development because the property right—the will in the thing—is the basis for the
rights of the person to life and liberty. The person claims himself as
he claims a property, through his will to own, to occupy, and to modify and transform himself: "it is only through the development of his
own body and mind, essentially through his self-consciousness's apprehension of itself as free, that he takes possession of himself and becomes his own property and no one else's" (57). Once a person gains
property in himself, his rights are inalienable. Since a person can
alienate only "single external things" (75, 65),

> therefore those goods, or rather substantive characteristics,
> which constitute my own private personality and the universal
> essence of my self-consciousness are inalienable and my right to
> them is imprescriptable. Such characteristics are my personality
> as such, my universal freedom of will, my ethical life, my
> religion. (66)

Through the exercise of the right to property, the person gains his inalienable rights to life and liberty.

By deriving the rights to life and liberty from the right to property,
Hegel evinces concern for the education and culturation *(Bildung)* of
the individual. A comparison with Locke may bring out Hegel's concern. Locke postulates the individual's property in himself as the
original: "every Man has a *Property* in his own *Person*. . . . The
Labour of his Body, and the *Work* of his Hands, we may say, are
properly his."[17] Locke assumes that the individual owns himself as
property and derives property in things from property in self.

From this difference in the derivation of rights flows a difference in
emphasis generally between Locke and Hegel. Since Locke begins
with the assertion that individuals own their minds and bodies, he regards that property as a given, not as a task for the individual nor as
a problem for his political philosophy. But Hegel sees that the individual's appropriation of himself as his own property—his self-

conscious apprehension of himself as free—is neither automatic nor easy. Thus, much of Hegel's political philosophy is devoted to developing and discussing the means whereby the individual can gain possession of, and property in, himself. Hegel defines rights broadly, including not only rights to "life, liberty, and estates" (57, 44), but also, for instance, rights to formal education (174), public services (242R), and subsistence (241), that is, to all that is necessary for the individual fully to appropriate and own himself. Similarly, Hegel sees *Bildung* as crucial for an individual to attain his rights to life and liberty, and to translate into actuality "what one is according to one's concept" (57), a free and rational being. The lessons the person learns in wrong, the subjective willing of morality, and the rational institutions of ethical life are all directed in part toward the education of the individual into all facets of ethical life and reason (187R). Freedom must "be earned and won through the endless mediation of discipline acting upon the powers of cognition and will."[18] To appropriate one's mind and body as one's own property is a long struggle in the claiming of one's self and the development of one's individuality.

As his emphasis on education suggests, Hegel insists that rights should not be seen as restrictions. He criticizes the "Kantian and the generally accepted definition of right" and law and the Lockean definition of natural law, both of which involve the "'*restriction* which makes it possible for my freedom or self-will to co-exist with the self-will of each and all according to a universal law'" or a natural law (29R), and which therefore see personality as a circumscribed, static concept, limited by law and society. For Hegel, on the other hand, personality is dynamic and capable of growth. The right to property expands the person by giving him an objective existence, a new mode of being, and a scope for the free determination of his free will. These are valuable and necessary for individual freedom and development. The individual must, of course, respect the property rights of others; but in Hegel's treatment this apparent restriction is in fact educative and developmental: for the person recognizes other property owners as persons and equals only through his respecting their property rights in contract (73). He thus attains an awareness of the social aspects of men (100, 208). By educating his will to restrain his desires, he develops moral ideas (104, 207).[19]

While a person's life and liberty, the most important parts of his personality, are inalienable (66), the person can alienate restricted and defined products of himself:

> Single products of my particular physical and mental skill and
> of my power to act I can alienate to someone else and I can give
> him the use of my abilities for a restricted period, because, on
> the strength of this restriction, my abilities acquire an external
> relation to the totality and universality of my being. (67)

As Hegel lectured,

> The distinction here explained is that between a slave and a
> modern domestic servant or day-labourer. The Athenian slave
> perhaps had an easier occupation and more intellectual work
> than is usually the case with our servants, but he was still a slave,
> because he had alienated to his master the whole range of his ac-
> tivity. (67A)

Because persons have inalienable rights, they cannot be in slavery,
serfdom, or any other status of involuntary servitude and personal
dependence. Because persons can alienate limited portions of their
time for wages, those whose labor on their own property does not
produce enough of what they desire or need can work for another, by
contracting for a limited period of time, while still maintaining personal independence and volition. Because the laborer can alienate
part of his labor time while nonetheless retaining his inalienable
rights, all unfree forms of subordinate work relationships are abolished as unright (57R), and "for the first time, liberty becomes, without any limitation, the principle of a society."[20]

7. The person is not only a private and separate being who expresses himself; as a person with a will, he also knows himself as "universal" in his "self-relation" (35). In other words, in thinking about
himself as an "I" or an ego, the person does of course see himself as a
particular single being; but he must also see other persons as persons
like himself, other egos as egos like himself, so that he can categorize
himself in or relate himself to the class or "universal" of "person" or
"ego" at the same time that he distinguishes himself from all other
persons or egos.

This universality or intersubjectivity of the person finds expression
in the person's property; it is implicit in and necessarily underlies the
developments and expressions of freedom and individuality in determinate action in objectivity, in man's liberation from nature, and in
the claiming of the right to life and liberty, all of which in some ways

require interactions among individuals. Property as a locus for inter-subjective interactions is also important in itself in the development of individual freedom and individuality.

Only with the actualization of the will in property can persons relate to each other. Indeed, this relating is an inherent part of property for Hegel, since the willing of property is not complete until the thing is "occupied" (51A); when the person occupies his property, his will becomes fully objective and apparent to him and to others so that they can recognize his will in the property. With the mutual recognition of property owners comes a basis for interpersonal life.

For Hegel, then, private property is not only a privatization; equally, it is a socialization. Requiring mutual recognition and the communication of that recognition, property is a basis for social communication. From property directly derives one institutionalized form of interpersonal life: contract, in which two property owners, mutually acknowledging each person as persons and as free, create in contract a common will to which each is bound (72–74). Contract remains a mode of interaction in the system of needs in civil society, and is regularized and formalized through the administration of justice.

In property, recognition, and contract, Hegel also finds the manifestations of spirit in objectivity. Persons recognize each other not as natural but as free beings; "only in such a manner is true freedom realized; for since this consists in my identity with the other, I am only truly free when the other is also free and is recognized by me as free" (Enc. 431A). For Hegel, spirit lies in this unity of each with all, a unity that is "indifferent to natural existence," a unity that maintains and transcends each, a unity that is inward: "this freedom of one in the other unites men in an inward manner, whereas needs and necessity bring them together only externally" (Enc. 431A).[21] Recognition in property and contract is the beginning of objective spirit, the unity of individuals not for purely natural or selfish reasons, but for recognized freedom in spiritual community.

Furthermore, for Hegel only through being objective in interactions with others can an individual fully cultivate himself; he must actualize his will and relate to others in a social setting. Without the social setting, the individual cannot gain nor maintain an educated development; an individual matured to adulthood in isolation is a theoretical fiction. Without the actualization of will, first in property and then in other actions, the individual would remain purely subjective and could not know the reality of his intentions; as Hegel lectured in a slightly different context, "the laurels of mere willing [without activity] are dry leaves that never were green" (124A). Additionally, part of the development of individuality requires attuning one's will to the wishes, feelings, and practices of others; through intersubjective action — in mutual recognition in contract, in interdependent arrangements like work, in explicitly rule-governed frameworks like the administration of justice, in voluntary cooperation in corporations, and in other social and political situations — the individual experiences social practices, learns to discipline his arbitrary whims, acculturates himself in new ways, and expresses himself.

Finally, for Hegel property also contributes to individuality because property maintains and accentuates the differences among humans (200R) and thus guarantees the existence of a complex, interdependent, differentiated, and multifaceted civil society and ethical life *(Sittlichkeit)*. Such an ethical life, with its many institutions, requires and encourages from individuals different modes of cognition, feeling, and action in order that individuals can express and develop themselves variously. [22]

8. It should be clear by now why, for Hegel, property is will-based, inherently unequally distributed, private property, and how it contributes to individuality. Property must be based on the will and be different from possession in order fully to differentiate man from nature and to allow for the creation of human and spiritual (as opposed to natural) interactions and ethical institutions. Property must be private because only private property for all guarantees that each and every individual must objectify himself, determine himself, and posit himself in externality in order to see and comprehend himself through his actions, to be social, and to create himself through acting on nature and in society; private property is the basis for the rights to life and liberty; and free work relations are possible only with private property. Everyone must own property, to guarantee for all its benefits, fully to separate man and nature, and to require all to participate in recognition and spirit; but the distribution is and must be unequal because humans are different and because ethical life requires variety and differentiation.

By the willful appropriation of the world, that is, by each man's owning property and developing and expressing himself in it, appropriating his mind and body, dominating nature, creating and comprehending social and political institutions, and recognizing others as free, men shape and maintain the spiritual world to serve human purposes and goals, and to assist human *Bildung*, self-knowledge, and self-creation. For Hegel, property is a political and philosophical necessity, essential for the development of men as rational beings, as individuals who are free.

9. Although property is essential for the full life of reason, Hegel acutely perceives that it is by itself not sufficient. Latent in property ownership are tendencies toward atomism and individual acquisitiveness that must be limited. For Hegel, the man of civil society does not try to accumulate property or wealth; rather, through the social dimensions inherent in property (51) and manifested in civil society, individuals develop and grow, cultivate their capacities and talents, and acculturate themselves from the natural and unreflective to the social and spiritual (187R). Through their positions in the division of labor, their choice of vocation, and their class membership, men become individuals who contribute a specific skill and product to the system of needs, who define themselves partially in terms of their work activities, and who through work cultivate themselves both in general culture and in the mores and morals of their professions (207; Enc. 527). By joining a corporation, individuals become recognized and respected members of the social whole; in a corporation, a member's subsistence is assured, and

in addition, this nexus of capability and livelihood is a *recognised* fact, with the result that the corporation member needs no external marks beyond his own membership as evidence of his skill and his regular income and subsistence, i.e. as evidence that he is a somebody. (253)

On the other hand, without corporation membership a man is "without rank or dignity, his isolation reduces his business to mere self-seeking, and his livelihood and satisfaction become insecure" (253R). While in contract everyone is recognized as equal on the basis of everyone's humanity (40), in civil society men are recognized and valued for their specific and regular contributions to society. Civil society is valuable for Hegel, then, not only because it is the playground of property, but also because its social arrangements lead men beyond concern with property accumulation and privatism to individuation, recognition, *Bildung*, and other types of individual development and satisfaction that transcend property's atomistic characteristics.[23]

Furthermore, Hegel confines individual private property to abstract right and civil society; by restricting contracts to "single external things" that are alienable (75R, 66), Hegel insists that the family and state are outside the realm of property, contract, and their concomitant attitudes and behaviors. Thus, the family is a locus of love and sharing, not contracts, privatism, and possessive individualism; and in the family private property becomes *Vermögen*, the family resources to be drawn on by all (171). The state is concerned with the good of the community as a whole, not the "will of all" (in Rousseau's words) nor the protection of property (in Locke's liberal terms); it is the focus of patriotism, not a means by which to maximize or guarantee private interests. In the state, private property is subordinated to rational political requisites (306). Because private property is transformed in the family and state, those institutions can hold society together against the centrifugal force of private property in a competitive system of needs; the state can direct social life to rational ends, not the interests of powerful groups; and state and family provide individuals with manifold types of interactions not available in institutions based solely on property and contract. While Hegel may begin the *Philosophy of Right* with private property, he stresses the social and developmental aspects of property, and he sees the family and state, essential spiritual institutions, as transcending property; for Hegel, property is but one moment — though a crucial one — of individual *Bildung* and freedom, ethical institutions, and spiritual development.

10. Although only one moment in the *Philosophy of Right*, private property is the cause of many of the problems in the world of objective spirit that Hegel presents. Most of the problems are marginal. Some drawbacks are inherent in property itself. For example, by putting his will into the external world, the person becomes, as Reyburn says, "liable to the lot and chances that external things suffer."[24] In determining himself to specific choices, the individual does have to renounce some possibilities; and a poor choice of vocation, for instance, can have some effect for a long time (though, since most vocations are reputable, the effect is not likely to be debilitating [Enc. 396A]). In a contract, persons relate to each other through things; in other words, human relations are reified.[25] These drawbacks are generally the obverse of benefits that are, to Hegel, overwhelmingly more important: for instance, the freedom to choose one's occupation is more important than the unfortunate effects of poor choices by a few individuals (185A); and reification in contract is the price for equality in contractual relations (74,77).

In addition, not everyone will transcend his property. The characteristics of a person too interested in his property rights are not appealing:

> To have no interest except in one's formal right may be pure obstinacy, often a fitting accompaniment of a cold heart and restricted sympathies. It is uncultured people who insist most on their rights, while noble minds look on other aspects of the thing. (37A)

Similarly, those who do not join a corporation remain at the level of pure self-seeking and asocial existence (253R).

Social effects related to private property in civil society also result in problems. For instance, mechanization threatens the liberating aspects of human labor (198) as well as the natural character of the agricultural estate (203A). Most serious, however, is a problem that Hegel unsparingly depicts: the physical and ethical corruption that comes from the highly unequal distribution of income and wealth in an active civil society composed of individuals who own capital (185, 243). The workings of the system of needs—with private property *(Eigentum)* and wage labor—lead to capital *(Kapital)* (200, 237).[26] When the economy is flourishing, "when civil society is in a state of unimpeded activity," the result is "the concentration of disproportionate wealth in a few hands" (244). The leisured wealthy suffer ethically, because they do not liberate themselves either from external nature through their own work (194R) or from their naturally given desires through social needs (194). At the same time, the activity of civil society results in the "subdivision and restriction of particular jobs" and "the dependence and distress of the class [*Klasse*, not *Stand*] tied to work of that sort" (243). For a member of this class, whose sole property is his labor, the result is poverty and misery, that is his exclusion from the physical and ethical benefits of society.

> When the standard of living of a large mass of people falls below a certain subsistence level—a level regulated automatically as the one necessary for a member of the society—and when there is a consequent loss of the sense of right and wrong, of honesty and the self-respect which makes a man insist on maintaining himself by his own work and effort, the result is the creation of a rabble of paupers. (244)

For Hegel, this poverty and misery is a necessary, not avoidable, consequence of civil society (245). Furthermore,

> Against nature man can claim no right, but once society is established, poverty immediately takes the form of a wrong done to one class [*Klasse*] by another. The important question of how poverty is to be abolished [*abzuhelfen*, not *aufzuheben*] is one of the most disturbing problems which agitate modern society. (244A)

In short, with the development of capital come social groups of the very rich and the poor, the ethical degeneration of both, and the continuing problem of a dispossessed and poverty-stricken class.

This problem of poverty is serious but not ultimately destructive. The state and public authorities can mitigate the problem in a number of ways: colonization (246), with its eventual geographical limits; redistribution of income by taxes or charity, which does "violate the principle of civil society" that all should work (245); and the assurance of a feeling of political rights on the part of the poor, a condition Hegel saw in England, because "poverty in itself does not make men into a rabble; a rabble is created only when there is joined to poverty a disposition of mind, an inner indignation against the rich, against society, against the government, &c." (244A). Conversely, problems within civil society help mature the state; a defined civil society focuses conflicts between rich and poor (rather than, for example, letting them dissipate through an escape valve like the American frontier) and thus forces state officials to reflect, deliberate, and choose consciously.[27]

Hegel sees the problems that attend property and capital, problems that result in suffering, misery, and anxiety. But these problems can be mitigated by the social institutions of civil society and by the family and the state; moreover, inseparably related to these problems of property is the distinctive and overwhelming value of modern ethical life: it is the highest development of freedom and individuality, a development in which property is an essential element. For it is only property that can institutionalize and guarantee man's objective existence, his liberation from nature and his natural being, his property in himself and his consequent rights, and his social and spiritual intersubjective activity.

11. At first glance, Marx seems to be as far from Hegel as possible on the issue of private property; in a famous (truncated) quotation, Marx asserts that " . . . the theory of the Communists may be summed up in the single sentence: Abolition of private property" (CM, II).[28] But the relation of Hegel's views to Marx's is in fact quite complex.

Marx explicitly discusses three forms of property in the modern world. The first is "self-earned," "individual" private property of all producers (CI, 762), a form of property that Marx sees as contributing to the individuality of the owner. "The private property of the labourer in his means of production is the foundation of petty industry," which is "an essential condition for the development . . . of the free individuality of the labourer himself" (CI, 761). Part of this individuality comes from creativity with social implements such as tools, which the artisan "handles as a virtuoso" (CI, 761). The independent peasant or handicraftsman must also practice, even if in a "small degree," his knowledge, judgment, and will in his work (CI, 361).

But petty industry is an undeveloped form of production; "it excludes co-operation, division of labour within each separate process of production, the control over, and the productive application of the forces of Nature by society, and the free development of the social productive powers" (CI, 762). Concurrently, it allows to the property-owning laborer "no diversity of development, no variety of talent, no wealth of social relations" (18thB, VII); he is isolated in his self-sufficiency. Because of this asociality of production and producer, for Marx petty industry is "compatible only with a system of production, and a society, moving within narrow and more or less primitive bounds. To perpetuate it would be . . . 'to decree universal mediocrity'" (CI, 762).

For Hegel also, "self-earned" private property, to the extent that it exists, produces a meager individuality. For this form of property lacks or denies the explicit social dimensions of property that Hegel sees as important — the recognition of others (40); the development of social needs and social work (194); banding together in corporations (255); and a self-conscious system of social rules (209) and political direction (258); the result of "self-earned private property" is a world of "dispersed atomic personalities," each "empty" in his singleness and lacking substantiality.[29] For Hegel as for Marx, individuality requires a rich social context for its full development and manifestation.

12. For Marx, petty industry has historically been "to a great extent . . . destroyed" (CM, II) by modern industry; "self-earned private property . . . is supplanted by capitalistic private property" (CI, 762). The distinction between these two forms of property is marked:

> [Bourgeois] Political Economy confuses on principle two very different kinds of private property, of which one rests on the producers' own labour, the other on the employment of the labour of others. It forgets that the latter not only is the direct antithesis of the former, but . . . grows on its tomb only. (CI, 765)

"Capitalist private property [has for its] fundamental condition the annihilation of self-earned private property; in other words, the expropriation of the labourer" (CI, 774).

This capitalist private property is the second form of property Marx discusses. He sees it as destructive of individuality. One immediate result of the gradual expropriation of the laborer is that the limited individuality within petty industry is eradicated. As Marx noted of the short span of two generations of French peasants when "the feudal lords were replaced by urban usurers," "small-holding property, in this enslavement by capital . . . , has transformed the mass of the French nation into troglodytes. . . . The bourgeois order, which at the beginning of the century set the state to stand guard over the newly arisen small holding and manured it with laurels, has become a vampire that sucks out its blood and brains and throws it into the alchemistic cauldron of capital" (18thB, VII). For the artisan, transformed under capitalism into industrial worker, the situation is the same: "it is the machine which possesses skill and strength in place of the worker [and] is itself the virtuoso" (G, 693; CI, 361).

Furthermore, the manifold relations Hegel saw between property and individuality do not exist with capitalist private property for Marx.[30] There is neither space nor necessity to describe in detail all of Marx's critiques; their content, complexity, and completeness can be readily indicated by touching on each of Hegel's major arguments. For Hegel, property allows the person an objective existence and scope for determinate, self-conscious action (see sec. 4, above). For Marx, capitalism is based on the continual, often violent expropriation of worker and capitalist (CI, 761–63); the many who are expropriated obviously lack whatever objectivity might be gained through property. The capitalist himself is sunk into his external existence and unable to extract himself from his property; he is subjected to the laws of capitalism lest he himself be expropriated (CI, 595) and is defined in terms of his externalities ("Money and Alienated Man"; CI, 72). Determinate action is eliminated in capitalism and replaced by abstract action: commodity production is based on abstract human labor (CI, 38); commodity exchange is "an act characterized by a total abstraction from use-value" (CI, 37). Self-conscious action is truncated before the dialectical process of externalization and its overcoming is completed; for Marx, in capitalism the worker externalizes himself in activity but cannot overcome the externalization; lost in the object of his activity, the worker is estranged. In his estranged activity, the worker "fashions against himself" a powerful "alien objective world" that "dominates and exploits him" and where appearances mystify rather than clarify how the world works ("Estranged Labour," E & G, 289–90; CI, 571; CIII, 827–30).

For Hegel, property is the proof of man's domination of and liberation from nature and his assertion of himself as a spiritual being (see sec. 5, above). For Marx, capitalism clearly involves the domination of nature on a historically revolutionary and progressive scale (CM, I). Part of capitalism's progressiveness is social; for instance, the development of human needs under capitalism is "an essential civilizing moment" (G, 287). But capitalist domination of nature also prevents liberation. It binds human beings to nature and to things. In their work, workers are reduced to their animal functions, their human dimensions suppressed or eliminated ("Estranged Labour," E & G, 292; CI, 231–302; CIII, 86). Labor itself is merely "a means to enable [the worker] to exist" (WLC, I), not a liberating life activity of self-realization (G, 307, 611). Social relations lose their human qualities and assume "the fantastic form of a relation between things" (CI, 72). Indeed, for Marx so little have human beings liberated themselves from nature that all existing societies are determined by the play of natural forces, not created by voluntary human action ("German Ideology," E & G, 424–30; G, 162).

For Hegel, the property right is the basis for the rights of the individual to life and liberty (see sec. 6, above). For Marx, the "sphere of simple circulation," the economic equivalent of Hegel's "Abstract Right," is "a very Eden of the innate rights of man. There alone rule Freedom, Equality, Property, and Bentham"; each buys and sells commodities freely, in equal exchange, disposing "only of what is his own," and acting from selfishness and private interest (CI, 176; G, 238). But the text of *Capital* involves taking abstract simple circulation and putting it into its concrete historical, social, and economic contexts; as the contexts become developed, "we can perceive," Marx writes, "a change in the physiognomy of our dramatis personae" (CI, 176) as well as of the other elements of simple circulation. In this contextualization, freedom disappears: the worker must work in order to survive, and he must work under the command of the capitalist and the conditions of capitalist production (CI, 487, 184, 488). So also does equality of exchange vanish, because the capitalist pays for labor power, receives labor, and thus can pocket the surplus value. "It is evident that the laws of appropriation or of private property, laws that are based on the production and circulation of commodities, become by their own inner and inexorable dialectic changed into their very opposite" (CI, 583). The apparently equal exchange between worker and capitalist is only "a mere form," "mystifying" a transaction of exploitation; for "what really takes place is this — the capitalist again and again appropriates, without equivalent, a portion of the previously materialised labour of others, and exchanges it for a great quantity of living labour" (CI, 583; G, 458).[31] At the same time, property is transformed drastically; "property in one's own labour, and free disposition over it . . . turn into the worker's propertylessness, and the dispossession of his labour" (G, 674; CI, 584). Even "Bentham" — individual self-interest — is changed, since self-interest is culturally determined (CI, 609n.) and buffeted by economic laws and ideological misunderstandings that frustrate its attainment (CIII, 826–30; G, 452–53).

For Hegel, property forms the ground for free, equal, and creative intersubjective activity (see sec. 7, above). For Marx, capitalist private property forms the ground for a class-based intersubjectivity characterized by struggle and for activity that is mystified and fetishistic. In the exchange for wage labor, the capitalist tries to expand the working day, the laborer to shorten it; each bases his position on the rights of buyer or seller. "There is here, therefore, an antinomy, right against right. . . . Between equal rights, force decides. Hence is it that in the history of capitalist production, the determination of what is a working-day, presents itself as the result of a struggle" (CI, 235), "a civil war" (CI, 295). Activity in capitalism takes on an alien, mystical, and fetishistic quality, since the intersubjective world that is created by human action is an alien world that people do not control (G, 197), a world in which the appearances of things are widely at variance from their essences (CIII, 817), a world where social connections among persons are transformed into social relations among things (CI, 72).

Looked at from a different perspective, it is clear that Marx criticizes capitalist private property precisely because it limits individuality, individual development and freedom.[32] It is instructive to attend to Marx's terms when he describes the oppression of the workers; he consistently moves beyond material and economic matters to issues of individuality, *Bildung*, and freedom. Such is clearly the case in the "1844 Manuscripts" like "Estranged Labour" and "Private Property and Communism." It is also true in the *Manifesto;* for instance, Marx writes: "In bourgeois society capital is independent and has individuality, while the living person is dependent and has no individuality" (CM, II). In the *Grundrisse*, Marx sees that the laborer gives up his human and creative powers to capitalist machines; "the accumulation of knowledge and of skill, of the general productive forces of the social brain, is . . . absorbed into capital" qua machines, and knowledge and skill become alien to the laborer (G, 694–95; CI, 360–61). Most strikingly, perhaps, is that throughout *Capital* Marx interjects remarks that go beyond the economic despite his own stricture on the limited scope of his book (CI, 354). Marx links capitalist division of labor to "industrial pathology" (CI, 363); in commenting on capitalism's preserving of capital but not labor, Marx notes that "more than any other mode of production, [capitalism] squanders human lives, or living labour, and not only blood and flesh, but also *nerve* and *brain*" (CIII, 88; my italics); and capitalism forces the laborer to become like a machine (CI, 349) or a living appendage to a machine (CI, 484), to be "crippled by life-long repetition of one and the same trivial operation" (CI, 488), and to be "made poor in individual productive powers" (CI, 361). In a caustic passage, Marx summarizes the result of the social and economic system based on capitalist private property:

within the capitalist system all methods for raising the social productiveness of labour are brought about at the cost of the individual labourer; all means for the development of production transform themselves into means of domination over, and exploitation of, the producers; they mutilate the labourer into a fragment of a man, degrade him . . . ; they estrange from him

the intellectual potentialities of the labour-process. . . . In proportion as capital accumulates, the lot of the labourer, be his
payment high or low, must grow worse. . . . Accumulation of
wealth at one pole is, therefore, at the same time, accumulation
of misery, agony of toil, slavery, ignorance, brutality, mental
degradation, at the opposite pole. (CI, 645)

Although the development of the productive powers of mankind under capitalism is a precondition for the new society that may develop
all dimensions of individuals in community, capitalist private property prevents the development of individuality and indeed suppresses
it by dehumanizing men while humanizing capital (CI, 645, 350).

Whereas Hegel links property essentially to the development and
manifestation of individuality, Marx links it to the warping and suppression of individuality. Even though less than a score of years separate Hegel's last lectures and writings on politics from Marx's works
that contain, in embryo at least, his whole system (e.g., "German
Ideology," CM, WLC), so that Hegel and Marx are both looking at
roughly the same, post–French Revolution, post–industrial revolution (or at least post–Adam Smith and Ricardo [189R]) world, the
differences between Hegel and Marx on property go to the bases of
their interpretations of society.

They do agree that capital results in groups of people whose individuality is stunted or twisted. For both Hegel and Marx, an ongoing
civil society produces capital and, with it, groups or classes of the
very rich and the very poor who suffer physical and ethical degradation (185; CI, 657); especially in times of economic activity a rabble
of paupers or poverty-stricken workers is created (243–45; G, 604).

But they disagree about the scope of capital's debilitating effects
and the power and inevitability of its self-expansion (253R; CI, 592).
Thus, they disagree about the size and importance of the capital-
related classes that emerge: for Hegel they are peripheral though
troubling to civil society; for Marx they are the central defining characteristic of capitalism. They disagree about the ability of noncapi-
talistic institutions to withstand the corrosive effects of capital. For
Hegel, the public authorities, administration of justice, and corporations—and especially the state and family—exist, and can domesti-
cate, mediate, and socialize the atomistic tendencies of private property and capital by acculturating individuals to a social individuality;
and a society containing private property can be subject to rational
control by a constitutional state. For Marx, however, the narrowness

of capital narrows individuals; the dynamics of capitalism control social interactions and political action; the objective divisions caused by capital cannot be mediated; and capital, driven by its own impulses, expands throughout social life and interactions.

They also disagree about work in a private property system: whether, as for Hegel, the externalization in work is dialectically overcome, the world that labor creates is a rational and rationally perceivable world of objective spirit, and the division of labor involves a deepening of individual insight—or whether, as for Marx, labor must be alienating and estranging, must create an alien world, and must issue in a division of labor whose results are pathological.

They disagree about the bases of exchange value (67), about the freedom or slavery of wage labor, about the locus of mediation in exchange (G, 171–72), about whether groups defined by their relation to production are estates *(Stände)* or classes *(Klassen)*—and from their different interpretations and answers, Hegel uncovers the task of comprehending the world, Marx the imperative to change it.

A Baedeker of disagreements on the meaning of private property could continue at great length: whether in Hegel's terms of work and interaction, reason and *Bildung*, or in Marx's terms of man's relations to other men, to nature, and to himself, private property is so basic to Hegel's comprehension of the modern world and Marx's critique of that world that almost every aspect of comprehension or critique is informed or affected by their disagreement on property.

13. Marx discusses a third kind of property: "socialised property," which is "for the producer, . . . individual property based on the acquisitions of the capitalist era: *i. e.* on co-operation and the possession in common of the land and of the means of production" (CI, 764, 763). Marx makes only elusive hints as to the overall character of the communist society based on socialized property; but some tentative conclusions can be drawn.

In this society, work becomes developing and liberating (G, 611). It is the case that "labour cannot become play, as Fourier would like" (G, 712); there will always be a realm of necessity: production to satisfy need, insurance, depreciation, and so on (Gotha, I). But the individual development and *Bildung* suppressed by capitalist private property will be released. Participation in the productive process will serve as "both discipline, as regards the human being in the process of becoming; and, at the same time, practice, experimental science . . . as regards the human being who has become, in whose head ex-

ists the accumulated knowledge of society" (G, 712). In this development, the worker liberates himself: "by thus acting on the external
world and changing it, he at the same time changes his own nature.
He develops his slumbering powers and compels them to act in obedi-
ence to his sway" (CI, 177). For Marx, "the overcoming of obstacles is
in itself a liberating activity," and, when this activity is directed by
human goals raised in the imagination, labor is "self-realization, objectification of the subject, hence real freedom" (G, 611).

Furthermore, man's relation to nature changes from exploitation.

> From the standpoint of a higher economic form of society [i.e. ,
> communism], private ownership of the globe by single individu-
> als will appear quite as absurd as private ownership of one man
> by another. [Men or societies] are not the owners of the globe.
> They are only its possessors, its usufructuaries, and, like *boni
> patres familias,* they must hand it down to succeeding genera-
> tions in an improved condition. (CIII, 776)

But this relation is not one of man's subordination to nature: "just as
the savage must wrestle with Nature to satisfy his wants, to maintain
and reproduce life, so must civilised man" (CIII, 820). He "starts,
regulates, and controls the material re-actions between himself and
Nature" (CI, 177). In highly technological society,

> No longer does the worker insert a modified natural thing as
> middle link between the object and himself; rather, he inserts
> the process of nature, transformed into an industrial process, as
> a means between himself and inorganic nature, mastering it.
> (G, 705)

To build on capitalism's "development of productive forces" and
mastery of nature is a major task for communist society ("German
Ideology," E & G, 427; Gotha, I).

Concurrently, in this society "the full and free development of
every individual forms the ruling principle" (CI, 592). With the development of productive forces and the consequent efficiency in society, "the saving of labour time [is] equal to an increase of free time,
i.e. time for the full development of the individual" (G, 711). "The
general reduction of the necessary labour of society to a minimum . . . then corresponds to the artistic, scientific, etc. develop-

ment of the individuals in the time set free, and with the means created, for all of them" (G, 706). Marx particularly stresses variegated
and multisided development; in perhaps his most famous remark
about communist society, he comments that it is "possible for me to
do one thing today and another tomorrow, to hunt in the morning,
fish in the afternoon, breed cattle in the evening, criticize after dinner, just as I like, without ever becoming a hunter, a fisherman, a
herdsman, or a critic" ("German Ideology," E & G, 425). But such
variety is possible not only in a bucolic world:

> Modern Industry . . . compels society . . . to replace the detail-
> worker of to-day, crippled by the life-long repetition of one and
> the same trivial operation . . . by the fully developed individ-
> ual, fit for a variety of labours, ready to face any change of pro-
> duction, and to whom the different social functions he per-
> forms, are but so many modes of giving free scope to his own
> natural and acquired powers. (CI, 488)

The technical developments of modern industry also suggest a variegated educational system for children, combining "productive labour with instruction and gymnastics" to produce "fully developed
human beings" (CI, 484). In communist society, the individual as a
member of the species will be able to exercise and manifest all his human capacities (CI, 329).

Objective and liberating labor, mastering nature and developing
the potentialities of mankind, nonetheless needs administration and
regulation (Gotha, I; "German Ideology," E & G, 425). In a society
of socialized property, the associated workers will give rational, voluntary, and conscious direction to develop the productive forces and
wealth of the society (CIII, 820); alien structures, chance, and irrational actions will be minimized or eliminated ("German Ideology,"
E & G, 424–30, 457–60).

In short, for Marx the wealth of communist society is multifaceted.
As he suggested in a series of rhetorical questions, "when the limited
bourgeois form is stripped away, what is wealth other than the universality of individual needs, capacities, pleasures, productive forces,
etc., created through universal exchange? The full development of
human mastery over the forces of nature, those of so-called nature as
well as of humanity's own nature? The absolute working-out of his
creative potentialities . . . ?" (G, 488). All this wealth is intersubjec-

tive; for "universally developed individuals," "social relations, as their own communal relations, are . . . subordinated to their own communal control" (G, 162).

14. On the issue of Marx's socialized property, Hegel and Marx seem to be diametrically opposed, not only because of Hegel's defense of private property, but because of his explicit objections to various schemes for "holding goods in common" (46R). While they may differ in terms of property, however, they manifest similarities about the general requisites for individuality.

In order to develop his individuality, the individual must objectify himself—through work for Marx, through private property and the activities of civil society for Hegel. The individual must liberate and develop himself—through consciously created needs (G, 325) and work for Marx, through conscious social needs (190–95), work (196), and the historical process of human labor that separated man from nature and is manifested in private property for Hegel (see sec. 5, above). The individual must develop his manifold capacities— through a flexible division of labor and variety of tasks for Marx, through his appropriating his own life and liberty and then acting in the different kinds of institutions of ethical life for Hegel. This development, for both Marx and Hegel, is not play (G, 172; 175R); "really free working, e.g. composing, is at the same time precisely the most damned seriousness, the most intense exertion" (G, 611). Individual *Bildung* for both involves discipline and effort. Finally, the individual's actions, to be truly free and to manifest his individuality, must occur in, and be guided by, a social setting, which for Marx is the community of associated producers or workers, and which for Hegel is the community of those who recognize each other as persons and as individuals and who live the same ethical life. And, for both Marx and Hegel (257–60), the community or the state as focus of ethical life must direct the society in rational, voluntary, and conscious ways, and not act merely naturally or out of the motives of selfishness or private gain.

While their general requisites for individuality are similar, Hegel and Marx differ on a number of key elements. For instance, they do define some concepts and activities—like labor—differently. Property is important in two crucial differences. The first difference can be illustrated by a specific example. Both Hegel and Marx see conscious social needs and work as central to the liberation and development of the individual; but Hegel adds as central also private property, the historical result of past work. Hegel here insists on manifesting in an actual, recognized institution (of property) the results of that past labor. He wishes to institutionalize and guarantee; and he wishes to do so in a conscious, recognized *will*-based manner. The sociality and consciousness of today's needs and work need to be assured, not left to tomorrow's whim, chance, or mistaken planning. Labor alone cannot provide that guarantee, as is shown by the unfree subordination in the "master-slave" dialectic and its aftermath. So Hegel gathers the results of historical labor and institutionalizes it as private property — guaranteed by law and recognition, a conscious and regularized product of will.

The second disagreement can be found in Hegel's explicit rejection of communism:

> The idea of a pious or friendly and even a compulsory brotherhood of men holding their goods in common and rejecting the principle of private property may readily present itself to the disposition which mistakes the true nature of the freedom of mind and right and fails to apprehend it in its determinate moments. (46R)

Hegel insists on determinateness, determination, the development of the particular or the specific. "Freedom of mind" cannot exist only through indeterminate generalities, as the "absolute freedom and terror" of the French Revolution showed; rather, freedom must exist at both the general (or "universal") level and at the specific (or "particular") determinaton: it must permeate every aspect of life. Hegel's stress on the determinate leads him to insist on private property within a free community, and equally to insist that each individual develop his own determinations through appropriating himself as his own property within a nexus of recognition of the universality and rights of himself and others as persons. Hegel wishes to hold fast to each moment of the dialectic; and property, as a determination of freedom in objective spirit, is a moment of freedom that must be retained.

From his emphasis on guarantees and determinations derive four major implicit criticisms, based on property, by Hegel against Marx. The first is that for Hegel's guaranteed institutions Marx substitutes human reason — the reasoned directives of the associated workers and the developed reason of individuals; for Hegel this substitution rates human reason too highly. The second is that Marx tends to presuppose or assume the characteristics that make men human beings, and he does not see those characteristics as needing to be proved, recognized, and guaranteed as human. For instance, in talking of labor in a crucial passage in *Capital,* Marx says, "we pre-suppose labour in a form that stamps it as exclusively human" (CI, 178). Marx relies on the human need for, and propensity to, labor to maintain labor's civilized content. For Hegel, the humanity of modern labor must be affirmed by institutions that reflect human will and consciousness, not just presupposed.[33] The third is that Marx appropriates the results of human history for his future society too readily. For instance, for Hegel men cannot be slaves because of the long historical development of Christianity and property; Marx accepts that men cannot be slaves while not accepting Christianity or property and thus while relying on the uninstitutionalized social activity and consciousness of the communist society to retain and maintain man's status as free. For Hegel, this consciousness needs determinate existence in institutions and laws in order to assure its continuance in consciousness and practice. Fourth, while Marx suggests that variegated human life can result from modern industry, he devotes little attention and fewer words to the problem of creating and maintaining a variety of associations and communities. Hegel sees the necessity of differentiated civil society and ethical life, with the differentiations clear and determinate in order to prevent a return to natural harmony or a move to a night in which all cows are black.

For Marx, on the other hand, Hegel's emphasis on guarantees, institutions, and laws is simply too conservative, too cautious; Hegel fails to see the material and social wealth latent in modern industry. Thus, while he has a full abstract ideal of individuality, he so hedges, limits, and mediates it that his ideal sinks back into the rather less lofty reality of early-nineteenth-century Western Europe. Since Hegel would institutionalize his ideal of individuality by means of the manifestations, laws, and determinations of property in civil society, his ideal sinks even more deeply into a morass of social divisions, conflicts, and poverty. Marx's criticism is especially telling because of Hegel's own admission of the ethical degeneration of rich and poor in his civil society that does contain capital. From Marx's point of view, Hegel wishes to guarantee a state of affairs that is in many ways corrupt or debilitating, whereas Marx wishes to use and build on the human potentials and capacities that are being developed in order to transcend contemporary limitations.

For Marx, Hegel is also too uncritical, precisely on the matter of capital (see sec. 12, above); although Hegel does see problems associated with capital and does expose the dilemmas of civil society (241–48), although he has approached or grasped many of the preconditions of Marx's analysis of capital (like the unequal social results of equal contracts), Hegel does not see the imminent self-expansion of capital (CI, 265), its insidious ability to impose itself throughout what Hegel calls ethical life and to transform that life, and the unmediatable divisions that it produces and reproduces. For Marx, Hegel's attempt to guarantee and institutionalize the individual and social moments of private property is bound to fail as capital, the results of private property, expands throughout society; Marx attempts to recognize and build on this expansion to transcend capital itself.

Hegel and Marx, then, see similar requisites for individuality. But they differ about the kind of property that would realize their ideals. For Hegel, only private property can produce full individuality: he sees private property as a way to guarantee individuality and make it determinate; he uses private property in order to bind, direct, and liberate individuals. For Marx, on the other hand, private property is a fetter, to be removed so that individuals can liberate themselves with socialized property. Generally sharing a common set of requisites of individuality, sharing the idea that property is related to individuality, Hegel and Marx differ drastically on what kind of property is the most conducive to the development and flourishing of individuality.

15. Although both Hegel and Marx, in their differing ways, tied property to individuality, their arguments have not fared well in the twentieth century. Despite their nominal adherence to Marx, contemporary communist societies generally ignore Marx's ideas, including his discussions of capital and his visions of a developed individuality based on socialized property. The continued existence of wage labor in communist societies should be a prima facie indication of the ignoring of Marx, who emphasized the intimate connection among private property or capital, division of labor, wage labor, and alienation. Wage labor is but the reverse of the coin whose obverse is capital (CI, 578n.); "therefore, the demand that wage labour be continued but capital suspended is self-contradictory, self-dissolving" (G, 308–9). Let contemporary "Marxist" rulers label their societies as they wish, nonetheless a system of wage labor and coerced division of labor is, for Marx, undergirded by capital, even if in a mutant form; and capital, mutant or pure, stunts, twists, and suppresses individuality.

Western liberal countries have failed to retain the links Hegel saw between private property and individuality. Property has been uncoupled from individuality and freedom as seen by Hegel, and no new bases for individuality have been developed. This separation has taken place in a number of different ways.

One is the growth of corporate property. A modern corporation, "however inherently concrete it may be, contains personality only abstractly, as one moment of itself. In an 'artificial person,' personality has not achieved its true mode of existence" (279R); property owned by a corporation does not contribute to individuality. Moreover, to the extent that Adolf A. Berle is accurate in seeing a pervasive split between ownership and management, modern shareholder property does not involve action in objectivity that Hegel saw as so crucial: "When an individual invests capital in the large corporation, he grants to the corporate management all power to use that capital to create, produce, and develop. . . . He is an almost completely inactive recipient . . . he must look elsewhere for opportunity to produce or create."[34]

A different separation has occurred with the rise of the welfare state, where "the new property" — as interpreted, for instance, by Charles Reich[35] — involves rights to income, services, and the like; it therefore lacks the moments of liberation implicit in social work in the system of needs for Hegel (194, 245). Indeed, since the new property entails rights against the government rather than rights exercised in a civil society with others having rights, it does not contain the elements of social recognition and sociality that Hegel saw as so crucial.

The clear distinction of man from nature, so important for man's liberation from nature according to Hegel, has been undercut in two quite different ways. One is the application of technical rationality — the rationality of man's domination of nature — to ever more numerous spheres of social life, as with Taylorism in the workplace and Skinnerian behaviorism in society. In *Walden Two*, Frazier, using his technology of behavior, looks to "what a few men can make of mankind."[36] What Hegel saw as liberating all men from nature and giving them all rights has, in the twentieth century, turned into a means whereby some men dominate many men as well as nature.

The second undercutting has occurred because of the environmental movement, with its various attempts to try to live in harmony with nature, to give natural objects legal standing or rights, and generally to reverse man's separation from nature. Hegel's analysis suggests that there may be serious implications for human rights lurking in environmentalism: to the extent that Hegel is correct in deriving human rights from man's separation from nature, those rights will be threatened by doing away with that separation.

Finally, it seems true that the process of expropriation, which Hegel saw as relevant just to the peripheral rabble, has continued in the West, with the result that individuals have less property that they can call their own, appropriate, act with, and define themselves with. Hannah Arendt has addressed this issue in ways that Hegel might not find foreign:

> Our problem today is not how to expropriate the expropriators, but, rather how to arrange matters so that the masses, dispossessed by industrial society in capitalist and socialist systems, can regain property. For this reason alone, the alternative between capitalism and socialism is false — not only because neither exists anywhere in its pure state anyhow, but because we have here twins, each wearing a different hat. [37]

T.W. Adorno addressed another dimension of the same question. Referring to the bourgeois individual, Adorno wrote: "since he no longer leads an independent economic existence, his character falls into contradiction with his objective social role. Precisely for the sake of this contradiction, he is sheltered in a nature preserve, enjoyed in leisurely contemplation." [38] The continued existence of the actuality of the rights to life and liberty and property is at issue.

On the other hand, the system of private property has been justified in the West on the grounds that it is very successful at producing wealth. But this relation of property and wealth has served only to distance property even further from Hegelian linkages to freedom and individuality, because liberation from hunger and the attaining of a comfortable level of material well-being are not necessarily related to — indeed, can subvert as likely as support — individuality and freedom. [39] To justify private property because of the wealth that results is to ignore individuality and freedom.

In short, Marx wanted the abolition of capital and the establishment of socialized property in order to liberate human individuality and freedom; in "Marxist" states, Marx's ideas have not been attempted. Hegel tied property to individuality because property involved action in objectivity, manifested man's separation from nature, led to the rights of life, liberty, and property, and allowed and

enforced intersubjective activity. With twentieth-century developments, each of these ties is becoming undone. The contemporary dilemma, then, is two-fold: What are or can be the bases of a sound individuality worthy of free human beings? What is or can be the description and justification of a system of property — private, social, or
whatever — that can contribute, if not to individuality and freedom
as Hegel and Marx would have it, to some important dimensions of
the good life for human beings?

NOTES

*I should like to thank Mitchell H. Miller, Jr., for detailed comments
on the first half of the chapter; they helped me in revising it. He is, of
course, not responsible for the remaining shortcomings.

1. John Stuart Mill, *Principles of Political Economy*, book II, chap. 1.
2. In this essay the term "property" usually means "private property"
   when it is used without modifiers; there are a few exceptions, which
   should be clear from the context. Also, the term "dimension" is frequently used as a nontechnical synonym for "moment."
3. G. W. F. Hegel, *Philosophy of Right* (1821), trans. with notes by T.
   M. Knox (Oxford: Oxford Univ. Press, 1945); Hegel, *Grundlinien der
   Philosophie des Rechts*, ed. Johannes Hoffmeister, 5th ed. (Hamburg:
   Felix Meiner, 1955). In conformity to the sensible continental practice, citations to the *Philosophy of Right* are placed in parentheses in
   the text and are according to section (not page) number; where the
   material cited is from the main text of the section, the section number
   alone is given; where it is from the "remarks" Hegel added to the text,
   the section number is followed by *R*; where it is from the "additions"
   which later editors appended to posthumous editions by collating student lecture notes, the section number is followed by *A*. The material
   in the *Philosophy of Right* is presented, in briefer compass, in G. W.
   F. Hegel, *Philosophy of Mind* (1830), trans. William Wallace (Oxford: Clarendon, 1894), which is part III of G. W. F. Hegel, *Enzy-
   klopädie der philosophischen Wissenschaften* (1830), ed. Friedhelm
   Nicolin and Otto Pöggeler, 7th ed. (Hamburg: Felix Meiner, 1969),
   cited in parentheses in the text, with the section number preceded by
   the abbreviations "Enc."
       The best treatments of Hegel's discussion of property are Joachim
   Ritter, "Person und Eigentum," in his *Metaphysik und Politik*
   (Frankfurt am Main: Suhrkamp, 1969) and Seyla Ben–Habib, "Natural Right and Hegel," Ph. D. dissertation, Yale, 1977. See also Peter
   G. Stillman, "Person, Property, and Civil Society in the *Philosophy of
   Right*," in Donald Verene, ed., *Hegel's Social and Political Thought:
   The Philosophy of Objective Spirit* (New York: Humanities, 1980),
   which complements this chapter.
4. "Personality" is a central but incomplete aspect of "individuality";
   abstracted from individuality, personality stresses the free will and ca-

pacity for rights, and includes natural characteristics (like appetites and physical appearances), that is, personality contains both universal and particular, not yet mediated to individuality (35, 37). Fully developed individuality, a distinctive dimension of the modern world, applies to the fully developed, concrete, individuated man of civil society. In the course of civil society, the moment of particularity in men is cultivated and acculturated through participation in universal communities so that particularity develops to individuality (187R). It might also be noted that, for Hegel and Marx, individuality and freedom are intimately related because only fully educated and developed individuals are able to comprehend the world and act rationally in it; in other words, only individuals with individuality are able through their knowledge and action to be free.

5. See John Locke, *Two Treatises of Government, Second Treatise*, chap. V, and Blackstone, *Commentaries*, book II, opening section on "Property in General."

6. To put Hegel's argument in the contemporary framework for the justification of institutions, the general justifying aim of property (or the justification of the system of property) is that private property contributes to individual freedom and individuality, as sections 4–7 below demonstrate; the specific distribution of property is considered by Hegel in the terms that everyone must have some property (to participate in its benefits) and that otherwise the distribution is determined by the play of civil society (which will produce inequalities).

7. Karl Marx, *Grundrisse*, trans. Martin Nicolaus (New York: Vintage, 1973), p. 485.

8. G. W. F. Hegel, *Philosophy of History*, (1858) trans. J. Sibree (New York: Dover, 1955), pp. 354–55.

9. I owe this insight to a lecture by Professor Mitchell Miller, Vassar College, February 21, 1977.

10. John Stuart Mill, *On Liberty*, as quoted in Hannah Arendt, "What Is Freedom?" in *Between Past and Future* (New York: Viking, 1968), p. 147.

11. See Peter G. Stillman, "Hegel's Critique of Liberal Theories of Rights," *American Political Science Review* 68, no. 3 (September 1974), p. 1088.

12. Karl Marx, *Capital* (New York: International, 1967), 1, p. 363n.

13. G. W. F. Hegel, *Phenomenology of Mind*, chap. V.C.a.

14. Ritter, "Person und Eigentum," sec. 6.

15. For an excellent beginning discussion of the importance of nature, see Emil L. Fackenheim, *The Religious Dimension in Hegel's Thought* (Bloomington: Indiana Univ. Press, 1967), chap. 4.

16. See G. W. F. Hegel, *Lectures on the Philosophy of World History: Introduction*, trans. H. B. Nisbet (Cambridge: Cambridge University Press, 1975), p. 115 (hereinafter cited as *World History*). For the references to Greek slavery, see ibid., p. 54; and G. W. F. Hegel, *Lectures on the History of Philosophy* (1892) (London: Routledge & Kegan Paul, 1955), I, p. 153. Like his slave, the Greek citizen was a

natural being; see *World History,* p. 97. Hegel's love of Greece was always tempered by his knowledge of Greek slavery; see also 67A.

17. Locke, *Second Treatise,* sec. 27.

18. Hegel, *World History,* p. 99.

19. For this point developed further, see Stillman, "Hegel's Critique of Liberal Theories of Rights," pp. 1091–92.

20. Ritter, "Person und Eigentum," sec. 9, and Marx, *Grundrisse,* p. 158.

21. Hegel, *Phenomenology of Mind,* chap. IV and IV.A. See also Ben–Habib, "Natural Right and Hegel."

22. For this paragraph, and my assertions about civil society generally, see Peter G. Stillman, "Hegel's Civil Society: A Locus of Freedom," *Polity* 12, no. 4 (Summer 1980), sec. 1.

23. A more finely developed argument in this paragraph would show that the "insufficiency" of property is only apparent, because the institutions of civil society by which Hegel limits acquisitiveness and atomism could be shown to be the inherent results of the concretization of abstract private property in civil society. A similar argument could be made in the next paragraph: the manifestation of spirit in property makes possible and requires noncontractual institutions, like family and state.

24. Hugh A. Reyburn, *The Ethical Theory of Hegel* (1921) (Oxford: Oxford Univ. Press, 1967), p. 126.

25. For Hegel, human relations are reified when the thing is a *medium* for interpersonal communication; for Marx, when the thing *is,* that is, takes on the qualities and attributes of, the individual.

26. Hegel does not justify capital; it simply follows from the play of private property in civil society. Among other implications, "Hegel's definition of property is neutral regarding questions of collective and individual ownership of the means of production" (Ben–Habib, "Natural Right and Hegel," p. 293 n. 59).

27. Hegel, *World History,* pp. 168–69.

28. Marx's works, as well as Hegel's, are cited in the text. In the case of the *Grundrisse* (abbreviated G); *Capital,* I (abbreviated CI); Karl Marx, *Capital* (New York: International, 1967), vol. III (abbreviated CIII); and the essays in Lloyd D. Easton and Kurt H. Guddat, *Writings of the Young Marx on Philosophy and Society* (Garden City, N.Y.: Anchor, 1967) (abbreviated E&G), citations are to the page numbers. In the case of the *Communist Manifesto* (abbreviated CM), *Wage Labour and Capital* (abbreviated WLC), *The 18th Brumaire of Louis Napoleon* (abbreviated 18thB), and the *Critique of the Gotha Program* (abbreviated Gotha), citations are to section numbers; quotations are in accord with Robert C. Tucker, ed., *The Marx-Engels Reader* (New York: Norton, 1972). Since this chapter's arguments could be easily documented by the "early" writings, I almost invariably refer to Marx's post–1848 writings.

29. Hegel, *Phenomenology,* chap. VI.C. It is not clear to either Hegel (62R) or even Marx (CI, 761) that this condition ever existed.

30. Most of Marx's comments consider property as originally justified by a

quasi–Lockean labor theory, not a Hegelian will-based theory. So Marx does not explicitly address Hegel's arguments. But Marx did criticize Hegel's treatment of property from his earliest writings, and his full criticisms can be readily inferred.

31. Thus, for Marx wage labor is quite literally slavery; the worker sells his life to the capitalist, who pays him for it piecemeal, a week at a time (G, 294).

32. I think Marx's basic criticism of capitalism has to do with capitalist property limiting individuality. For some further development of this theme, see George G. Brenkert, "Freedom and Private Property in Marx," *Philosophy and Public Affairs* 8, no. 2 (Winter 1979), pp. 122–47.

33. Habermas shares Hegel's concern; see Jürgen Habermas, *Toward a Rational Society* (Boston: Beacon, 1970), p. 118.

34. Adolf A. Berle, *The 20th Century Capitalist Revolution* (New York: Harcourt, Brace and World, 1954), pp. 30–31.

35. Charles A. Reich, "The New Property," 73 *Yale Law Journal* 734–87 (April 1964).

36. B. F. Skinner, *Walden Two* (New York: Macmillan, 1977), p. 279

37. Hannah Arendt, *Crises of the Republic* (New York: Harcourt Brace Jovanovich, 1972), p. 214.

38. T. W. Adorno, *Minimum Moralia,* quoted in Jürgen Habermas, *Legitimation Crisis* (Boston: Beacon, 1975), p. 127.

39. See Jürgen Habermas, *Theory and Practice* (Boston: Beacon, 1973), p. 169.

PART III

THE RIGHT
TO PROPERTY

7

THOUGHTS ON THE RIGHT
TO PRIVATE PROPERTY

J. ROLAND PENNOCK

"Everyone has the right to own property alone as well as in the association of others." So it is proclaimed in the "Universal Declaration of Human Rights." (Article XVII, the second item of which reads, somewhat redundantly, "No one shall be arbitrarily deprived of his property.") And yet we hear much today of the contrast between property rights and human rights, the clear implication being that the former do not belong in the category of those rights that are "human," that they belong to a different order of rights than those of life and liberty, for instance, or perhaps welfare. In fact, a contributor to this volume, in a book on the subject of rights, while conceding rather grudgingly that property rights do at times assist in the implementation of the liberal principle, expresses "skepticism about the value of rights [in the strict sense] to private property as any very prominent part of political societies in our time."[1]

From the demise of the *Lochner Case* until recent times, the U.S. Supreme Court has distinguished between property rights and personal rights, tending to place the former in a decidedly subordinate category. More recently, however, the Court appears to have had second thoughts on this matter. Justice Stewart, writing for the Court, has declared that "the dichotomy between personal liberties and property rights is a false one. Property does not have rights. People have rights. . . . In fact, a fundamental interdependence exists between the personal right to liberty and the personal right to property. Neither could have meaning without the other."[2] Perhaps more impressive, because coming from a scholar whom no one would designate "conservative," is the conclusion of Laurence Tribe that "the at-

tempt to distinguish the rights protected during the *Lochner* era
from the preferred rights of [communication and expression, political participation, religious autonomy, and privacy and personhood]
in terms of a supposed dichotomy between economic and personal
rights must fail.[3]

Perhaps what all this adds up to is no more than Ritchie's conclusion that "the confusions which permeate the theory of natural rights
comes out most conspicuously of all in the case of the right to property."[4] Why this should be so and, more specifically, why modern
writers, unlike Rousseau for instance, are reluctant to list property
rights among the Great Rights, are questions to which I shall give
only passing notice. Doubtless the fact that the specific form of property rights varies greatly from one jurisdiction to another has something to do with it. Probably the ease and subtlety with which property rights may be used to dominate other important rights has also
contributed to this situation. I would also suggest that John Locke
must bear some of the blame for confusion in this field and for di-
verting the attention of political philosophers from the most fruitful
paths of analysis respecting that right that he was so concerned to justify. Accordingly, in this essay I shall treat the great Locke with be-
nign neglect.[5]

In view of the fact that this volume is concerned especially with
"the concept" of property, it will do no harm to begin with a brief
reference to the meaning of that concept. It is a legal concept, and it
implies a right, a legal right at least. It is defined as "the right to possess, use, and dispose of something."[6] For this reason I referred above
to the Declaration of Human Rights as being mildly redundant: if
there is a right to property, a right to ownership is implied. Just what
this right entails, to be sure, is subject to wide variations, according
to the circumstances of time and place. It is seldom if ever absolute,
unless in some very limited sense of that term. The point is constantly
reiterated that the so-called right to property is in fact a "bundle of
rights." Following and simplifying Honoré, Lawrence Becker, a contributor to this volume, has enumerated those rights in a list including the right to possess, the right to use, the right to manage, the
right to enjoy the income, the right to the capital, the right of security, and the right of transmissibility, among others.[7] I have already
suggested that the great variety of types of ownership made possible
by variations in these constituent elements of the overall concept help
account for the confusion about the right to property. Yet it hardly

seems that this explanation is sufficient, for much the same could be said about the right to liberty (although it is not, as such, a legal concept, as property is). Liberty includes, or may include, all sorts of freedoms — to speak, to publish, to worship, to associate with others, to marry the mate of one's (and the other's!) choice, to move about, to contract, to work, to strike, to loaf, and so on. And, as with property, these constituent elements are subject to varying definitions and limitations. Even the right to life is subject in some degree to similar variability of extent. When does it begin and when does it end? Does it include the right to commit suicide, elective abortion, euthanasia, and so on? It hardly seems likely, then, that the tendency in modern times to deny to property an equal standing with life and liberty, as regards the "right to," can be fully accounted for by the fact that it can be analyzed into a number of constituent rights, or that its boundaries are uncertain.

Perhaps a few additional remarks are in order regarding the right to "own" property. Clearly it does not entail that everyone should *have* property, good thing though that might be. Certainly it does entail that everyone should be *permitted* to own property, and, if this adds anything, that they should have the *opportunity* to obtain ownership of property.

The concept of property itself, it may also be remarked, subject to wide variations though it is, would seem to entail that property, however defined, cannot be "taken" for public use, without just compensation. (What constitutes a "taking" and how the "just" amount of compensation is to be determined are problems with which I shall not deal.) Likewise property should not be taken (in a broader, but still vaguely defined sense) without due process of law, without fair procedures and just cause. And to all of this it should be added that a right to property in a particular thing may be forfeited by the misuse of that thing, as by the use of a boat for illegal purposes; for example, smuggling.

Turning from these preliminaries to the heart of the matter, the *justification* of some sort of private property rights, of *an* institution of private property, does not appear to me to be a difficult task. What I shall say about it by no means exhausts the subject, but it seems to me to be sufficient to establish rights to private property, pace Flathman and Grey, as playing a valuable as well as a prominent role in modern societies. Indeed, I would classify it as one of the Great Rights.[8] Hardly anyone has denied that property in some form appears to be essential for any society, and that therefore its institution cannot be unjust. Even Proudhon, whose name is ineradically connected with the phrase "property is theft," did not condemn all that the term includes. While denying the concept of property, he asserted the *right* to possession.[9] How inescapable is the concept is highlighted by a modern definition of the term: "Property is the name for a concept that refers to the rights and obligations and the privileges and restrictions that govern the behavior of men in any society toward scarce objects of value in that society. . . . Socially sanctioned customs or police-enforced laws, which define rights and obligations about ownership, control competition for . . . desired goods. What is owned is property."[10]

Anyone familiar with the development of the American West, as depicted for instance in Michener's *Centennial* (in book or TV form), will have a graphic picture of what happens when population grows to the point that scarcity of valued objects creates a significant tension between demand and supply.[11] The point is made in briefer and more scholarly fashion by those who have applied the tools of economic analysis to the law. The work of Richard Posner is typical. He begins by pointing out that no would cultivate land, with all the labor that entails, if others were free to help themselves to the product.[12] Possibly a cultivator, singly or in league with others, could, by the use of force and threats of force, keep such marauding under some semblance of control; but if he did he would in effect have established at least an embryonic property system, with its attendant rights.[13] It is unnecessary, I believe, to elaborate upon this point. That has been done by others and is now sufficiently obvious.

A slightly, but only slightly, different point is made by Garrett Hardin's justly famous "The Tragedy of the Commons."[14] Picture a pasture open to all. If disease, wars, and similar destructive circumstances keep the numbers of both men and beasts at a reasonable level, all may be well. But when someone gets the idea and the ability to double his herd, and thereby his welfare, trouble begins. Even though all realize that too many cattle will ruin the pasture, to the detriment of all, each family finds it to its interest to follow the example of the first free enterpriser. By ineluctable logic the basis for the welfare of all will be destroyed unless by some means they create and enforce property rights. This does not necessarily mean "enclosure," individual plots of land, although historically, perhaps for good reason, that has been the usual solution. It might mean common ownership, with some mechanism for determining and enforcing the use rights of the members. But in any case a property system would have been established. In the first place, the land would have to be protected against use by outsiders. "Public" as well as "private" property must be protected by a set of rights and obligations. But this is only the beginning. The rights of individual members of the in-group, the rightful users, would have to be defined and protected against incursion by other members of the group. These rights might fall far short of what we generally think of as entailed by property rights, but that is only because we think within the boundaries of our own experience. A method of acquiring one or more cattle must be established; the number that a family (whether or not varying with the size of the family) may graze on the commons must be determined; and their freedom to allow these cattle to graze unimpeded either by other members of the group or by outsiders must be protected. (These musts, of course are not logical musts, but they are practical requirements in the light of human experience.) Even if no more than this is entailed, a system of legal rights and obligations corresponding to the concept of property has been established, even though, for instance, the rights in questions are nontransferable (whether by trade, sale, gift, or inheritance).

It may be objected that I have assumed private ownership of the cattle, even if not of the land. That is true, and the assumption is not logically entailed. The cattle, too, might be jointly owned "public property." It would still be property for the reason outlined above. But apart from this, presumably the work obligations of the group members would have to be established and likewise their rights (which need not be equal) to participate in the product. In the absence, at least, of a completely arbitrary dictatorship, some system of rights, properly designated property rights, would have to be established and enforced. Further, at least in any sizable aggregation of people, a completely arbitrary ruler, Rex, would be practically impossible, as Lon Fuller shrewdly demonstrated.[15] A powerful autocrat might seek to enforce a set of rules affecting scarce, valued entities, but he could succeed in doing so only if the rules were internalized by most of the members of the society—that is to say, unless the rules embodied moral as well as legal rights and obligations.[16]

What I hope to have established thus far is simply that something that comes under the concept of property rights as defined above, at least for any but the smallest and simplest of societies (and probably even for them), appears to be inescapable. It is requisite to human life, at least on any but the very lowest level of existence. Although this proposition is minimal, and one would think hardly controversial, it does provide a useful, perhaps sufficient foundation for that "universal" right proclaimed in the Declaration of Human Rights. It seems probable, however, that the Declaration meant by "the right to own property" rather more than has been argued for above. In any case, it is of interest to know whether something more than that can be established as a universal and perhaps inalienable right of man. If not a "natural right," then at least a "human right" (for those who make that distinction). We could push utilitarian analysis much further than we have in this direction. Utiliterian arguments for private property with many, if not all, of the features pertaining to that term in our society can certainly be made. In fact, they have been made to a sufficient extent that I shall forgo that line of reasoning at this point and turn to another kind of analysis. When people assert a "natural" or "human" or "universal" right to property, a "fundamental" right, the terms have more evocative connotations than are suggested by the utilitarian analysis. This fact does not prove that the utilitarian analysis is not exhaustive, but it at least encourages other lines of thought.

In truth, it is the utilitarian analysis that is relatively new, while deontological statements go back to antiquity. Among the Ten Commandments "Thou shalt not steal" ranks along with killing and lying as a universal prohibition. It is sometimes said that the natural law tradition did not embody the right to property. It is true, for instance, that Seneca spoke of a golden age, an age of innocence, a state of nature in which neither coercive government nor property existed. What is to be noted, however, is that the reference is to a stage in which human nature is at a primitive stage of development. As it did develop, so the theory went, it developed both vices and virtues unknown to early man. Among the vices were avarice; and the great institutions of society, coercive government and property, were both consequences of, and remedies for, vice.[17] Moreover, the earliest writers on property in Justinian's *Digest* (Labeo and Nerva Filius, in the first century A.D.) treat property as arising naturally from the occupation or capture of what previously belonged to no one.[18] "It would seem clear," concludes Carlyle, ". . . that those writers who make no distinction between the *jus naturale* and the *jus gentium* looked upon the institution of private property as being primitive, rational, and equitable." And Florentinus, who does distinguish between the two kinds of *jus*, holds that property belongs to the *jus naturale*.[19]

Coming down to modern times, Blackstone is sometimes cited as denying that property is from natural law. Careful reading shows that he assumes the contrary, holding that stealing is wrong by nature. What has perhaps misled some scholars is that he does argue, and is mainly concerned to argue, that the *definition* of property and the determination of how property rights are to be enforced are matters to be resolved by the civil law.[20] The same could be said of the right to life. On the matter of property as a natural right, the French and American Declarations left no doubt. The Virginia Declaration of Rights (1775) listed as "inherent rights" "the enjoyment of life and liberty, with the means of acquiring and possessing property." The French Declaration of the Rights of Man and of Citizens (1789) declared that "the end of all political associations is the preservation of the natural and imprescriptible rights of man; and that these rights are liberty, property, security, and resistance to oppression," while one of their later declarations (1795) defined property as "the right to enjoy and to dispose of one's goods, one's revenues, the fruits of one's labor and industry."

Of course these proclamations are in themselves mere assertions. They remind us of a long and continuing history, now echoed in the United Nations Declaration, of a general and vigorously asserted belief that something called "the right to property," spelled out a bit more fully than this in the French statement of 1795, is of a fundamental nature, on a par with the rights of life and liberty. The very reason that led Bentham to call such assertions "nonsense on stilts," their rhetorical nature and their apparent claim to a standing more nearly absolute than anything that finds its support in utilitarian calculations, provides impetus for examining this claim more carefully. Much has been said on this subject, by writers at least as far back as Aristotle, and I have no wish to repeat it. What I do wish to stress, though, is the way in which property is bound up with the self. The etymological connection with the concept of the self is well known (Latin *proprius*, not common with others, own, individual). What I wish to emphasize is the deep psychological reason underlying this connection. It appears to be essential to the sense of identity, and to human dignity, including self-respect.[21] I must be entitled to say of various things "this is mine" — maybe to assert my right to keep, use, or sell it, but possibly also to be in a position to give something of me to you. Likewise to receive something from you that was part of you and now becomes part of me is also a treasured capacity. We value certain things because they unite us, sometimes to the person from whom they came, sometimes to past experiences. As I sit at my typewriter, I look at my library. Each of those books is (in my mind) filled with associations, with feelings, that make it part of me. Someday, on moving to smaller quarters, I may have to part with them. Many of them I know I shall never use again; yet the thought of parting with them is painful. It will indeed be giving up part of my self. Perhaps they are part of my "security blanket." It would be a great mistake to believe that, as we outgrow our childhood security blankets, we no longer have need for anything that takes their place. The kind of security, the kind of identity, that one finds in his closest human (and animal!) associates is not to be sharply distinguished from the part of the self that encompasses inanimate as well as animate objects.

To some extent of course this feeling does not depend upon ownership. But the psychological tie between a person and the house in which he or she lives is certainly more filled with significance, with emotional overtones, if he or she owns it than merely renting it or, I feel sure, if it is provided by the state for his or her use. We take pride in ownership, not just in our homes, but in all sorts of things. Although pride is often associated with conceit or arrogance, the term is also defined as "a sense of one's own dignity or worth; self-esteem."[22] Of course, it is not simply the ownership of something that makes us take pride in it. We may own things of which we are ashamed. But if we own something that we value and that is valued by others and contributes to their respect for us, certainly the resulting enhancement of our self-respect owes something to the fact that it is our property. If it was subject to being taken away from us at any time and for no good reason, if indeed others were as free to use it as we were, the effect would be very different. There is no need, I think, to enlarge further on this rather simple but certainly fundamental psychological fact.

My property may also serve as a concrete indication of my work, my accomplishments. It may be recognized as reflecting my taste, my values, and so, if my values are widely shared, enhance my self-esteem and my dignity. Or, like almost anything one owns, anything one has purchased from his or her earnings, whether or not possessing any distinctive character, property may be thought of, both by the owner and by others, as an indication of desert.[23] One must tread carefully here, and I shall have more to say momentarily about the limits to the kind of justification I am attempting to establish. But let it be noted now that this argument cuts both ways. A person's income may not be deserved, or be so considered. For the moment all that needs to be said on this point is that the justification of the institution of private property does not need to cover all cases of ownership. With property, as with other rights, the limits of moral rights seldom coincide with those of legal rights. In fact, as regards the Great Rights—life, liberty, property, and the like—they should not coincide. Legal, especially constitutional rights, as William Ernest Hocking argued, are presumptive rights.[24] Both to prevent overly narrow interpretation of the law and, more important, to develop individual responsibility, the law must allow elbow room, room to err and even to abuse. Those who talk of "liberty but not license" are treading on dangerous territory if they apply this formula to the law. The fact that rights may be abused is not necessarily an argument for their legal limitation. It is likewise true that the broad terms in which the Great Rights are normally stated call ultimately for more precise definition with consequent restriction. This is especially true when they deal with a whole institution such as that of property; but the difference is one of degree, not of kind.

To this point, then, I have argued that *some form* of the institution of private property is a matter of moral right in any society. That is to say, it is of basic importance that it should be possible for individuals to acquire articles that are scarce and are valued in their society; that this acquisition should be recognized as rightful (ownership); and that they should be protected against being deprived of these goods without just cause, either by other individuals or by the state itself. (In short, the rights in question are claim rights, not mere liberties.) I have sketched two independent forms of justification for this institution: one utilitarian and the other more deontological in nature. In referring to the second as "more" deontological, I mean that it is directly derived (causally) from what I take to be generally accepted intrinsic values. I have said nothing about how far this right should extend in the direction of what kinds of things may be acquired, or how the property may be used, transferred, and the like. It seems self-evident that neither the utilitarian nor the deontological justification would be satisfied unless some considerable extensions of the minimal concept were embodied in the institutions.

With exceptions to be noted as I proceed, I do not intend to embark upon the mammoth undertaking of defining the proper extent of the right to property. In any case, such an enterprise would have to deal in terms of what would be appropriate or morally requisite under given circumstances, for it is only the general character of the institution that could be established as a universal right.

Further comments are called for with respect to the two independent justifications I have offered. While to a certain degree they may be said to operate in tandem, this is by no means wholly the case. The closer one is related to his property, the more important is the psychological argument. When I say "closer," in this context, I have in mind psychological closeness although it would be a mistake to suppose that this quality and physical proximity are unrelated. But other facts influence the "bite" of this argument; intangible property, if it is in the form of, say, shares of stock, may possibly be psychologically less close than one's car, while the same might not be true of an original idea or an artistic creation. Perhaps a more important variable is the sheer amount (market value) of property one owns; and also (operating in the opposite direction) the proportion of it that is threatened.

These last points do not necessarily mean that the more property one has or the less it is psychologically part of oneself the less important it is as the subject of rights. Sometimes — possibly mostly — utilitarian considerations may become more important as the psychological justification becomes weaker. In any case, the former may be strong enough to justify the same sort of property rights that apply to property of the more intimate variety. Whether or not this is so, or under what conditions and to what extent it might be so, I do not intend to argue. I merely make the point that these two independent types of justification may apply in varying degrees to different kinds of property and to different property situations, and that they need not increase or decrease together in persuasiveness, bu that even the exact opposite is possible.

Further, it will matter what is the nature of the threat. Rights to property are not, at least in the common sense of the word, "absolute." They must yield, on occasion, to other considerations, other rights. One of the most obvious of these is the right of the government to tax for the general welfare — a right that may be stronger if what constitutes the general welfare has been determined by a process in which those who are being taxed have had a share. In other ways, property may be taken for public use. But here we have come across an important distinction, because, under the American Constitution at least, property may be "taken" for use only with "just compensation."[25] From the owner's point of view, unlike the case of taxation, the selection of his or her property for taking is accidental. A few people's property will be taken for the benefit of a great many; and those few are not selected by any criterion of justice, such as ability to pay. What this distinction brings out is that an extremely important aspect of property rights—as with the rights to life or liberty—is that they should not be destroyed arbitrarily, without just cause. Not only must the public be the beneficiary but the persons whose property is taken must be selected—if all are not affected equally—in accordance with some just principle—and, by compensation, the cost spread throughout the relevant political unit. Questions about the taking of property, then, generally have to do with distribution; that is, they have to do with the selection of a particular kind of property or of particular owners of property. The rights involved, although they are property rights, are also rights involving the question of equal treatment—like treatment of like cases. It is, in short, with the *equal* right to property, as with Hart's "equal right to liberty" that we are dealing in most "taking" cases.

However, one can imagine cases involving the basic right to property itself. Suppose the government proposes to confiscate all "instruments of production." Let us leave aside the question of definition and also the matter of any exemptions that may be granted to very small productive enterprises. Short of doing away with the institution of private property altogether, this comes about as close as is imaginable to a direct conflict with the justifications I have offered for that institution. Here the question of the rights themselves, not simply their just distribution, or the just distribution of otherwise justified "takings," would be at issue. It would go far beyond the scope of this discussion to say anything about the merits of such an action— which in any case could be considered only in the light of the particular circumstances—beyond what has already been said. It would have to meet the test of utility, but more than this it would have to confront those elements of right that derive from human dignity, in each of the cases involved. Whether the latter could be accomplished by any degree of utility or whether it would have to have a deontological foundation is a question of ethical theory in which I do not propose to become involved.

Property rights may be limited when they conflict with each other and with other basic rights — this point needs to be reiterated and amplified. Conflict with other property rights, as when a house is blown up to prevent a fire from spreading out of control, raises no problem of principle. The only property right that might arise is whether or not the cost should be spread beyond the owner. Far more important issues present themselves when, for example, the rights to property and liberty clash. Nor can they be settled by the important fact that each is dependant upon the other. That proves only that neither must be totally extinguished. The most important case of this kind arises when large property holdings give the owners such power that it seriously impinges upon the liberty of others. Both rights (property and liberty) are, in part, rooted in considerations growing out of human dignity. To that extent the issue will have to be decided by how significantly human dignity is infringed on each side. But of course utilitarian considerations will also be of utmost importance. While the very existence of the institution of private property is not involved in such an issue, the proposed remedies and the theories and factual assumptions upon which they are founded (e.g., as to the extent to which liberty is in fact being limited) so restrict and threaten the hitherto respected rights of property that much more than matters of just distribution of the costs is involved. The threat goes to the heart, even though it is not fatal. It is not surprising, then, that arguments arising out of this issue are among the most fundamental and deeply felt in modern society. They frequently tend to be cast in terms of the validity of the very institution of private property. Fortunately for the viability of the polity and of society itself, the remedies of taxation and welfare statism are not of the all-or-nothing variety; they admit of variations of degree almost without limit.

Perhaps the matter can be further clarified by pointing out that the rights of life and liberty, like those of property, may sometimes be overridden or, alternatively, may be defined in such a way that they are not all-inclusive of the subjects to which their everyday meaning refers. In fact, it might even be argued, as to the rights to life and liberty, as is generally admitted with respect to property, that they are bundles of rights rather than each being a single right. This fact is most obvious with respect to liberty, but even with life one soon finds oneself talking about the right to killing in self-defense or to save the life of others, the right to have one's life protected, the right to be provided with the necessities of life, the right to commit suicide, euthanasia, and so on.

In sum, I have argued that the case for an institution of private property is fundamental, that it has both utilitarian and deontological foundations, and that these justifying considerations do not apply equally in all situations. I do not attempt to discuss what should be the limits of property rights (what elements of the "bundle," and how much in each case, should be included); but I hope that what I have said may be somewhat clarifying as to how one should go about answering such questions for a given society at a given period of its history. I have not attempted to compare my approach with that of Lawrence Becker or those of others who have dealt with the problem since the time of Artistotle, leaving that to the reader; nor have I touched upon all the arguments — not even all the valid arguments — for the institution of private property.

Perhaps one point calls for further comment. Property rights, like the rights to life and liberty, are frequently in tension with the equality component of the concept of justice, however one may define that component. In arguing that the resolution of the resulting problems must give weight to both utilitarian and deontological considerations (such as desert, need, and justifiable expectations, with which I have not dealt, feeling that they have been sufficiently discussed elsewhere), I do not mean to preclude the acceptance of a theory, be it neoutilitarian or Rawlsian, that comprises them all, giving to each its due consideration. But somehow, I believe, each of these elements must be given weight. The question Rawls raises is whether that weighing can be done once and for all, in formulaic fashion. While remaining skeptical of such a solution, I retain an open mind.

NOTES

1. Richard E. Flathman, *The Practice of Rights* (Cambridge: Cambridge Univ. Press, 1976), p. 227.
2. Lynch v. Household Finance Corp., 405 U.S. 538, 552 (1972). Three justices dissented but did not take issue with this pronouncement. Two of the other justices took no part in the decision.
3. Laurence H. Tribe, *American Constitutional Law* (Mineola, N.Y.: Foundation, 1978), p. 574.
4. David G. Ritchie, *Natural Rights* (London: George Allen & Unwin, 1924), p. 263.
5. Since I disagree with Whelan's interpretation of Locke, it is perhaps fitting to make a few remarks on Locke at this point. In my view Locke took for granted, while occasionally expressing, his belief that the right to property, like, as a matter of fact, the right to liberty and the right to life, was subject to regulation by law once the civil society

was established. Note, for instance, the *Second Treatise*, sec. 50, where he states, "For in governments the laws regulate the right to property, and the possession of land is determined by positive constitutions." And again, sec. 89, where he says that each gives up power to enforce the law of nature to the political society and authorizes that society "to make laws for him as the public good of the society shall require." Finally, on this point, in sec. 120, he declares that men enter into society "for the securing and regulating of property." With respect to inheritance, while in general he certainly took this institution for granted, he was careful to state in sec. 190 that "Every man is born with . . . *a right before any other man*, to inherit, with his brethren, his father's goods [italics mine]." Note that he is careful not to assert an actual right to inherit, but simply a natural right to be preferred in inheritance over other men except for his brethren.

6. *Webster's New World Dictionary* (Cleveland and New York: New World Publishing, 1959).

7. Lawrence C. Becker, *Property Rights—Philosophic Foundations* (London: Routledge & Kegan Paul, 1977), chap. 2.

8. See Flathman, op. cit., p. 203. In speaking of "justification", I do not attempt the impossible—*proof* of validity—which sometimes seems to be the standard that Flathman would apply to Becker. See his chapter in this volume, below pages 221–43.

9. Pierre-Joseph Proudhon, *What Is Property? An Inquiry into the Principle of Right and Government*, trans. B. R. Tucker (New York: Dover, 1970), p. 280.

10. Ernest Beaglehole, "Property," *International Encyclopedia of the Social Sciences*, ed. David L. Sils (New York: Macmillan, 1968), vol. 12, p. 590.

11. James A. Michener, *Centennial* (New York: Random House, 1974).

12. Richard A Posner, *Economic Analysis of Law*, 2d ed. (Boston: Little, Brown, 1977), chap. 3.

13. For an interesting study showing how the development of scarcity (in this case caused by increased demand) leads to the establishment of property rights in land, see Harold Demsetz, "Toward a Theory of Property Rights," *American Economic Review* 57 (1967), pp. 347–59, reprinted in Eirik G. Furubotn and Svetozar Pejovich eds., *The Economics of Property Rights* (Cambridge: Ballinger, 1975), chap. 3.

14. *Science* 162 (1968), pp. 1243–48; reprinted in Bruce A. Ackerman, ed., *Economic Foundations of Property Law* (Boston: Little, Brown, 1975), pp. 2–11.

15. Lon L. Fuller, *The Morality of Law* (New Haven: Yale Univ. Press, 1964).

16. This, incidentally, seems to me to provide part of the answer to Flathman's contention that Becker's argument for the necessity of property rights renders otiose his argument in support of their moral justification. That which is inescapable cannot at the same time be morally required; so much is true. But what is inescapable may be a system of moral rules, the precise nature of which is not determined.

Further, the necessity in question is not a logical necessity; rather, it takes the form of the hypothetical "*if* a society is to continue as a society," or, better, "become" a society, "then a system of moral rules corresponding to the concept of property must come into being."

17. See A. J. and R. W. Carlyle, *A History of Medieval Political Theory in the West* (New York: Barnes and Noble, n.d.), vol. 1, pp. 23–25.

18. Ibid., p. 51.

19. Ibid., pp. 52 and 54.

20. See William Blackstone, *Commentaries on ʾhe Law of England* (Philadelphia: Rees Welsh, 1902), vol. 1, p. 54, and vol. 2, p. 2. At the first point cited, Blackstone speaks of theft, along with murder and perjury, as *mala in se*, "forbidden by the superior laws." Clearly he held that a person's property ought to be protected in the same way as his life and liberty. The fact that he did not mention it in the preceding sentence ("natural rights, such as life and liberty, need not the aid of human laws to be more effectually invested in every man than they are,") appears to indicate only that property was more in need of laws for its definition than the other two, but not for its moral support in "the superior laws." Frederick Whelan, in his essay in this volume, holds that Blackstone's recognition of "property," as according to natural law, does not imply that *private* property can claim this support. I shall not argue the point here, but it seems to me unlikely, judging both from the context in Blackstone and from the times in which he wrote and his general outlook, that he intended by implication (through the failure to qualify the word "property" by the word "private") to make this important distinction between private and public property.

21. I pass by the problem of defining "human dignity" (except as I have associated it with "self-respect" and "sense of identity") and also of justifying the great value we set upon it. Philosophers differ as to *why* it is of such value, but they seem to be generally in accord on the proposition that it *is* of the highest value. See, for a helpful discussion of the subject, Herbert Spiegelberg, "Human Dignity: A Challenge to Contemporary Philosophy," in Rubin Gotesky and Ervin Laszlo, eds., *Human Dignity: This Century and the Next* (New York: Gordon & Breach, 1970), pp. 39–64.

22. *Webster's New World Dictionary* (Cleveland and New York: World Publishing Co., 1958).

23. A side remark. It is sometimes argued that the concept of earnings makes little sense in modern society, where what one "produces" is so dependent upon matters for which one can take no credit—upon capital, upon inventions, upon the cooperation of others, to mention only the most obvious factors. But surely this is at best a half truth. If you pay me one hundred dollars to do a job for you, even though I use your tools and follow your instructions, you must believe that I have added to the value of whatever I was working on by at least one hundred dollars' worth, at your valuation. It is true that I might not have been able to do whatever I did without training paid for by others; but

the fact remains that I added, in your estimation, one hundred dollars to the value of your property, when I had the option, despite my training, of refusing to create this value. I am not supporting a labor theory of value nor trying to ground the right to property upon Locke's reasoning, but merely to show a weakness in one of the lines of attack that is sometimes made on that and other theories of property.

24 *Present Status of the Philosophy of Law and Rights* (New Haven: Yale Univ. Press, 1926), chap. 6.

25. The question of what constitutes a "taking," and whether it should be considered an all-or-nothing matter or one of degree, has been considered in other chapters of this volume. (See the contributions of Ackerman, MacRae, and Scanlon.) It seems clear that the present law on the matter in the United States makes a crude fit, at best, with a just system of property rights.

8

THE MORAL BASIS OF PROPERTY RIGHTS

LAWRENCE C. BECKER*

The work of the philosopher consists in assembling reminders
for a particular purpose.
— Ludwig Wittgenstein, *Philosophical Investigations*, 127

The justification of property rights entails three kinds of problems.
One is the problem of general justification: Why should there be any
property rights at all—ever? Another is the problem of specific justification: Given that there should be property rights of some kind,
what kind(s) should there be? What sorts of things should be owned,
and in what ways? The third is the problem of particular justification: Given that a specific kind of property is justifiable, who, in particular, should have title to existing pieces of it?

Important conceptual (and to that extent philosophical) issues are
embedded in each of the justificatory problems. For example, fitting
the wide variety of types of property rights to existing social, economic,
and political conditions is part of the problem of specific justification. And the concepts of native title, prescription, and adverse possession figure prominently in the problem of particular justification.

But it is general justification that seems most obviously and purely
philosophical, and so it is not surprising to find the bulk of philosophi-

*For important bibliographical help, as well as stimulating conversations,
I am indebted to several of my colleagues at Hollins College: Theodore E.
Long, William P. Nye, Art Poskocil, and Wayne G. Reilly. Thomas Grey,
Richard Flathman, Abraham Edel, and others at the 1977 American Soci-
ety of Political and Legal Philosophy meetings also helped greatly.

cal work on property devoted to things like the labor theory of property acquisition, the justification of a system of private as opposed to
public ownership (or the other way around), and the connections between rights to liberty and rights to property. The thought is that until one knows whether — and how — property rights in general can be
justified, one is not likely to get very far with problems of specific and
particular justification.

The controlling idea of this paper, however, is that although philosophical work on property rights may correctly *begin* with questions
of general justification, it cannot end there. To ignore, or at any rate
slight, the conceptual problems of specific and particular justification is indefensible. That means, I fear, that philosophical work on
property — taken as a whole — is indefensibly narrow. What I want to
do here is to contribute to its broadening.

In particular, I want to develop an admittedly artificial but useful
distinction — one between the moral basis of property rights and the
moral arguments for them.[1] The moral basis, as I conceive it, is a set
of facts about the human condition: facts about human needs, propensities, and behavior from which (together with judgments about
values, duties, and virtues) moral arguments for and against property rights can be built up. It is from just such facts, or what they
supposed to be facts, that traditional theorists built up their accounts
of property.[2] They talked about acquisitiveness, greed, envy, the
need for security, the existence of surplus value, the consequences of
alienated labor. From such considerations, not only did they draw
arguments for and against the general justifiability of property
rights, they also often tried to sketch in a few details about what specific sorts of property rights there should be — whether there should
be private property in land, for example, or an unrestricted right to
transmit one's property to others by means of a will.

One cannot simply rely on traditional accounts of the moral basis
of property, however. In the first place, much of the anthropological, sociological, and psychological data in such accounts are now regarded as erroneous — or at any rate, too speculative to be very useful. And at least as far as I know, the last systematic attempt to get an
overview of such materials, for the purpose of thinking about property rights, was a book published in 1931.[3] Much has happened in
the intervening years to render that book inadequate. Second, as already noted, the interest of philosophers has been predominantly
with general justification, and a few Hobbesian commonplaces[4]

about the human condition will usually suffice to ground such a justification. So even the traditional accounts—which give much more prominence to these matters than do current accounts—tend to rely on a terribly impoverished analysis of the moral basis of property.

It is time to begin the process of enriching these considerations, to make a start at taking them beyond the commonplaces used for general justification to the point where they will be of some use in theorizing about specific and particular justification. The eventual philosophical aim of this enterprise (if you will pardon the paraphrase of Epicurus[5]) is to answer the question of which forms of property, if any, can be said to be natural and necessary; which natural but not necessary; and which neither natural nor necessary but merely the product of extravagant invention.

To do this, one must summarize material from sociology, ethology, economic anthropology, theories of social organization, comparative economics, and social psychology. (Modern economic theory—both developmental theory and "impact" theory—is of course also crucial, as is modern political theory. Happily, I am able, here, to leave those materials to others.) Since I am not expert in any of these fields, what I have to say about them should be carefully examined for the sorts of errors characteristic of amateurs. My justification for taking on this task rather than leaving it to the relevant experts is threefold. First, as I have indicated, it needs to be done. Second, assembling the relevant materials into a form suited to a discussion of property rights is essentially a conceptual (and to that extent philosophical) problem. So I am not entirely outside the realm of my professional competence. Third, these matters need to be put into a form useful to political philosophers. The 1931 book mentioned earlier was virtually ignored by lawyers, philosophers, and political scientists, as evidenced both by the paucity of references to it and by the substance of philosophical work on property rights. The latter, my own included, when it makes reference to human behavior at all, tends to rely on the same old commonplaces found in seventeenth-, eighteenth-, and nineteenth-century writers. As I hope to show, the moral basis of property rights includes much more than that.

THE CONCEPT OF OWNERSHIP[6]

Property rights, as I will deal with them here, are the rights of ownership. In every case, to have a property right in a thing is to have a bundle of rights that defines a form of ownership. Many futile debates (e.g., over the existence of "primitive communism") have owed their existence to a failure to be clear about the varieties of ownership—thus the varieties of property rights. So I want to pay careful attention to definitional matters.

A. M. Honoré has given an analysis of the concept of full ownership[7] that with some modifications, provides a very clear overview of the varieties of property rights. I have found his analysis—or rather, my version of it—to be an adequate tool for analyzing every description of ownership I have come across, from tribal life through feudal society to modern industrial states. The definition of the elements of ownership that he identifies will vary from society to society, as will the varieties of ownership that are recognized. But ownership is always, as far as I can tell, analyzable in the terms he proposes. I shall therefore apply his analysis to "primitive" and archaic societies as well as to modern ones.[8]

The Elements of Ownership

Honoré identifies eleven elements of the notion of ownership. Each of the elements is capable of variation, both in its definition and in the range of things to which it applies. Full ownership is the concatenation of all the eleven elements, in whatever way they may be defined.

The number eleven is not sacred, however. As Honoré is careful to point out, it is possible to combine or split some of the elements into others. The test of success in what he has done is not the discovery of immutable atoms of the concept of ownership, but rather the ability of the analysis to advance understanding. Accordingly, because I find it helpful to do so, I have split one of his elements into three, and propose to use the following list of thirteen:

1) *The right (claim)*[9] *to possess*—that is, to exclusive physical control of the thing. Where the thing is noncorporeal, possession may be understood metamorphically.

2) *The right (liberty) to use*—that is, to personal enjoyment of the benefits of the thing (other than those of management and income.)

3) *The right (power) to manage*—that is, to decide how and by whom a thing shall be used.

4) *The right (claim) to the income*—that is, to the benefits derived from foregoing personal use of a thing, and allowing others to use it.

5) *The right (liberty) to consume or destroy*[10] — that is, to annihilate the thing.

6) *The right (liberty) to modify* — that is, to effect changes less extensive than annihilation.

7) *The right (power) to alienate* — that is, to carry out *inter vivos* transfers by exchange or gift, and to abandon ownership.

8) *The right (power) to transmit* — that is, to devise or bequeath the thing.

9) *The right (claim) to security* — that is, to immunity from expropriation.

10) *The absence of term* — that is, the indeterminate length of one's ownership rights.

11) *The prohibition of harmful use* — that is, one's duty to forbear from using the thing in ways harmful to oneself or others.

12) *Liability to execution* — that is, liability to having the thing taken away as payment for a debt.

13) *Residuary rules*[11] — that is, the rules governing the reversion to another, if any, of ownership rights which have expired or been abandoned. This category includes rules as various as those for determining the reversion of rights upon the expiration of leases, for determining the heirs in cases where the power to devise or bequeath does not exist, for determining the disposition of property left by intestate deaths, and for determining the disposition of abandoned property.

As should be readily apparent, the first nine elements are rights of various sorts, and the remaining four elements are rather different — essentially defining limitations (or the absence of them) on the rights. Each of the elements is capable of a variety of definitions. The prohibition of harmful use may shade into a requirement of productive use; the right to income may be subject to taxation; security may be limited by eminent domain; and so on. Full ownership — that is, the concatenation of all these elements — therefore has as many different varieties as there are different definitions of the elements.

Varieties of Ownership

More important, many varieties of ownership, and thus of property rights, do not reach the level of full ownership. A trust fund, for example, can be one's property even though one does not have the right to manage it, consume the capital, or bequeath the income to others. This point is crucial in the reading of both law and economic anthropology, where one finds varieties of ownership quite foreign to our ordinary notions.

How minimal a set of these elements can count as a variety of ownership in law need not trouble us long. (The notion of a moral property right is more complicated, and I shall not deal with it here.) For property rights in law we may argue as follows: the final four elements are not rights at all and so obviously cannot stand alone as a variety of property rights. The right to security seems similarly parasitic on other elements: Immunity from expropriation of what *right?* is always a question that must be answered in applying this element. So it too cannot stand alone. But I suggest that any of the remaining eight rights (possession, use, management, income, consumption or destruction, modification, alienation, and transmission) *can* stand as a variety of *legal* ownership when it is supplemented by some version of the right to security. That is, I suggest (on the bases of nothing stronger than my understanding of English) that if anyone holds even one of these eight rights plus security—and therefore any bundle of rights that includes one of the eight plus security—then it makes sense to say that that person has a property right. (I assume that any of these rights that is *not* secured—that is, that is subject to expropriation by the state at any time, by any process, for any reason—would *not* count as a private property right.) No doubt the thought of a person having the right to consume or destroy but not to possess is strange. But it is not necessarily a contradiction; and surely it constitutes what could reasonably be called a property right. Similarly for the others.

The varieties of property rights, then, consist of any set of the thirteen elements that includes at least one of the first eight plus security. There are 4,080 such combinations.[12] Full ownership, as I have said, is the concatenation of all the elements. Full *exclusive* ownership is full ownership, by an individual or a group, in cases where no other individual or group has any form of ownership in the same thing.

With these definitional matters out of the way, I want to turn to a final preliminary: a summary of the moral arguments for property at the level of general justification.

THE GENERAL JUSTIFICATION OF PROPERTY RIGHTS

At the outset of this chapter, I urged a distinction between the moral basis of property and the moral arguments for it. I want now to review the moral arguments (at the level of general justification) as a preface to what I have to say about the moral basis. This is necessary not only because the moral basis contributes to the general justification of property but also because the problems raised by the general justifications—what I call the "coordination problem" and the "compatibility requirement" (see below)—partly define the ways in which the moral basis is relevant to the process of specific and particular justification. And one of the aims of this paper is the broadening of philosophical discussion to include more work on specific and particular justification.

It should be noted that throughout what follows I am speaking of the justification of an institution of *private* property—even when the modifier "private" is not used. When I speak of public ownership, I will always use an appropriate adjective.

The Plurality of General Justifications.

I have argued in *Property Rights*[13] that there are at least four sound and independent lines of general justification for private property.

The first may be called the Locke-Mill version of the labor theory. It is essentially a "why not?" argument, asserting that when labor produces something that would otherwise not have existed, and when that labor is beyond what morality requires of the laborer, and when others suffer no loss from being excluded from enjoying the fruits of the labor, then property rights for the laborer (in the fruits of the labor) can be justified.

The second line of general justification may be called the labor-desert version of the labor theory. It holds that when labor produces something of value to others—something beyond what morality requires the laborers to produce—then the laborer deserves some benefit for it. Sometimes the only (or most) appropriate benefit is a property right in the things produced (or in something else of value). When this is the case, property rights can be justified.

The third line of general justification consists of a complex of considerations of utility, framed in terms either of economic efficiency or of political and social stability. All of these considerations are directed to the task of showing that a system of property rights is necessary for human happiness. This is essentially Hume's argument, complicated by the later developments of utilitarianism and economic theory.

The final line of general justification may be called the argument from political liberty. It assumes (as does the utility argument) that some measure of acquisitiveness among humans is inevitable and goes on to assert that effective prohibition of all acquisitive activity would require a comprehensive and continuous abridgment of people's liberties that is at best unjustifiable. Further, it holds that the acquisitive activities which must be permitted in a just society will require regulation, lest each person's acquisitive acts interfere with others' liberties. It concludes that a system of property rights is a justifiable way of regulating acquisitions so as to preserve liberty.

Each of these four lines of general justification is both complemented and limited by the others. The labor-desert argument, for example, justifies property rights only when the laborer produces something of value to *others*—for only then can a laborer be said to deserve a benefit (from others). The remaining arguments complement this, however, by justifying ownership in cases where it results in no loss to others (the Locke-Mill version of the labor theory), where ownership has utility, or where it must be permitted to preserve liberty.

On the other hand, there are clearly cases in which considerations of utility conflict with those of liberty, or desert-for-labor. In those cases the arguments limit, rather than complement, each other. Conflicts among the arguments are "limiting" in the sense that they confine the justificatory adequacy of each argument to cases in which it either faces no opposition or faces opposition of demonstrably inferior strength. A "justification" of property rights, as the term is used here, requires an "all-things-considered" argument. One cannot accurately assert that the labor theory "justifies" anything if the results it yeilds are contradicted by a utility argument of equal weight.

The general justifications for property are also limited, in the same way, by some standard *anti*property arguments. Just as it is possible to show that in general a system of private ownership has utility, so too it is possible to show that some systems of ownership, in some social circumstances, lead to social *in*stability—to a net *dis*utility. Further, it can be shown that some systems of private ownership tend to produce and perpetuate unjustifiable socioeconomic inequalities. Such antiproperty considerations limit the effectiveness of the general justifications of property rights every bit as much (in principle) as conflicts among the proproperty arguments do.

The Coordination Problem.

This plurality of general justifications—and the existence of antiproperty arguments—yields what I call the coordination problem for the theory of property rights. Conflicts must be managed. When considerations of liberty require or permit property rights while utility forbids them, or when some version of the labor theory justifies property while the antiproperty argument from socioeconomic inequality does the opposite, then a decision has to be made about which set of considerations will be controlling. Are we to have, at bottom, a utilitarian theory? Or a libertarian theory? Or a labor theory? Or are we to take an essentially antiproperty position and hold that only in the absence of antiproperty objections can property rights be justified?

It is my contention that none of the "dominance solutions" is acceptable for the general theory of property rights. This is so because the four lines of property argument — as well as the standard antiproperty ones — are all *independent* and of *presumptively equal weight*. They are independent in the sense that, though they have some assumptions in common, none is reducible to any other. They are, in my view, of presumptively equal weight because, although it may be demonstrable that in *some* circumstances one should be subordinated to another,[14] I can find no justificatory strategy that yields the conclusion that, in general, any one of the lines of argument ought to have priority over the others. It is therefore not warranted to start with a utilitarian theory of property, a libertarian one, or an egalitarian antiproperty position and then compromise it from time to time with other considerations. It is rather necessary to begin with the recognition of the irreducible plurality of pro- and antiproperty arguments, and the (rebuttable) presumption that the arguments are of equal weight. The "coordination problem" will then be to define the ways in which the arguments act on each other, to complement or to limit, and to identify the circumstances in which, and the way in which, conflicts among the arguments can be resolved.

The Compatibility Requirement.

The solution to the coordination problem is a prerequisite to work on specific and particular justification because such arguments must be compatible with the *general* justifications as coordinated. That is, the specific sorts of ownership one hopes to justify, as well as the particular instances of it, cannot (on pain of logical inconsistency) violate whatever restrictions on *all* forms and instances of ownership are imposed by the general justifications of property. If, for example, utility and egalitarian arguments combine — in the absence of opposition from the labor theory and libertarian arguments — to prohibit the transmissibility of significant amounts of wealth by bequest, then one will obviously not be able to give a successful defense of current inheritance laws or any instance of their operation.

Summary

To summarize, then, this severely compressed overview of the problem of giving a general justification of property rights: Of the three levels of justificatory problems, those having to do with general justification clearly have logical priority. The specific forms of property one will be able to justify, and the particular instances of ownership one will be able to justify, will be limited by the restrictions and requirements placed on all ownership by general justifications. Further, there are at least four independent and sound lines of general justification, plus some standard antiproperty arguments, all of which are of presumptively equal weight. Each of these arguments both complements and limits the others. Thus, the general theory of property [15] must both solve the coordination problem and define the compatibility requirement. That is, the general theory of property rights must provide a way of resolving conflicts among (general) pro- and antiproperty arguments, and it must spell out in detail the restrictions these arguments place on specific and particular justification.

It is with the coordination problem and the compatibility requirement that I think the moral basis of property can be of most use. Assumptions about the human condition are embedded in each of the general justifications for property, and from those assumptions, together with certain formal properties of the arguments (e.g., their presumptively equal weight), one can derive some guidance for problems of specific and particular justification. [16] But as I mentioned at the outset, the elements of the human condition appealed to by the general justifications are (intentionally) minimal—the Hobbesean commonplaces. A much richer set of considerations is needed if we are ever to get beyond the rather vacuous pronouncements on inheritance law, private property in land, native title, and so forth, so common in political philosophy. (We need to know, for example, something about the variety of property arrangements that have served various societies well, and under what social circumstances they broke down or changed. We need to know such things just in order to apply the utility argument—and the antiproperty arguments—to questions of specific and particular justification.)

THE MORAL BASIS OF PROPERTY

I turn now, then, to the the central topic of this paper—the set of considerations about the human condition I have called the moral basis of property. What I shall do is present a brief summary of some of these considerations (but by no means all of them), draw some preliminary conclusions, and indicate some directions for future study.

A bit needs to be said about methodology, however. The material from the social sciences presented below is, of course, description and theory about what human beings *actually* do and what institutions *actually* exist or have existed. It is not directly about what people *ought* to do or about what institutions *ought* to exist. It can, however, enter into moral argument in an important way if the following assumptions are made:

First, I take it to be true by definition that a finite moral argument cannot provide a justification for every one of its premises (without being circular). One part of the problem of avoiding moral skepticism can thus be defined as putting a nonarbitrary stop to the process of (noncircular) reason giving. An argument that goes on forever, in an infinite regress of reason giving, is forever unsatisfactory because it is forever incomplete. An argument that is circular, or that is truncated arbitrarily, is no argument at all.

Second, I shall assume that an acceptable strategy for putting a nonarbitrary stop to reason giving is to shift the burden of proof to the skeptic by showing that the "starting point" for a given justification, though unsupported by argument, is nonetheless not an arbitrary assumption. It may be nonarbitrary if, for example, an alternative is literally inconceivable. (It is in this sense that people have claimed that the law of contradiction is not an arbitrary assumption.) Or the starting point may be nonarbitrary because (again, perhaps, like the law of contradiction) it is not a thing that one ever *does* "assume," in the usual sense of the term; that is, it may fail to be an arbitrary assumption simply because it is not, in fact, an assumption at all. Such starting points are not in principle incontestable, but they do shift the burden of proof onto the skeptic: if they have not been arbitrarily chosen (a fortiori, because they have not been chosen at all), and if there is no reason to *reject* them, then their use in argument cannot be unjustifiable. At worst it could only be a matter of indifference.

The use I wish to make of the elements of the moral basis of property is that of a nonarbitrary starting point for argument. If in fact certain sorts of property rights are universally recognized, for example, I shall assume that—in the absence of countervailing arguments—they need no justification.[17] The nature and scope of this justificatory strategy should become clearer in what follows.

The Universality of Property Rights

From roughly the middle of the sixteenth century through the first quarter of the twentieth century it was commonly believed among Western property theorists that in many primitive societies the concept of ownership was wholly unknown. Such primitive communism, as it was called, was characterized by common possession and use of valuables rather than by anything corresponding to our notions of individual, joint, or even common ownership.[18]

Naturally enough, writers found conflicting uses for such information. Some saw property-free society as an ideal to be reachieved. Others saw it as an early stage in socioeconomic evolution that we were well rid of.[19] In any case, the notion of primitive communism persisted in academic debate well into this century.[20]

Careful study of the anthropological evidence, however, beginning perhaps with Rivers[21] and Malinowski,[22] and culminating in the development of economic anthropology in the 1930s and 1940s,[23] has set the record straight. More quickly than legal scholars[24] (though without very much conceptual precision) anthropologists recognized that the notion of ownership was very complex. They saw that property rights were typically complexes of use rights, possessory rights, rights to income, management, alienability, and so on—many varieties of which looked very little like what earlier writers apparently had in mind when they thought of ownership. (Apparently these earlier writers were using only someting like the notion of full exclusive ownership. If they read a report of a society in which no individual or group had exclusive use of, say, the fishing canoes, they concluded that those canoes were not "owned." They drew similar conclusions when they found other elements of the notion of full ownership missing.)[25] In any case, an appreciation of the varieties of property rights that fall short of full ownership forces a radical reevaluation of the anthropological evidence. It becomes clear that ownership can be divided, not only in the sense of joint and common tenancies, but in the sense that different people can hold different sorts of property rights in the same thing. Someone who holds a right to the possession and use of a piece of land may be said to have (partial) ownership of it, even though the rights to income are held in common by the society as a whole.

When property rights are seen in this light, and together with the wealth of detailed ethnographic studies now available, it is easy to show that private property rights of some sort exist everywhere.[26] Indeed, it is possible to argue that they are a *necessary* feature of social organization. To quote Irving Hallowell:

> If the core of property as a social institution lies in a complex system of recognized rights and duties with reference to the control of valuable objects, and if the roles of the participating individuals are linked by this means with basic economic processes, and if, besides, all these processes of social interaction are validated by traditional beliefs, attitudes, and values, and sanctioned in custom and law, it is apparent that we are dealing with an institution extremely fundamental to the structure of human societies as going concerns. For . . . property rights are institutionalized means of defining *who* may control various classes of valuable objects for a variety of present and future purposes and the *conditions* under which this power may be exercised. Since valuable objects in all human societies must include, at the minimum, some objects of material culture that are employed to transform the raw materials of the physical environment into consumable goods, there must be socially recognized provisions for handling the control of such elementary capital goods as well as the distribution and consumption of the goods that are produced. Consequently, property rights are . . . an integral part of the economic organization of any society.[27]

It does not follow, however, that any specific system of property rights is necessary for social organization, even once a set of general social circumstances is specified. Indeed, the variety of systems that will work in any given set of circumstances is impressive. Here again, the "earlier" writers were quite mistaken, this time, for example, in things like tracing the origin of property in land solely to the rise of agriculture. In fact, property in land — common, joint, and individual — occurs in many hunting and gathering societies, whereas in others it does not.[28] Increasing scarcity may cause a movement toward private property arrangements,[29] but then again it may not.[30]

In the West, until the late nineteenth century a movement toward full private ownership corresponded with the demise of feudalism, the rise of capitalism, and industrialization.[31] But the movement has reversed since.[32] And industrialization in the Soviet Union has been accomplished with quite a different property system.

The correlation of specific systems of property rights with the other elements of social organization[33] — as well as with the environments in which societies find themselves — would be of obvious importance. And perhaps some useful generalizations can be drawn. I cannot do it, however. Every attempt I have made is refuted by a counterexample actually observed in the field. The data indicate that, although property rights exist everywhere, what is necessary about them is just *that some exist*. It appears that many specific systems of ownership are compatible with any set of environmental conditions and social structures.

Territoriality, Acquisitiveness, and Egoism

The argument given above for the necessity of property rights (and thus the explanation for their universality) was sociological. I want to turn now to some issues in sociobiology, ethology, and social psychology.

If existing human beings are necessarily territorial, acquisitive, and egoistic (whether for reasons of genetics, psychology, or sociology), then much seems to follow for the theory of property rights. The liberty to pursue egoistic goals, and the liberty to acquire and keep both territory and other valuables, will be seen as fundamental human needs. Such needs create a powerful presumption in favor of the justifiability of social institutions (e.g., systems of private property rights) that satisfy those needs.

Not all (proposed) human needs create such a presumption, of course. If there are dispositions toward altruism, toward sharing, toward cooperation, and toward the achievement of intimacy in social relationships, then the liberties to act out those dispositions will also be fundamental needs — needs that may create presumptions in favor of social institutions that conflict with private property.

Property theory in our century is remarkable for its avoidance of these issues.[34] But the avoidance is in part justifiable. The current data on territoriality, egoism, altruism, individual distance, cooperativeness, acquisitiveness, and the like seem to be of very little constructive use. The data have significant destructive uses, of course. Early attempts to prove the existence of an acquisitive instinct in humans (whether from the supposed existence of primitive communism or the supposed prevalence of collecting behavior in children) have been debunked.[35] The Social Darwinists' evolutionary argument for the primacy of egoism and selfishness has been exploded.[36] And incautious interpretations of ethological material, to the effect that territoriality, aggression, and dominance structures have a preponderant role in human behavior have had to be revised.[37]

But constructive guidance for property theory, drawn from these materials, is very thin. Part of this is due to their lack of specific applicability to property rights, and part of it is due to their equivocal results. To explain:

The work on territoriality and individual distance is fascinating,[38] but its applicability to any specific form of property rights is highly questionable. Territoriality, to the extent that it is a human species characteristic, is clearly as much a group phenomenon (whether of family, clan, tribe, or nation) as it is an individual one. And the "territorial imperative" for individuals — which is what would be related to private property rights — is clearly satisfiable in so many ways as to provide little or no foundation for arument. If a fixed term, inalienable, untransmissible lease on an apartment will satisfy it as well as full ownership of a house (and I know of no evidence to suggest the contrary), then the territorial imperative gives virtually no commands to a property theorist. Similarly, the work on individual distance, although giving support to arguments for very minimal rights to privacy and freedom from trespass of one's personal boundaries, also gives no guidance to property theorists. There is much cultural and individual variation in the distances demanded by people — whether for intimate encounters, casual conversations, or living arrangements. It thus hardly seems possible to use such data in arguments for or against specific forms of property.

The equivocal nature of these materials with respect to property rights issues is another problem. Humans demand private spaces and set various sorts of interpersonal distances for carrying on social relationships, but they also seek the sort of conviviality and intimacy that depends on ignoring (while not violating) personal boundaries.[39] If humans are instinctually aggressive and violent, they are also instinctually loving. The ethological evidence is equally strong for each.[40] If egoism and selfishness are genotypic traits now — due to their evolutionary adaptiveness—then so are cooperation and altruism. Evolutionary theory supports the existence of both sorts of traits. [41]

In short, the sociobiological materials on the sorts of species characteristics of interests to property theorists are not (now) of much use. The work in these fields should be watched, however, for the *possibility* of a significant contribution to property arguments is there. And the contribution made, if it ever is, could push property theory either way: toward an extension of full private ownership or toward the reverse.

Reciprocity

Of much more immediate use than the material from sociobiology is some sociological work in exchange theory—the attempt to give a general account of the social function of exchanges of goods and services.

The obvious place (for modern westerner) to start in trying to understand exchange is with a narrow economic assumption: that exchanges of goods and services are to be understood in terms of the perceived self-maximization of economic value on the part of each participant. But this does not take one very far in explaining anthropological data such as the potlatch[42] and the Kula exchange.[43] In fact, exchange in very many primitive societies has an aspect that initially puzzled Western observers: the requirement of reciprocity (and the consequent lack of any significant economic profit for the participants).

Some elements of reciprocal exchanges could be understood along standard economic lines, of course. Malinowski describes the ritualized exchanges of fish for garden produce between coastal tribes and inland tribes in the Trobriand Islands as an obvious economic necessity.[44] Rates of exchange exist; money, too, in some primitive societies. And examples of the profit motive, greed, sharp business practice, and theft are plentiful. But the institution of the obligatory exchange of gifts of equal value is widespread enough—and central enough to the structure of those societies in which it has a prominent place—that it struck some observers as an important thing to study. And the topic has more than historic interest. Reciprocal exchanges pervade modern societies as well. Some are ritual—for example, the giving of Christmas gifts. Others are embedded in etiquette—for example, returning dinner invitations.

There are two competing approaches to social exchange theory.[45] One, traceable to Durkheim, has a collectivist character. "Social facts" are primary, and social exchange is seen primarily as a function of social structure. This approaches emphasizes what has been called *generalized* exchange — transactions in which people do not get reciprocity directly from the individual(s) to whom they give but depend instead on complex social processes to produce the reciprocal benefit. An example is what Peter Ekeh calls *chain generalized exchange* — a series of transactions in which A gives to B; B gives to C . . . and Z gives to A.[46] Such exchanges are taken to be expressions of more fundamental social structures and processes. That is, it is supposed that the social *structures* (kinship or whatever) come first, and generalized exchange grows up as a way of preserving, enhancing, and symbolizing them.[47]

The other approach to social exchange theory is more individualistic. It begins with face-to-face transactions and argues that social structures are at least in part functions of such transactions. Peter Blau's work in exchange theory is an example of this approach, and it deserves attention from property theorists for reasons I shall shortly mention.[48]

In outline, Blau's account is as follows: (1) Begin with what he calls the forces of social attraction, defined as whatever may cause people to seek contact with each other. In Maslovian terms, these forces may be survival needs, security needs, or self-needs. (2) Action in accord with such forces stimulates reciprocal exchange transactions. To get what one wants from others (without force or fraud), one ordinarily has to provide something of comparable value to those others. (3) As long as the exchange is reciprocal (i.e., of roughly equal valuables), social equilibrium is maintained. (4) But just as surely as the forces of social attraction stimulate exchange, so too exchange stimulates status and power differentiation. Some people will find themselves at a disadvantage in exchanges and will have to rely on force or fraud in place of reciprocity, or they will have to reciprocate by substituting deference or subservience for, say, material goods. (5) Those who find themselves at a considerable advantage in exchanges, with the resultant benefits of power and status, will try to institutionalize and legitimate those advantages. (6) Those who are at a disadvantage will resist the institutionalization and legitimation of status and power differentials. (7) The resultant dialectic between the advantaged and disadvantaged explains a good deal, Blau thinks, about *all* social institutions, however simple or complex, however central or peripheral to the social order. And it all rests on the notion of reciprocity.

This is not the place to discuss the details and scope of Blau's views or to assess the opposing "collectivist" accounts of social exchange. It is enough for present purposes to point out that, however incomplete this account may be, the processes it describes are indisputably pervasive in, and central to, human life as we know it. The relevance of this material to the moral arguments for and against property should be clear. To the extent that a specific system of property rights tends to produce and perpetuate inequalities of power and status that make reciprocity among members of a social order difficult or impossible, and to the degree that such lack of ability to reciprocate is unjustifiable (whether for reasons of fairness or reasons of utility), then one will have powerful support for the antiproperty arguments from inequality and disutility.

The Labor Principle

I turn back, now, from sociological theory to anthropological data — specifically, to data relating to laborers' entitlements to property. The practice of assigning to some laborers at least some of the rights of ownership in the things they produce appears to be a universal one.[49] I shall call the basis of this practice the labor *principle* — to distinguish it from the moral argument for property which I have called the labor "theory."

The labor principle, however, if it is to characterize a universal social practice, must be stated in a highly qualified way. For example, one must state it so as to take account of the fact that in many cultures whole groups of people (e.g., children, women, slaves) are systematically excluded from holding some sorts of property. Their labor is thus not always recognized with property rights, even in a society that grants others nearly full ownership over the things they produce. Further, it is often the case (in primitive societies and thoroughly socialistic ones as well) that laborers obtain only very limited sets of ownership rights for their efforts, for example, the right to distribute the meat from a kill, perhaps reserving the hide, sinews, and choicest portions of meat for oneself, but otherwise taking a share equal to that of people who did not make the kill themselves.[50] It is only a very restricted form of the labor principle, then, that can be said to be universal.

Even so, the universality is impressive. If one looks only at personal articles (clothing, personal adornments, household implements, toys) and at rather simple productive goods (e.g., spears, hoes, axes), and if one then looks at actual practices rather than whatever formal legal or moral code may exist, the labor principle can be stated in a much less qualified way. It seems that all recorded societies (for which we have such data) recognize *in practice* laborers' entitlements to purely personal articles and simple productive goods the laborers have produced.

The reason(s) for the universality of the labor principle have not been systematically explored by modern social science.[51] People make remarks indicating that they think the reasons are obvious[52] and then mention the sense of "psychological appropriation" of a thing that accompanies producing it.[53] The thing becomes "identified" with its maker, not only in the maker's mind, but in the minds of those who have seen it made. But remarks, however intuitively clear, are one thing; sound social psychology is another. It would be illuminating for property theorists to have the benefit of a defensible psychological theory explicity relating the labor principle to something like Maslow's hierarchy of needs. If it were then possible to relate forms and levels of need satisfaction to social development, one might have quite a powerful basis for moral argument at the levels of specific and particular justification.

In any case, for whatever reasons, the labor principle describes a social practice that is a fixture of human society. Its scope is often limited by the systematic exclusion of some groups from full citizenship in the social order. The entitlements it gives are often limited to very restricted forms of ownership—or to ownership over a very restricted range of things. But for the purposes of moral argument, it seems fair to conclude that the burden of proof is on those who would restrict or limit it, not on those who would act in accord with it.

Property and the Right to Use

A rather different, and striking finding in the anthropological and historical data on property rights concerns the extent to which owners' use rights are typically restricted. In some primitive societies, for example, the people who own major means of production like canoes have an obligation to keep them in use.[54] An owner may refuse to take the canoe out himself, but he must allow others to do so on demand. Similarly in some agricultural societies: fallow land can be used for gardening by anyone, even without getting the owner's permission.[55] In Europe, as late as Grotius, one finds references to an analogous principle of "innocent use" with respect to land.[56] (The origin and scope of the principle is somewhat obscure, but it seems to have come down from archaic law and to have prohibited owners from taking legal action against trespassers as long as they were in no way interfering with the owners' use of the land.) Of course in our own case one of the thorniest conceptual and political questions about property concerns the extent to which the government can compromise an owner's use rights (e.g., by zoning regulations) without running afoul of the constitutional prohibition of the taking of property without compensation.

In short, it is safe to say that use rights are everywhere among the most restricted of the rights that make up the notion of full ownership. Indeed, even in Honoré's *list* of the elements of full ownership (see above, pages 190-91), one such general restriction is included: the prohibition of harmful use. As Honoré points out, although in some legal systems "no harmful use" may mean no more than "no active use of a thing to do physical injury to people," in other legal systems it includes a prohibition of economic and/or aesthetic injury, and in still others shades into a requirement for productive use.[57] What is true in this regard of developed legal systems (Honoré's frame of reference) seems clearly true of societies in general, developed or not.

It is not possible, however, to correlate restrictions on use rights in any *simple* way with things like scarcity, or political, social, and economic development. One might think, for example, that the more urgent the social need for something that is privately owned, necessarily the more severely would the owner's use rights be restricted. Some societies provide evidence of this.[58] But other societies—even some exhibiting a considerable degree of cooperativeness—have in fact dealt with scarcity by making owners' use rights *more* exclusive rather than less exclusive.[59]

Similarly for social, political, and economic development. One might think that as social, political, or economic roles and structures become more specialized, and the members of society more complexly interdependent, use rights would necessarily be compromised. But the growth of Anglo-American property law since feudal times defies a straightforward analysis of this type. A movement *toward* full ownership coincided with increasing complexity until the late nineteenth century.[60]

Even if no "simple" correlations can be found, however, there is one striking observation of some importance for property theory. Beginning with the "static" fact of the typically restricted character of use rights, and then looking for "dynamic" correlations with changing social structures, convinces one that *in practice*, use rights have always been vulnerable to significant and more or less continuous redefinition. Their vulnerability appears nearly as great, in fact, as that of the right to income (which is nearly always subject to taxation). Our current problems with land-use policy and environmental law are not aberrations in this regard. The fragility of use rights (relative to most other property rights) is the rule, not the exception.

Property and Rights to Transfer

If use rights are often heavily restricted, rights to transfer property are sometimes altogether absent. In many primitive societies, as well as feudal societies in the Western tradition, property in land passed only by fixed rules of inheritance; owners could not transmit it by will.[61] Further, in feudal societies *inter vivos* transfers of land at first required permission of the lord. In some primitive societies, such transfers were forbidden altogether. In short, free alienability of property, and the power to dispose of one's holdings through a will, are rather recent accretions to the notion of ownership—neither natural nor necessary to human society per se.

This point can be made more intelligible by a brief excursion into comparative economics, specifically into the work of Karl Polanyi and his followers.[62] Polanyi maintained that modern economic theory is an inadequate tool for understanding the economics of primitive and archaic societies; indeed, inadequate for handling very much of anything that existed prior to the seventeenth century. This is so, he held, because modern economic theory, whether socialist or capitalist, is essentially the theory of market exchange, and market economies are an aberration in human history. It is not that *markets* were unknown in primitive, archaic, and feudal societies, but simply that it is inaccurate to characterize their economic systems as market economies (and thus inappropriate to analyze their systems solely in terms of the theory of market exchange as developed by modern economists).

Polanyi identified three fundamental forms of economic exchange. [63] One is *reciprocity*, in which an individual, household, or tribe exchanges goods with others out of mutual social obligations based on friendship, kinship, or some status hierarchy. These exchanges in fact create and maintain a stable supply of goods and services, but they are embedded in underlying social institutions (e.g., kinship structures) that have much broader functions. They are characterized by the absence of profit (hence the name "reciprocity") and lack the familar supply-and-demand dynamics. Modern economic theory is largely inapplicable to such transactions.

A second fundamental form of economic transaction, according to Polanyi, is *redistribution*, in which producers turn over their goods and/or labor power to some central authority where it is pooled with others and then redistributed. Here the exchange from producer to authority is a product of political or religious obligations, and the redistribution is based on anything from recognized moral, political, or religious principles to the whim of the authority. Again, Polanyi implies, the analytical tools of modern economic theory are largely beside the point.

The third form of economic transaction is *market exchange*. It is this form of exchange — in which individuals or groups offer goods or services to anyone willing and able to pay an acceptable price — with which modern economic theory is designed to deal.

Polanyi acknowledges that all three fundamental forms of economic exchange have existed in all societies of record. But he argues that economic systems as a whole must be classified by reference to which form of exchange is the dominant one, how it dominates the others, and how it is supplemented with the other two types. Helen Codere, [64] following Polanyi, thus characterizes systems in which reciprocity predominates as *social economies* (because exchanges come predominantly out of the task of fulfilling broader social obligations). Systems in which redistribution predominates are called *political economies* — to bring out the fact that exchanges occur primarily in fulfillment of political obligations. Systems in which market exchange predominates are *market economies*.

Polanyi's contestable historical and normative claims (e.g., that market economies are a recent and rather deplorable aberration in human history) need not concern us here. What is important for present purposes is, first, the fact that his analytical framework fits the available data on primitive, archaic, and modern economies. There are at least these three fundamental forms of economic exchange, and recorded economic systems do tend to be dominated by one sort or another, with the remaining ones in subsidiary roles.[65]

The second thing of importance here is the light Polanyi's analysis sheds on the "naturalness" of different forms of ownership—specifically, but by no means exclusively, on the very restricted rights found in many primitive and archaic societies. In this light it is clear, for one thing, that a general argument for the utility of free alienability and transmissibility can be sound only if one assumes the existence of a market economy—or at any rate, only insofar as one assumes a movement toward market exchange of the relevant goods. Social and political economies may require very different arrangements.

It is thus quite unlikely that any general theory of property will include *unrestricted* rights to transfer, for it has long been admitted that the labor theory does not support them,[66] and I see no way to make the argument from political liberty carry the whole burden of justification (at least in the fact of opposition from the utility argument and nonsupport from the labor theory). The justification, of rights to transfer must therefore take place at the level of specific justification, and the central, *general* truth about such justifications is that they will be controlled by what sort of economy one is faced with.

Some Other Areas of Research

The considerations I have advanced are by no means exhaustive of the moral basis of property, of course. They are intended to reopen an old field, not to enclose it. But some tentative conclusions for property theory can be drawn from them. Before doing that, however, I want to make a few remarks about some areas of research I have not yet mentioned, areas whose results I suspect will one day be very important parts of the moral basis of property rights.

Personality Theory

It has sometimes been remarked that property is necessary for the full development of personality. I say "remarked" rather than "argued" because aside from Beaglehole's criticism of the notion,[67] I have not been able to find a significant and sustained argument on the subject. What one *can* find is a scattering of remarks, such as Aristotle's contention that property is connected to the development of the virtue of generosity,[68] and Hegel's suggestion that property acquisition is something natural to the exercise of human freedom and will.[69] Some work in modern personality theory seems tantalizingly close to such concerns (e.g., on territoriality and "spacing" behavior), but I know of no serious attempt to relate it to property theory.

The result is that when one turns to what is perhaps the most obvious source of data for the moral basis of property—that is; personality theory—one finds very little help. Putting aside Freudian speculation about anal retentiveness and its relations to miserliness, kleptomania, and collecting behavior, it is hard to find material of more than simply suggestive value.

Part of this is no doubt due to the constraints of experimental science. Ways of testing territoriality and spacing behavior virtually suggest themselves. Property rights, however, are evidently much more difficult to deal with.

Even so, one would think that personality theorists could make a direct and significant contribution to property theory. The study of "agency" surely has relevance to the normative problems of liberty. And the development of personality may in fact involve the psychological appropriation of things. I hope that we will see some work of this sort in personality theory soon.

The Theory of Political Development

The results of work in comparative politics—particularly systems and functional analysis—may one day have an important impact on property theory. At present, the results seem too general to be of much use, but I shall indicate briefly where I think the future importance may lie.

Some theorists[70] have proposed the thesis that the development of political systems from traditional forms (e.g., patriarchy, patrimony, feudalism) through historical bureaucratic empires to modern democratic and authoritarian forms is characterized most fundamentally by ever increasing role and structure specialization, substructure autonomy, and "secularization" of the political culture. If this is so, *and* if the future direction of development can be predicted, then it may be possible to argue for the functional necessity of certain forms of property.

It is of course possible to make functional arguments concerning the *current* situation, but in the absence of defensible judgments about the probable course of development, they are rather weak. They are vulnerable to the standard normative challenges to preserving the status quo. If other sorts of systems have worked, and are morally better, then why preserve this one?

So the interesting material will come, I think, from the theory of political development. But as I say, the results so far seem to be too general to be of much use for property theory.

Obligations to Future Generations

One final remark before I turn to some conclusions. Work from economics, psychology, ecology, and other sources that bears on the questions of saving and/or providing for future generations will clearly have an important impact on the specific justification of property rights. I refer here not to work that is in itself normative (i.e., that constitutes an argument for or against obligations to future generations), but rather to work that is part of the basis for such normative arguments. What constitutes an economically efficient savings principle, for example? What, if any, foundation does personality theory supply for various versions of the right to transmit? These and other questions, which need answers for other reasons as well, also need answers for the purposes of property theory.

Economic Theory

This is, of course, already addressing the problems of specific justification directly. Arguments about the impact of various property systems on production, or on the economy as a whole, are numerous and illuminating. Hypotheses about the connections between property arrangements and economic development—or socioeconomic institutions—have also been advanced. No philosophical account of the moral basis of property can be complete without taking these matters into consideration.[71]

CONCLUSIONS

Perhaps enough has been said, for present purposes, about the substance of what I have called the moral basis of property—enough to indicate its importance to property theory. I want to conclude by drawing some tentative conclusions from the material just presented, conclusions that illustrate the sort of contribution such considerations can make to the general theory of property rights.

Most of the conclusions to follow are in the forms of *rebuttable presumptions*. Considerations drawn from the moral basis of property do not establish normative judgments either directly or conclusively. Rather, they help to establish principles upon which it is reasonable to act in the absence of countervailing evidence. (I shall make no comment here on what would count as countervailing evidence or on the likelihood of its being found.)

The Necessity of Property

The leading conclusion from this survey of the moral basis of property is undoubtedly a presumption in favor of the conclusion that an extensive system of private ownership is a necessary feature of human societies. This conclusion is drawn directly from reflection on the fact that ownership has many varieties, and that, once the wide variety in forms of ownership is recognized, extensive systems of private property appear to be universal. The burden of proof is thus surely on anyone who holds that a propertyless society—whatever that might mean— is a possibility. [72]

The significance of this presumption is questionable, however. It gives no guidance on the issue of what sort of things (beyond the consumables necessary for survival) should be privately owned and in what way. Further, the varieties of ownership cover such a wide range—from the mere right to use to full ownership—that it is questionable whether the bare presumption in favor of *some* extensive system of ownership advances moral argument at all.

The Possibility of Plurality

Combined with some other conclusions, however, the presumption in favor of the necessity of property begins to look stronger. For one thing, it is clear from the anthropological and historical evidence that there must be a presumption in favor of the "naturalness" and functional adequacy of a wide range of sorts of property systems— even given very similar social and environmental circumstances. Arguments for the functional necessity of a specific sort of property system, no matter how severe the environment or well defined the social conditions, are thus highly unlikely to succeed. One is likely to be able to find examples of similar societies, in similar circumstances, that managed very well with quite a different system of property rights.

The Presumption Against Full, Exclusive Ownership

However, this general rule, is subject to exceptions. A presumption against full, exclusive ownership of anything other than items produced or purchased solely with one's labor is derivable from the (apparent) absence of such a practice in human history. Private ownership of things other than the products of purely pesonal labor seems always to be either less than full or less than exclusive.

The Vulnerability of Use Rights

Further, use rights are properly vulnerable to continuous redefinition. The recognition of rights by a social order has the character of a promise — a guarantee that mere utility for an individual or for the social order as a whole will not justify interference with the right holders' liberties, justify a change in their powers and immunities, or justify a change in the duties of others. But promises can be conditional. Just as we all understand that the government's promise to secure to us the right to our income is subject to the condition that taxes may be levied, so too the promise of the right to use must usually be understood as subject to conditions. One such condition (always present, though defined in widely divergent ways) is the prohibition of harmful use. But the virtual ubiquity with which use rights are subject to other conditions (e.g., the possibility of rezoning) shifts the burden of proof to those who wish to establish a stonger sort of use right.

The Labor Principle

A strong presumption in favor of securing to laborers some fairly extensive property rights over the fruits of their labor is clear. This too is a universal practice that puts the onus of proof on its opponents.

The Possibility of Reciprocity

In potential conflict with the labor principle, however, is support from exchange theory for the contention that the antiproperty arguments from inequality and disutility must be weighted very heavily in specific justification. The functional importance of maintaining the capacity for reciprocal exchanges among all members of a society, and the role property rights obviously can play in this task, enhances the importance of those antiproperty arguments.

The Nature of Property Theory

Undoubtedly other conclusions could be drawn from the material here presented, but I shall content myself with one final remark. The problems of specific justification reveal themselves here as *doubly* subordinate. They are, of course, subordinate to the results of general justification through what I have called the compatibility requirement — that is, the requirement that specific forms of property must be compatible with the requirements placed on all ownership by the general justifications of property rights. But the evidence from the theory of economic systems suggests that specific justification is subordinate in yet another way — subordinate to prior normative decisions about the fundamental nature of the economic system. The type of economic system one wants to maintain (whether a social, political, or market economy, for example), will obviously be a decisive factor in many aspects of specific justification. (Free alienability, for instance, is required by market exchange). The possibility of getting a prior justification of specific forms of property which would then determine decisions about the fundamental nature of the economic system seems so remote as to be negligible. I have elsewhere[73] carefully considered the inventory of arguments for property rights, and I find no glimmering of an argument that could be that powerful *at the level of specific justification*. It seems more than likely, then, that progress with specific justification will be helped not simply by the considerations I have labeled the moral basis of property; it will *depend* on such considerations — particularly those drawn from comparative economics and politics.

NOTES

1. A remark on my use of the term "moral." By a moral argument I mean an "all-things-considered" argument — one not limited to considerations of prudence alone or duty alone or utility alone, but one that includes all such considerations (as well as any others that are relevant). Secondarily, of course, a subsidiary argument, taken *as a part* of such an "all-things-considered" approach will often be referred to

as a moral argument. Whether the concept of morality implicit in this usage is a defensible one in terms of ordinary and/or philosophical language does not concern me here. (I have argued elsewhere that it is. See "The Finality of Moral Judgments," *Philosophical Review* 82 [1973], pp. 364–71.) All-things-considered arguments, at any rate, are what moral philosophy must ultimately concern itself with. The moral basis of property, then, consists of all those facts about the human condition that are relevant to an all-things-considered argument for or against property rights.

2. By "traditional theorists" I mean those writers on property who lived and wrote before the emergence of modern social anthropology in the first decades of the twentieth century.

3. Ernest Beaglehole, *Property: A Study in Social Psychology* (London: George Allen & Unwin, 1931).

4. E.g., the scarcity of goods; the limited generosity and altruism of humans; and their relative equality. See Thomas Hobbes, *Leviathan*, chaps XIV and XV; and the elegant summary by H.L.A. Hart in *The Concept of Law* (Oxford: Clarendon, 1961), pp. 189ff.

5. Epicurus, *Principal Doctrines* XXIX. His remark there concerns desires, not property.

6. I have covered these matters in more detail in chapter 2 of *Property Rights: Philosophic Foundations* (London and Boston: Routledge & Kegan Paul, 1977). In some respects I think the brief treatment here is superior to the one in the book. Here, for example, I have improved the list of elements.

7. A.M. Honoré, "Ownership," in A.G. Guest, ed., *Oxford Essays in Jurisprudence*, First Series (Oxford: Clarendon, 1961), pp. 107–47.

8. Throughout this paper I shall use "modern society" to refer to postmedieval societies of a large scale, whether industrialized or not. "Archaic societies" refers to those of ancient Greece Rome, Egypt, the large-scale ancient societies of the Near and Far East, and comparable societies in the Americas (e.g., the Incas) and Africa (e.g., Dahomey). "Primitive" is a term of convenience, and one that has had an ugly history. But the alternatives anthropologists have proposed (e.g., preliterate, nonliterate, peasant, small scale, and so on) are all equally misleading as attempts to refer to that group of small-scale, nonindustrialized, mostly nonliterate, mostly non-money-economy societies to which I want to refer. I trust the imprecision and (unintended) derogatory connotations of "primitive" will be offset by the usefulness it has by reason of familiarity.

9. I shall use the Hohfeldian categories of rights, somewhat renamed. "Claim rights" entail the existence, for specifiable others, of definable duties with respect to the right holder. "Liberty rights" entail only the absence of claim rights against the right holder. "Power rights" correlate with liabilities in others; "immunity rights" correlate with disabilities. For W.N. Hohfeld's presentation of the distinctions, see his *Fundamental Legal Conceptions* (New Haven: Yale University Press, 1919).

10. This right (consumption and/or destruction) plus the next two (modification and alienation) are all grouped together by Honoré under the heading, "the right to the capital." In *Property Rights*, I followed his usage, but I have since come to believe that it is advantageous to split up the category. One has read, for example, of a tribe in which certain timbers for the building of huts may not be modified by the owner even though they (apparently) may be alienated.

11. I have here retained Honoré's title for the element but have changed the exposition. See his in "Ownership," op. cit., pp. 126-28.

12. There are $2^8 - 1$ (i.e., 255; combinations of the first 8 elements. Each of these may either stand alone with the right to security or be combined with any subset of the remaining 4 elements. There are thus 2^4 (i.e., 16) variations possible on each of the 255 combinations (16 × 255 = 4,080). This number should not be taken too seriously, of course. There is some arbitrariness in dividing ownership into 13 (or 11, 9, or 15) elements. And each element may be defined in various ways as well. The important point is simply that there are *very many* varieties of ownership no matter how the concept is cut up.

13. The substance of this section is a summary of chapts. 3 through 9 of my *Property Rights*.

14. Rawls says, for example, that he claims priority for liberty only in the case of modern industrial societies. See *A Theory of Justice* (Cambridge: Harvard Univ. Press, 1971). pp. 541-48.

15. The general theory of property includes, but is not limited to, the general justification of property rights. The general theory also includes work on the coordination problem, the compatibility requirement, and whatever can be said "in general" about specific and particular justification.

16. See my attempt in chap. 9 of *Property Rights*.

17. I have argued at length for the general applicability of this method of justification to the problems of moral skepticism in *On Justifying Moral Judgments* (London and New York: Routledge & Kegan Paul and Humanities Press, 1973).

18. See, for example, the relevant discussion in Ch. Letourneau, *Property: Its Origin and Development* (New York: Charles Scribner's Sons, 1896).

19. See ibid for a combination of the two.

20. For an attempt to rebut the modern anthropologists' interpretation of the evidence, see William Seagle, *The Quest for Law* (New York: Knopf, 1941), chap. 5, pp 50-57.

21. W.H.R. Rivers *The Todas* (London: Macmillan, 1906).

22. Bronislaw Malinowski, *Crime and Custom in Savage Society* (New York: Harcourt, Brace, 1926).

23. Particularly the work of Raymond Firth and Melville Herskovits.

24. For a fairly late legal account that is conceptually unsophisticated in comparison with the anthropologists working at the same time, see A.S. Diamond, *Primitive Law* (London: Longmans, Green, 1935), Chap. 24, pp. 260-76.

25 Both Seagle, *The Quest for Law*, and Diamond, *Primitive Law*, perpetuate this mistake.

26. See the excellent summary of the data in Melville J. Herskovits, *Economic Anthropology* (New York: Knopf, 1952), with the "universality conclusion" on pp. 326–29. Herskovits's theses about the economic functions of property are highly contestable. He does not, for example, take account of Karl Polanyi's work (see references, n. 62, below). But his summary of the raw data is admirable.

27. A. Irving Hallowell, "The Nature and Function of Property as a Social Institution," *Journal of Legal and Political Sociology* I: 115–38 (1943), and reprinted as chap. 12 of his *Culture and Experience* (Philadelphia: Univ. of Pennsylvania Press, 1955), pp. 236–49. The quotation here is from pp. 246–47 of the reprint.

28. Herskovits, op. cit., chaps. 15 and 16.

29. See Raymond Firth, *Social Change in Tikopia* (London: George Allen & Unwin, 1959), p.159.

30 Herskovits, op. cit., reference to the Eskimos on p. 372.

31. For an excellent summary of these matters, beginning with English feudal law, see Thomas F. Bergin and Paul G. Haskell, *Preface to Estates in Land and Future Interests* (Brooklyn: Foundation, 1966).

32. Witness the growth of land use and planning law, the income tax, antitrust law, inheritance taxes, and so forth.

33. "Other elements of social organization" here include kinship and marriage structures, legislative and judicial processes, and the like. What counts as a necessary element of social organization is a matter of some debate. But it is enough for my purposes to take just those that are universal (as far as we know) in societies that have survived for several generations.

34. By "property theory" I mean attempts to justify or disjustify property rights—whether at the general, specific or particular level. I do not include attempts to explain or describe the existence of various property rights. Some of the descriptive and explanatory material does involve itself with these issues. See Ernest Beaglehole, op. cit.

35. See Beaglehole, op. cit., parts II and III.

36. In the latter part of the nineteenth century, in fact. See P. Kropotkin, *Mutual Aid, A Factor of Evolution* (New York: Knopf, 1922). Originally published in the 1890s as a series of articles.

37. See Edward O. Wilson, *Sociobiology* (Cambridge: Harvard Univ. Press, 1975), chaps. 11 and 12.

38. See ibid., chap. 12, for a summary of the animal data; and Edward Hall, *The Hidden Dimension* (New York: Anchor Books, 1969), for the material on individual distance as applied to humans.

39. See Abraham Maslow, *Motivation and Personality* (New York: Harper, 1954).

40. See Irenäus Eibl-Eibesfeldt, *Love and Hate: The Natural History of Behavior Patterns* (New York: Holt, Rinehart & Winston, 1971).

41. See Robert L. Trivers, "The Evolution of Reciprocal Altruism," *Quarterly Review of Biology* 46, no. 4 (1971), pp. 37–57; and the

summary in Wilson, op. cit., chap. 5.

42. "Potlatch" is the name given to a practice—common among some tribes of American Indians in the Pacific Northwest—of large-scale ceremonial distribution of goods. The recipients were obligated to take gifts and give something even greater in return at a potlatch of their own. See Philip Drucker, "The Potlatch," in George Dalton, ed., *Tribal and Peasant Economies: Readings in Economic Anthropology* (Garden City, N.Y.: Natural History Press, 1967), pp. 481–93. This article is reprinted from Drucker's *Cultures of the North Pacific Coast* (Chandler, 1965), pp. 55–66.

43. The Kula exchange, an intircate, obligatory passing of gifts among the Trobriand Islanders, is described by Malinowski in "Kula: The Circulating Exchange of Valuables in the Archipelagoes of Eastern New Guinea," first published in *Man*, no. 51 (1920), pp. 97–105, and reprinted in Dalton, ed., *Tribal and Peasant Economies*, pp. 171–184.

44. Ibid.

45. Here I am relying on Peter Ekeh, *Social Exchange Theory: The Two Traditions* (Cambridge: Harvard Univ. Press, 1974). For an argument to the effect that reciprocity (the basis of Blau's theory of exchange as summarized below) is a universal moral demand, see Alvin W. Gouldner, "The Norm of Reciprocity: A Preliminary Statement," *American Sociological Review* 25 (1960), pp. 161–78.

46. The Kula exchange is like this. Other types of generalized exchange identified by Ekeh are two forms of what he calls "net" (as in network) generalized exchange. One is focused on individuals: in a series of transactions, ABCD give to E; ABCE give to D; ABDE give to C; ACDE give to B; and BCDE give to A. Think of farmers helping each other in turn at harvest time. The other form of net generalized exchange is focused on groups. Again in a series of transactions, A gives to BCD; B gives to ACD; C gives to ABD; and D gives to ABC. (Think of each member of a bridge club entertaining the whole group.) In each case, just as in chain generalized exchange and in "restricted" or "mutual" exchange between two parties, reciprocity can be achieved. See Ekeh, op, cit., pp. 51–54.

47. Although "collectivist" exchange theory is not as clear to me as I would like, and consequently I feel uneasy about commenting on it further, its proponents do not appear to deny that what they call "restricted" exchange—that is, mutual exchange between two parties, whether groups or individuals—does function in the way described by "individualist" theorists (below).

48. See Peter M. Blau, *Exchange and Power in Social Life* (New York: John Wiley, 1967).

49. Herskovits, op, cit., pp. 372ff.

50. See Herskovits, op. cit., chap. 17.

51. I can find no specific references to such work, for example, in the past forty-five years of *The International Index of Social Science Periodicals*.

52. E.g., Herkovits, op. cit., p. 380.

53. Beaglehole, op. cit., p. 300.

54. See Malinowski, *Argonauts of the Western Pacific* (London: George Routledge and Sons, 1922).

55. Firth, op. cit., p. 159.

56. Hugo Grotius, *De jure belli ac paci,* translation of the 1646 edition by F.W. Kelsey and others (Oxford: Clarendon, 1926), II, II, XI.

57. One should not suppose that it is only rights to the means of production that are typically limited in this way. Nuisance law in developed societies, and less formal prohibitions in primitive societies, show that use rights over even the most personal sorts of property are restricted.

58. Herskovits, op. cit., references to the Eskimos.

59. Firth, op. cit., p. 159.

60. See, for illustrative material, Bergin and Haskell, op. cit.

61. For a review of the practices of primitive societies, see Beaglehole, op. cit., pp. 244–47. Bergin and Haskell, op. cit, contains material on English feudal law.

62. The most convenient source for the material presented here is George Dalton, ed., *Primitive, Archaic and Modern Economies: Essays of Karl Polanyi* (New York: Anchor Books, 1968). Dalton provides a lucid introduction and bibliography. For some of the empirical support for Polanyi's analytical framework — as well as much of the theoretical material itself — see Karl Polanyi, Conrad M. Arensberg, and Henry W. Pearson, eds., *Trade and Market in the Early Empires* (New York: The Free Press, 1957).

63. Economic exchange means the exchange of material goods (or money) and productive services. It should not be confused with *social* exchange, which is sometimes treated as all exchange other than economic, but which in my view is better regarded simply as exchange per se — of which economic exchange is a part. The reason I favor the latter course is that otherwise economic exchange tends to be identified too closely with market exchange, much to the confusion of all.

64. Helen Codere, "Exchange and Display," *International Encyclopedia of the Social Sciences* (1968).

65. For one who reads extensively in economic anthropology first, as I did, Polanyi's analysis is both revelatory and utterly convincing. The work of Durkheim, Rivers, Malinowski, Mauss, Firth, Herskovits, and others is beautifully synthesized by it. The general outline of Polanyi's position is perfectly consistent with their *data* (though not always with their speculations about their significance), and makes sense of them in a way that the anthropologists themselves do not. The same is true of the criticism of Polanyi (and followers) which I have read: it does not challenge the usefulness of the analytical framework. It challenges the polemical character of the presentation and the claim that modern market analysis is largely inapplicable to primitive and archaic societies. See, for example, Edward E. LeClair, "Economic Theory and

Economic Anthropology," *American Anthropologist* 64 (1962), pp. 1179, 1203.

66.   See Becker, *Property Rights*, chap. 4.

67.   Beaglehole, op. cit., part III.

68.   Aristotle, *Politics* at 1263b.

69.   G. W. F. Hegel, *Philosophy of Right,* trans. T. M. Knox (Oxford: Clarendon, 1942), pp. 37–41.

70.   Specifically, Gabriel A. Almond and G. Bingham Powell, Jr., *Comparative Politics: A Developmental Approach* (Boston: Little, Brown, 1966).

71.   For a useful overview of some of these matters, see Frederic L. Pryor, *Property and Industrial Organization in Communist and Capitalist Nations* (Bloomington: Indiana Univ. Press, 1973), chap. 9, pp. 336–74.

72.   It might be wondered whether this method of argument—from the existence of a universal practice to a normative presumption in favor of it—has embarrassing results with respect to male supremacy. It does not. If it can be shown that the social position of women has everywhere, in every society of record, been inferior to that of men, then there is indeed a rebuttable presumption in favor of such practices. But I take it as settled that any such presumption has long since been destroyed (e.g., by reference to existing and historic social circumstances that make the subordination of women dysfunctional, and by reference to the injustices done to individuals by such practices). And of course it is far from clear that male supremacy *is* a universal practice. As has been pointed out even by one who is basically unsympathetic to modern feminism, the data on the position of women in primitive and historic cultures are largely unreliable. See E. E. Evans-Pritchard, *The Position of Women in Primitive Societies and Other Essays in Social Anthropology* (New York: The Free Press, 1965), pp. 37–58, at pp. 38–43.

73.   Becker, *Property Rights.*

9

ON THE ALLEGED IMPOSSIBILITY OF AN UNQUALIFIED DISJUSTIFICATORY THEORY OF PROPERTY RIGHTS

RICHARD E. FLATHMAN

Prima facie, rights to property are doubly objectionable, doubly dangerous. They are objectionable first just because they are a species of rights. If rights are anything approaching the moral, legal or political "trumps" that Ronald Dworkin says they are, then in having a right to X Able has a dangerously powerful weapon against anyone who may have reason to object to X.[1] And if the right is to property it warrants Able, as Blackstone put it, in exercising "sole and despotic dominion . . . over the external things of the world,"[2] that is over resources that may be vital to the interests, objectives or well-being of other persons. This dominion, of course, may be qualified in various ways, doubtless including some Blackstone did not anticipate. But it remains the case that just insofar as Able has rights, to that extent he has a weapon against all others.

A further feature of rights and especially of rights to property should be noted at the outset. It can be described by saying that the idea of rights, as such, is devoid of any principle of moderation. Insofar as Able has a right to free speech, he can exercise that right as frequently and as assertively as he wishes; he is at liberty to spend all of his days delivering harangues. Similarly, if Able has a right to acquire property, he can follow the example of such exemplary characters as the Rockefellers, Mellons, and Vanderbilts and accumulate rights in so much capital that it is virtually impossible for him to spend as rapidly as he "makes," acquire vast and choice estates that sit unused for months or years at a stretch, and deprive all of mankind by purchasing great quantities of rare and beautiful objects to be hoarded in private places.

These features of property rights have from time to time generated deep skepticism concerning their justifiability. There is a perhaps recessive but nevertheless persistent strain of anti property thought and sentiment in the record of reflection about property rights. And quite properly so. The features we have been discussing are unattractive in themselves, and the factual record concerning property acquisition, as Professor Becker has put it, "is a sordid one," replete with "injustice" and "inequity."[3] Perhaps there are nevertheless adequate, convincing justifications for maintaining some version of the institution or practice of property rights. But powerful objections to this practice cry out for explicit and systematic justification.

Or so it would appear. We have rehearsed the foregoing tolerably familiar considerations because the implication that property rights as such demand justification has been vigorously denied. As with other widely encountered arrangements and institutions such as political authority and obligation, the edge of the demand for a justification for property has been blunted by both practical political and philosophical objections against the enterprise of essaying a general justificatory or disjustificatory theory. As a practical political matter, the practice of maintaining rights to property has been a generally popular feature of numerous societies and communities. To quote Blackstone once again, "There is nothing which so generally strikes the imagination and engages the affections of mankind"[4] as do rights to property. Perhaps for this reason theorists from Plato to More to Marx who have questioned property rights in a radical manner, and utopian communities that have attempted to abolish such rights, have been dismissed as eccentric, misguided, or worse.

The ubiquity and general approbation of the practice has itself been offered as a kind of theoretical justification for it. According to a familiar line of thought (which might be styled Burkean), a practice that has been widely adopted, steadfastly maintained, and generally approved is thereby shown to have the best possible justification. Some such disposition may lurk beneath the arguments we will shortly be considering. Certainly the "Burkean" position is intended to deflect abstract, systematic assessment of property rights — and hence to deflect one possible impetus to change in the experience that is alleged to justify them. But it must be emphasized that the Burkean appeal to experience leaves open the possibility that humankind's experience with property rights might change — might change in ways that substantially alter judgments concerning them and their justifiability.

However, arguments intended to generate yet more categorical objections to general, philosophical assessments of the institution of property are abroad. The most insistent of these is the natural rights position according to which (as in Robert Nozick's recent version[5]) the right to acquire property is a normatively given or primitive attribute, which it would be *morally* wrong to question. Another, less dogmatic, and hence philosophically more respectable argument, contends that general justifications or disjustifications for property are necessarily afflicted by some species of absurdity or incoherence. According to this view, the traditional philosophical enterprise of attempting a general justificatory or disjustificatory theory of property is fated, not just to the kind of error that Burke would have predicted for it, but to a deeper philosophical failing, incoherence or meaningless.

Professor Becker's writings (on property and on metaethical questions generally)[6] present a complex and challenging version of this latter position. For this reason, because his arguments raise a variety of important philosophical questions of great generality, and not least because his position could be taken to support an unwarranted complacency concerning a major but dubious feature of our arrangements, his arguments deserve critical examination. With the foregoing intuitive and perhaps merely native skepticism about property rights as a backdrop, the remainder of these remarks are given to such an examination. Although we will not defend a categorical anti-property position, we will try to show that Becker fails to discredit the possibility of such a position. We will also suggest that the most plausible general justificatory theory of property rights, which in our view is utilitarianism, not only keeps the possibility of such a position open but by its own logic must take that possibility very seriously.

In claiming that Becker holds general justificatory theories of property to be incoherent we are admittedly contradicting his explicit statements to the contrary. He concedes that "general justification . . . seems [the] most obviously and purely philosophical variety," finds it "not surprising" that "the bulk of philosophical work" is at this level,[7] and even allows that question "having to do with general justification clearly have logical priority."[8] Thus he agrees that "one is not likely to get very far with problems of specific and particular justification" until "one knows whether — and how — property rights in general can be justified."[9] "Philosophical work on property," therefore, "may correctly begin with questions of general justification," and Becker claims no more than that "it cannot end there."[10] Accordingly, a considerable part of his paper and yet a larger proportion of his book attend to theories that aspire to provide general justifications or disjustifications for property rights.

The present interpretation, therefore, rests on the implications of the main arguments he advances, of which there are three, as follows: (1) If appropriately conceptualized, the empirical study of past and present human affairs and arrangements shows that property rights are a universal, arguably a necessary, feature of human societies. (2) Critical examination of general theories of property rights (including antiproperty theories) shows that no single theory "dominates" either the subject matter or (therefore?) its competitors among general theories. There is an "irreducible plurality" of such theories, all of which are "sound, independent and of presumptively equal weight." Thus, we must abandon the quest for a "dominance solution" to general justificatory questions about property and "coordinate" the several presumptively equal theories in the course of justifying or disjustifying specific forms and particular distributions of property rights. (3) A suitably conducted social scientific analysis of human beings and human societies can hope to identify "a set of facts about the human condition" that will provide "a moral basis" or "non-arbitrary starting point" for moral arguments concerning property rights. The program of this chapter is to take up these arguments in the order just listed, commenting *inter alia* on their merits and on the uneasy relations among them.

PROPERTY RIGHTS AS A UNIVERSAL AND NECESSARY FEATURE OF HUMAN SOCIETIES

"Property right," "ownership" and related concepts, Becker argues, following A. M. Honoré,[11] are family resemblance terms under the rubric of which a considerable variety of elements (13 in Becker's view) have been brought together in what is indeed a "prodigous diversity"[12] of combinations (no less than 4,080 by Becker's computations).[13] Realizing this allows us to dispose of the discredited view that some "primitive" societies were without the concept and the practice of property rights. If we operate with a suitably capacious conception of ownership, Becker argues, "it is easy to show that private property rights of some sort exist everywhere."[14] In short, Wittgensteinian premises about language, mediated by A. M. Honoré's application thereof to "ownership," plus a conceptually sophisticated anthropology, yields the conclusion that rights to private property are a universal phenomenon.

This by no means modest finding is much less than the entire yield of Becker's potent combination of authorities. The finding of universality would support the "Burkean" argument noted above. But it could not exclude the possibility of a morrow that witnessed the abolition of all 4,080 members of this (truly extended) family. More to the present point, it could not exclude the possibility of a conclusive argument that all 4,080 variants are moral abominations that ought to be abolished. The possibility of such an argument is excluded, however, by Becker's further contention. "[I]t is possible to argue," he goes on to say, "that they [property rights] are a necessary feature of social organization."[15] Now, as Hobbes somewhere says, that which is necessary arises not for deliberation. If property rights are not only universal but necessary, any philosopher attempting a *general* justification or disjustification of them would be pretending to a kind of intellectual purchase that is simply not available.

Becker hastens to caution against a familar type of misinterpretation of the evidence to which he is responding. Early economic and legal anthropologists, operating with an overly restricted concept of ownership, mistakenly concluded that numerous societies were devoid of property rights. The analogous error in respect to the improved (perfected?) anthropological accounts would be the contention that some "specific system of property rights is necessary for social organization."[16] The evidence does not support such a thesis. What the data indicate is that, while property rights exist everywhere, "what is necessary about them is *just that some exist*."[17] This leaves abundant room for philosophizing about the "specific" questions of just which type, form, or variant of property rights would be best suited to this or that social organization and about the "particular" question of how those rights ought to be distributed. The metatheoretical point that matters here, of course, is just that these are the *only* questions left open to question. Despite the remarks quoted earlier, it is the clear implication of Becker's necessity thesis that what have passed for general theories of property is one of three things: confused or disguised theories of specific and/or particular justification; metatheoretical remarks that are either demonstrably mistaken or that demonstrate the incoherence of putative general justifications; absurdities. And the practical upshot (one could hardly say the moral upshot) of the argument, one may suppose, is that we might as well resign ourselves to life with some form or other of property rights.

Let us take up the argument by considering the three elements of which it consists, namely: (a) Honoré's Wittgensteinian explication of "property" and "ownership"; (b) the claim that property rights are "found everywhere"; and (c) the inference that they are necessary to social organization.

The present commentator has no quarrel with the "Wittgensteinian" approach to the definition of ownership. Nor is he competent to question the substance of Honoré's analysis of the standard "incidents" of ownership. But does this analysis support the conclusion that property rights exist "everywhere" (whatever, exactly, is meant by that conveniently vague term)? Honoré says that his analysis is of "mature legal systems," and he leaves open the question whether it holds for societies, organizations, or whatever that do not fall into that category.[18] On the basis of extensive reading in legal and economic anthropology, Becker finds that Honoré's analysis, in only slightly modified form, does work for all of the societies discussed in those materials. Hence his claim that property rights are universal.

Our first objection to this argument concerns the conceptual verisimilitude and perspicuity of the accounts on which it is based. As noted, Becker himself stresses the distortions introduced by the inappropriate conceptualizations employed by nineteenth- and early-twentieth-century anthropologists. Those conceptualizations were inadequate, according to Becker, because they were based on an overly narrow understanding of ownership in *their own* (i.e. the anthropologists' own) societies. But what reason does Becker have for thinking that the latterly improved understandings of ownership in mature legal systems (simply granting that the anthropologists in question did employ something like Honoré's conceptualization) itself better prepares scholars to analyze societies that manifestly differ from their own in important ways? Does he have independent evidence against the possibility that one conceptual distortion has been succeeded by another?

The skepticism we are expressing is grounded in that very Wittgensteinian understanding of language from which Becker seems to be proceeding. For Wittgenstein, most concepts take their meaning from the uses to which speakers put them in the course of the activities, practices, and forms of life in which those speakers are engaged. We are not in a position to prove that concepts such as "possession," "management," "alienation," and "transmission" (which in varying forms and combinations, are among the incidents of ownership in mature legal systems) have no equivalents or close analogues among the Azande, the Zulus, the Hopi, and so forth. But a minimum of knowledge about other differences between those societies and those from which Honoré's analysis is built up is enough to generate our skepticism.

Let us nevertheless assume that analogues to these concepts are indeed to be found, albeit in a great diversity of forms and combinations, "everywhere." It is not yet clear that it follows from this assumption, especially if one is working from recognizably Wittgensteinian premises, that it is helpful or enlightening to insist that property rights are a universal phenomenon. Can we imagine Wittgenstein concluding his analysis of such concepts as "game" and "understanding" by trumpeting the generalization that games and understanding are universal phenomena? The answer is pretty clearly negative. And the reason it is negative is just that such generalizations, even if in some sense true, deflect us from the point that Wittgenstein is most anxious to establish. "[I]t is our *acting*, which lies at the bottom on the language-game [italics mine]."[19] Where the acting differs, generalizations based on linguistic or grammatical similarities are seriously misleading. Is there a universal pattern of *acting* in respect to ownership? Perhaps. But the least that must be said is that this remains to be shown.

These doubts about the universality thesis, of course, are anything but irrelevant to the necessity thesis. If property rights are not universal, then neither are they necessary. Equally, if the sense in which property rights are universal is insignificant or unenlightening, then the same will be true of the sense in which they are necessary. Because we have only suggested, not established, our objections to the universality thesis, we cannot claim that those objections prove Becker's necessity thesis false or insignificant. But then neither has Becker proved the universality thesis. Until he does so, he too is debarred from simple reliance upon it in arguing for the necessity thesis.

There is however at least one objection to the necessity thesis that is independent of the discussion thus far. Unless Becker has some heretofore unappreciated solution to the Humean principle of induction, he can hardly claim that "the data" themselves are sufficient to "indicate" that property rights are necessary to all social organizations. Even if we grant universality, necessity remains to be established.[20]

The most extended argument Becker presents for the necessity thesis is made via a passage he quotes from the sociologist Irving Hallowell. "Since [sic] valuable objects in all human societies must include, at the minimum, some objects of material culture that are employed to transform . . . raw materials . . . into consumable goods, there must be socially recognized provisions for handling the control of such elementary capital goods as well as the distribution and consumption of the goods that are produced."[21] Thus far we have an assertion of a kind familiar to readers of structural-functional sociological *theory*. Certain functions, it is alleged, must be performed *if* a society is to maintain itself; *therefore* certain structures or arrangements, which perform those functions, are necessary. Even if we waive the well-rehearsed objections to this mode of reasoning,[22] Becker's endorsement of the inference Hallowell draws from it is a truly arresting example of begging the question at issue. "Consequently," Hallowell continues, "property rights are . . . an integral part of the economic organization of any society."[23]

No doubt property rights are one familiar device for "handling the control of elementary capital goods" and for regulating the distribution of consumables. Equally, in societies for which the hypotheticals Hallowell had earlier[24] enunciated are true, property rights are "extremely fundamental." But what in this argument demonstrates that property rights are the only possible device for doing these things?

Strictly speaking, of course, the answer to this question is "nothing whatsoever." Judging from the passage Becker quotes, Hallowell had found that property rights performed this function in numerous societies and, drawing on a deeply controversial general theory, illicitly transformed an empirical generalization into a necessary truth. Whatever Hallowell may have been doing, the most likely explanation for Becker's use of the passage seems to be along the following lines. Becker is operating with a highly latitudinarian concept of ownership, one that gives plausibility — although perhaps an illicit plausibility — to the claim that property rights are universal. This concept of ownership was derived from an analysis of societies in which property rights arguably do "perform the functions" that Hallowell discusses. Thus when Becker has satisfied himself that the same concept is at work in all societies, he implies that the property rights denoted by the concept do the same job in all societies.

THE IRREDUCIBLE PLURALITY OF GENERAL JUSTIFICATORY THEORIES OF PROPERTY RIGHTS

A. Metatheoretical arguments

On its face Becker's argument under this heading stands in a con-

tradictory relationship to the arguments we have considered under
(1). If property rights are a universal and necessary feature of human
affairs, then general justificatory theories such as Locke's, Hume's,
and Mill's—to say nothing of antiproperty theories such as More's,
Marx's and Proudhon's—should be otiose and indeed absurd. Rather
than rejecting them for this reason, however, Becker accords these
theories serious philosophical attention. His objection seems to be not
that the philosophical enterprise they prosecute is a priori untenable
but simply that they have failed to bring it to its intended conclusion.

By this second line of argument, however, Becker intends to reinforce the conclusion that a truly general justificatory or disjustificatory theory is some species of impossibility. In the case of the second
argument, this result is expressed in the proposition that there is an
irreducible plurality of sound and independent justificatory theories.
Although aspiring and even pretending to entire generality (to
"dominance"), the celebrated theories of property rights do not and
could not attain this objective. Hence, as before we have no choice
but to "coordinate" partial but complementary theories as we deal
with specific and particular questions. We should also note at once
that the conclusion of this second line of argument goes importantly
beyond the first in one unsettling (from our perspective) respect. The
first argument teaches us to resign ourselves to property rights as an
ineluctable feature of our affairs. The second teaches that an indeterminate but evidently substantial array of property rights will always (and necessarily?) be justified. We find ourselves in that happy
state that only philosophy (or at least its consolations) can produce,
one in which the ineluctable coincides with the morally defensible.

How does Becker know that avowedly encompassing and dominant
theories are and must be no more than partial and complementary?
The detail of his arguments for this view consists in close, consistently
incisive analyses at two levels. Most immediately, he examines the
major extant theories of property, assessing each taken alone, and
working out the relationships among them. This discussion takes
place against the backdrop of a yet wider investigation, reported in
his earlier work,[25] of the major extant theories of moral justification
generally. The two investigations have led Becker to analogous conclusions. Just as the plurality of sound property is irreducible, so are
the three sound and independent theories of moral justification. The
proproperty arguments from labor, liberty, and utility can and must
be coordinated with one another and with what is "sound" in antiproperty arguments. At the higher level of abstraction, deontologi-

cal, teleological, and agathistic theories of moral justification can and must be coordinated. The logic of the overall scheme suggests the intriguing and ambitious program of achieving an overarching coordination between the two levels. Becker makes some suggestions along these lines, but the latest of his work known to this commentator (the paper in the present volume) moves in the equally ambitious direction taken in argument (3), that is, toward a social scientific "basis" for all theories of property. Perhaps he entertains the profoundly ambitious (and profoundly eighteenth-century) project of finding such a basis for moral argumentation *tout court*.

These conclusions challenge a range of widely received views in moral and political philosophy—perhaps most emphatically the views of the theorists on whose work he comments. It is no doubt in part for this reason that his views appear to be strongly counterintuitive. Given the radically different premises from which Hume's utilitarian defense of property and Locke's labor theory begin, how could the two theories possibly be reconciled? And how could either of them be "coordinated" with the contention that property rights of any kind are a moral outrage? At the higher level, and especially coming after a decade of assertions by deontological moralists that utilitarianism is morally bankrupt, how can Becker claim that these types of theories, as well as moral agency or virtue-and-vice theories, are not only compatible but positively complementary?

The soundness of Becker's several conclusions must of course depend finally on the particular arguments he makes for them one by one. Space will not allow dealing with the higher order arguments, and we must rest with two observations concerning them: first, they are important contributions to metaethics; second, although they are in a general way compatible with the property argument, they do not themselves demonstrate that argument. Neither can we examine the property argument in the detail that its quality invites, but in (2.b) below we comment on key points in Becker's assessment of the theories he finds sound and independent.

It must be said at once, however, that we will not understand how Becker so much as gets his program of argumentation going if we do not appreciate its relation to the position canvased under (1.a) above. This same association will prove to be crucial to the very uneasy relationship between (2) and (3), and indeed to the peculiar combination, presented by the overall theory, of modest, almost complacent descriptivism and a philosophical hubris that (given

Becker's invocation of the name) must be disturbing whatever rest Wittgenstein's shade would otherwise be enjoying.

As we have seen, "property" and "ownership" mark an extended family of elements and combinations of elements. No single theory captures or dominates this entire array. Utilitarian theory is sound as a justification for some subset of the diversity, liberty theory another, and so on. And some known forms and distributions of property are shown by antiproperty theories to be morally unacceptable. Thus the irreducible plurality of sound, independent, and presumptively equal theories is explained by the fact that the subject of those theories, what they are theories of, is itself diverse. There could be a single dominant theory only if there were a single phenomenon. As things stand (and of course as they will remain as regards the history of property to this juncture), a general theory is possible only in the weak sense of one (such as Becker's) that charts the relationship among the irreducible diversity of more limited constructs.[26]

This interpretation of (2) provides an additional perspective on the issues discussed above in respect to (1.a) We can explore these issues further by noting respects in which Becker's procedure is, and some in which it is not, recognizably Wittgensteinian in spirit. He seems to follow Wittgenstein in contending that the phenomenon of property is given or constituted by the concepts, practices, arrangements, and so forth that in fact obtain in various forms of life. Theorizing about property consists in assembling reminders about (as we might call them) these Wittgensteinian facts.[27] The vice that most commonly vitiates such theorizing is a "craving for generality"; it is the attempt to impose a pattern or uniform assessment on what is in fact a diverse array. Proceeding in this spirit, Becker insists that the diversity of the Wittgensteinian facts requires a plurality of theories.

But a plurality of theories about *what*? Does the vast array of instances that Becker has gathered under the rubric "property rights" constitute a single phenomenon in any useful sense? For purposes of establishing the universality and necessity of property rights, Becker insists that they do. But is not this move on his part a giving way to a particularly ominous instance of that characteristic impulse to philosophical error? Let us put the objection another way. Did theorists such as Locke and Hume, Mill and Marx have anything approaching Becker's entire array in mind when they argued for and against property rights? Would they or their intended audiences have regarded, for example, the uses of fallow land in primitive agricultural societies as a relevant source of support for or counter- examples to their arguments?[28] *Should* they have done so if they had been proceeding from Wittgensteinian premises?

Without claiming to have definitive answers to questions such as these, what is striking is that Becker wants to have it both ways in respect to them. For purposes of identifying the subject matter of property theory he adopts an extraordinarily encompassing concept of property. For purposes of conducting and assessing such theorizing he insists upon the sui generis, deeply and irreducibly plural character of the phenomena that fall under that concept. The combination of the two moves virtually guarantees the conclusion that a dominance solution is unobtainable. More serious, it virtually guarantees the conclusion that some property rights will be found to be justified. Whatever else might be said about them, these moves are much too debatable, much too clearly in tension with one another, to still skepticism about the institution of property rights as it has presented itself to those theorists — and their societies — with whom Becker is in fact concerned.

B. Substantive Arguments

As has been noted, in at least one respect Becker seems to accept this judgment. The arguments we have been discussing thus far are external to the particulars that make up theories such as Locke's, Hume's, Marx's, and so forth. One would have expected that his views under (2.a) would lead him either to reject these traditional theories without reference to their particulars or at least to assess them from a perspective controlled by the metaethical arguments. True, his analysis of these theories also leads him to the "irreducible plurality" conclusion. But it does so primarily on the basis of critical analysis of the particulars of major extant theories. (This is fortunate in at least one respect; even if we reject (1.c) and (2.c), we can profit from his excellent discussions of Locke, Mill et al.)

As indicated, we will limit our comments on these discussions to a few salient points. Our objective will be to suggest (we cannot hope to prove) that utilitarianism has a better claim to dominance in the justificatory theory of property than Becker allows. In the perspective announced at the outset of this paper, this conclusion is of course welcome. It is welcome, not because it itself demonstrates that no property rights can ever be justified, but because it keeps that possibility philosophically open and hence deprives such property rights as may be justified in this or that circumstance of the privileged standing that various of their defenders have attributed to them.

Of the four sound justificatory theories, two are labor theories, one is an argument from liberty, and the last is a utilitarian argument. In saying that these four arguments are sound Becker apparently means that when they are properly formulated they are subject to no *generally* convincing objections. Perhaps each of them justifies no more than a limited array of property rights. But the soundness of each of them is proof against the contention that *no* property rights of any sort can *ever* be justified. In short, Becker is claiming, quite apart from arguments (1), (2.a), and (3), that anyone who advances a categorical antiproperty argument can be demonstrated to have committed some error of reasoning.

i. Arguments from labor

In his paper in the present volume Becker states that "the Locke-Mill version of the labor theory" is sound, a conclusion he claims to have argued for in detail in his *Property Rights.*[29] As we read the latter discussion, however, it does not in fact make such an argument. It contends, and rightly in our view, that at most this theory can justify Hohfeldian liberties (as opposed to claim rights or rights in the strict sense) and indeed that there is no sound general argument for the view that people are *entitled* to *property* because of any labor they have performed.[30] He accepts, as we see just below, an argument for the principle that people sometimes *deserve something* in return for their labor. But it is entirely possible that this something will *never* be a property right. Because we find Becker's own arguments against the Locke-Mill theory convincing, we need not discuss that theory here, and we add only that Becker's arguments are very skillfully marshaled and deserve the attention of anyone who has puzzled over this curious and curiously influential theory.

The second, or "labor-desert" version of the labor theory, is of Becker's own devising. His arguments nevertheless cast considerable doubt on the theory and certainly do not demonstrate that it must be accepted as justifying at least some property rights. He begins by replacing "entitlement" by "desert," contending that the latter is "a constituent of the notion of morality per se" and cannot be questioned without "calling into question the whole enterprise of passing moral judgment on people for their conduct."[31] Granting this for purposes of the present discussion, the question then arises whether it will necessarily (must in some time and place) be the case that a property right is what one deserves for one's labor. In the formal rendition of his argument Becker puts the crucial premise as follows:

> When, in terms of the purposes of the labor, nothing but property rights in the thing produced can be considered a fitting benefit for the labor, and when the benefit provided by such rights is proportional to the value produced by the labor, the property rights are deserved.[32]

Is there conclusive reason to think that the two conditions specified by this formulation will sometimes (or at least sometime) be satisfied? With his usual candor Becker shows that those conditions are not satisfied in respect to numerous widely established and staunchly defended property rights. More important, so far as we can find he nowhere gives any reason to think that those conditions will (must be) satisfied under some circumstance or other. In the absence of such an argument (and given that the notions of "fittingness" and "proportionality" slide over notoriously difficult questions about the commensurability of values), why should antiproperty theorists such as More and Proudhon give up their insistent and explicit objections to just this premise? For them property rights can never be a fitting reward for labor — or for anything else — just because such rights are always morally unacceptable. Becker has not demonstrated the contrary.

ii. The argument from political liberty

Here is Becker's schematic formulation of the argument for property rights from political liberty:

> (1) It is a fact that human beings will try to acquire things, control them, exclude others from their use, modify them, and use them as wealth.
> (2) The effective prohibition of such activities — i.e., the elimination of private property altogether — would require a comprehensive and continuous abridgment of people's liberty which (even if it were possible to carry out) is at best unjustifiable and at worst flatly prohibited by the existence of political liberties to which people are entitled, morally.
> (3) The regulation of acquisitive activities, by what amounts to a system of property rights, is likewise required to preserve liberties to which people are entitled.
> (4) Therefore, property rights are justifiable.

This is, of course, only a *general* justification, for it does not specify what sorts of things people are entitled to own, and what sorts of property rights they are entitled to have in those things. And it makes property a derivative, rather than a fundamental, right; it assumes the prior justification of an extensive system of political liberty.[33] In his concluding discussion of this argument, Becker comments that "The crucial premise here is . . . [2], and the justifiability of a (minimal) system of political liberties is all that is required" in order to establish the soundness of this argument for property rights.[34] This comment faithfully reflects the initial discussion in chapter 6, an abbreviated defense of minimal political liberties that makes almost no mention of the right to private property as such. Thus, in this argument Becker treats the right to private property as an entailment of the argument for political liberty.

This contention is subject to a number of objections. The most basic of these is that there is a profoundly important difference between justifying Hohfeldian liberties and justifying the claim rights or rights in the strict sense of which, as Becker says elsewhere, property rights are examples. Able's Hohfeldian liberties impose nothing more on Baker than the "no-right" to contend that Able's acting on those liberties is legally or morally wrong.[35] But Able's right in the strict sense to property imposes very definite and substantial obligations on Baker. For this reason alone rights in the strict sense can never be justified in terms of liberty *simpliciter*. At a minimum the contribution they make to Able's liberty must be weighed against, and justified despite, their interference with the liberty of Baker.[36] Thus, on purely formal grounds Becker's third argument for property rights is unsound.

This first difficulty is a part, but not more than that, of the objection that antiproperty theorists have commonly made to the argument from political liberty. Leaving to one side the full range of inequalities that, as Robert Nozick persuasively argues,[37] invariably develop around property rights, the dominion that some of these give Able over all other persons is harmful and morally repugnant. Able should no more be allowed the "liberty" to acquire such dominion than he should be allowed the liberty to use physical violence against others, to libel and defame others, and so forth. True, "human beings will try to acquire things," and prohibiting them from doing so "would require a comprehensive and continuous abridgment of . . . liberty." But equally human beings will try to kill, harm, slander, and cheat others, and the prohibition of these acts abridges liberty. But most of us would not use the word "liberty" in the last sentence. And the antiproperty theorist, convinced that the disposition to "acquire things" is (a) deeply unfortunate and (b) itself an alterable consequence of the history of property relations and their illicit justification, will not use it in the sentence before. Antiproperty theorists may be mistaken in this view, but Becker's argument does nothing to demonstrate that they must be mistaken.

iii. The argument from utility

Despite his claim about the "presumptive equality" of the four sound theories of property, Becker himself accords a certain primacy to the utilitarian theory. Utilitarian arguments are "central" to justifying property rights. If arguments of this type "cannot provide at least a partial rationale for the institution, it is doubtful if anything can." A "negative result here would conflict with the attempt to justify property on other grounds — and might overwhelm those other grounds. A careful analysis of the arguments [from utility] is thus required."[38]

As indicated, we are inclined to agree with these judgments. But it should be noted at once that the judgments will be rejected out of hand by numerous theorists of property rights and of rights in general. Becker presents a balanced account and assessment of what is essentially the Humean version of the utilitarian argument for property. But although he recognizes that it is *rights* in the strict sense to property that must be justified, he never addresses the objection that utilitarianism simply has no place for the moral and political "trump" that is a right. For utilitarianism, this objection runs, the propriety of doing or having X turns on its consequences for an aggregate end state called the general or greatest happiness. Thus, rights are at most of derivative and instrumental standing; they are valuable only isofar as they contribute to the general happiness. Moreover, the decision to establish a right can represent, again at most, a judgment that doing or having X has theretofore maximized the general happiness. Because this judgment must be based entirely on, can be nothing more than, a summary of past experience, it is constantly vulnerable to revision. Thus, the notion that a right is an established claim or warrant that of certainty holds against some more or less clearly identified range of objections can have no place in the theory.

If this objection to utilitarianism is well founded, and if utilitarianism is nevertheless the *most* plausible of the general justificatory theories of property rights, we have strong support for a categorical antiproperty position. And of course the objection is well founded if one takes Bentham's doctrine to be the canonical form of utilitarianism and if one means by a right an intrinsic, natural, or inherent moral attribute that is absolute or indefeasible regardless of such allegedly heteronomizing contingencies as the beliefs and values actually held by participants in a practice and the consequences of the rights as assessed by reference to those beliefs and values. But we agree with Becker that there are no such attributes in any "useful sense" and with his related judgment that we are not in fact faced with a choice between "the rigidity and ultimate mystery of seventeenth century natural rights theory" (or, we would add, its late-twentieth century analogues) and "the ruthlessly forward-looking concerns of [certain] utilitarian and revolutionary socialist theories."[39] Moral and political orders, which are the very paradigms of practices that sustain rights, nevertheless engage in a great deal of weighing up, balancing, attending to consequences, and so forth of kinds that natural rights theory condemns as incompatible with "taking rights seriously." And numerous utilitarians for example, Hume, J. S. Mill, Henry Sidgwick, and G. E. Moore, and contemporary exponents such as Richard Brandt, Rolf Sartorious, and T. M. Scanlon—have explicitly rejected the unqualifiedly maximizing or aggregationist doctrine usually attributed to Bentham. They have insisted that there are cases in which Able's interests are more important than the supposed aggregate or cumulative interests of Baker, Charlie, and Dog. In the case of J. S. Mill, his account of rights in *Utilitarianism* and in *On Liberty* clearly depends on the view that it will sometimes be worse to support the qualitatively less important aggregate interest of Baker, Charlie, and Dog over the perhaps lonely and idiosyncratic but qualitatively vital interests of Able. And as Becker's account reminds us, David Hume, Mill, and later self-designated utilitarians have found an important place in their theories for rules and institutions and for the idea, vital to the concept of a right, that rules and institutional arrangements are of great moral import.

Of course intricate and as yet unresolved problems are involved in constructing a utilitarian theory of rights, and we cannot resolve them here. But not all of these often discussed problems are with utilitarianism. Some at least among them are with the rights — especially the rights to property — and recurrent beliefs and arguments concerning them. If property rights are intuitively objectionable and indeed dangerous, it is not necessarily a fault in utilitarianism that it gives systematic, theoretical expression to those intuitions and provides criteria and procedures for limiting the dangerous and objectionable characteristics of whatever property rights seem on balance to be justifiable.

With this thought in mind we can conclude our discussion of Becker's argument from utility. If only because of the difficulties with the other extant arguments, Becker is correct that the argument from utility is the most plausible general justification for property rights. We believe that he is also correct that this argument alters widely accepted understandings of what a property right is or should be and places narrow limits on the property rights that can be justified in the societies and polities that we know. (Despite our criticisms of Becker, and especially our perhaps overdrawn suggestion that he is complacent about property rights, it should be acknowledged that he stands as a forceful critic of views that celebrate them uncritically.) We must nevertheless quarrel with his claim that the utilitarian argument excludes (or contributes to the exclusion of) the very possibility of a sound categorical antiproperty theory. Whether hedonistic, eudaemonistic, or ideal, whether act or rule, extreme, restricted, or some other variety, all utilitarian theories make the justification of property rights depend finally on their satisying the principle of utility. Because it is contingent whether property rights (or rights of any sort, or any practice or institution) do in fact satisfy that principle, it is always possible that they can be shown not to do so.[40] However deeply we may be socialized or encultured into our practices of property rights, however philosophically satisfied we may now be concerning their justifiability, the possibility always remains open that we will come to see that they are moral abominations which should be eradicated root and branch from our affairs. Not the least of the advantages of utilitarianism as a general theory of property rights is that it allows us to justify certain limited rights to property without depriving us, as Becker would apparently do, of this possibility.

THE MORAL BASIS OF PROPERTY RIGHTS

By the moral basis of property rights Becker means "a set of facts about the human condition: facts about human needs, propensities, and behavior from which (together with judgments about values, duties and virtues) moral arguments . . . can be built up."[41] These facts are to be taken over by philosophy from the several social sciences in order to provide a foundation for the moral arguments, which it is the task of philosophers to develop.[42] Such facts would undergird

Becker's argument (1) by identifying the (presumably causal) forces or agencies that explain the universality and necessity of property rights. They would both deepen and extend his argument (2), the first by providing "non-arbitrary starting points"[43] for the several sound theories of general justification, and the second by helping to "coordinate" the several sound theories in the course of applying them to specific and particular questions.

One feels a strong temptation to amplify Becker's own admissions about the weaknesses of social science. But because most of his own inferences from it are thus far tentative and conjectural, we resist this temptation and conclude with two further remarks about the logic of the relationships between his argument (3) and his arguments (2) and (1).

The most obvious difficulty concerns the relationship between the idea of an irreducible plurality of independent theories and the idea of a factual moral basis for such theories. If Becker succeeds in establishing such a moral basis, the plurality of independent theories will have been eliminated at least in the sense that henceforth all sound theories will be built up from the same factual base. It is presumably for this reason that the moral basis of the several theories will help us to coordinate them as we decide specific and particular questions. To put the point polemically, establishing a moral basis for property theory will give us, if not a dominant general theory, at least a single foundation for all theories.

There is a further point in this same connection. The conjectures that Becker has thus far advanced strongly suggest that the moral basis will establish the dominance of one of the existing justificatory theories in at least one additional sense: some one theory will be shown to be exclusively correct for a range of questions to which all of the theories had previously addressed themselves in a sound manner. (His discussion of the "labor principle" and the support it seems to afford the labor-desert theory is the clearest instance.)[44] It is of course possible that Becker advanced the irreducible plurality thesis as no more than provisionally true — as true only until a proper moral basis had been developed. But he does not say this, and in general he does not attend sufficiently to the implications of argument (3) for argument (2).

This argument (3) poses a related and wider problem. Earlier we criticized Becker for treating as universal a concept of property rights that is in fact drawn from, and may well be distinctive to, mature legal systems. A set of conceptual facts that have "Wittgensteinian" standing in some number of societies is uncritically adopted as a basis for analyzing relations in societies in which these concepts (may) have no such standing. Argument (3) presents the same kind of difficulty in aggravated form. Social scientific facts are to provide the starting points for moral argumentation about property relations wherever they occur — that is, regardless of the setting in which they are encountered and experienced. Of course numerous social scientists will have no difficulty with this idea. They proceed from the Durkheimian premise that characteristics that differentiate societies and social contexts, especially the "Wittgensteinian" concepts that make up "the words of everyday language," are superficial, confused, and indeed ideological. The job of the social scientist is to penetrate beneath such "confused impressions of the crowd" to the "social facts." The latter, as Becker seems to agree at least in part, explain and make possible uniform, objective assessments of the apparently diverse realities of social life.[45]

This understanding of social inquiry is deeply controversial in philosophical circles. It has been condemned with particular vigor by avowedly Wittgensteinian theorists such as Peter Winch, Norman Malcolm, and A. I. Melden, philosophers who would surely insist that Becker's third argument is entirely incompatible with the Wittgensteinian assumptions that apparently inform his argument (1.a).[46] True, this position is widely thought to be extreme. Other philosophers of social science argue that "social scientific facts" can and for some purposes should be combined with "Wittgensteinian facts" in explanatory constructs and theories.[47] But these more latitudinarian theorists nevertheless place a good deal more weight on the delicate and indeed problematic character of such conceptual amalgamations than do the social scientists on whom Becker relies.

It is, in short, something of an understatement to say that complex philosophical issues surround Becker's third argument. As with other issues that have emerged in the course of our exploration, we can only raise, not resolve these difficult questions. We conclude by noting a related but further complexity that presents itself with particular urgency owing to his claim that argument (3) contributes to his goal of banishing categorical antiproperty theory.

Justifying and disjustifying property rights is a practical activity; it aims to convince the participants in moral practices to accept or reject certain arrangements. Whatever their other merits, arguments cast in a conceptualization that is alien to participants will not, indeed cannot, bring about this result. When Becker has satisfied his philosophical audience that Hallowell's structural functionalism, Maslow's need hierarchy, Ekeh's chain generalized exchanges, and so forth are compatible with a meaningful conceptualization of property relations, it will remain to make these notions available to participants in those relations and to convince those participants that arguments based on them deserve their moral allegiance. Until these further steps have been successfully taken, participants disposed to a deep skepticism about property rights will have been given no reason to give up that skepticism. Happily, such is the condition in which they are left by Becker's entire discussion.

NOTES

1. Ronald Dworkin, *Taking Rights Seriously* (Cambridge: Harvard Univ. Press, 1977).
2. William Blackstone, *Commentaries on the Laws of England,* book II, chap. I, par. 2.
3. Lawrence C. Becker, *Property Rights* (London: Routledge & Kegan Paul, 1977), p. 27; hereafter Becker, 1977
4. Blackstone, op. cit.
5. Robert Nozick, *Anarchy, State and Utopia* (New York: Basic Books, 1974)
6. Becker, 1977; Becker, "The Moral Basis of Property Rights," chap. 8 of this volume; Becker, *On Justifying Moral Judgments* (New York: Humanities Press, 1973) hereafter Becker, 1973.
7. Becker, pp. 187–88, above.
8. Ibid., p. 196.
9. Ibid., p. 188.
10. Ibid.
11. A. M. Honoré, "Ownership," in A. G. Guest, ed., *Oxford Essays in Jurisprudence,* First Series (Oxford: Clarendon, 1961).
12. Cf. Ludwig Wittgenstein, *Philosophical Investigations* (New York: Macmillan, 1953), vol. 2, p. xi.
13. Becker, chap. 8, p. 192, above.
14. Ibid., p. 199.
15. Ibid., italics added.
16. Ibid.
17. Ibid., p. 225. Italics Becker's.
18. Honoré, op. cit., pp. 108–9.
19. Ludwig Wittgenstein, *On Certainty* (Oxford: Basil Blackwell, 1969), par. 204.
20. At one point Becker does simply equate the two theses. "What counts as a necessary element in social organization is of course a matter of some debate. But it is enough for my purposes to take just those which are universal (so far as we know) in societies which have survived for several generations." Becker, above, n.6, fn. 33. Just why this assimilation of the two theses is allowed by his purposes is not explained. But

if we were to take this passage seriously the argument for the necessity thesis would amount to an elementary mistake in reasoning.

21. Quoted in Becker, above, p. 199.

22. See, for example, among many others: Ralf Dahrendorf, *Class and Class Conflict in Industrial Society* (Stanford: Stanford Univ. Press, 1959); Lewis Coser, *The Functions of Social Conflict* (London, 1956); Max Black, ed., *The Social Theories of Talcott Parsons* (Englewood Cliffs, N.J.: Prentice-Hall, 1961); Ernest Nagel, *The Structure of Science* (London: Routledge & Kegan Paul, 1956); Brian Barry, *Sociologists, Economists and Democracy* (Chicago: Univ. of Chicago Press, 1978).

23. Becker, above, p. 199.

24. See the first part of the passage that Becker quotes, ibid.

25. Becker, 1973.

26. Perhaps we should note what Becker's argument, on this reading of it, does *not* amount to. It is not, for example, the contention that the several theories are equally sound in the weak sense that in fact they all reach the correct conclusion concerning some aspects of property. For example, it is not like John Rawls's concession that utilitarians generally reach (although for the wrong reasons) the correct moral conclusions about slavery. Nor is it like the view about punishment, advanced by H. L. A. Hart and Anthony Quinton, according to which a correct theory of punishment must be a combination of utilitarian and retributive elements. If there is an analogue to Becker's position in the recent literature it is probably H. L. A. Hart's argument that morality consists in a number of distinct spheres or "dimensions." Thus, we need some species of deontological theory to cope with "right" and "wrong," "rights" and "justice," a utilitarian theory to handle "good," "interests," "welfare," "the common good." See John Rawls, *A Theory of Justice* (Cambridge: Harvard Univ. Press, 1971); H. L. A. Hart, *Punishment and Responsibility* (Oxford: Oxford Univ. Press, 1968); Anthony Quinton, "On Punishment," in Peter Laslett, ed., *Philosophy Politics and Society,* First Series (Oxford: Basil Blackwell, 1956); H. L. A. Hart, "Are There Any Natural Rights?" *Philosophical Review* 64 (1955), pp. 175–91.

27. Cf. the epigraph to Becker, chap. 8, above.

28. Cf. ibid., p. 205.

29. Ibid., p. 193.

30. See Becker, 1977, pp. 32–48, esp. p. 44.

31. Ibid., p. 49.

32. Ibid., p. 54

33. Ibid., p. 75.

34. Ibid., p. 102.

35. See my *The Practice of Rights* (London and New York: Cambridge Univ. Press, 1976) chap. 2.

36. See ibid., Introduction, chaps. 2, 7, and 8.

37. Nozick, op. cit., esp. pp. 160–64.

38. Becker, 1977, p. 159.

39. Ibid., p. 4.

40. Becker in effect concedes this at one point in his discussion of Hume. "Therefore, a system of property rights is necessary (*or very nearly so*) if individuals are to achieve (the means to) even a reasonable degree of happiness." Ibid., p. 58; italics mine.

41. Becker, above, p. 188.

42. Ibid., pp. 188–189.

43. See ibid., p. 197; and Becker, 1973, chaps. 7 and 8 for his discussion of this notion.

44. Becker, pp. 204–05.

45. See Emile Durkheim, *Suicide,* esp. the Introduction (Glencoe: The Free Press, 1951); and *The Rules of Sociological Method* (Glencoe: The Free Press, 1938), chap. 2.

46. See Peter Winch, *The Idea of a Social Science* (London: Routledge & Kegan Paul, 1958); Norman Malcolm, *Dreaming* (London: Routledge & Kegan Paul, 1959); A. I. Melden, *Free Action* (London: Routledge & Kegan Paul, 1961).

47. See esp. Alasdair MacIntyre, "The Antecedents of Human Action," in B. Williams and A. Montefiore, eds., *British Analytic Philosophy* (London: Routledge & Kegan Paul, 1966).

10

SLAVERY, SOCIALISM, AND PRIVATE PROPERTY

HILLEL STEINER *

If slavery is not wrong, nothing is wrong.

— Abraham Lincoln

Upon what grounds can slavery be condemned *categorically*? The vicissitudes of the continuing debate on the economic efficiency of slavery, in both the ancient and the modern world — and even when, as is but recently the case, the slave's own living standard is subsumed in the social calculus — only serve to remind us of what we already know: that social utility, however reckoned, affords no foundation for the unqualified rejection of any institution or practice. Perhaps, then, the cruelty and indignity attendant upon slavery can be pressed into service for this purpose. But again, although the concept of the "happy slave" or the "noble slave" may be only an invention of slavery's apologists and a heuristic device used by moral and political philosophers, this phrase is nevertheless not a contradiction in terms. Its instanceability disqualifies the slave's humiliation as a firm basis for the universal condemnation of that "peculiar institution."

We advance a little way in the desired direction if we say that slavery is wrong because it deprives persons of liberty. But only a little way, because it is an awkward but undeniable fact that the abolition of slavery also deprives persons of liberty. Slavery is a legal condition.

*This paper would contain many more errors of judgment and presentation were it not for the advice and criticism I have received from Patrick Day, John Gray, Ian Steedman, Robert van der Veen, Ursula Vogel, and the editors of this volume.

Its abolition requires a legal enactment and, more specifically, an enactment abrogating certain property rights. In what sense is such an enactment liberating? Clearly, it has the effect of extending the range of actions which the emancipated person may perform or forbear without legal interference from others. In extending to him rights enjoyed by nonslaves, it expands the sphere in which his conduct is subject only to his own determination. Yet evidently the abolition of this legal condition, in abrogating certain rights, must be understood to curtail the liberty enjoyed by some members of society. For the range of legally unobstructable actions open to slaveowners is necessarily and drastically reduced by such measures. Sharing an enthusiasm for personal liberty, they might well fail to see the elimination of their property rights as in any way a contribution to its advancement.

Might we say, then, that abolition can be understood to expand the *total amount* of liberty in society and, therefore, that a conclusive justification for the indictment of slavery resides in its being restrictive of that magnitude? But again, there is no very straightforward sense in which an increase in some persons' liberty, secured at the expense of a reduction in others', can be said to entail a net increase in liberty. Perhaps those who have seen slave emancipation as expanding total personal liberty in society, have believed it to have this consequence on the grounds that some kinds of liberty are more important than others. However, such a belief unwarrantedly equates "more important liberty" with "more liberty." Moreover, the equation of "more important liberty" with "more liberty" raises the thorny and not irrelevant issue of "more important to whom?"[1] And in suggesting that different kinds of liberty can be morally graded, it reintroduces the element of contingency into the grounds for the rejection of slavery that, as was indicated in the first paragraph above, deprives such rejections of any categorical status. For if the ranges of action opened to emancipated slaves are considered more important than those available to unexpropriated slaveowners, this must be because that former set of activities is expected to produce more desirable results than the latter. But such expectations, like any others, need not be fulfilled.

Thus Isaiah Berlin, quoting the epigram "Freedom for the pike is death for the minnows," has interpreted it to mean that "the liberty of some must depend on the restraint of others."[2] The concept of liberty, as has been argued elsewhere, is such that it makes no sense to speak of it as being enlarged or diminished—much less, maximized or minimized—within a society, but only as being distributed in a certain way.[3] Nor, therefore, can liberty be said to be accorded or denied priority by any particular set of social institutions.

Nevertheless, many writers and political figures have held that the minimization of noncontractual legal restrictions on individual liberty—slavery being the paradigm case—is the essential mark of a free society. And it is this belief that is usually identified as the distinguishing feature of classical liberalism. The progressive transition from "status to contract" is, for instance, the central theme of the Whig interpretation of history. Maurice Cranston expresses what is unquestionably a common view when he says, "By definition, a liberal is a man who believes in liberty."[4] But if, as I am suggesting, we can assess societies only in terms of their interpersonal distributions of liberty and not in terms of their aggregate amounts of liberty, then it is plain that H. L. A. Hart is much nearer the mark in claiming:

> that the principle that all men have an equal right to be free, meagre as it may seem, is probably all that the political philosophers of the liberal tradition need have claimed to support any programme of action even if they have claimed more.[5]

Certainly the historic tasks of liberalism, consisting in the abolition of the legal privileges and disabilities associated with slavery and serfdom in their developed and vestigial forms, can readily be understood as programs for realizing *equal* liberty, and were so understood by writers such as Locke, Kant, and the early Spencer in setting out the implications of their natural rights positions.[6]

I shall take it, then, that the principle entitling each person to equal liberty furnishes the grounds for a categorical condemnation of slavery. What follows is an attempt to explore the implications of this principle and to display the requirements it imposes on any legal order that embodies it. Hart, in the passage quoted above, describes this principle as being of "meagre" appearance. I shall try to show that it is neither quite so meagre as it may seem, nor is its prescriptive imposition exhausted by the items characteristically found on classical liberal agenda.[7]

Legal systems consist essentially of enforceable rules and, therefore, consitute sets of rights and correlative duties. To apply a normative standard—such as the equal liberty principle—to a legal system is to attempt to ascertain whether the set of rights constituted by that system's rules conforms to the requirements of that standard.

Rights are a certain kind of claim that individuals may make one against another. Like any other term, the word "rights" has certain logical properties such that, if a claim lacks those properties or possesses properties incompatible with them, it cannot be a right. And if it cannot be a right, it cannot be constituted by the rules of a legal system.

One property of rights is that they can be exercised. We speak of persons exercising their rights or of being prevented by others from doing so. A right thus denotes a sphere of action, a domain within which the right holder may act—or compel others to act—as he chooses, and must not suffer interference by others with the execution of his choices. This fact about the concept of "a right" allows us to infer a criterion for assessing the coherence of a set of rights, that is, a criterion for determining whether the prescriptive impostions of a rule or set of rules can intelligibly be called rights: *a set of rights must be such that it is logically impossible for one person's exercise of his rights within that set to interfere with another person's exercise of his rights within that same set.* [8] I do not, of course, mean to suggest that our systems of, say, legal rights meet this requirement in any simple and straightforward way. If they did, and if there were no dispute about the facts of the cases in question, our courts would presumably be empty of all persons except those appearing to be sentenced on uncontested charges. Rather the point is that, in adjudicating between opposing claims, the court is determining which contestant was within his rights and which was not. [9] The court cannot find for both the plaintiff and the defendant on a single charge. Thus, where one person's rightful action can interfere with another's rightful action, the underlying structure of rights is incoherent inasmuch as it is constituted by rules that are, by implication, mutually inconsistent and to that extent prescriptively meaningless. The rules of such a system imply, of one and the same act, that it is both permissible and impermissible.

Hence the characteristics of a set of mutually consistent rights-constituting rules are discovered by considering the conditions under which different persons' actions cannot interfere one with another. All actions consist in some kind of motion: the passage of some body from one place to another, the displacement of some material substance from one portion of physical space to another. Interference by one individual's action with another's occurs if, and only if, at least one of the material or spatial components of the one action is identical with one of the material or spatial components of the other ac-

248   HILLEL STEINER

tion. Let us call the material and spatial components of an action its *physical components*. It follows that one individual's action cannot interfere with another's if, and only if, none of their respective physical components is identical. A rule or set of rules assigning the possession or exclusive use of each particular physical object to particular individuals, will, if universally adhered to, exclude the possibility of any individual's actions interfering with those of another in any respect. Such property rules would thus assign, to individuals, ranges of permissible and inviolable actions — rights — composed of their uses of their allotted bundles of physical objects. And the set of rights thereby prescribed would satisfy the previously stated condition of being coherent, inasmuch as the exercise of any one of them could not constitute an interference with the exercise of any other of them.[10]

Our problem is thus one of delineating the basic features of a set of rights embodying the principle of equal liberty. And it is to this theoretical task that classical liberalism has preeminently addressed itself. As was suggested above, however, liberals have failed to trace out fully the implications of the equal liberty principle. Correctly believing that the minimization of noncontractual legal restrictions (on the kinds of activities individuals may pursue) is a *necessary* condition of equal liberty, many of them have mistakenly assumed that it is also a sufficient condition of that state of affairs. In consequence, much laissez-faire thinking of the eighteenth and nineteenth centuries, as well as much current writing in that tradition, betray an erroneous if understandable view of the kind of juridical framework required to realize equal liberty. We *do* find, in the work of Locke, Kant, Spencer, and latterly Nozick, attempts to grapple with the difficulty presently to be examined. And some of these attempts are acute and painstaking indeed. But none of them is successful in closing what remains a serious hiatus in the liberal argument — an omission that can be understood to have been made good by arguments offered from a putatively opposed moral and political commitment.

What is the nature of a set of property rights embodying the principle of equal liberty? One kind of property right that this evidently entails — and that has historically been taken to be so entailed — is each person's title to his or her (physiologically) own body. Having a right to a body means, as with a right to any object, being entitled to the possession or exclusive use of that body. Thus Nozick:

> The central core of the notion of a property right in X, relative
> to which other parts of the notion are to be explained, is the
> right to determine what shall be done with X.[11]

Being entitled to the use of a body means, as with an entitlement to
any animate object, being entitled to the *labor* of that body. A slave
is a slave inasmuch as he lacks any such right.[12] But one's body cannot constitute the whole of one's domain of equal liberty, since, while
the body or parts of it must comprise some of the physical components of any of one's actions, it necessarily cannot be the only such
component. Thus, individuals' entitlements under the equal liberty
principle must extend to objects external to their bodies. It is the formulation of this aspect of their entitlements that has traditionally
given rise to issues of considerable complexity.

Specifically, the difficulty has been to formulate an entitlement to
nonhuman physical objects that is universal in its incidence *and* that
does not have the logical effect of noncontractually conferring the
ownership of (part or all of) one person's labor upon another. Thus,
Nozick has rightly observed that most commonly proposed principles
of distributive justice

> institute (partial) ownership by others of people and their ac-
> tions and labor. These principles involve a shift from the classi-
> cal liberals' notion of self-ownership to a notion of (partial)
> property rights in *other* people.[13]

Any distributive principle that, in making noncontractual assign-
ments of property to individuals, either restricts the kinds of use to
which it (and it alone) may be put by them or confiscates and reas-
signs the results of those uses, paradoxically implies that what belongs to one person by right may be disposed of by another by right
and, in particular, that some have a right to the persons of others.[14]

For these reasons, many laissez-faire theorists have drawn the conclusion that the distributive impositions of equal liberty cannot be
such as to allow the permissibility—much less the necessity—of regulating individuals' nonforcibly acquired property, or of confiscating
and redistributing objects with which they have "mixed their labor."
To reject this conclusion is to affirm that some have a noncontractual
title to the fruits of others' labor, hence to the labor embodied in

those objects, and thus by extension to the persons whose labor that is.[15] This is tantamount to affirming the permissibility of slavery. It is these considerations which have led writers such as Locke, Kant, Spencer, and Nozick to adopt the view that the only kind of objects to which the strictly distributive requirements of the equal liberty principle *do* apply are those that do not embody human labor: namely, natural resources.[16] However, the accounts offered by these and other writers, concerning the nature of these requirements, differ significantly.

Indeed the "land question," as it came to be called, considerably exercised liberal and radical thinkers from the late eighteenth until the early twentieth century. But it was gradually submerged beneath the ascendancy of utilitarian influences in economics specifically, and the optimizing claims of laissez-faire theory generally. Utilitarianism's eschewal of natural rights and, in particular, neoclassical economics' rejection of the earlier classical view—that there are theoretically important asymmetries between the conditions respectively governing different production factors' effects on the creation and allocation of values—fostered the undue neglect that, until very recently, has been accorded to the problem of what *original* (i.e. non-contractual) entitlements or endowments rightfully accrue to all individuals. Often implicit in such neglect was an acceptance of the legitimacy of whatever property titles currently happened to enjoy legal sanction, that is, regardless of whether they derived from forcible acquisition.

But the limitations of neoclassical economics, and especially its incapacity to identify welfare-maximizing or productively efficient allocations *that are not distribution relative*[17]—as well as the familiar and related inability of utilitarianism to underwrite any form of personal inviolability—have lately generated renewed interest among liberals in theories of just distribution and, therefore, in the question of what it is that each individual is originally entitled to. As was noted above, natural rights thinkers have been at one in asserting that these original entitlements pertain to natural resources, but they have differed in their characterizations of such entitlements. Thus, we are offered the following diverse interpretations of the kind of right involved: for a historically limited time, each person was entitled to "as much and as good" natural resources as others (Locke); an original community of land gives way to unlimited private titles through positive personal acts of occupancy (Kant); each person has an equal title to the land by virtue of his equal share in society which owns it (Spencer); each person may appropriate unlimited amounts of natural resources, provided he compensates others for any net loss of well-being they incur as a result of their loss of liberty to use the appropriated object (Nozick). In each case, except that of Spencer, the private title thereby acquired is held to be one to an object that can rightfully be transformed or transferred only as its appropriator chooses,[18] and thus constitutes a permanent bequeathable property right.

It was earlier remarked that liberals are mistaken in believing the traditional injunctions of laissez-faire to prescribe the sufficient condition of equal liberty. The efforts of natural right thinkers to make good the implied ommission — by supplying an account of original appropriative rights — were described as acute but, in the event, unsuccessful. Hence it is to this desideratum that reference was made in reporting a serious hiatus in the liberal argument. In the remainder of this paper I shall try to show (1) why the attempts of liberal writers to eliminate this hiatus have failed, and (2) the kind of account which may be adequate to this task.

Consider, first, Locke's construction of individuals' original rights. The claim that for a limited (early) historical period each person was entitled to appropriate a quantitatively and qualitatively similar collection of natural resources is open to the unanswerable objection — noted by Nozick — that a right of historically limited validity and, thus, of less than universal incidence, cannot be constituted by any set of moral rules that extend the same kinds of right to all persons. The titles thereby established can preclude historically later persons from exercising the same kind of right. Hence the set of rights constituted by Locke's rule fails the test of coherence outlined previously. The same criticism applies to Kant's even more unbounded right of first occupancy, which betrays a rather uncharacteristically slavish adoption of the contemporary conventions of German jurisprudence and of the positive provisions of Roman law from which they derived. Thus, Spencer observes:

> For if *one* portion of the earth's surface may justly become the possession of an individual, and may be held by him for his sole use and benefit, as a thing to which he has an exclusive right, then *other* portions of the earth's surface may be so held; and eventually the *whole* of the earth's suface may be so held. . . . Observe now the dilemma to which this leads. Supposing the entire habitable globe to be so enclosed, it follows that if the land-

owners have a valid right to its surface, all who are not landowners, have no right at all to its surface. Hence, such can exist on
the earth by sufferance only. They are all trespassers. Save by
the permission of the lords of the soil, they can have no room for
the soles of their feet. Nay, should the others think fit to deny
them a resting-place, these landless men might equitably be ex-
pelled from the earth altogether. . . . it is manifest that an exclusive possession of the soil necessitates an infringement of the
law of equal freedom. For men who cannot "live and move and
have their being" without the leave of others, cannot be equally
free with those others. [19]

Spencer's view that each person is entitled to an equal share of natural resources — a right exercised through his equal membership in society — avoids the difficulties besetting Locke's and Kant's formulations, but raises other questions to be examined presently.

Nozick's revision of the Lockean construction also fails, but its failure has the merit of helping to clarify the basic difficulty in specifying individuals' original entitlements and, thereby, indicating the direction in which a solution to this problem may be sought. Nozick
suggests that what is required for an appropriation of natural resources to be rightful is that the appropriator must compensate all
others who are thereby deprived of the level of well-being they might
otherwise have expected to attain. This proviso generates a series of
conceptual problems among which are: (1) that the compensation
owed is logically indeterminable due to the proviso being circular, inasmuch as nonappropriators' net loss of well-being is not identifiable
independently of the amount of compensation owed them;[20] (2) that
Nozick's suggested index of well-being — market prices — is distribution relative and thus cannot consistently be treated as a parameter
for determining the very distributive entitlements of which it is necessarily a function;[21] and (3) that market prices cannot in any case be
taken to represent every person's valuation of every object, without
rendering inexplicable why people ever engage in market exchange.[22]

More interestingly, Nozick's proviso, in requiring that compensation be paid out of their holdings, imposes restrictions on what owners may do with their nonforcibly acquired property, and licenses
confiscation of it. Thus, as he concedes, his proviso on appropriation
dictates noncontractual restrictions on the freedom to dispose of
one's holdings — precisely that freedom that lies at the heart of laissez-faire doctrine.[23] Finally however, this complex proviso fails to es-

cape the very objection with which Nozick initially taxes Locke and
that motivates his revision of Locke's formulation. For there appears
to be no way in which the compensation proviso can be interpreted so
as to yield a right of historically unlimited validity. This is because an
appropriator can neither know, nor therefore compensate for, the
loss of well-being incurred — in consequence of their being deprived
of the use of the appropriated object — by persons who do not yet exist. For Nozick, as for Locke, the incidence of appropriative right is
unavoidably confined to historically earlier individuals. As such, it
cannot form an element of a coherent set of rights and it cannot be
consistent with the requirements of equal liberty.

It is not unilluminating to reflect upon what it is about the "human condition" that renders so intractable the problem of formulating an original entitlement of universal incidence. If the world in
which we live were (self-contradictorily) one of unlimited natural resources, there would be no difficulty about applying Locke's simple
"as much and as good" requirement over an unlimited span of time
and, thus, on a universal basis. Indeed, that requirement would be
superfluous. That no world can be one of unlimited natural resources is painfully apparent to us today, confronted as we are on all
sides by pollution and raw material shortages, to say nothing of the
prospect of general ecological disaster. On the other hand, that this
necessary truth may have been less than fully apprehended by earlier
liberal writers is perhaps indicated in Locke's hesitantly extenuatory
remark that "in the beginning all the World was America;"[24] in some
classical economists' optimistic classification of clean air and water as
"free gifts" of nature; and in the utterly extravagant claim of that
nineteenth-century popularizer of laissez-faire doctrines, Harriet
Martineau, that

> As the materials of nature appear to be inexhaustible, and as
> the supply of labour is continually progressive, no other limits
> can be assigned to the operations of labour than those of human
> intelligence. And where are the limits of human intelligence?[25]

Their entertainment of such beliefs renders more understandable, as
was earlier observed, the erroneous conception entertained by many
laissez-faire theorists of the juridical framework required to confer
equal liberty upon each individual: namely, the conception that only
the right of self-ownership and the absence of any (other) noncontractual restrictions on conduct are necessary. Owning oneself, one

could proceed to "mix one's labor" with any amount of natural resources without running the risk of thereby depriving others of the
same liberty.[26] Such a belief readily licenses, if it does not necessitate,
the attribution of poverty to idleness—an attribution that, viewed in
this context, betokens little of the inhumanity and self-serving hypoc-
risy with which its subscribers have frequently been charged.

If we are sadder and wiser than some of our forebears concerning
the exhaustibility of natural resources, there is nevertheless an alternative—if equally unwarranted—hypothesis under which the Lockean requirement could constitute a nonenslaving original right of
universal incidence. Some brief consideration of this condition will
also help to shed light on the nature of our problem and on the con-
traints governing its solution. Suppose that the membership of the
class of persons were historically constant in identity and, therefore,
in number. In this circumstance, and even allowing that natural resources are limited, it would in principle be possible for Locke's rule
to apply universally. Each person would be originally entitled to—
and could rightfully mix his labor with—a collection of natural resources such that a quantitatively and qualitatively similar collection
was left for every other person. Having acquired his equal share of resources, each person would be entitled to dispose of them as he
wished and in the absence of any forcible interpersonal transfers,
each person's holdings would at all times be in conformity with the
universal enjoyment of the right of self-ownership.

But this supposition of constant identity is (contingently?) untrue.
Consider, then, another contrary-to-fact condition under which the
Lockean requirement could operate to create a right of the requisite
kind. Let us now suppose, not that all persons are at all times con-
temporaneously existing beings, but rather that the total number of
persons who are yet to exist is always knowable. In this circumstance,
too, the Lockean rule could assign determinable natural resource entitlements to all individuals. Again, however, the supposition is
groundless, and not merely because this datum was unavailable to
our ancestors. For it is true that such a datum could be, and could
have been, knowable in the circumstance of an appropriately designed and *enforced* population control program. But this possibility
is irrelevant here since any such program would necessarily violate
existing persons' rights of self-ownership—that right which is presupposed by any right to nonhuman objects. Not owning themselves,
slaves are logically debarred from owning anything else.

A final and more complex counterfactual assumption will serve to

complete our delineation of the source of the difficulty. Imagine that
the membership of the class of persons, though neither constant nor
(numerically) knowable, is divided into an indefinite number of generations, which, however—and unlike human generations as we
know them—do not overlap one another in time. That is, imagine
that successive human generations are serially ordered in the same
manner as generations of agricultural crops and that the members of
any one generation share no element of contemporaneity with the
members of any other generation.[27] The pertinence of this supposition is as follows. If all existing rights holders initially confront the
same supply of natural resources at the same time, the Lockean rule
would constitute an original right of universal incidence. Each person would be entitled to an equal share of whatever natural resources
were left. Nor would the exhaustibility of natural resources pose a
problem for this rule in respect of the original entitlements of members of later generations. For the assumption of completely nonconcurrent generations allows us to extend the jurisdiction of this rule. It
was previously noted that natural rights thinkers believed that individuals' original rights—the rights they possess noncontractually—
could pertain only to natural resources. This is because any original
entitlement to man-made things would confer upon some individuals
a noncontractual title to the labor and, thereby, to the persons of
others. It would thus violate the requirement of equal liberty and
constitute slavery. But it would seem beyond dispute that dead men
cannot be slaves. When one has ceased to exist, one is, so to speak,
liberated from the danger of having one's liberty curtailed. And so
the noncontractual assignment to others, of the titles to those objects
that embody a deceased individual's labor, cannot be said to constitute an augmentation of their liberty at the expense of a diminution
in his. It cannot be said to violate the equal liberty principle. Now, in
a world of entirely non-concurrent generations, the collection of objects that initially confronts all existing rights holders at the same
time consists of whatever natural resources remain *and* of man-made
objects embodying the labor of only deceased individuals. A right to
an equal portion of *all* these objects on the part of each rights holder
would at once be a right of universal incidence and one that does not
assign to some a noncontractual title to the labor of others, since
there are no "others."

The immediate objection that might be raised against this argument is that deceased persons may have bequeathed their possessions
to members of the subsequent generation and hence that any non-

contractual allocation of these objects entails a forcible violation of
the right that owners have to dispose of their property as they wish.
Indeed, we are all familiar with Burke's view — a view entailed by this
objection — that the dead can and do have rights against the living.
Clearly, this claim raises questions of far greater complexity than can
satisfactorily be handled here. But it seems to me that there is at least
one consideration that counts — and counts decisively — against its acceptance. This consideration arises out of the requirements of the
equal liberty principle itself. For any individuals who have rights
against one another are necessarily encumbered with duties to on
another. What duties, then, do the dead owe to the living? Is it possible for them to act in dereliction of such duties? Suppose there can
be such duties and such derelictions. In any case, one thing is certain: the equal liberty principle imposes upon all rights holders the
duty to deprive no one of his original entitlement. If the dead remain
rights holders, how must they act — or, more precisely, how must they
have acted — to fulfill this duty? Presumably, they owe it to each subsequent (as well as current) rights holder to insure that the supply of
natural resources available for his appropriation is as great as that
which was available to each of them. They have a duty to appropriate no more than would leave such a remainder. But we have already
seen that the condition for this remainder to be knowable is that the
number of subsequent rights holders be knowable. And we have already noted that this condition cannot be fulfilled. Members of earlier generations cannot fulfill a duty to respect the original entitlements of their posterity because there can be no such duty. It follows
that deceased persons are not part of the network of rights holders
comprehended by the principle of equal liberty, that this principle
cannot sustain any right of bequest, that the dead can have no rights
against the living. Their possessions, embodying their labor, are as
eligible to constitute the original entitlements of others as are unap-
propriated natural resources. [28]

This finding, however, avails us little in our quest for a nonenslaving right of universal incidence, once we relax our assumption that
human generations are entirely nonconcurrent. The foregoing argument — that the principle of equal liberty sustains no right of bequest — was, of course, constructed independently of that assumption
and its validity is not affected by an admission of the fact that successive generations do share some element of contemporaneity. But the
relaxation of the assumption of nonconcurrence does throw back into
question the identity of the kinds of object which can permissibly

constitute each individual's original entitlement. We cannot now include man-made objects *simpliciter*, since, apart from the irrelevant fact that these are already owned by the living persons, many or all of them can embody the labor of living persons.

With the relaxation of this third counterfactual assumption, we appear to have exhausted the range of alternative possible circumstances in which an original right—bearing the features required by the equal liberty principle—can be formulated along Lockean or semi-Lockean lines: that is, along lines that confer on each person a noncontractual title to a particular bundle of objects. The aspects of the human condition that render the problem so intractable consist in the indefinite reproducibility of persons and the nonreproducibility of natural resources. If either of these conditions did not obtain, our problem would be soluble along Lockean lines. Because they do obtain, most attempts to formulate individuals' original entitlements have consisted either in (1) assigning original rights to things to only some persons (classical liberalism), or (2) assigning original rights to things to all persons, but the rights thereby assigned dictate the constant redistribution—or disassignment—of assigned things and their manufactured derivatives, and thus noncontractually confer the ownership of some living persons' labor on others (various other moral and politiical theories). Both formulations are inconsistent with the principle of equal liberty, since the first lacks universality and the second underwrites slavery.

An indication of the direction in which a solution to these difficulties is to be sought is, I believe, to be found in the proposal offered by the early Herbert Spencer. Although, in his view, the principle of equal liberty can support no restriction on free exchange nor on what individuals may rightfully do with what is theirs, it does at the same time encumber all persons with the duty to respect the entitlement of each to an equal share of natural resources. This entitlement takes the form of each person's being an equal shareholder in society, which, as a joint-stock company, owns all such resources and leases them to individuals or groups for a specified period.[29] Now, this proposal raises two difficulties, one of which we have already encountered. The exhaustibility of natural resources makes it possible that, with the expiration of leases, there may no longer be any assets which revert to shareholders for their further disposition. That is, leaseholders may have mixed their labor with all available natural resources.[30] The second problem engendered by Spencer's formulation has to do with the nature of the liberty conferred upon an individual by virtue of his entitlement, not to specific objects, but to a stock-holder's share in jointly owned objects. Can a right to participate in collective decisions affecting the disposition of jointly owned assets sensibly be construed as affording to each individual the domain of inviolable choice that the equal liberty principle purports to confer upon him? It seems fair to say that Spencer's account, suggestive as it undoubtedly is in many respects, fails to come to grips with either of these difficulties, and that their solution—if they can be resolved—involves an altogether more profound departure from prevailing ar-rangements than he contemplated. Let us consider them each in turn.

The first difficulty has to do with what can permissibly he owned by society construed as a joint-stock company. If it is to be only natu-ral resources, if only unused resources are what revert to collective disposition when leases terminate, shareholders who are members of later generations may find themselves lacking any original entitle-ment. If, however, what reverts to society are *all* unconsumed ob-jects—all objects that have not, so to speak, become parts of lease-holders' persons in a strictly physical sense—no problem arises in respect of later shareholders' deprivation.[31] To this proposal it might be objected that, although it protects the right of self-ownership to the extent that it leaves intact each individual's exclusive title to his own person, it nevertheless also violates that right by conferring upon shareholders the titles to objects embodying leaseholders' labor. As such, this formulation appears to assign original ownership of (part of) some persons' labor to others. This objection is, however, ground-less, because the entitlement of shareholders to objects embodying leaseholders' labor is not an original but a contractual one. No one can be originally or noncontractually entitled to the labor of an-other. But leaseholders, in contracting terminal leases for the use of shareholders' assets, would thereby be contracting to relinquish all unconsumed (including labor-embodying) objects to shareholders when those leases expire. Leaseholders' labor is contracted, not con-scripted nor confiscated.

Our second difficulty revolves around the wider and more troubl-ing issue of whether the personal inviolability associated with one's exclusive ownership of some objects can equally be associated with one's shared ownership of all objects. Notice that if everyone enjoys an equal right to determine the disposition of the same set of objects, there is a clear sense in which the demands of the equal liberty prin-ciple are at least formally fulfilled.[32] Perhaps, then, we should let the analysis end at this point. But one would, I think, be understandably dissatisfied with such a conclusion to an argument about individuals' natural rights or original entitlements, inasmuch as it appears to display them as being purely procedural and not substantive. Rights to be heard, to participate, to have one's preferences counted, and so forth are just not the same as rights to have one's practical choices fulfilled. And the personal liberty implicit in the latter would seem intuitively to be not merely different from, but also more significant than, that implicit in the former—even if, as in the present case, the range (of objects) over which individual choices are exercised is inversely greater in the former than in the latter.[33] I do not know, nor do I propose to consider here whether this intuition is ultimately justifiable. Suffice it to say that the reasons why we commonly hold a substantive right to be more significant for personal liberty than a procedural one are as follows. A substantive right endows its owner with a domain of decision making such that, barring unforeseen circumstances, the outcomes of the choices he makes within that domain cannot permissibly be contrary to his preferences or values. But the same cannot be said of a procedural right. For such an entitlement is one to make choices in a decision-making process, the outcomes of which possess the crucial property that they *can* permissibly be contrary to a chooser's preferences or values even if no unforeseen circumstances intervene. Since we are only too aware of the possibility of the formation of persisting majorities and permanent minorities, we are generally loath to construe the possession of a procedural right—such as a right to vote—as conferring more than an adjunctive and relatively attenuated form of personal liberty upon its owner.

The question to be answered, then, is whether, we are forced to conclude that the rights of shareholders—those rights that, I have argued, are individuals' natural or original rights—cannot but be of a procedural character. And to this the answer is, I think, no. Again, Locke is a helpful guide. He suggests that the essence of something being a person's property is that it cannot be disposed of by others without his consent.[34] If we interpret each shareholder's title as a right that none of society's assets be disposed of without his own consent, the right we thereby confer on each individual is a substantive and not a procedural one. It gives him an indefeasible claim against anyone disposing of an asset in a manner to which he has not given his approval. All persons have a duty to forbear from dispositions of this kind. It is, indeed, a right of similar form (thought of different content) that Rawls confers upon each person in the "original position," when he requires that principles of justice be chosen unanimously. There would thus be good grounds for describing his theory as one that takes as its prescriptive starting point each person's natural or original right to determine the "basic structure" of his society.[35]

Let me end this somewhat protracted argument by summarizing its main points and clarifying a subsidiary one. We began by asking for the grounds upon which slavery can be condemned categorically and located these grounds in the principle of equal liberty. This principle was taken to confer upon each individual an original or noncontractual right to his own person and, hence, to his own labor. Our problem thus became one of formulating a right to nonhuman objects — the receptacles or fields of labor — that would possess two properties: (1) that it is capable of being exercised by all individuals, regardless of their temporal locations; and (2) that it does not confer, upon any individuals, a noncontractual title to the labor of others. This right was shown to consist in the title to an equal shareholding in all nonhuman objects — a title that makes any permissible disposition of these objects subject to its owner's consent. What I have admittedly not attempted to explore in this chapter are the sorts of bargaining mechanism and institutional structure required to sustain such a right. For although their nature is obviously of the first importance, it is equally clear that the question of what they would be like is conceptually distinct from that of the form of the principle they are to embody. Little is gained from blurring this distinction, and it may be profitable to treat the two issues separately.

What can be said, however, is that these mechanisms and structures — whatever specific forms they might assume — appear to bear certain central affinities to *some* conceptions of socialism. That is, they appear to be the necessary conditions for realizing that socialist injunction that requires that no one be unjustly deprived of the fruits of his labor: that the circumstances in which any individual enters into a contractual relation of exchange must be equitable ones.[36] Socialist theories that place principal emphasis on the *exploitative* character of such exchanges in nonsocialist societies are theories that imply the adequacy of the kind of right outlined above for the realization of socialism. One might therefore say that socialism, thus conceived, is the embodiment of the principle (equal liberty), if not the practice, of classical liberalism. On the other hand, those conceptions of socialism that assign primary importance to distribution according to need — and that, in that respect, suggest that welfare states are approximations to socialism — cannot be seen as embodied in this right and may well be incompatible with it.[37]

Finally it should be observed that, in saying the requisite right must be of this character because of *inter alia* the indefinite reproducibility of rights holders, we are not positing duties to future generations as the grounds for this right. The grounds for the right taking this form are conceptual, not moral. It is quite true that this is a right that can be enjoyed by all members of an indefinite number of future generations. But the reason the right must be of this kind has nothing to do with duties to them. Rather, it is that only this right guarantees that persons who are born at different times, but who nevertheless share some element of contemporaneity, can all be said to be equally free with respect to one another. It is in constructing a right conferring equal liberty upon all persons whose existences are at least partially concurrent, that we *pari passu* confer rights on members of future generations. These are rights they hold against their contemporaries, but not against their entirely noncontemporaneous predecessors. For under the equal liberty principle there are no duties to nonexistent persons, be they dead or as yet unborn.

NOTES

1. Indeed, defenders of slavery have celebrated it as "the beneficent source and wholesome foundation of our civilization," "Moral and civilizing, useful at once to blacks and whites," "the highest type of civilization yet exhibited by man"; cited in J.E. Cairnes, *The Slave Power* (London and Cambridge, 1863)), p. 169. See also R.B. Davis, *The Problem of Slavery in Western Culture* (Ithaca, 1966), esp. part II.
2. *Four Essays on Liberty* (Oxford, 1969), p. 124.
3. Hillel Steiner, "Individual Liberty," *Proceedings of the Aristotelian Society* 75 (1974–75), pp. 33–50, esp. pp. 48–50.
4. "Liberalism," *The Encyclopedia of Philosophy*, ed. P. Edwards (New York, 1972), vol. 4, p. 458.
5. "Are There Any Natural Rights?" *Philosophical Review* 64 (1955), pp. 175–91; p. 176.
6. Cf. J. Locke, *Second Treatise*, chap. II, sec. 4, and chap. IV; I. Kant, *The Metaphysical Elements of Justice*, ed. J. Ladd (Indianapolis, 1965), pp. 33–45; H. Spencer *Social Statics*, 1st ed. (London, 1851), pp. 75–109.
7. Thus, although the equal liberty principle is the only grounds for a categorical rejection of slavery, it also serves as grounds for condemning forms of servitude other than the historically familiar institution of chattel slavery; cf. n. 12, below.
8. For a full account of the conditions that must obtain for this criterion to be satisfied, see my "The Structure of a Set of Compossible Rights," *Journal of Philosophy* 74 (1977), pp. 767–775.
9. I leave aside here the important question of whether the court's

verdict reports a discovery or a decision: in the former case, the respective contestants' rights and duties are previously determined; in
the latter, they are created *ex post*. I also leave aside the question of
whether there can be *ex post* duties.

10.   Cf. Steiner, "Individual Liberty," and "The Structure of a Set of
      Compossible Rights."

11.   Robert Nozick, *Anarchy, State and Utopia* (Oxford and New York,
      1974), p. 171.

12.   What are the referential limits of the concept of slavery? This intricate
      and troubling issue is not a purely semantic one. For the general con-
      dition of involuntary servitude — or, more specifically, the involuntari-
      ness of the relation of servitude — seems susceptible of an indefinite
      number of gradations. In *Progress and Poverty*, Henry George offers
      the following observation: "Place one hundred men on an island from
      which there is no escape, and whether you make one of these men the
      absolute owner of the other ninety-nine, or the absolute owner of the
      soil of the island, will make no difference either to him or to them. In
      the one case, as the other, the one will be the absolute master of the
      ninety-nine — his power extending even to life and death." (London,
      1884), p. 268. How would our appraisal of this society be affected if
      the ownership of the island were vested in *two* of the hundred persons?
      For an illuminating account of another dimension in which grada-
      tions of involuntary servitude arise, see Nozick's "Tale of the Slave,"
      op. cit., pp. 290–92, and the earlier argument of Spencer, from whch
      Nozick's is derived, in "The Coming Slavery," *The Man versus the
      State* together with *Social Statics*, 2d ed. (London, 1892), pp. 315–16.
      Davis, op. cit., chap. 2, provides a useful resume of the historical dif-
      ficulties in delimiting the institution of slavery. One of the reasons un-
      derlying the frequent situating of various other forms of servitude on a
      continuum with slavery is set out in n. 15, below. That said, it is nev-
      ertheless important to remember that there are significant conceptual
      differences between chattel slavery and other relations of servitude —
      differences that, under certain conditions, have been of the utmost
      practical consequence for persons in such relations. I am grateful to
      my colleague, Ursula Vogel, for insistently reminding me of this fact.
      See also M.I. Finley "A Peculiar Institution" *Times Literary Supple-
      ment*, July 2, 1976, pp. 819–821.

13.   Op. cit., p. 172.

14.   Such principles are incoherent; cf Steiner, "The Structure of a Set of
      Compossible Rights."

15.   A number of writers have queried the validity of this inference; that
      is, they have denied that the premises 'X owns L' and "X mixes L with
      O" imply that "X owns O." They suggest that one could equally con-
      clude that X loses L; cf. Lawrence Becker, *Property Rights* (London,
      1977), p. 34; Nozick, op. cit., pp. 174–75. It seems to me, however,
      that the inference is unimpeachable, given the two considerations
      conventionally assumed in drawing it: (1) that O is an object owned by
      no one; and (2) that to own something is to have an exclusive entitle-
      ment to dispose of it. Doubts as to the validity of the inference may, in

part, be due to the fact that the conclusion is slightly misstated in the above form. Strictly speaking, it should read *not* "X owns O" *but rather* "X owns OL," since the inference in fact contains a suppressed premise that immediately precedes the conclusion—namely, "X thereby creates OL." If one denies the properly stated conclusion—if one affirms "X does not own OL"—it follows that persons other than X may dispose of OL and, hence, of L. And this directly contradicts the first premise, "X owns L."

16. Cf. Locke, op. cit., chap. V; Kant, *The Philosophy of Law*, ed. W. Hastie (Edinburgh, 1887), part I, chap. II, sec. 1 (this chapter is omitted from the Ladd edition of the same work, op cit.); Spencer, *Social Statics*, 1st ed., chap. 9; but compare this with the revised 1892 edition of the same work, pp. 60–65, and with his *Justice* (London, 1891), chap. 13 and Appendix B, which reflect the utilitarian tendencies of Spencer's subsequently developed Social Darwinist beliefs; Nozick, op. cit., pp. 174ff.
17. No maximizing calculus can operate in a distributive vacuum; cf. n. 21, below.
18. And as is chosen by anyone whom it is tranferred through an unbroken series of nonforcible transferences.
19. Spencer, op cit., pp. 114–15.
20. Cf. Hillel Steiner, "Nozick on Appropriation," *Mind* 87 (1978), pp. 109–10.
21. See, for example, Peter Newman, *The Theory of Exchange* (Englewood Cliffs, 1965), p. 50: "prices are not given exogenously in the exchange situation, from the outside so to say, but are intrinsic to the problem embedded in the individuals' . . . preferences and initial endowments of goods."
22. Cf. Hillel Steiner, "The Natural Right to the Means of Production," *Philosophical Quarterly* 27 (1977), pp. 41–49; p. 46.
23. Nozick, op. cit., pp. 178ff.
24. Locke, op cit., chap. V, sec. 49.
25. *Illustrations of Political Economy* (London, 1832–34), quoted by H. Scott-Gordon, "The Ideology of Laissez-Faire," in A.W. Coats, ed., *The Classical Economists and Economic Policy* (London, 1971), p. 194.
26. It was conceded by some that, for later individuals, this might only be possible at the frontiers of their (or another) society—a concession that at once betrays the chief lacuna of this theory and suggests the importance of the notion of "the frontier" for some forms of liberalism.
27. We might introduce a grain of realism into this fable—and indirectly be more true to crops at the same time—by specifying that this entirely unshared contemporaneity subsists between generations of *moral agents*, that is, between generation of persons who have attained maturity or the "age of reason" and who are, therefore, rights holders.
28. For a convincing (though more qualified) criticism of the claim that the dead can have rights against the living, see E Partridge, "Posthumous Interests" (paper read at the Annual Meeting of the American Philosophical Association, Western Division, 1978). One might have

thought that the fact that Burke's emphatically antinatural rights theory entrenches this claim as its fundamental prescriptive premise, might have given the proponents of classical liberalism cause for some hesitation in endorsing a right (of bequest) that entails that claim.

29. In practice, Spencer suggests, such leases should be tendered on the basis of competitive bids.

30. Henry George's solution to the problem discounts the importance of assigning land on the basis of terminal leases and proposes, instead, that society impose a tax on the site value of land, i.e., on its value independent of the value of improvements made upon it — in short, its rent. But, apart from the empirical difficulties of applying this proposal, it falls prey to the same (second) objection made above to Nozick's appropriation proviso: namely, that the valuation in question, being based on market prices, make the just distribution a mathematical function of the prevailing distribution.

31. In an earlier paper I suggested an intermediate position: what belongs and reverts to society need only be the means of production (cf. "The Natural Right to the Means of Production"). This appears to be unsatisfactory in a theoretically important respect. For although the concept of "means of production" may be sufficiently precise for most exercises in economic analysis, it is ultimately and seriously indeterminate in its reference. Forests are viewed in one way by nature lovers, in another by timber manufacturers. Even the modest toothbrush, so beloved of poltical philosophers concerned with the present sort of issue, is apparently a most useful instrument in the finishing of various decorative metals. Thus, whether an object is a capital good or something else is, in the final analysis, contestable and dependent upon respective individuals' particular preferences and priorities. And it is therefore clear that to designate only some kinds of object as constituting what rightfully belongs to society — as what each shareholder has an equal natural right to — would be to favor some individuals' preference sets at the expense of others'. To say this is not, of course, to preclude the (highly probable) possibility that shareholders may frequently wish to renew many existing leases. We are here concerned only with the formal question of where an object's ownership ultimately resides, not with what disposition of it shareholders would commonly find to be optimally advantageous.

32. See Nozick's imaginative discussion of an analogous point in his chapter, "Demoktesis," op. cit., pp. 227–92.

33. "Inversely greater" in the following sense. Let x be the number of right holders in a society. Under an equal partition of objects among separate owners, each individual would have a personal title to particular objects which amount to $1/x$ of all objects. But where all objects are collectively owned, each shareholder's dispositional choices range over $x/1$ of all objects, i.e., all objects. One can of course say that (formally) each shareholder has a $1/x$ *chance* of exclusively determining the disposition of all objects.

34. Locke, op. cit., chap. XI, sec. 138 passim.

35. Cf. John Rawls, "The Basic Structure as Subject," *American*

Philosophical Quarterly 14 (1977), pp. 159–65.

36. On this view, the equity of these circumstances depends upon the equity of the distribution of preexchange property rights — what is referred to in microeconomics as *endowments* (cf. n. 21, above).

37. The distinction between these two conceptions of socialism — and the tensions between them — are noted by Anton Menger, *The Right to the Whole Produce of Labor* (London, 1899; reprinted, New York, 1970), p. 5 passim.

PART IV

PROPERTY AND OTHER RIGHTS

11

LIBERTY, PROPERTY, AND EQUALITY

JEAN BAECHLER *

I am very much embarrassed. On the one hand, the topic poses a
problem to which the solution is plain. Political liberty obviously depends on private property. Property generates inequality. And inequality menaces liberty. These truths can be obliterated only by
ideological passions that fasten upon the last two propositions and
forget the first. And so we are led, by one way or another, to some
kind of political despotism.

On the other hand, if one wishes to ground these truths in reason,
it would take a book. Here I shall present what is essentially an outline of their rational demonstration, at the risk of appearing somewhat elusive and terse.

This demonstration may be divided into four distinct lines of
analysis and argument: (1) liberty implies private property; the connection between the two is conceptual; it may also be demonstrated
by way of an analysis of a model of a regime of pure liberty; (2) historically liberty has been based on private property; (3) logically
property gives birth to inequality; and (4) inequality is a hypothetical
menace to liberty in that *if* one were to attempt entirely to eliminate
it, liberty would perish.

LIBERTY AND PROPERTY: THE CONCEPTUAL CONNECTION

A conceptual definition of liberty implies private property as both
a sphere of autonomy and a locus of initiative. If this straightforward

* Translated by John W. Chapman

conception of liberty is challenged as controversial, then one may proceed by pointing to situations in which liberty is clearly absent.

Liberty is denied in a condition of *oppression*, understood as the imposition on a person of a choice by an external will or constraint. Here is an *absolute definition* of liberty, in which it means the possibility of choice among a range of opportunities without interference from anybody. Liberty is also denied in a situation of *coercion* where an external will or constraint is injected into a sphere of autonomy. Here we have a *negative definition* of liberty as a sphere within which one can act or not as one pleases. Finally, liberty is absent in a state of *subjection*, taken to mean the deprivation of opportunity freely to participate in group decisions. Subjection produces a *positive definition* of liberty, liberty as freedom of participation.

Now, each of these definitions of liberty logically implies the other two. Absolute liberty disappears if coercion and subjection combine to reduce a plurality of choices to a single necessity. Negative liberty vanishes if oppression and subjection together destroy autonomy. And positive liberty evaporates when oppression and coercion unite to preclude participation in group deliberation.

It follows from these logical relations that a regime of liberty, conceived as a form of organization of power in a polity in which freedom is the supreme value, conceptually implies the autonomy and initiative *appropriate* to citizens. Hence property is only a way of naming *autonomous centers of decision*, men who choose and direct the destinies of a free society. In this sense, property is that which is proper to citizenship.

But this kind of conceptual analysis always runs the risk of appearing to be merely tautological. So I will continue the demonstration of the identification of property with autonomous centers of decision by constructing a model of a free state, pure and simple.

THE MODEL OF A REGIME OF LIBERTY

Unhappily, construction of the model is very long. But I ask for the reader's indulgence, and I will mark only the principal steps of the analysis.

Imagine an entity—in the sense of a unity of action, which can be either an individual or a collective—that is sovereign, egoistic, and calculating. I understand by *sovereign* that this agent is the absolute master of the power at its disposal. By *egoistic*, I mean that it always pursues its interests to the full extent of the power that it has, or to the point where it meets with resistance from others of its kind. By *calculating*, that it is capable of balancing exactly the costs and benefits of all its decisions.

Given such an agent, the question is: On what terms would it consent or associate with the others? It would be guided by a triple calculation. This would indicate that in giving up sovereignty and constraining egoism, the entity could gain security, prosperity, and liberty at very advantageous prices. The essentials of the demonstration are as follows.

Before association, each individual agent lives in a condition of permanent insecurity. For each, wielding its power in a sovereign and egoistical manner, can decide at any moment that preemptive attack on another is to its advantage. Since there is, by hypothesis, no communication among these creatures, none can know whether it would be strong and clever enough to survive any and all assaults. Each lives then always under the gun, in the presence of potentially violent death.

After association, however, *security* is guaranteed by mutual renunciation of the use of force. Certainly any of the associates may be attacked by an enemy or betrayed by a fellow. But in either case, the coalition of power permits each to expect a favorable outcome. To associate means then to leave a condition of insecurity for one of security by each giving his power, not to someone else, but rather to himself as a member of the association.

Again before association, the individual is condemned, by the particularities of his own nature and by technical constraints, to a state of perfect ineffectiveness, indeed to the level of a degraded animal. Once associated with others, each is assured of something better than zero effectiveness and hence of at least a minimum *prosperity*.

So long as each is on his own, individuals cannot know absolute liberty, since all are condemned through poverty to acting on the basis of natural necessities. Moreover, they cannot know of negative liberty, since each is open to attack at any moment. Nor can they experience positive liberty. For each is governed by both natural constraints and the sovereign decisions of the others. Only after the formation of the association do the three definitions of freedom come into being, thanks to the acquisition by all of efficiency, security, and publicly stipulated rules of the social game.

In abandoning his sovereignty and in confining his egoism, each individual makes an indefeasible calculation, but he also runs an enormous risk. For the power renounced by all does not go out of existence. For it has been transferred to the group and remains always at its disposal. Not only does power remain in existence, but it is also actually enlarged by the very fact of association. Moreover, if this enlarged power should be captured by one or a few of the associates, the others would be deprived, certainly of their security and their liberty, and very likely of their prosperity.

In consequence, the calculation to associate can escape absurdity—in the strong sense of being logically contradictory—only on the condition that the associating parties insure themselves against these risks. The precaution that must be taken is essentially a balancing of power. How is this to be accomplished?

POWER BALANCING AND PRIVATE PROPERTY

The number of associates forces a choice between two alternative solutions. In very small face-to-face groups any menacing will to power displayed by a member will be countered by the instantaneous coalition of all the others against him. And the ambitious will be eliminated by being put to death, or by exile, quarantine, or simple mockery. But once we leave the face-to-face society, we become dependent upon those highly complex equilibriums of power that are truly political.

In abstract terms, we can say that a political regime can guarantee its members security, prosperity, and freedom only on the imperative condition that each member or coalition of members constitute *autonomous centers of decision*. Autonomous, that is to say, neither independent—because then there would be no association—nor absorbed by the association—since there would then be no guarantee. This requirement of autonomy is the rational foundation of the distinction between the public and the private. The private is that space where the centers take their autonomous decisions; the public is the space where the rules of the association are defined and the problems to which it gives rise are resolved.

If we call *democratic* a regime of this type, we postulate that a democratic regime is founded partly on the fixing of sovereignty in the individuals who make it up, and partly on making and maintaining the distinction between the public and the private. Notice that the private is note merely that which is not public. The private is not to be conceived in passive terms. Is is an active force insofar as it is a center of decision and a locus of *initiative*.

What does all this have to do with private property? Precisely speaking, "property" is only a word used to designate the autonomous centers of decision, or again that which is *proper* to the individual or a coalition, that which is private.

It is remarkable that all languages combine the two senses of "property," as that which is proper to someone or something and as that which pertains to someone.[1] We speak also of that which is appropriate to someone or something, and of some thing being appropriated by someone. The expression "private property" is a pleonasm. One cannot speak of "public property" without conceptual and logical contradiction. But the private nature of property does not prejudge its *individual* or *collective* character. A property can remain private when it is owned by a group so long as that group does not compose the whole society.

Now we know the "form" of property, but we are still ignoring its "content." The content of property is nothing other than that which is contained in an autonomous center of decision. This content may be classified under two rubrics. In the first we find the body, the opinions, the beliefs, the initiative, the temperament, the character, and so on, of the individual. These are the properties of an individual, understood as a unity of social action, and this individual may be either a person or a collectivity. The other content of property takes the form of the results of individuals' activity: the productions, the savings, the acquisitions, and so on, that we refer to as property. This distinction between properties and property is founded, at least in French, in ordinary language, that is to say, in common usage.

Conceptual analysis and the analysis of rational deliberation and calculation thus reinforce one another to show that without a private sphere power can be monopolized to kill liberty. The associates could be stripped of all initiative and freedom emptied of all content. Liberty then very clearly demands property in the sense of a sphere of autonomous initiative. Does historical analysis confirm this connection?

PROPERTY AND LIBERTY

To verify the proposition that democratic regimes are effectively founded on autonomous centers of decision, that is, on the properties or the property of their members, I will examine four historical types of democracy. These are paleolithic, segmentary, neolithic or agrarian, and capitalist democracies. Needless to say, what follows is an attempt at analysis conducted at a very high level of generality.[2]

PALEOLITHIC DEMOCRACY

By paleolithic democracy I mean to refer to the political regime of *bands*. This was the normal condition of humanity for perhaps hundreds of thousands of years, and some peoples still continue in it.[3]

These societies, such as the Eskimoes, the Shoshone Indians, the Bochimans, and the Nambikwaras, are very small, on the order of several dozens of individuals. And they are democracies pure and simple. They are not Rousseauist or utopian societies based on group unanimity. Rather, these are polycentrist democracies. For power rests with autonomous centers of decision, the proprietors.

In such societies property in the form of individual or family ownership of the land is not in question. Ordinarily hunter-collectors are interested only in the resources of a territory.[4] Each band should have enough land to take care of its needs. And usually these small groups are not warlike.[5] But they do rigorously delimit their domains, and they may even establish no-man's-land barriers between themselves to keep the peace. In case of demographic pressure or internal conflict, the group splits, and a new territory is established. Thus each band bases its sovereignty and independence on the exclusive use of a territory, which we may refer to as its property. The communal land is not subdivided into parcels held by individuals. For the game is mobile, and there is no regular cultivation of grains and fruit. Hence agricultural property and the private hunting territory are both impossible and useless.

Moreover, these peoples have very little by way of durable goods, given their seminomadic way of life. They save practically nothing. They really have no private property, only their personal property and properties, and these are sufficient to constitute within them centers of autonomous decision. It is a grave mistake to think of paleolithic men as lacking individuation. They are real individuals, with personal passions and interests, fantasies and enthusiasms.

In conformity with our theoretical analysis, sovereignty resides, not in the band but in its constituent members. No superior has either the power or the authority to impose decision on the autonomous heads of families. These people are natural anarchists; all decisions are based on deliberative unanimity. If agreement cannot be obtained, the group simply breaks up.

SEGMENTARY DEMOCRACY

This is a form of social and political organization that is based on a plurality of units at the bottom and on their automatic regrouping at higher levels. At each level of organizations these segmental units have about the same strength and so offset and neutralize one another. At the limit—this is the case with the Nuer and the Tiv, but it appears to be exceptional—the whole group, segmented and yet culturally unified, may unite against an enemy. The question is: Where does property reside in the segmentary societies?

The numbers involved are very large. About seven hundred thousand people in the case of the Tiv in Nigeria. And their social and political structure is very complex. It follows that regulations about space will be very strict and precise, especially since these societies engage in horticulture and even some agriculture. By and large, each level of segmentation has its territory, at least when each segment is united and its members not scattered among the others. The lowest level of organization is a family group that traces its lineage about three generations back. The land is distributed at this level, and we can speak, therefore, of individual ownership.

The remarkable thing about these segmental societies is a switch of autonomy and initiative from the individual to some degree of segmentation. Power is essentially patriarchal, and each head of family takes part in collective decisions. If there is a chief, his power is negligible, and he functions essentially as a symbol of group unity.

The big difference between paleolithic and segmentary democracy is that in the latter the minimal lineage becomes the basic unit of social action instead of the individual, as in the former.

NEOLITHIC DEMOCRACY

The neolithic revolution marks a decisive rupture with the past. Democracy, instead of being the norm, becomes the exception. Indeed, there are no really democratic regimes to be found. And the postneolithic regimes, down to our own day, even when they tend toward democracy, are always more or less oligarchic. But even oligarchies are less frequent than autocratic and charismatic regimes.

In ancient Greece as in the Roman Republic, and in the West, both medieval and modern, autonomy is based on rural property in the shape of the domain. The *oikos* becomes the ideal and object of aspiration. The combination of a private sphere as autarkic as possible, purely and simply beyond the law, and active public participation becomes the model of social and political organization. This model was sometimes inscribed on the land in the form of the enclosure, within which the proprietor was absolute master.

The connection between autonomy and the rural domain was maintained at whatever level of society the distinction between the private and the public obtained. Indeed, the great domains were able to become so strong as to absorb or to ignore the public. They were not so much autonomous as independent and anarchic. This politico-agrarian ideal was finally incorporated in Article 544 of the Napoleonic Code: "property is the right to enjoy and to dispose of things in an absolute manner, so long as the use is not prohibited by law." Note also that this right is an individual right, not of families.

CAPITALIST DEMOCRACY

I understand by capitalism a type of social organization that tends to encourage and to reward economic efficiency. Elsewhere I have tried to show that this type of social organization requires a certain kind of political organization, in which the distinction between the public and the private is established and maintained, in which the state is separated from civil society.[6] History shows that capitalism is the form of social and economic organization that arises naturally in the absence of political impediments.[7]

However, in a capitalist environment so specified, individual property, which is so strikingly present and natural in the preceding case, becomes increasingly problematic. Why this is the case may be outlined as follows.

In the first place, economic growth never ceases to reduce the significance of agricultural land. Property becomes identified less and less with the rural domain and more and more with capital goods and consumers' durables. Moreover, the properties of the individual person, his capacities and talents, become increasingly significant. And the connection between the new forms of property and freedom is less evident. In fact, this connection is less well grounded, because the new property does not guarantee autonomy. Today a talented individual or a Parisian proprietor is obviously less autonomous than a fourteenth-century Swiss mountaineer.

Second, property can be a clear obstacle to the interests of the majority. And so arise the questions of expropriation or nationalization, both of which are quite inconceivable in the agrarain world.

Third, private ownership makes possible unearned and unjustified windfall returns. The phenomenon of urban ground rent is a case in point.

Fourth, property can become a hindrance to economic development and prosperity by enhancing structural rigidities. Governmental protection of small business, for example, can impair the efficiency of markets.

Fifth, corporations continue to grow in size and complexity. Management separates from ownership and then itself tends to become less entrepreneurial and more routine.

Finally, there appears the problem of the legitimacy of corporate authority.[8] The new managers dispose of tremendous power both within and without the corporation.[9] And the distinction between the public and the private comes to be felt as a contrast between democracy and oligarchy.

All of these tendencies and problems are real. It is not mysterious that the relation between private property and liberty, so clear to the thinkers of the seventeenth to the nineteenth centuries, should become obscure, and even inverted, in nineteenth-century ideologies and in the mind of the public today. That inversion is quite understandable, and it accounts for the coming of the new egalitarianism.

JUSTICE, EQUALITY, AND EQUITY

Like the concept of liberty itself, the concept of equality is highly ambiguous and hence subject to various interpretations. If we wish to discover a logical connection between private property and inequality, we must settle upon a clear understanding of the diverse meanings of equality. The Aristotelian distinctions are very useful for this purpose. Aristotle distinguished between numerical equality, which we shall call equality; proportional equality, which we shall call justice; and equity, understood as the correction of the inevitable rigidities of justice. These distinctions may be given a more precise formulation.

Equality may be defined in terms of an equal distribution, as for example, exactly similar slices of cake at a birthday party. Justice may be defined as a graduated distribution, in which each gets proportionally larger pieces of the cake on the basis of some established criterion. Equity then consists in the correction of the just distribution in the light of some superior criterion such as harmony, charity, or generosity.

The question is whether a regime of liberty implies equality, justice, or equity. Undoubtedly the answer is equality. The implication may be demonstrated by recalling our previous analysis.

LIBERTY AND EQUALITY

Recall how we postulated beings that are sovereign, egoistical, and calculating. Before they form an association, the relations among these creatures are governed by the relative strength of each, that is· to say, by force and cunning, used by each of them to advance its interests as far as possible. Over such creatures diffidence and mutual fear reign, and insecurity is general and ever present. Now, if strength is unequally distributed, the stronger will certainly take more than their share of what there is to be had. On the other hand, if strength is equally distributed, competition will operate to generate inequality. For these calculating egoists will form coalitions, some of which are bound to be more powerful than others.

Our analysis of their motivations showed that they would create an association, the terms of which are renunciation of sovereignty and violence in return for security, prosperity, and liberty. Given that the supreme objective of the associates is liberty, their compact would not be acceptable to all, and indeed would not work, if the inequality of power that obtains in the "state of nature" were to be transposed into civil society. If this were the case, the stronger could and would put down the weaker. It follows, therefore, that the first condition of a free society is rigorous equality of power of its members.

It may seem that one could insist upon equality of power and also subscribe to principles of justice and equity. But this is not so. For power consists in a relation between wills and is not something that can be divided up and distributed without regard for human differences. Riches, prestige, talent, beauty, intelligence, eloquence, indeed any criterion that could be adopted as a criterion of justice would affect the distribution of power. The rich would then have more power than the poor, the wise more than the ignorant, and so on. It follows, therefore, that if our creatures are to be really equally powerful, they must be equal in all respects.

An important empirical consequence of this logical analysis is that every democracy always tends downwardly toward equality. Equality upward is precluded, of course, by human differences. Indeed, this explains why the most universal passion present in human societies is envy.[10] People cannot bear that others should be more fortunate and have more.

And envy is the democratic passion par excellence! It is an essential engine of regulation in both the paleolithic and segmentary democracies. There enviousness operates effectively to contain all of those natural inequalities that threaten equality of power. And on the contrary, in the neolithic democracies, or rather oligarchies, and above all in the capitalist democracies, human differences are magnified by the institution of private property. Inequality is inherent in, and fostered by, these societies. These logical and empirical points require historical elaboration.

PROPERTY AND INEQUALITY IN HISTORICAL PERSPECTIVE

Private property has, so to speak, two distinct vectors, an internal vector marked by self-reliance and autonomy, and an external vector that expresses itself through the initiatives of individuals. The first tendency does not disturb equality. But the second one does, depending upon historical circumstances.

In paleolithic democracy, property is centered on the individual. And all of the possible aspirations toward inequality of power are without a focus. One may think that a person stronger than the others could subject them to his will. But this is not the case. For an individual is always weaker than a coalition. And coalitions can form instantaneously in the face-to-face society, and they will always be victorious. The danger of individual tyranny is constant, but so is vigilance against it. In the band the watch is always on for signs of hubris.

Moreover, there is no scope for economic initiative that could lead to inequalities of wealth and income, and so to inequalities of power. Saving is impossible. And anyway there is nothing to invest in. Nor can a large family aspire to power, given the demographic constraints imposed by the environment.

In the segmentary democracies, property is centered on the lineage. The situation is very much like that of paleolithic democracy. The autonomy of each segment can be threatened only by the appearance of a stronger group. But the system is evidently designed precisely to confront segments of equal power, at whatever level the confrontation takes place. Within the basic lineages, wealth is redistributed on the basis of strict equality. It is true that at the political level of segmentation there can be accumulation of wealth by chiefs. But this does not lead to an inequality of power, for the common expectation is that chiefs are generous redistributors. Hence, inequality can spring from neither property nor from the family. And these systems of social organization tend to reproduce themselves indefinitely.

Neolithic democracy is based on the rural domain. The domain is an enterprise, that is, it is a place where people seek to employ scarce resources in the most efficient manner. Needless to say, some are more sucessful than others, and in the course of time great proprietors emerge to dominate the rest. Then the reformers, like Solon and the Gracchi, appear on the scene and attempt to restore the conditions of democracy.

Capitalist democracy depends on many autonomous centers of decision, not just on economic enterprises, but also on pressure groups, universities, clubs, and talented and ambitious individuals. All of these centers, and not only the enterprises, are in a state of permanent competition, in which there are both winners and losers. The losers abandon their autonomy. Thus the rural exodus, in this perspective, is a gigantic operation of expropriation and concentration of enterprises. The gainers enrich themselves at the expense of the losers. In other words, the outcome of competition is that the number of autonomous centers of decision decreases, and those that remain increase their weight and influence. And these growing centers become hierarchically organized to cope with complexity. In these bureaucratic pyramids, power is necessarily distributed unequally from the top to the bottom. Otherwise there would be mutual paralysis as in the segmental systems.

The interplay of these forces determines that the development of a capitalist democracy will be characterized by the existence of an indefinite number of autonomous centers of unequal importance, in the more important of which power and authority will of necessity be distributed drastically unequally. This unequal distribution is not unjust. Justice requires that each be given his due. It is just that a great painter should have more prestige than the mediocre, but unequal. It is just that the head of a great corporation should be paid and respected more than a small shopkeeper, but again not equal.

Unhappily, the generational nature of human life works to corrupt justice. Families are able to pass on advantages and opportunities without regard for the merits of specific individuals. But it would be fatal for liberty to attempt a systematic redistribution of opportunity for each new generation.

Thus inequality, whether it is just or not, necessarily goes along with private property in the neolithic and capitalistic democracies. In what ways does this inequality pose a threat to liberty?

INEQUALITY AND LIBERTY

Inequality endangers liberty in two ways: directly, by reducing the liberty of the majority of people; and indirectly, by generating irrational attempts to restore equality. These tendencies threaten democracy itself.

A direct threat to democracy derives from a proposition established earlier. Power is not a thing; rather it is a relation or a tension between two wills. Anything that influences this relation or tension affects power itself. For example, a woman's beauty confers power, at least over those who are attracted by her type of beauty. To be rich means to be able to control, in a certain measure, the actions of those who are dependent on your wealth for survival, and so on.

Assume, as common sense suggests, that in society everyone is permanently immersed in various and discontinuous relations of power, in the family, in companies, and other organizations. These relations can be inverted in the case of any individual; a person is dominant in the family and dominated at work. Now, each person can be given an index of power, an index that combines and summarizes all the power relations, both positive and negative, in which he is enmeshed. Construction of such indices is not empirically out of the question. Suppose, then, that we get them made. Then everyone could be ranked against all of the others. We would have a scale for society that runs from more to less of the powers of its members.

From these premises we may derive a theorem, namely, that the distribution, or curve, of power is the same as the distribution, or curve, of liberty. This is a logical deduction. Since, in actuality, liberty consists in plurality of choice, autonomy, and participation, and power is an asymmetrical tension between two wills, it follows that the dominated will is less free than the dominant will. It follows also from the tension between wills that their respective liberties can be infinitely combined in a range from perfect reciprocity to total subjection of one party to the other. This why the words we use tend to mislead us, because our language attempts to capture reality with essences. But between liberty and servitude there are many nuances that the essentialism of our vocabulary leads us to overlook.

What will be the shape of such a hypothetical distribution of power? It will certainly take the shape of a Pareto, that is, skewed distribution. In practice, power is a scarce good that is distributed by the outcomes of multiple competitions among members of society. That power should be scarce derives from its very nature. If it were a free good, each person would have an infinite quantity of it, and no one could impose on another. Power is not only desirable in itself but is also as a means, of course, to obtain other goods. One could even go so far as to claim that power is the supreme value in the human comedy, and not wealth, as we are tempted to think by a kind of optical illusion created by the last two centuries of Western history. Before our era, power to grab and to hold is what counted in human affairs.

A scarce good submitted to free competition tends to be divided between a minority of great beneficiaries and a majority of small, great and small being calculated on a per capita basis. In fact, the majority gets the biggest part of the cake, but because of their numbers, each person in the majority gets only crumbs. Thus, our theorem is flanked by a corollary: the distribution of power, and the distribution of liberty, translates into a distribution between a minority who have a lot of both power and liberty, and a minority who have little, again always calculating per capita.

This analysis goes to show that even in a perfect democracy an oligarchical structure is inescapable, because of all the inequalities that influence the distribution of power and the scarcity of power itself. It is equally the case that oligarchy endangers in varying measure the freedom of the majority. At one extreme the majority is servile as in the cases of the Greek city-states and the high Middle Ages. At the opposite extreme, the majority has a good deal of freedom as in the Western democracies since 1945. Above all, one comes across intermediate situations where the majority has in reality little freedom and yet is not oppressed. In this connection, eighteenth-century England and the Venetian Republic come to mind. It all depends on history, national temperament, and the environment.

OLIGARCHY AND LIBERTY

If oligarchy by its very nature limits the freedom of the majority, still it remains constant that oligarchy—and this is a point of capital importance—does not endanger the polycentric structure of the political regime itself. If one defines a liberal regime in terms of the absence of a monopoly of power or, which comes to the same thing, by the division of power among several autonomous centers of decision, then it is clear that oligarchy tends toward democracy, and not toward autocracy. In practice, oligarchs tend to have substantially the same amounts of power, since the stronger eliminate the weaker. Thus, competition tends to re-create the original division of power, in which several centers exist in a condition of equilibrium. Whether the oligarchs are aristocrats, businessmen, or organized groups, they always control property, people, and resources, the enduring foundations of autonomy and initiative.

Moreover, it can be shown that oligarchies possess long-term stability. Recall our central line of argument. When a small number of more or less equal competitors exists, none has a strong interest in getting rid of another. For the spoils would be dispersed among all of the others; otherwise one of the oligarchs would get the upper hand. Besides, no one would get enough to make the struggle worthwhile. In other words, no established oligarch has a rational interest in assault for gain. On the other hand, no one is likely to be mulcted by another, for the intended victim can always resort to a defensive coalition. He will not want for allies, for others have a rational interest in their own future security. It follows that none has a reason for preemptive attack. Consequently, established oligarchs do have a positive interest in reaching an accommodation among themselves, in defining the rules of the game, and in mutual survival. Each rationally seeks to avert either a monopoly of power or an Hobbesian struggle. The only rational solution for all is construction of a unified polity, in which power is allocated among several autonomous, not independent centers of decision. Historically oligarchies have been monarchies, well tempered.

Oligarchy is a stable structure of power that is in direct contradiction with autocracy. And given favorable circumstances, even an apparently rigid oligarchy will drift toward actualizing its latent democratic potentialities. However, this process of democratization will not redistribute power in a nonskewed manner, nor will it so redistribute liberty. Rather, the rules of the game will be rewritten so as to confer rights on the majority. Thus, new autonomous centers of decision come into being in the form of pressure groups, unions, and so on. These new countervailing powers raise the general level of freedom in society. This is exactly what happened in Western Europe between the eleventh and twentieth centuries.[11] There society moved from the savage competition of feudalism to limited monarchy and then to polyarchal democracy.

In sum, oligarchy is Janus faced. On the one hand, it supports freedom by dividing and balancing power. On the other hand, it limits freedom, because it constrains the majority. It is precisely this ambiguity that renders possible lack of liberty for all. Our contemporary

egalitarians neglect the positive side of oligarchy and fasten upon its
defects.

OLIGARCHY AND RESTRICTED LIBERTY

Once an oligarchical society is on the road to democracy and
evolves an ideal of perfect democracy, difficulties are bound to arise.
We have demonstrated that perfect democracy implies equality and
that practical democracy is able, at best, to assure justice. This incongruity between the ideal and reality is the source of what we may
label "the party of equality." In every democracy, this so-called party
aspires to the ideal. And this faction has every chance of flourishing.
For the majority has an interest in listening to it, and the oligarchs
find it difficult to justify their advantages. So they wish to be democrats also. In particular, the hereditary nature of inequality of opportunity gives some of the elite a bad conscience, and they join up
with the egalitarian faction.

Let us pass quickly to the next historical stage in which this faction
comes to power and tries to put its program into action. Two great
choices then present themselves. In the terminology that we adopted
earlier, the first alternative is to temper justice with equity without
attempting to equalize. The second is to disregard equity and over-
ride justice in order to achieve equality. We have either a politics of
redistribution or the death of liberty, perhaps both.

We are now so well acquainted with redistribution that only a few
remarks about it will be sufficient. Its "spirit," as Montesquieu would
say, is clear. This is to permit competition freely to generate inequalities, to produce a just distribution, in which each person gets the
power, wealth, and prestige that he merits. Given distribution on the
basis of competitive merit, then some of the accumulated goods and
advantages are redistributed downward. This practice corresponds
exactly with our definition of equity. It is the modern avatar of Aristotelian friendship or Christian charity, with this difference: the latter are free expressions of individual wills, whereas redistribution as
we know it is imposed by the state. One notices that the amount redistributed on an equitable standard is open, for there is no higher
criterion in terms of which the amount could be precisely determined. Between public relief of atrocious poverty and absolute
equalization lies an infinity of intermediate points that a society can
reach depending on a constellation of considerations, namely, previous history, national character, influence of egalitarian intellectuals,
and so on.

THE POLITICS OF REDISTRIBUTION

One could show, and experience begins to confirm analysis, that as equity enlarges setbacks become more and more certain. The analysis would revolve around several main points. Those who are being redistributed against have the means to defend themselves against what they rightly think is injustice. And so they compensate themselves in devious ways. The aggrieved slacken their efforts and threaten to kill the goose that lays the golden eggs. They engage in "internal emigration" or join the "brain drain," and so on.

Insofar as redistribution is accomplished through publicly subsidized education, health, and culture, the advantage taken of these subsidies depends upon the distribution of aptitudes, which are themselves tied to social position. Moreover, provision of educational opportunity is doomed to disappointment, for the structure of occupations, at least in the short run, is quite independent of the supply of educated persons. And increasing equality of educational opportunity appears to have negligible influence on social mobility. [12]

Finally, it is highly probable that the effort to institutionalize unwilling equity will miscarry. There will be redistribution of advantages among the middle classes and some transfer from the top to the bottom. [13] But the politics of redistribution, taken by itself, has every chance of falling to its lowest common denominator, namely, public relief of misery.

EGALITARIANISM AND ITS CONSEQUENCES

Hence there arises a revulsion against the policy of equity and an intensified desire for equality. A politics of equality can do nothing other than violence to social reality in an attempt to make it coincide with the ideal; for egalitarianism is always based on systematic expropriation.

It is remarkable how the two meanings of property reappear in the notion of expropriation. One transfers property into the public sphere and thereby make possible the complete absorption of the private by the public. But through expropriation one seeks also to transfer into the public dimension of life the properties, the attributes, of individuals. This is the deep meaning and significance of the ambition avowed by all the totalitarians to create a "new man!" [14] This notion of the "new man" is a perverse way of affirming that the individual is not an authentic agent, indeed ought not to be morally free and spontaneous in the formation of his motives and character.

Rather, the private personality must be restructured, forced into a new mold, gotten rid of.

The suppression of private property and individual properties is always tantamount to destruction of autonomous centers of decision. It is nothing less than murderous metamorphosis of the private into the public. Public power can be divided and contained only if the public is counteracted by private power, the state by society. Expropriation tends inevitably, therefore, toward concentration of power, toward some kind of autocracy. By pursuing equality beyond the limits of equity, the egalitarian faction leaves behind the democratic logic of liberty and passes into the autocratic logic of servitude. [15]

I began by asserting that the connection between inequality and restriction of liberty was hypothetical. Now one can see why. The passage from one internal logic or dynamic to the other cannot take place in an organic and imperceptible manner. It presupposes a rupture of the social fabric, indeed a revolution, in which the extreme egalitarian faction emerges victorious.

THE DEATH OF LIBERTY?

We may now put aside theoretical for empirical analysis and ask the question: What are the conditions in which the revolution that I have portrayed could actually take place in a modern polyarchal regime? No general answer is possible. It all depends on the circumstances that obtain in each polity, on its history, its culture, its elites, and its people. The course and configuration of international politics are, of course, also relevant.

But one cannot predict the time and place of the death of liberty as the outcome of massive revulsion against human inequality. Only a historical, retrospective analysis would be possible, and that would reveal the point beyond which one cannot go in the quest for equality at the expense of justice and equity. Here and now, the best we can do is to forecast the existence of that point of no return.

PROPERTY AND PERSONALITY

My analysis has been explicit enough to permit me to dispense with a summary. From freedom to serfdom I have traced a very strong thread. Powerful social and political dynamics are pushing us from the one to the other. The transition is not inevitable, however. But its very possibility should put us on guard against the dangers that a democracy courts if it should attempt to achieve its overt ideal. It is not the nature of ideals to be realized. One should not even hanker that they could be.

The heart of the analysis resides in the concept of property that we have developed. By identifying property with the private and with autonomous centers of decision and initiative, I do not think that I have done violence either to our language or to the facts of human life. I may very well have done violence to those mental habits that would confine the meaning and significance of property to things and possessions. While these habits may have been appropriate in the agrarian world that we have left, they strike me as regressive and blinding error in the closing years of the twentieth century.

In reality, private property is only an extension of the properties of individual personalities. Its essence remains as unalterable as those properties in the absence of which human personality would not exist. Together private property and personal attributes demarcate the sphere of the private without which power knows no limits. To expropriate is not only to oppress the expropriated in their persons and goods; it is also to release the public power from all restrictions.

Theoretical analysis and historical experience coincide. Liberty and property form an indissoluble unity in society and politics. If one aspires to preserve the liberal philosophy of life, the irremediable damage that liberty and property inflict on human equality must be accepted. And we must cling to justice tempered by equity. One may hope that better understanding of the dialectical relations between liberty, property, and equality will foster liberal aspiration.

NOTES

1. In Greek, ἴδιος and τὰ ἴδια ; in Latin *proprius and proprietas*; in German, *eigen* and *Eigentum*; in English, *proper* and *property*; and in Italian *proprio* and *prorietà*; in French, *propre* and *propriété*.
2. I deal more thoroughly with some of these matters in my *Le pouvoir pur* (Paris: Calmann-Lévy, 1978).
3. Recent studies that bear on the nature of paleolithic man and life include: Lionel Tiger and Robin Fox, *The Imperial Animal* (New York: Dell, 1972); George Edgin Pugh, *The Biological Origin of Human Values* (New York: Basic Books, 1977); Edward O. Wilson, *On Human Nature* (Cambridge: Harvard Univ. Press, 1978); and Mary Midgley, *Beast and Man: The Roots of Human Nature* (Ithaca, N.Y.: Cornell Univ. Press, 1978).
4. On the emergence of private property rights, see H. Demsetz, "Toward a Theory of Property Rights," in Erik G. Furubotn and

Svetozar Pejovich, eds., *The Economics of Property Rights* (Cambridge: Ballinger, 1974).

5. See Marvin Harris's analysis of the Yanamamo's warfare in his *Cows, Pigs, Wars and Witches: The Riddles of Culture* (New York: Vintage, 1978).

6. See *The Origins of Capitalism*, trans. Barry Cooper (Oxford: Basil Blackwell, 1975).

7. I demonstrate this proposition in *Origins of Capitalism*, and it finds firm confirmation in the following historical studies: Douglass C. North and Robert Paul Thomas, *The Rise of the Western World: A New Economic History* (Cambridge: Cambridge Univ. Press, 1973); and Fernand Braudel, *Afterthoughts on Material Civilization and Capitalism*, trans. Patricia M. Ranum (Baltimore: The John Hopkins Univ. Press, 1977).

8. This is a major concern of Charles E. Lindblom in his *Politics and Markets: The World's Political-Economic Systems* (New York: Basic Books, 1977).

9. On the men of the *grandes ecoles* and the *grands corps*, see Ezra N. Suleiman, *Elites in French Society: The Politics of Survival* (Princeton: Princeton Univ. Press, 1978).

10. I explore the connections between human passions and ideologies in *Qu'est-ce que l'ideologie?* (Paris: Gallimard, 1976).

11. For a theoretical treatment of the passage from serfdom to freedom, see Evsey D. Domar, "The Causes of Slavery or Serfdom: A Hypothesis," a paper presented to the Economic History Association, August 28, 1969.

12. An excellent analysis of this phenomenon is to be found in Raymond Boudon, *Education, Opportunity, and Social Inequality: Changing Prospects in Western Society* (New York: John Wiley, 1974).

13. For the situation and trends in England, consult J. E. Meade et al., *The Structure and Reform of Direct Taxation* (London: George Allen & Unwin, 1978).

14. For example, Georgi Smirnov, *Soviet Man: The Making of a Socialist Type of Personality*, trans. Robert Daglish (Moscow: Progress Publishers, 1973).

15. To avoid any ambiguity, we add that autocracy is not founded on equality; quite the contrary. Autocracy is much more inequalitarian than democracy. The difference is that inequality wounds democracy but not autocracy.

12

JUSTICE, FREEDOM, AND PROPERTY

JOHN W. CHAPMAN

Over twenty years ago Bertrand de Jouvenel observed that "Preoccupation with justice is . . . the political preoccupation *par excellence* and it is no bad thing that 'social justice' should be the obsession of our time."[1] That obsession has since become the debate of the century. Jouvenel was inclined to think that argument over justice would prove to be both inconclusive and divisive if men came to think of it, not as an attitude of mind, but as a configuration of society, as "social justice." For this kind of justice involves irreducible and incommensurable criteria such as needs, merits, and initiatives. And agreement could not possibly be reached as to their relative weights. Maybe it was not such a good thing after all that we have become fixated on distributive as contrasted with commutative or catallactic justice. But we certainly have. And now there is nothing for it other than to think our way through—some would say, out of—the issues and implications of "social justice," in particular its implications for freedom and for private property.

I propose to go about this by first surveying the moral gradient the debate has assumed. Then I shall examine the more prominent stations erected along the line of descent, or ascent, as the case may be. Many stations may turn out to be less sturdy than their architects would have us believe. At the end of the journey we should at least have a better idea of what the real issues and alternatives are. For some visions of the just society may be not only morally defective but actually unworkable in that they envisage some inconceivable transformation of human nature. Others may be based on mistaken readings of history, or misunderstandings about the theory of economic organization, or failure to appreciate the significance of property

289

rights for both freedom and economic efficiency. The real argument
may be over philosophies of life and ideals of personality. And some
conceptions of "social justice" may be deadly for social and political
equilibrium. As de Jouvenel says, "to keep the game of Politics within
the rules, the stakes must be kept moderate."[2]

In the West today many people appear to be disenchanted with economic rationality. They think that economic justice demands greater
equality of income and ownership, perhaps even abolition of private
ownership, that somehow we can do better than "welfare liberalism"[3]
based on semicapitalist democracy. Under the banners of social justice and freedom, but above all in the name of equality, the search is
on for new and better forms of economic and political organization,
for a political economy puported to be more human and democratic.

THE EGALITARIAN TELEOCRATIC GRADIENT

The first imposing station on the moral gradient I call, in the language of Michael Oakeshott, the morality of individuality. This is the
classical liberal philosophy of life to be found in the works of de
Jouvenel, Oakeshott, F. A. Hayek, Sir Isaiah Berlin, Edward Shils,
and Robert Nozick.[4] Here I shall attend primarily to the thinking
of Hayek and Oakeshott as representatives of economic and moral
individualism.

Our second station is occupied by Alan Gewirth, who deliberately
takes his stand between the "extreme," as he calls them, positions of
Nozick and John Rawls. According to Gewirth, "the two extremes
overlook, respectively, the claims of severe economic need and the
claims of desert as based on voluntary effort and accomplishment."[5]
We may label his position the morality of freedom and well-being.

C. B. Macpherson has named the third point on the gradient
"revisionist liberalism."[6] But I shall designate it the morality of welfare liberalism or compensatory reciprocity. Its supreme exponent is,
of course, John Rawls.[7] At the heart of this outlook on life one may
discern, in the words of Oakeshott, "a disposition to identify oneself
as a partner with others in a common enterprise and as a sharer in a
common stock of resources and a common stock of talents with which
to exploit it."[8]

The sign says "market socialism" at the next station down, or up,
the line. It was designed by Oskar Lange and built by Tito and the
Yugoslavs. The new stationmaster is Charles E. Lindblom.[9] Whether
an economy based on the market, private profit, and public ownership is properly referred to as "socialism" is certainly a question.

Anyway, according to Lindblom, the workers' control experiments suggest that "private property and private enterprise are not, as socialists used to believe, the principal targets of democritization of the workplace. The target is instead a hierarchical and authoritarian structure of authority in the enterprise, whether resting on private property or not."[10]

Into sight now comes the morality of "altruistic collaboration,"[11] followed by that of "equal concern and respect."[12] At the first of these sites, competitive efficiency is replaced by an ideal of human cooperation, whether efficient or not. At the second, equality of opportunity and the criterion of competitive merit have been displaced by the ethic of "reverse discrimination," and private property has been reduced to "personal possessions." We have come a long way from the classical liberal morality of individuality.

And now we reach C. B. Macpherson's ideal of "creative solidarity,"[13] organized through participatory democracy and a command economy based on abolition of private property. No Maoist or Titoist heresy is to be found here. Abundance apparently prevails despite obvious signs of scarcity, and somehow "society regulates the general production," as Marx affirmed desirable in *The German Ideology*.

At the end of the line we come to a stop at the Franciscan morality of nearly "absolute egalitarianism," as preached by Roberto Mangabeira Unger.[14] Here the ultimate tyranny of individual distinction and merit is to be overcome through democracy organized as a welfare-corporate teleocracy, from which private property has been, of course, banished. Perhaps Michael Oakeshott was mistaken to say, "no European alive to his inheritance of moral understanding has ever found it possible to deny the superior desirability of civil association without a profound feeling of guilt."[15]

From the proponents of individuality to the apostle of community, at every station along our route we have been offered moral packages in which justice, freedom, and property are differently related. At the top of the gradient private property loomed large with moral, economic, and political significance. At the bottom, it has altered its meaning completely and become the paramount instrument and expression of human division and domination. Let us listen more closely to the disputants.

THE MORALITY OF INDIVIDUALITY

At the core of this ethic or ethos is an ideal of personality, a vision

of essentially private men, independent and self-reliant, men who go
their own ways in life, and who find their lives not so much rivalrous
as complementary. They are not much given to envy, being rather
mutually appreciative. Their mutual independence is rooted in their
character, and they experience their properties as extensions of their
selves. They are ambitious and expansive for both self and family.
But they are essentially moral, not "possessive," individualists as
C. B. Macpherson would have us view them. Their individualism
shows itself as much in culture and religion as it does in their economic aspirations.

These persons, individuated and rationalized, their consciences
developed and brought into line with natural inclination, appeared
in early modern Europe.[16] Their moral psychology disdained natural
law and demanded natural rights; they thought of society and government in terms of contract and trust; and their conception of justice, best expressed by John Locke, was almost entirely procedural.
The rule of law was designed to protect the substance of their natural
rights to life, liberty, and property. Individual freedom and self-af-
firmation are their supreme values. In their eyes, propertyless men
were dependent men, bound to be both corrupt and dangerous to
political equilibrium.[17]

Today the most powerful exponents of this morality, although with
somewhat contrasting moral and economic emphases, are Michael
Oakeshott and Friedrich A. Hayek. Oakeshott's ideal men are civil
associates whose relations are defined by law and governed by common sentiments of justice. He regrets the prevalence of dependent
men and even more that independent men have been tamed into af-
fluent role performers by their Baconian inspirations. Oakeshott's
ideal individuals seem to exhibit an austere indifference to economic
activity, and rightly so. For the economy is not a realm of choice in
his eyes, and so it deflects men from their moral vocation. Unlike
Hayek's ideal men, Oakeshott's can never flourish in a world dominated by economic ambitions or concerns.

But neither Oakeshott nor Hayek has any use for "social" justice or
the redistributive state. Hayek thinks social justice is a deadly "mirage." After men, equal before the law, have dealt with one another
in the market, and catallactic justice has been done, nothing is left to
divide, and no one would have authority to divide it anyway. Even if
there were an authoritative redistributor with something to distribute, no practicable criteria exist on the basis of which a share-out
could be made. To Hayek "social" justice is just another self-serving

ideology that the organized use to defend themselves against, and to pervert, market forces to the detriment of all.

Naturally Hayek deplores egalitarianism. "Equality of the general rules of law and conduct . . . is the only kind of equality conducive to liberty and the only equality which we can secure without destroying liberty."[18] A competitive economy based on private property is the institutional guarantee of freedom. "It is competition made possible by the dispersion of property that deprives the individual owners of particular things of all coercive powers."[19] In this perspective, private property is a way of organizing the inescapable competitiveness of life so as to support and promote freedom, economic efficiency, and growth. Moreover, a market economy imposes its own forms of responsibility. There is no need to politicize all of life in an attempt to subject economic authority to democratic accountability.

In an open society, so conceived, much that happens is due to chance, and about this "random-walkness" nothing can be done. A desert-based conception of justice cannot be applied to the workings of a market economy. Hayek is even dubious about seeking to create equality of opportunity, for inequality of opportunity is "inevitably connected with the effectiveness of that discovery procedure, which the market order constitutes."[20] And all a progressive income tax does is to make it more difficult for the aspiring to displace the established.

Hence freedom under purely procedural justice is Hayek's formula for the long-run good of man. Any tampering with this formula by way of planning and controlling runs contrary to the advance of civilization itself. "The desire to eliminate the effects of accident, which lies at the root of the demand for 'social justice,' can be satisfied in the field of education, as elsewhere, only by eliminating all those opportunities which are not subject to deliberate control."[21] Indeed, in a progressive society apparent injustice is unavoidable; it is one of those contingencies that the ethically mature will learn to put up with. The open society cannot be justified in the name of any substantive conception of justice. Rather, it offers, over time, the best chances that men can hope for and have. To choose freedom entails acceptance of the resultant inequalities. It means banking on those chancy and unpredictable initiatives that the demand for "social justice," to say nothing of outright socialism, would stifle. "Even the poorest today owe their relative material well-being to the results of past inequality."[22]

In practice, Hayek's version of the morality of individuality takes on the form of an evolutionary utilitarianism. People are entitled to that which they are allocated by an impersonal system that maximizes welfare over the long run. This is too economistic a philosophy of life to suit his fellow moralist of freedom, Michael Oakeshott.

FREEDOM AND WELL-BEING

Alan Gewirth argues that men, purposive agents that they are, logically are bound both to claim for themselves, and to accord to one another, equal and effective rights to freedom and well-being. From his standpoint, a world like Hayek's "may not make adequate provision for rules that protect each person's right to well-being."[23] In Gewirth's morality of freedom and well-being these basic rights have to be adjusted so as to come into rational balance. In practice, this objective would appear to require, not equalization of wealth and income, but provision of a minimum standard of living combined with promotion of equality of opportunity.

Gewirth says that "What is of central importance . . . is not that wealth or property itself is to be equalized but rather that, beyond the minimum required for basic goods, persons have as nearly as possible equal chances for developing and utilizing their own capabilities for successful agency."[24] Injustice consists in the imposition of "a severe inequality with regard to basic well-being."[25] The right to basic well-being evidently limits the right to property to some unspecified degree. But with reference to both wealth and income, Gewirth asks not that they be distributed equally, "but rather that the means of acquiring them be distributed equally so far as possible."[26] He recommends advancing equality of opportunity by enhancing through education and effective family nurture the ability of all to work.

Gewirth's principles of political economy are strikingly similar to those of Sir Henry Phelps Brown, who says that "the main cause of the inequality of pay is the inequality of abilities to work. There are great difficulties in the way of breaking the link between pay and ability, and prescribing equal pay for unequal work. The best way to reduce the inequality of the effect is to reduce that of the cause."[27] For the sake of economic efficiency and justice, both advocate policies designed to enable people to compete more effectively within the market. Very likely, Gewirth would subscribe to dispersion of property along lines proposed by J. E. Meade.[28]

We can regard Gewirth's morality of freedom and well-being as a temperate modification of classical liberal individualism, at the heart of which is the equal right to freedom, conceived as equality of opportunity.

WELFARE LIBERALISM: COMPENSATORY RECIPROCITY

Elsewhere I have compared Rawls's theory of justice to a Gothic cathedral.[29] If you look at it from the sides, or from the front and the back, it is a vast and imposing pile of analysis and argument. But from the air its plan stands out starkly. Our sense of justice calls us to correct and to compensate for the accidents and contingencies of life, for these are undeserved and hence arbitrary from a moral point of view. The sense of justice "reveals what the person is, and to compromise it is not to achieve for the self free reign but to give way to the contingencies and accidents of the world."[30] An instinct for reciprocity lies deep within the nature of man, a bedrock foundation for the moral ideal of the just person. Moreover, cool, prudential reason itself dictates that we arrange our affairs to maximize the long-term prospects of the least advantaged, given the constraints of greatest equal freedom and fair equality of opportunity. We achieve reflective equilibrium, a condition of moral unity and stability, when our rationality coalesces with the most fundamental of our moral feelings.

Rawls's ideal society, based on the morality of compensatory reciprocity, does contain a large element of pure procedural justice. It is a constitutional democracy based on a market economy in which capital may be either privately or publicly held. But at the center of his social, substantive conception of justice is the "difference principle," which requires that distributional outcomes must maximize the advantages of the disadvantaged. Justice dictates that the fortunate compensate the unfortunate.

And so Rawls installs in his government a distribution branch, whose function is to insure satisfaction of the difference principle. Once everything has been done that can be done to promote fair equality of opportunity, and the economy has generated a distribution of income and wealth, apparently there would still be a question as to just how much this distribution branch would still have to do.[31]

With specific reference to inheritance and gift taxes, Rawls says that the branch would act "gradually and continually to correct the distribution of wealth and to prevent concentrations of power detrimental to the fair value of political liberty and fair equality of opportunity."[32] As did Gewirth, and unlike Hayek, Rawls subscribes to

J. E. Meade's principle of contrived property dispersal. Again like Gewirth, he would probably find compelling Sir Henry Phelps Brown's distinction between salutary actions taken *before* the market and disruptive action *within* the market. [33]

According to Lester C. Thurow, disequilibrium in the capital markets generates "instantaneous fortunes" that are really unearned, but are then managed well and passed on. [34] Presumably Rawls would wish the government to deal with this kind of clearly unproductive gaining.

In addition to these measures, Rawls sees the distribution branch devising a scheme of taxation to raise the revenue that justice requires. He considers a proportional expenditure tax among others. Clearly he seems to think that the distribution of income, despite the steps take to insure general fairness and to deal with property, may still fail to reflect the difference principle. His theory of justice calls for equalization beyond that stipulated by Gewirth's criterion, avoidance of "severe inequality of well-being." And, of course, Rawls envisages equalization well beyond Hayek's "minimum" to be provided for those who are unable to make their way in the market. [35]

The question that naturally arises is: How far can equalization be pushed in accordance with the difference principle? We tend to assume that in the light of this principle most Western societies are excessively unequal. My impression is that Ronald Dworkin, for one, makes this assumption. But is it correct? Recall that Rawls's criterion can be violated also by overequalization and thereby injustice done.

POLITICAL ECONOMY AND JUSTICE

Consider the modern economy as portrayed by Phelps Brown in *The Inequality of Pay*. On the whole and over time, the economy presents a picture of massive economic rationality. Differentials in earnings tend strongly to depend upon differences in intelligence, education, experience, skill, and responsibility. Historically, changes in these differentials depend on changes in supply and demand. There is a good deal of intergenerational mobility. Distribution of individual earnings appears to depend in a reasonable way upon differentials in ability to work. Income from property is much more unequal than is income from work. But the importance of property income has greatly declined in comparison with earnings. Education operates to compress differentials, although it does not seem to have much effect on intergenerational mobility, the rate of which has been both high and stable for some time. Some human potentialities, perhaps a good deal, are being lost through lack of family encouragement.

Suppose now that Rawls's distribution branch feels that greater equalization than has already been achieved is desirable in order, say, to foster greater self-respect on the part of the disadvantaged. And so it begins to push even harder against the distribution of income and wealth generated by economic rationality and corrected along the lines discussed above. To finance larger transfers, the branch imposes higher taxes and more progressive taxes. At some point this policy is bound to violate the difference principle by giving rise to both disincentives and perverse incentives. Has that point been reached? Recent experience is conclusive that the answer to this question is yes, at least for some of our welfare states.

According to David R. Cameron, there has been dramatic expansion of the public economy in advanced capitalist and semicapitalist societies.[36] These have become, he says, "tax states." In some cases, for example Sweden, the explanation is primarily ideological; in others, for example the Netherlands, expansion of the public economy has to do with dependence on international trade. Compared with the United States, Japan, Italy, and Spain, the high expansion countries have achieved greater equality at the cost of lower rates of private capital accumulation. In Sweden the percent of population below the poverty line, according to *The Economist*, is now less than 4, whereas in the United States its remains above 12.[37]

In Sweden, according to Melvyn B. Krauss, people have begun to evade taxation.[38] They trade work for leisure and engage in barter. Krauss estimates that between 1950 and 1977, public sector spending in Sweden rose from 24 to 64 percent of GNP. The impact on incentives has been severely adverse, and the Swedish economy appears to be in deep trouble.[39] In Britain, a similar revolt against "welfare liberalism" is taking place, accompanied by economic turmoil and collapse of the public sense of justice.[40] In the United States a federally sponsored experiment with a negative income tax shows that such a tax impairs incentives to work.[41]

It would appear that the economic morale of a country and its public sense of justice are both dependent upon adherence to rational political economy. The case of Sweden is particularly instructive in this respect. Apparently what the Swedes have done is to maximize the advantages of their least advantaged in the short term by undermining incentives to point of serious inefficiency. Surely this means that they are not maximizing the long-term prospects of the disadvantaged, as Rawls's difference principle demands. Indeed, the difference principle has been violated in an unexpected manner, not by preserving unnecessary inequality, but by attempting to achieve too much equality. The limits of "welfare liberalism" have come into sight. In the spring of 1979, the Conservative party came to power in Britain, pledged to policies that would restore incentives to work and save.

MARKET SOCIALISM

Although Rawls looks with favor on Meade's "property-owning democracy," he is willing to consider a market-socialist society as an appropriate way in which to institutionalize his theory of justice. This kind of an economy has won the approval of Charles E. Lindblom.

According to Lindblom, "Yugoslavia may presage the gradual development of a greatly more efficient and equitable economic order. In destroying the historical connection between market system and private enterprise, Yugoslavia may—it is at least a possibility—have set itself and the world on a new course."[42] He sees the Yugoslav workers' council type of organization as the real alternative to the modern corporation, which he thinks is inconsistent with political democracy. "The executive of the large corporation is, on many counts, the contemporary counterpart to the landed gentry of an earlier era, his voice amplified by the technology of mass communication. . . . More than class, the major specific institutional barrier to fuller democracy may therefore be the autonomy of the private corporation."[43] This is certainly an arresting speculation, that "market socialism" may be the royal road to freedom, democracy, efficiency, and justice. Can Lindblom be right?

Comparative history strongly suggests, if it does not outright demonstrate, that private property is crucial to formation of just and open societies. M. I. Finley compares the experience of ancient Greece and Rome with that of the tyrannical Middle Eastern empires. He points out that "the Graeco-Roman world was essentially one of private ownership, whether a few acres or of the enormous domains of Roman Senators and emperors, a world of private trade, private manufacture."[44] It is impossible, he says, "to translate the word 'freedom,' *elutheria* in Greek, *libertas* in Latin, or 'free man,' into any Near Eastern language, including Hebrew, or into any Far Eastern language for that matter."[45] And according to Fernand Braudel, "In the vast world of Islam, especially prior to the eighteenth century, land ownership was temporary, for there, as in China, land legally belonged to the prince. . . . When the lord died, his seigneury and all his possessions reverted to the Sultan of Istanbul or the Great Mogul of Delhi."[46]

Inspired by Clausewitz's analysis of military escalation and absolute war, Jean Baechler holds that "Capitalism is the state the economy must attain when nothing arises to hinder its law, that is, the law of efficiency."[47] His comparison of Western and Eastern civilizations leads Baechler to conclude, "*The expansion of capitalism owes its origins and its raison d'être to political anarchy.*"[48] In this respect the Western experience was unique. Politics was unable to dominate economics as it did throughout the East. The result was sustained economic growth that culminated in the industrial revolution.

Comparative European political and economic history supports the global findings of Braudel and Baechler. According to the economic historians, North and Thomas, "Efficient organization entails the establishment of institutional arrangements and property rights that create an incentive to channel individual economic effort into activities that bring the private rate of return close to the social rate of return."[49] Imperfectly stipulated, or unenforced, property rights greatly constrain the productivity of a society, as do political restraints on the extent of markets. They say that "the differences in the performance of the economies of Western Europe between 1500 and 1700 was in the main due to the type of property rights created by the emerging states in response to their continuing fiscal crisis."[50] During this period, there was sustained growth in the Netherlands and in England, relative retardation in France, stagnation and decline in Spain. In conclusion, North and Thomas assert that by the eighteenth century, "a structure of property rights had developed in the Netherlands and England which provided the incentives necessary for sustained growth. These included the inducements required to encourage innovation and the consequent industrialization. The industrial revolution was not the source of modern economic growth. It was the outcome of raising the private rate of return on developing new techniques and applying them to the production process."[51]

The historically decisive role of private property, both material and intellectual, in the development of productive and liberal societies would seem to be beyond question. Those civilizations and societies prospered in which economic freedom and a desert-based conception of justice were established. They are also the cradles of political democracy.

What of today? Has our situation so changed that we no longer need private property as a foundation for political freedom, and so presumably we could if we wished safely go over to "market socialism"? Is the market alone a sure foundation for political freedom, or is capitalism, or at least some kind of mixed economy, also required? In the opinion of one political economist, "The Yugoslav and Hungarian instances confirm what one would suppose *a priori*: the market is crucial, but ownership is, so to speak, *secundus inter pares*."[52] It does seem exceedingly likely that both social and political equilibrium depend upon private property that amounts to "concrete authorities capable of restraining Power."[53] Our present forms of economic organization would have to be, both morally and politically, gravely defective to make "market socialism" worth the risk. Is it? After all, as Peter Wiles writes, "The discovery that competition plus direct owner-management makes self-interest a very tolerable motive is the first great discovery in modern economics."[54]

HISTORY AND THEORY

Lindblom would have us believe that the capitalist firm and the modern corporation are historical accidents, the products not of economic logic, rather of disparity of bargaining power. Could this be so in a civilization in which men had come to have rational attitudes toward themselves, their societies, and nature itself? Recall Phelps Brown's analysis and explanation of the distribution of income and the rationality that the distribution displays. He points out further that "the sense that higher qualifications should be more highly paid may not be merely conventional, but rest upon a categorical judgement of fairness that goes deep in human nature."[55] This suggests that the forms of economic authority we have developed are also ratonal. Whereas if Lindblom is right, Western societies would be deeply incoherent, amalgams of distributional rationality and organizational irrationality. This may be possible, of course, but it would certainly seem unlikely.

Further doubt is cast on Lindblom's thesis by the effort made in recent years to explain the economic rationality of property rights and to advance the theory of economic organization. North and Thomas's analysis of European economic history is a remarkable demonstration of the explanatory power of the new ways of thinking.

Understanding of property rights, their formation and alteration, turns on their use as incentives in the historical drive toward greater efficiency, toward minimizing all costs, including information, transaction, and negotiation costs. In economic language, "property rights develop to internalize externalities when the gains of internalization become larger than the cost of internalization."[56] The economic rationale of private ownership is that "This concentration of benefits and costs on owners creates incentives to utilize resources more efficiently."[57] Demsetz goes on to apply this way of thinking to landownership, copyright, and patents, and the modern corporation. He reveals a paradigm in which there are dual tendencies. The first is a tendency for ownership to rest with individuals. And the second is a tendency for the extent of an individual's ownership to enlarge to the point where all costs are minimized.

In the creation and operation of the corporation, "De facto management ownership and limited liability combine to minimize the overall cost of operating large enterprises. . . . What shareholders really own are their shares and not the corporation. Ownership in the sense of control again becomes a largely individual affair."[58] In this realistic perspective on ownership, legalized exit of shareholders through organized trading of securities functions further to minimize the impact of externalities, in this case, externalities in the shape of the behavior of corporate executives, the real owners of the modern corporation.

In the later article, this type of analysis is applied to the emergence of the classical capitalist firm. The firm is shown to be a more efficient way of organizing productive activity than would be a system based on mutual contracting and profit sharing. The crux of the argument is that "the cost of team production is increased if the residual claim is not held entirely by the central monitor. . . . if profit sharing had to be relied upon for *all* team members, losses from the resulting increase in central monitor shirking would exceed the output gains from the increased incentive of other team members not to shirk."[59] The authors go on to claim that "If this were not so, profit-sharing with employees should have occurred more frequently in Western societies where such organizations are neither banned nor preferred politically."[60] The reference to political preference is, of course, to Yugoslavia. And in this connection, remember John Stuart Mill's hopes and expectations for producers' cooperatives and their failure to become widely established.

Contrary to Lindblom's indictment of corporate authority, Alchian and Demsetz conclude that the modern corporation is not an authoritarian organization. "The contractual structure arises as a means of enhancing efficient organization of team production."[61] If they are correct in their analysis of the rise of the corporation, then both Lindblom and Marx are mistaken in their understanding of economic history and given to mistaking rationally grounded economic authority for arbitrary power. The new theory of economic organization explains concentration of economic authority in terms of its efficiency and so challenges all theories that treat economic authority as just another form of irrational and unjustified domination.

Our excursion into economic history, the economics of property rights, and the theory of economic organization does not lend support to Lindblom's endorsement of "market socialism" based on workers' self-management. One rather wishes that Lindblom had dealt explicitly with these alternative interpretations of economic history and the logic of economic organization and authority. Nevertheless, "market socialism" provides an insecure foundation, at best, for political freedom and equilibrium. And it appears to be more the product of political ideology than of economic rationality. Moreover, in Yugoslavia "market socialism" appears to encourage perverse incentives that make for both injustice and inefficiency. Wiles says, "probably genuine capitalist competition within Yugoslavia would bankrupt its self-managed enterprises. For where labour is less alienated it is mostly, and in the short run, less efficient."[62]

These considerations seem to me to justify as prudent a skeptical response to Lindblom's speculative proposal that "market socialism" offers a democratic solution to the problem of corporate authority. It may well be that an economic logic has been at work to shape our institutional history. The outcome of this logic is the creation of distinctively economic types of authority that have their own justification in terms of rationality and efficiency. If this is the case, then we should be wary of trying to replace such authority with apparently more democratic forms of economic organization. Rather, our situation calls for recognition that economic and political authority are essentially different kinds of authority, each of which has its distinctive justification and function. And we need not assume that the only techniques by which authority of either kind can be controlled are political. An open society offers equality of opportunity to acquire economic authority on the basis of competitive merit.

CORPORATE CAPITALISM AND DEMOCRACY

Robert A. Dahl shares Lindblom's belief in the supposed incongruity of capitalism and democracy. Hence he proposes that we "give priority to political ends over economic ends, to liberty, equality, and justice over efficiency, prosperity and growth, a priority that the commitment to corporate capitalism reversed both in theory and in practice."[63] He thinks that it was "by an extraordinary sleight of hand" that Locke's defense of private property, suitable for an agrarian order, was transferred into the world of corporate enterprise.[64] Apparently ideological considerations, rather than disparity in bargaining power, account for the rise of corporate capitalism. Nevertheless, Dahl agrees with Lindblom that corporate capitalism cannot be rationally justified, that it has brought injustice in the form of inequality, and that it constitutes a serious impediment to political democracy.

To remedy these evils Dahl puts forward two proposals. He says that "considerations of substantive distributve justice would seem to require a considerable reduction in inequalities in wealth and income."[65] Second, he thinks, "the criteria of procedural democracy ought . . . to be applied to the government of firms."[66] By the criteria of "procedural democracy" he means political equality, effective participation, and enlightened understanding.

Unfortunately, Dahl does not attempt to specify how much redistribution his conception of justice would require, although he does seem willing to impair efficiency for the sake of equality. In this case, a problem that we noticed earlier would arise. Present equalization harms the long-term prospects of the least advantaged and so would violate the Rawlsian difference principle.

Nor does Dahl attempt to describe how "procedural democracy" is to be installed in the modern corporation. But, as does Lindblom, he appears to assume that the only way to legitimize and to control corporate authority is to politicize it. Assuming that this could even be done, the costs would certainly be very high. Indeed, I should think prohibitive in a world lurching toward greater scarcity. Unhappily or not, economic authority concentrates, as does effective ownership itself, because concentrated authority is efficent. Moreover, in the modern corporation vast disparities in "enlightened understanding" are inherent and unsurmountable. As Kenneth J. Arrow points out, "majority rule is no model for organizations with functionally differentiated elements among its membership, such as firms and universities."[67]

Finally, Dahl's concept of "procedural democracy" ignores the fact that democracy means competition, as I believe Raymond Aron once remarked. Equality of opportunity and systemic competition are hard to improve on as means for legitimating economics and competitive politics. And I see no incongruity between competitive economics and competitive politics, nor any need to try to reduce the procedures of the one to the procedures of the other.

ALTRUISTIC COLLABORATION

Lindblom's morality of "market socialism" retains competition and aspires to economic efficiency. Not so the morality of "altruistic collaboration." In his book against Rawls, Brian Barry contends that "in matters of political, social and economic organization altruistic collaboration is worth giving up a good deal of efficiency for."[68] The trouble with Rawls is that he is insufficiently egalitarian, and perversely so. Given his moral premise that our natural assets and social advantages are undeserved, Barry claims that Rawls should have advocated a much more equal distribution of income and wealth than he does. But Rawls holds on to the notion of necessary incentives. He insists, according to Barry, that "people must be paid their marginal product in order to attract them into occupations where they are most needed and once there induce them to perform conscientiously."[69] But in Barry's best of worlds, "people would be willing to regard the fact that some job needed doing as itself a salient motive for doing it. If this were so then the need for pay differentials would be greatly reduced."[70] Barry realizes that reliance on "moral incentives" is unrealistic. And then, in a startling manner, he pushes on to coercion.

"It is characteristic of Rawl's liberalism that for him the paramount value in relation to occupations is freedom of choice."[71] The workers' sovereignty principle has to go. Barry proposes "to spread the nastiest jobs around by requiring everyone, before entering higher education or entering a profession, to do, say, three years of work wherever he or she was directed."[72] This system would be supplementd by an annual "call-up." Such interference with occupational choice would, of course, be inefficient, and this Barry is quite prepared to accept. But the justice of these practices, he says, would "be difficult to deny."[73] Barry's brand of egalitarian justice overrides freedom. And freedom of choice of occupation is a right to which great importance has been attached in the West.

Much of what has been said about other of the lower points on the moral gradient applies also to Barry's egalitarian and purportedly cooperative socialism. He ignores the danger that socialism poses for political equilibrium. Indeed, he is prepared to accept not only occupational coercion but also political repression as the price of "justice."[74] Moreover, his preferring justice, as he understands it, to freedom may also mean preferring it to the welfare of the least advantaged. Are people this envious, this interested in avoiding relative deprivation? Justice conceived as enforced "altruistic collaboration" is not only self-contradictory on the face of it; it would also seem to rest on an incoherent theory of human nature, rendering people at one and the same time both too altruistic and too envious.

Finally, Barry is cavalier about economic efficiency. Is it the case that people would willingly, trade efficiency for equality, and stick to the deal, once they experience and understand its consequences? They did not in Czechoslovakia. And now we have a revolt against "welfare liberalism" in both Sweden and England. Pursuit of an egalitarian ideal against the grain of human nature frustrates human ambition and energy, is socially divisive, and sacrifices long term for present advantage. Pushed to an extreme, pursuit of this ideal infringes freedoms, without which everyone will be worse off than they otherwise would be.

EQUAL CONCERN AND RESPECT

Barry's morality of "altruistic collaboration" is not put forward as an interpretation of liberalism, but rather as an alternative to it. However, Ronald Dworkin's rather similar morality of "equal concern and respect" is advanced as "the liberal conception of equality."[75] This is the conception of equality that has always been at the root of liberalism. But we failed to appreciate the significance of this kind of equality until Rawls produced his theory of justice. According to Dworkin, the right to equal concern and respect "must be understood to be the fundamental concept of Rawl's deep theory."[76] This right, Dworkin holds, is absolutely fundamental. But even Rawls did not clearly see that this is the case. Dworkin says, "the right to equal respect is not, on his account, a product of the contract, but a condition of admission to the original position."[77]

A more straightforward reading of Rawls, I would suggest, shows that the "condition of admission" is not possession of Dworkin's fundamental right, but rather capacity for having a sense of justice, the possession of which is crucial to Rawls's understanding of what it means to be a person. Moreover, in Rawls's lexical ordering of his principles of justice, liberty, and equality of opportunity take precedence over equality. Rawls may be something of an egalitarian liberal, but he does not accord equality priority over liberty as Dworkin would have us do.[78]

Application of Dworkin's right to "equal concern and respect" to the issues of income distribution and private property produces the following results: "The liberal . . . finds the market defective principally because it allows morally irrelevant differences, like differences in talent, to affect distribution, and he therefore considers that those who have less talent, as the market judges talent, have a right to some form of redistribution in the name of justice." On the score of property, he says, "The liberal will . . . accept some right to property, because he will count some sovereignty over a range of personal possessions essential to dignity."[79] Evidently a "liberal" society is egalitarian, perhaps highly egalitarian, and confines private ownership to "personal possessions." Perhaps Dworkin is best described as a "collectivistic liberal," if indeed we can use the word "liberal" at all with reference to his thinking. In any event, operationally speaking, his ideal is open to all of the objections that we have raised against socialism.

CREATIVE SOLIDARITY

C. B. Macpherson advances a morality of "creative solidarity" (my label) as the great alternative to the moralities of individuality, freedom and well-being, compensatory reciprocity, and "market socialism." In the light of his ideal, as is the case with Barry and Dworkin, these are all defective visions of the good for man, mainly by way of being insufficiently egalitarian and communitarian. They do not recognize "the equal right of every man and woman to the full development and use of his or her capabilities."[80] According to Macpherson, "the enjoyment and development of one's capacities is to be done for the most part in conjunction with others, in some relation of community."[81] In practice, this means that democracy must become "participatory," for "only throught actual involvement in *joint political action* can people transcend their consciousness of themselves as consumers and appropriators.[82] In this way would Macpherson bring to completion that process of psychological and moral transformation that Marx thought he saw in the dialectics of capitalism itself.[83]

In Macpherson's ideal society, participatory democratic institutions, envisaged as a pyramidal councils system, are combined with what economists call a "command economy." "A fully democratic society requires democratic political control over the uses to which the amassed capital and the remaining natural resources of the society are put. It probably does not matter whether this takes the form of social ownership of all capital, or a social control of it so thorough as to be virtually the same as ownership."[84] So great is his aversion to market relations among men, Macpherson never even entertains the possibility of organizing his economy along the lines of Yugoslav "market socialism."[85] Indeed, he proposes to substitute participatory democracy for the market. How this could be done in modern societies I cannot see. Anyway, somehow people are expected to reach agreement on an economic plan and not to have a plan imposed upon them, as is the case with the command economies that we know. Perhaps we have never seen a genuine "command economy," that is, one based on "creative solidarity." Nevertheless, Macpherson is working with a conception of a general will that finds expression not in moral and legal rules, as Rousseau conceived it, but in a set of integrated economic priorities and policies, to which all contribute and subscribe. So long as men remain as they are, the cost of the contemplated negotiations is inconceivable.

This morality of "creative solidarity" is ultimately derived from a curious kind of "property" right that Macpherson calls the right "to a kind of society."[86] But I fail to see how it strengthens Macpherson's case for his ideal by phrasing it in terms of property right. Is this not to slip into rhetoric? What he needs to make is a utilitarian argument to the effect that democratic, command-economy socialism, is workable and will maximize human fulfillment. This he does not do, preferring instead to continue his crusade against liberalism.

According to Macpherson, "The central problem of liberal-democratic theory may be stated as the difficulty of reconciling the liberal property right with that equal effective right of all individuals to use and develop their capacities which is the essential ethical principle of liberal democracy."[87] As we have seen, in the West, and only in the West, did there arise under liberal auspices efficient property rights and efficient forms of economic organization and authority. By and large and over the long run, the inequalities associated with these developments served freedom, and increasingly so as opportunity became more equal. Given their differences and the circumstances that men face, it is impossible to eradicate inequalities from human life. The best we can do is to work against those inequalities that hinder equal freedom, that is, equality of opportunity, and let men sort themselves out on the basis of their aspirations and comparative advantages. Each will have done the best he could, and it is pointless to ask for more, to set up an irrelevant moral alternative. In this light and contrary to Macpherson, Western liberalism has offered, and continues to offer, a coherent philosophy of life.

By comparison with the liberal tradition of the West, Macpherson's teleocratic egalitarianism raises all sorts of misgivings. Is it the case that we are so thoroughly social as he and Marx appear to think? We all have our own plans of life, as Rawls and the autonomist liberals recognize. Macpherson would have us believe that apathy brought on by inequality has been the bar to participatory democracy. But what of the negotiating costs? Political authority, like economic authority, tends to concentrate, because, happily or not, concentrated authority is efficient. We would have to be much more deeply, and irrationally, political animals than we are to be willing to absorb the costs of Macpherson's vision of participatory democracy.

Could agreement be reached on so detailed a plan as to render the market obsolete? There is good reason, given the diversity of human wants and goals, to think that an attempt to do so would only exacerbate conflict. No matter what economic priorities and plans were democratically decided on, some people and very probably many would be bound to feel oppressed, unless indeed we are morally transfigured. Only then could individualism and collectivism fuse in the manner Macpherson desires. Moreover, as Wiles shows, " 'Freedom under socialism' logically entails a *caesura* between the political and the economic orders."[88] If this is the case, then Macpherson is really asking for what is morally and psychologically impossible, a way of life that is inconsistent with rational human nature as we know it.

I am inclined to think, therefore, that the fatal defect of the morality of "creative solidarity" is its incoherent moral psychology. Although he wants both individual creativity and social solidarity, Macpherson never tells us how these are to be brought together. Does not John Passmore's charge against Marx apply equally well to him? "To attempt to describe in detail a society which is at once unified and creative would have brought to light the fatal contracdictions inherent in the whole enterprise."[89] It is not enough conceptually to conjoin command-economy socialism and participatory democracy and to affirm that such an institutional melange will work for human freedom and development, given the reasons we have advanced for thinking that it would miscarry. Even if the command economy has never really been tried, every historical instance we have of it from those palace-and-temple complexes, of which M. I. Finley writes, to the present, has been an authoritarian affront to both freedom and equality.

ABSOLUTE EGALITARIANISM[90]

At the end of the line we come to Roberto Mangabeira Unger's morality of nearly "absolute egalitarianism." Again the label is mine. I say "nearly," because it is not clear how far Unger thinks we could move in the direction of his ideal. Moreover, his use of concepts like "corporation" and "organic," and his conception of a "hierarchy" of communities all would seem to imply some tension with absolute equality. Nevertheless, his basic complaint against the moralities of individuality and compensatory reciprocity is that they both wrongly assume that "social relations can be emptied of any element of personal dependence or domination without it being necessary to establish the precise ends for which power ought to be exercised."[91] The ends that Unger has in mind now lie latent in human nature, awaiting extraction by way of total democratization of life.

From this angle even John Rawls takes on the guise of an aristocrat, a latter-day purveyor of *noblesse oblige.* He would have the able look after the disadvantaged, whereas the only truly moral response to human inequalities is to submerge them in the full democracy, toward which the welfare–corporate state is already tending. And the proponents of individuality are but apostles of domination. They urge us to ignore human differences and to get on with our own lives, accepting the structures of authority that arise among us as morally justified, necessary for the getting of what we all want and value. But in societies based on either the morality of individuality or compensatory reciprocity, or even on Macpherson's creative solidarity, genuine authority does not exist, only "tranquil exercise of power, which men call authority."[92]

In the truly just society only those ends and values to which men have openly and democratically consented count as valid expresions of their human nature. Anything else is, and has been down the ages, a dictate of the superior, whether they style themselves Mandarins, Brahmins, aristocrats, or Western liberals. This is moral Franciscanism, or is it moral Jacobinism, *à l'outrance!*[93]

Unger speaks of a morality of "sympathy" that he understands as a "hypothetical condition in which the greatest individuality is allied with the greatest sociability."[94] This ideal is to be approached through a society composed of "organic groups," in which direct democracy is practiced. In this way the shared goals, above all that of equality, that are inherent in, and now lie hidden in, our humanity will be brought to light. In Unger's utopia rights to property do not exist, considerations of economic efficiency are meaningless, and economic authority based on competitive merit fades away. "The democracy of ends in the organic groups consists in the progressive replacement of meritocratic by democratic power in the ordinary in-stitutions of society and, above all, in its occupational groups."[95] Radical equality is somehow to lead freely to monolithic unity of pur-pose as individuality is maximized. For the first time true justice would enter the world as men escape from domination and depen-dence through sympathetic communion and pursuit of democrat-ically elicited common goods.

The problem of justice arises, I would suppose, because human be-ings are not naturally equal and are condemned to live in scarcity. To attempt to deal with human inequalities by transcending them, as Unger does, is to move from the world of morality and politics into a religious realm. Indeed, it is to move right off the map of human justice. Again I think, as in the case of Macpherson's "creative soli-darity," that Unger's morality of sympathy is based on a mistaken con-ception of our moral psychology. We are simply not so constituted as to maximize together our individuality and our sociability. There can be no human society that is both creative and fully unified on the basis of nearly absolute egalitarianism. Unger's is an essentially relig-ious ideal, not of this world, the pursuit of which would only destroy autonomy, inflame enviousness, and place us at the mercy of the men of power. Once people have become individuated and rational as we have, there is no going back past Machiavelli.

ISSUES AND ALTERNATIVES

Looking back now over the ground we have traversed, I would of-fer the following observations on the nature and structure of our great debate. If we take Rawls's morality of compensatory reciprocity as our benchmark, then to his left, up the gradient, lie the classical or autonomist liberals; the proponents of procedural justice; individ-ualism; private property; economic rationality; and, with the excep-tions of Hayek and Nozick, equality of opportunity. Perhaps Alan Gewirth's morality of equal freedom and well-being best exemplifies a moderate and commonsensical version of the classical liberal philosophy of life.

To Rawls's right, as we go down the gradient, we move in the direction of increasingly egalitarian moralities. The egalitarians appear to be captivated by a Marxian ideal of cooperative, as distinguished from compensatory, reciprocity, for which there is no warrant in our moral experience, at least since our hunting and gathering days. The equality and cooperative solidarity characteristic of prehistoric bands or good families does not translate into a workable social ideal, although this psychic heritage may well help to account for our endemic discontent with modern society. Our genetic ambivalence, the tension between our individuality and our sociability, obviously informs and structures the debate over justice and its relations to freedom, equality, and property.

Given our intrinsic ambivalence, it seems to me that societies are best conceived as Hegelian-Calder mobiles, in which the divergent components of our nature operate to balance one another. In institutional terms, the central balance that sustains freedom in all its forms in our modern societies is that between economics and politics conceived as interpenetrating and yet distinct and autonomous spheres of activity. To destroy this balance would not release creativity and establish harmony. The real alternatives are balanced equilibrium or authoritarian order. Hegel's distinction between civil society and the state still prevails.

Nevertheless, as we go down the egalitarian gradient the economic dimension of life disappears into the political. Economic authority and inequality are to be gotten rid of through abolition of private property, democratization of the corporation, displacement of Benthamite by moral incentives, disregard for economic rationality and efficiency, and finally transcendence of market relations. This is a prescription for total politicization of life, for concentration and unification of economic and political authority that would, given everything we know about human nature and history, offer prizes, competition for which could not be other than ferocious, an eruption of what Hobbes understood by diffidence. Without the independence provided by private property and the market, political and economic authority would amalgamate into pure power, would surely turn into what the egalitarians call "domination."

Still the antipathy of the extreme egalitarians to the market economy is understandable and from their standpoint well founded. As we have seen, minimization of costs through market processes does tend to concentrate economic authority in the form of effective or de facto ownership. Although industrial societies are far less unequal than their predecessors, still the market may appear unjustly to magnify human inequalities. For these tend to cumulate multiplicatively, as J. E. Meade and Phelps Brown have shown. This phenomenon is the main inegalitarian consequence of economic rationality and our reliance on the market. It cannot be defeated by increasing equality of opportunity, only mitigated. For increasing equality of opportunity may well have meritocratic as well as equalizing implications. And direct action against economic inequality and authority runs up against two barriers. It first begins to violate the Rawlsian difference principle by worsening the prospects of the disadvantaged, and then it begins adversely to affect their present welfare.

THE LOGIC OF EGALITARIANISM

The extreme egalitarians, Unger and Macpherson, do not drift into teleocratic politicization of life. They are driven there by the logic of their moralities. Once market relations among men are seen as inherently immoral and fatal to community, some kind of totally planned and politicized economy is the only alternative left open to them.[96] And their claim that modern societies are naturally skidding toward corporatist planning may well be wishful thinking.[97] In any event, both Unger and Macpherson, so concerned are they with "domination," appear insensitive to the market's contribution to freedom and to the necessity for a social balance of power, to which private property makes an indispensable contribution. Their presumption that acceptance of their institutional recommendations would bring about a requisite transformation of human nature and attitudes lacks empirical foundation in our historical psychology. Even if we were to attempt to slake the thirst of our hunting-and-gathering ancestry for equality and sharing at the cost of depersonalized economic rationality, it is not a deal we could stick with, given the individuated and Benthamite incentives at work within us. Human nature can change and has changed, but not in the direction dictated by the logic of egalitarianism.

The basic trouble with Barry's morality of altruistic collaboration and Dworkin's equal concern and respect is that both are driven to flirt with coercion to achieve their aims. The one is prepared to dispense with workers' sovereignty, and the other with equality of opportunity. Here we see egalitarian justice in direct conflict with individual rights. Moreover, these moralities display a simplistic and careless view of private property, so strikingly announced in

Dworkin's willingness to confine it to "personal possessions" for the sake of human "dignity." One would have thought that personal independence and social equilibrium are at stake as well in the case for private property. They neglect the vital systemic dimension of the justification of the right to property.

DIMENSIONS OF PROPERTY

Today we are told to stop thinking of property as things — capital equipment, durables, and the like — and to think about it in a more sophisticated manner, as a "bundle" of rights. The "bundle" conception of property, it seems to me, fails adequately to take account of a distinction that emerges from our analysis of the great debate, namely, the distinction between property as wealth and property as a form of economic authority, the effective ownership that corporate executives possess. We need to take a functional as well as a legal view of property. From a functional standpoint, property as economic authority is going to be present in any economy. And property as economic authority is something that is competed for both within and between economic enterprises. It is a form of authority that is and can be kept more or less self-controlling and self-regulating. Corporate authority should not be assumed to be illegitimate merely because it is not subject to democratic, political forms of accountability. Moreover, competion for economic authority offers an avenue for human ambition that would otherwise flow into politics.

Property as wealth, on the other hand, performs a background, stabilizing function. Like the academic practice of tenured appointment, property as wealth operates to secure the freedom of those who do not have it as well as of those who do.

From the functional point of view, what we really want are forms of property that taken together serve both to promote economic efficiency and to protect rights. I very much doubt that we would be willing, in a Rawlsian condition of "reflective equilibrium," to consider just a structure of property rights that failed to do both of these things. This suggests that into any final justification of property rights considerations both of utility and systemic support for individual freedom must enter. Only myopic and politicized egalitarians would disdain the benefits of an economically and politically effective system of property rights, with its attendant inequalities, and in the name of justice attempt to equalize by getting rid of property as wealth. Prop-

erty as economic authority cannot be done away with in any economy. The only question is whether authority is efficient or not.

LINDBLOM'S MARKET SOCIALISM

In this light, the case for "market socialism," as expounded by
Lindbolm would seem to be both historically and theoretically
flawed. And it would involve us in what I sense to be unacceptable
political risks. Moreover, "market socialism" relies on Benthamite incentives. This being so, there is no point to eliminating wealth as an
incentive to both work and innovation. If you are going to rely on the
motive of private profit anyway, it is pointless to object to private
wealth on moral grounds. To adopt "market socialism" would be a
tremendous gamble for little, if any, returns.

Since our society is open to institutional competition and evolution, presumably self-managed, communally owned forms of enterprise should be able to take hold where people find them both morally attractive and economically effective. Some kind of general organizational equilibrium may naturally and spontaneously come
about, an equilibrium that is fully consistent with security of political
freedom.[98] Clearly, preservation of institutional competition is the
more prudent and more liberal course to follow.

Moreover, is it not likely that full-fledged "market socialism" is an
essentially unstable form of political economy, dependent on dictatorship, however moderated? In the absence of political constraints,
Yugoslavia might very well have evolved in a capitalist direction,
given the historically demonstrated economic rationality of private
property. Perhaps "market socialism" is a plant that can grow only in
the shadow of the Soviet Union, a deterred Soviet Union, one may
add. This brings us to the real alternatives.

WELFARE AND CLASSICAL LIBERALISM

The moralities of welfare and classical liberalism have much in
common, although rather less than Hayek would seem to think when
he says about Rawls that "the differences between us seemed more
verbal than substantial."[99] And sometimes, not always, Rawls does
write in a manner that bears Hayek out. Both moralities share a preference for procedural justice, although Rawls is obviously not the
stringent proceduralist that Hayek and Oakeshott are. Both moral-

ities are alert to the importance of Benthamite incentives and to the desirability of economic effectiveness, although Rawls less so than the classical liberals. They both dismiss the extreme egalitarian moralities out of hand. Both want societies of independent, self-reliant men, conscious of their own worth, indifferent to invidiousness and the promptings of envy, men who are not rivalrous and yet unafraid of competition, and who can make their own lives in what Rawls calls a "social union of social unions." Rawls views democratic politics as not much better than regulated grabbing, and Hayek would put a stop to it by restricting legislation to general rules. The spirit of Hayek's "evolutionary utilitarianism," the expression that I used earlier to sum up his outlook, is certainly similar to that embedded in Rawls's "difference principle." Both seek to serve the long-run good of man.

Nevertheless, Hayek and Oakeshott write off "social" justice as meaningless, whereas Rawls does his best to formulate a rationally and emotionally acceptable theory of social justice. The classical liberals insist on the economic and political necessity and beneficence of private property, whereas the welfare liberal is prepared to contemplate a market-socialist economy. How can we explain these obviously significant differences between these two expressions of liberalism?

NATURE AND SOCIETY

Hayek says, "Nature can be neither just nor unjust."[100] I take this to imply that Rawls's compensatory attitude toward life is inappropriate or unfounded. According to Rawls, "The natural distribution is neither just nor unjust; nor is it unjust that men are born into society at some particular position. These are simple natural facts."[101] But then he goes on immediately to argue that "What is just and unjust is the way that institutions deal with these facts. . . . In justice as fairness men agree to share one another's fate."[102] Rawls's theory of social justice and his conception of human society are designed to deal in a fair way with the arbitrariness of fortune. This is a very different attitude toward life and society from that which Hayek takes. And it differs also from the views of Oakeshott as expressed in the following passage: "the civil condition and a state understood in terms of civil association postulates self-determined autonomous human beings seeking the satisfaction of their wants in self-chosen transactions with others of their kind."[103] Oakeshott's beings deal with one another as ultimately separate individuals; they have no common fate in which they share.

We are in the presence of ultimate moral, perhaps even religious or metaphysical, intuitions between which one may choose or fluctuate.

For I see no rational or empirical way to resolve this question as to what life and society ought to be. Argument over what goes on in Rawls's "original position," of which there has been so much,[104] provides no way out. For in the "original position" the dictates of rationality are tailored to support, not to evoke, the basic moral intuition that issues in the morality of compensatory reciprocity.

Hayek thinks that a morality of sharing would prove fatal to the freedom and well-being that the open society has to offer. But this is a forecast, not a demonstrable truth. All we can say is that if the consequences of acting of Rawls's theory of justice proved to be morally unacceptable, we could and would abandon it. The consequences I have in mind have to do with kinds of persons a Rawlsian society produced. And here we find a moral criterion that is common to classical and welfare liberalism, namely, an ideal of personality. No theory of justice that in practice worked against human autonomy and independence would be acceptable in a liberal civilization. Any form of society or economy that worked to create what Oakeshott calls "dependent" men would clearly violate the spirit of liberalism.

JUSTICE, FREEDOM, AND PROPERTY

At the heart of the liberal philosophy of life is the idea of equality as the equal right to freedom, to equality of opportunity. Hayek sometimes refers to equality of opportunity as an illusion, but he always insists that his vision of the open society gives every man the best chance in life that he can have. Alan Gewirth explicitly endorses equality of opportunity as the primary objective of public policy in the just society. And Rawls calls for "fair" equality of opportunity and sees no conflict between this principle and his difference principle. In the crucial case of education, he says, "the difference principle world allocate resources in education . . . so as to improve the long-term expectation of the least favored. If this end is attained by giving more attention to the better endowed, it is permissible; otherwise not."[105] I presume that allocation of educational resources on the basis of competitive merit works to further the prospects of the least favored.

In this perspective, a liberal theory of justice would hold that inequalities are justified so long as they are both the outcomes of, and necessary conditions for, freedom. As John Plamenatz well said, "inequalities of power must, in a free and equalitarian society, arise out of freedom and must also serve it."[106] It is not to be assumed, as the egalitarian exponents of social justice tend to assume, that all the inequalities that arise in modern society are forms of "domination." The liberal will wish to distinguish between those inequalities that foster freedom and equality of opportunity and those that hinder or are destructive of freedom.

In an efficient economy, open competition on the basis of equality of opportunity generates differentials in income, wealth, and economic authority. Given human differences, these inequalities are inescapable if we are to have, sustain, and increase the wealth in which all share. This wealth serves freedom, for its is the foundation and context of all the opportunities that a modern society affords its members. If its positions are open and all have access to the education that they can manage and that fits them for the positions to which they aspire, that is to say, if there is fair equality of opportunity and fair competition, then the society is well on its way to meeting the criteria of liberal justice. It will not be a perfect society, for complete equality of opportunity is unattainable so long as wealth functions not only to maintain political equilibriums but also to influence politics and policy, so long as there are families that inherit wealth and influence their children for better or for worse. But being what we are it is the best we can do, and recent attempts to equalize the human condition confirm this conclusion.

The liberal just society provides plenty of room for private property as an incentive to industry, as an avenue of self-expression and disclosure, as an efficient form of economic authority, and as a counterweight to government. Inequality of property, whether effective or sleeping property, does not imply unequal freedom or injustice. Inequality of property is just so long as it is a necessary feature of an institutional structure that fosters, indeed maximizes, human freedom. In a genuinely liberal society justice, freedom and property stand in a relation, not of opposition, but of mutual justification and support.

NOTES

1. Bertrand de Jouvenel, *Sovereignty: An Inquiry into the Political Good*, trans. J. F. Huntington (Cambridge: Cambridge Univ. Press, 1957), p. 139.

2. de Jouvenel, *The Pure Theory of Politics* (Cambridge: Cambridge Univ. Press, 1963), p. 190.

3. I borrow the idea of "welfare liberalism" from Gerald F. Gaus, "The Convergence of Rights and Utility: A Study of Rawls's and Mill's Liberalism" (Ph.d. diss., 1979), University of Pittsburgh.

4. See Oakeshott, *On Human Conduct* (Oxford: Clarendon, 1975); Hayek, *Law, Legislation and Liberty: A New Statement of the Liberal Principles of Justice and Political Economy,* 2 vols. (Chicago: Univ. of Chicago Press, 1973, 1976); Berlin, *Four Essays on Liberty* (London: Oxford Univ. Press, 1969); Shils, "The Antinomies of Liberalism," in Research Institute on International Change, ed., *The Relevance of Liberalism* (Boulder, Colo.: Westview, 1978), pp. 135-200, and "An Age of Embarassment," *Encounter* 51 (October 1978), pp. 82-95; and Nozick, *Anarchy, State, and Utopia* (New York: Basic Books, 1974).

5. Gewirth, *Reason and Morality* (Chicago: Univ. of Chicago Press, 1978), p. 313.

6. Macpherson, *Democratic Theory: Essays in Retrieval* (Oxford: Clarendon 1973), Chap. 4.

7. Rawls, *A Theory of Justice* (Cambridge: Harvard Univ. Press, 1971).

8. Oakeshott, op. cit., p. 324.

9. Lindblom, *Politics and Markets: The World's Political-Economic Systems* (New York: Basic Books, 1977).

10. Ibid., pp. 332-33.

11. See Brian Barry, *The Liberal Theory of Justice* (Oxford: Clarendon 1973).

12. See Ronald Dworkin, *Taking Rights Seriously* (London: Duckworth, 1977); and "Liberalism," in Stuart Hampshire, ed., *Public and Private Morality* (Cambridge: Cambridge Univ. Press, 1978), pp. 113-43.

13. Macpherson, *The Life and Times of Liberal Democracy* (Oxford: Oxford Univ. Press, 1977), Chapter 5. For a comparison of the principles of genuine Marxism, Maoism, and Titoism, see P. J. D. Wiles, *The Political Economy of Communism* (Cambridge: Harvard Univ. Press, 1962), chap. 17.

14. Unger, *Knowledge and Politics* (New York: The Free Press, 1975).

15. Oakeshott, op. cit., p. 321.

16. On the formation and nature of liberal personality, see Oakeshott, op. cit., pp. 235-45; John Plamenatz, "Liberalism," in Phillip Paul Wiener, ed., *Dictionary of the History of Ideas* (New York: Charles Scribner's Sons, 1973), vol 3; Zevedei Barbu, *Problems of Historical Psychology* (London: Routledge & Kegan Paul, 1960), Chaps. 5 and 6; and my "Toward a General Theory of Human Nature and Dynamics," in J. Roland Pennock and John W. Chapman, eds., *Human Nature in Politics: Nomos XVII* (New York: New York Univ. Press, 1977) pp. 292-319.

17. See J.G.A. Pocock, *The Machiavellian Moment: Florentine Political Thought and the Atlantic Republican Tradition* (Princeton: Princeton Univ. Press, 1975), part III; and H. T. Dickinson, *Liberty and*

Property: Political Ideology in Eighteenth Century Britain (New York: Holmes and Meier, 1978).

18. Hayek, *The Constitution of Liberty* (London: Routledge & Kegan Paul, 1960), p. 141.

19. Ibid.

20. Hayek, *Law, Legislation and Liberty*, vol. 2, *The Mirage of Social Justice*, p. 10.

21. Hayek, *The Constitution of Liberty*, p. 385. For a comparison of Hayek and Rawls , see my review of *The Mirage of Social Justice,* in 16 *Journal of Economic Literature* (March 1978) , pp. 96-98 .

22. Hayek, *The Constitution of Liberty*, p. 44.

23. Gewirth, op. cit., p. 290.

24. Ibid., p. 209.

25. Ibid., p. 216.

26. Ibid., p.246.

27. Phelps Brown, *The Inequality of Pay* (Oxford: Oxford Univ. Press, 1977), p. 332.

28. The Institute for Fiscal Studies, report of a committee chaired by Professor J. E. Meade, *The Structure and Reform of Direct Taxation* (London: George Allen & Unwin, 1978), pp. 512-14.

29. "Rawls's Theory of Justice," *The American Political Science Review* 69 (June 1975), pp. 588-93, p. 588.

30. Rawls, op. cit., p. 575.

31. According to Robert Paul Wolff, "it would require very considerable power to enforce the sorts of wage rates, tax policies, transfer payments, and job regulation called for by the difference principle. The men and women who apply the principle, make the calculations, and issue the redistribution orders will be the most powerful persons in the society, be they econometricians, elected representatives, or philosopher-kings." *Understanding Rawls* (Princeton: Princeton Univ. Press, 1977), p. 202.

32. Rawls, op. cit., p. 277.

33. Phelps Brown, op. cit., p. 329.

34. According to Thurow, to eliminate or reduce disequilibrium in the capital markets, "The simplest procedure would be to abolish the current corporate income tax, but to require that all firms distribute all of their earnings and depreciation allowances to their stockholders." *Generating Inequality: Mechanisms of Distribution in the U.S. Economy* (New York: Basic Books, 1975), p. 202. Mr. Ray A. Kroc, the MacDonald's hamburger man, went in worth from $50 million to $500 million in five years. Ibid., p. 235.

35. Hayek, *The Mirage of Social Justice*, p. 85.

36. Cameron, "The Expansion of the Public Economy: A Comparative Analysis," *The American Political Science Review* 72 (December 1978), pp. 1243-61.

37. *The Economist*, (February 3, 1979), p. 65.

38. Krauss, "The Swedish Tax Revolt," *Wall Street Journal*, February 1, 1979.

39. See John Vinocur, "Sweden's Economic Success Sours," *New York*

Times, March 24, 1978.

40. See Andrew Knight, "Tax Me, I'm British," *New York Times*, March 8, 1978; and Jeremy Hardie, "The Pound Out of Your Pocket," *Times Literary Supplement*, March 10, 1978.

41. See Robert Reinhold, "Minimum Income Test: Pros, Cons," *Pittsburgh Post-Gazette*, February 8, 1979.

42. Lindblom, op. cit., p. 343. Note also his statement that: "as Marx saw more clearly than the classical economists, the historically given distribution of wealth is such that, when potential suppliers of capital and potential suppliers of labor contemplate joining with each other in an enterprise, the suppliers of capital have the necessary exchange or bargaining power to insist that authority be in their hands rather than in the hands of the workers. Not by logic, but by history, owners of capital have become the owners of the enterprise." Ibid., p. 105.

43. Ibid., p. 356.

44. Finley, *The Ancient Economy* (Berkeley: Univ. of California Press, 1973), p. 29. "The Near Eastern economies were dominated by large palace- or temple-complexes, who owned the greater part of the arable, virtually monopolized anything that can be called 'industrial production' as well as foreign trade . . . and organized the economic, military, political and religious life of the society through a single complicated, bureaucratic, record-keeping operation for which the word 'rationing,' taken very broadly, is as good a one-word description as I can think of." Ibid., p. 28.

45. Ibid.

46. Braudel, *Afterthoughts on Material Civilization and Capitalism*, trans. Patricia M. Ranum (Baltimore: The John Hopkins Univ. Press, 1977), p. 73. He says, "the Chinese state showed constant hostility to the spread of capitalism." And in eighteenth-century Cairo the great merchants "were devoured by political society." Ibid., pp. 72 and 74. On Russian patrimonialism and its fateful consequences, see Richard Pipes, *Russia Under the Old Regime* (London: Weidenfeld and Nicolson, 1974).

47. Baechler, *The Origins of Capitalism*, trans. Barry Cooper (Oxford: Basil Blackwell, 1975), p. 56.

48. Ibid., p. 77. Baechler compares the histories of Byzantium, Imperial China, and Japan. In the last, a weak government led to a flourishing market economy, as in the West.

49. Douglass C. North and Robert Paul Thomas, *The Rise of the West: A New Economic History* (Cambridge: Cambridge Univ. Press, 1973), p. 1.

50. Ibid., p. 97 "The fiscal policy of the French Crown . . . did almost everything conceivable to thwart the spread of an extensive market and thereby surrendered the gains that lay therein." In Spain, "As the Crown's financial difficulties increased, seizure, confiscation, or the unilateral alteration of contracts were recurrent phenomena which ultimately affected every group engaged in commerce or industry as well as agriculture." Ibid., pp. 122 and 131.

51. Ibid., p. 157.

52. P. J. D. Wiles, *Economic Institutions Compared* (New York: Halsted Press, 1977), p. 484.

53. Bertrand de Jouvenel, *Power: The Natural History of Its Growth,* trans. J. F. Huntington (London: Batchworth 1952), p. 256. On the relations between economic and political history, see also the following: E. Lipson *A Planned Economy or Free Enterprise: The Lessons of History,* 2d ed (London: Adam & Charles Black, 1946); Albert O., Hirschman, *The Passions and the Interests: Political Arguments for Capitalism before Its Triumph* (Princeton: Princeton Univ. Press, 1977); Joyce Oldham Appleby, *Economic Thought and Ideology in Seventeenth-Century England* (Princeton: Princeton Univ. Press 1978); and Thomas A. Horne, *The Social Thought of Bernard Mandeville: Virtue and Commerce in Early Eighteenth Century England* (London: Macmillan 1978).

54. Wiles, *Economic Institutions Compared,* p. 16.

55. Phelps Brown, op. cit., p. 330.

56. H. Demsetz, "Toward a Theory of Property Rights," in Erik G. Furubotn and Svetozar Pejovich, eds., *The Economics of Property Rights* (Cambridge: Ballinger, 1974), pp. 31-42; p. 34.

57. Ibid., p. 39.

58. Ibid., p. 42.

59. A. Alchian and H. Demsetz, "Production, Information Costs, and Economic Organization," in Furubotn and Pejovich, op. cit., pp. 303-25; p. 314.

60. Ibid., p. 315.

61. Ibid., p. 324.

62. Wiles, op. cit., p. 136.

63. Dahl, "On Removing Certain Impediments to Democracy in the United States," *Dissent* (Summer 1978), pp. 310-24; p. 317.

64. Ibid., p. 315.

65. Ibid., pp. 321-22.

66. Ibid., p. 322.

67. Arrow, *The Limits of Organization* (New York: Norton, 1974), p. 79.

68. Barry, op. cit., p. 168.

69. Ibid., p. 156.

70. Ibid., p. 162.

71. Ibid., pp. 162-63. As for the principle of workers' sovereignty, Wiles says that "it is of far greater social and political importance than consumers' sovereignty." *Economic Institutions Compared,* p. 185.

72. Barry, op. cit., p. 164.

73. Ibid., p. 165. Barry's devotion to equality at times would seem to lead him into serious misunderstanding of Rawls. He thinks that Rawls bases self-respect entirely on equal possession of civil and political liberties. "That equality of self-respect may be as much or more hindered by inequalities of wealth or power themselves apparently does not occur to him." Ibid., p. 32. Rawls seems to be quite aware of this consideration. Indeed, it is the reason why he is prepared to contemplate pushing equalization beyond the barrier of economic rationality.

74. Ibid., p. 142. He says, "unlike Rawls, I am prepared to allow for the possibility of a politically repressive society with other advantages (perhaps Yugoslavia) being judged more highly than a society (perhaps Italy) which offers parliamentary democracy and, on the whole, the liberal freedoms, but is immensely corrupt and unjust in social and economic matters."

75. Dworkin, *Taking Rights Seriously*, p. 273.

76. Ibid., p. 181.

77. Ibid.

78. On Dworkin's claim that his conception of equality is implicit in classical liberalism, see the following: Martin Diamond, "The Declaration and the Constitution: Liberty, Democracy, and the Founders," *The Public Interest* 41 (Fall 1975), pp. 39-55; Thomas Pangle, "Rediscovering Rights," *The Public Interest* 50 (Winter 1978), pp. 157-60; John M. Blum, *The Burden of American Equality* (Oxford: Clarendon, 1978); and J. R. Pole, *The Pursuit of Equality in American History* (Berkeley: Univ. of California Press, 1978). The classical liberals, including the American founders and their descendants, were not so much interested in equality as in liberty, independence, and opportunity. After all, the founders were men who saw their opportunity to become independent and took it. According to Blum, " 'Distinctions in society,' Jackson wrote, and Lincoln agreed, 'will always exist under every just government. Equality of talents . . . or of wealth cannot be produced by human institutions.' Every man, he continued, was equally justified to protection by law 'in the full enjoyment of the gifts of Heaven and the fruits of superior industry . . . and virtue,' but no laws could alter 'natural and just advantages,' natural human distinctions." Op. cit., p. 10. Pole points out that "a genuinely egalitarian ideology would conflict with the American system of incentives, which was just as important to the public conscience and probably more popular." He concludes, "It is the individual whose rights are the object of the special solicitude of the Constitution and for whose protection the Republic had originally justified its claim to independent existence." Op. cit., pp. 351 and 358. Bernard Schwartz argues that Rawlsian justice is incompatible with the American Bill of Rights. *The Great Rights of Mankind* (New York: Oxford Univ. Press, 1977), pp. 228-30.

79. Dworkin, "Liberalism," in Stuart Hampshire, ed., *Public and Private Morality* (Cambridge: Cambridge Univ. Press, 1978). pp. 113-43; pp.137 and 138-39. See also "What Rights Do We Have? in *Taking Rights Seriously*, pp. 266-78.

80. Macpherson, *The Life and Times*, p. 114. On the difficulties inherent in the notion of "full" development, see John Plamenatz, *Karl Marx's Philosophy of Man* (Oxford: Clarendon 1975), pp. 347ff.

81. Macpherson, *Life and Times*, p. 99.

82. Ibid., p. 100.

83. "Marx points out that the capitalist form of production necessarily stresses the need for social togetherness and mutual co-operation in the productive process. This statement contradicts the individualistic

model on which capitalist economic theory operates, and this antagonism between capitalist theory and practice ultimately causes the capitalist mode of production to fetter its own development. The antagonism can be resolved only in socialism." Shlomo Avineri, *The Social and Political Thought of Karl Marx* (Cambridge: Cambridge Univ. Press, 1968), p. 176.

84. Macpherson, *Life and Times*, p. 111.

85. Earlier Macpherson attempted to derive support from Rousseau for his hostility to the market by interpreting Rousseau's rhetorical remarks about wealth as "a prohibition of the purchase and sale of free wage labour." Ibid., p. 17. On my reading of it, Rousseau was simply expressing his view that excessive inequality is incompatible with freedom.

86. Macpherson, "Capitalism and the Changing Concept of Property," in Eugene Kamenka and R. S. Neale, eds., *Feudalism, Capitalism and Beyond* (New York: St. Martin's, 1975), pp. 104-24; p. 121. For a persuasive critique of Macpherson's way of thinking about property, see Alice Erh-Soon Tay, "Property and Law in the Society of Mass Production, Mass Consumption and Mass Allocation," *Archives for Philosophy of Law and Social Philosophy* 10 (1978), pp. 87-106. She points out that he is awkwardly, if not illegitimately, using the concept of property to state "a radical political demand for the socialization of large-scale property and social institutions." Ibid., p. 100.

87. Macpherson, "Liberal-Democracy and Property," in C. B. Macpherson, ed., *Property: Mainstream and Critical Positions* (Toronto: Univ. of Toronto Press, 1978), pp. 199-207; p. 199.

88. Wiles, *Economic Institutions Compared*, p. 462.

89. Passmore, *The Perfectibility of Man* (London: Duckworth, 1970), p. 238. Notice also that Yugoslav Marxists are having second thoughts about Marx's theory of human nature. See Svetozar Stojanovic, *Between Ideals and Reality: A Critique of Socialism and Its Future* (New York: Oxford Univ. Press, 1973); and Mihailo Markovic, *From Affluence to Praxis: Philosophy and Social Criticism* (Ann Arbor: Univ. of Michigan Press, 1974). And compare with these the orthodox fatuity of Georgi Smirnoff, *Soviet Man: The Making of a Socialist Type of Personality* (Moscow: Progress Publishers, 1973).

90. For a more extensive appraisal of Unger's views, see Gerald F. Gaus and John W. Chapman, "Anarchism and Political Philosophy: An Introduction," in J. Roland Pennock and John W. Chapman, eds., *Anarchism: Nomos XIX* (New York: New York Univ. Press, 1978).

91. Unger, op. cit., p. 168.

92. Ibid., p. 64.

93. Note Oakeshott's description of the anti-individualist, op. cit., p. 278: "one intolerant not only of superiority but of difference, disposed to allow in all others only a replica of himself, and united with his fellows in a revulsion from distinctness."

94. Unger, op. cit., p. 217.

95. Ibid., p. 268.

96. On the morality of markets and market relations, see H. B. Acton,

The Morals of Markets: An Ethical Exploration (London: Longman, 1971); Gerald Dworkin, Gordon Bermant, and Peter G. Brown, eds., *Markets and Morals* (New York: John Wiley, 1977); and, of course, Hayek's writings.

97. Wiles thinks Hayek's fears on this score are much exaggerated. "The real point is that fundamentally most societies are incapable of political freedom. . . . They are not on the Road to Serfdom, they never left it." *Economic Institutions Compared*, p. 466. See also W. L. Weinstein, "Is Britain Becoming a Corporate State?" in R. I. Tricker, ed., *The Individual, the Enterprise and the State* (New York: John Wiley, 1977), pp. 137–69.

98. On the difficulties involved in restoring political freedom once it has been lost, see Robert A. Dahl, *Polyarchy: Participation and Opposition* (New Haven: Yale Univ. Press, 1971).

99. Hayek, *The Mirage of Social Justice,* p. xiii.

100. Ibid., p. 32.

101. Rawls, op. cit., p. 102.

102. Ibid.

103 Oakeshott, op. cit., pp. 314–15.

104. Among other studies, see Norman Daniels, ed., *Reading Rawls: Critical Studies on Rawls' A Theory of Justice* (Oxford: Basil Blackwell, 1975).

105. Rawls, op. cit., p. 101.

106. Plamenatz, "Equality of Opportunity," in Lyman Bryson et al., eds., *Aspects of Human Equality* (New York: Harper, 1957), pp. 79–107; p. 105.

PART V

LEGAL THEORY, PROPERTY, AND THE CONSTITUTION

13

SCIENTIFIC POLICYMAKING AND COMPENSATION FOR THE TAKING OF PROPERTY

DUNCAN MACRAE, JR.

The institution of private property is formally defined by a body of law and judicial decisions, but it is also informally defined by the everyday understandings that citizens have of property; and it has been influenced increasingly by systematic views of property that are propagated through the law schools and the legal literature by economists and other scholars. The tensions among these various sources of law are the subject of Ackerman's analysis.[1] He proposes a broad debate that will help to resolve them and focuses this proposal on alternative views of property and compensation associated with judicial roles that he refers to as the "Scientific Policymaker" and the "Ordinary Observer." In commenting on his proposal, I shall first restate it and then argue that a broader notion of Scientific Policymaking, illuminated by sociology as well as economics, can guide us in taking citizens' views into account; but that this notion of policymaking ought not to be located exclusively in the legal profession or the judiciary.

TWO VIEWS OF PROPERTY

Ackerman points to a serious disparity between a view of property that is coming to characterize the teaching of law schools, on the one hand, and a view more characteristic of laymen and judges, on the other. The increasingly prevalent position among lawyers, influenced by economists, is that property is a bundle of separable rights, some of which may be taken or transferred while others remain. That of the layman and the courts is more nearly that property involves control of a "thing" — a bundle of rights that are seen as inseparable and that belong as a bundle to one person or another. Ackerman designates the former view as that of "legal property," the latter as "social property" recognized by actual social interactions and control over things.[2]

The focus of Ackerman's analysis is the "takings" clause of the Fifth Amendment: "nor shall private property be taken for public use, without just compensation." Supported by this clause, persons who consider themselves deprived of property by governmental action bring cases to court. The courts' interpretations of the clause, and commentaries on them in the legal literature, are the materials with which Ackerman works.

A growing group in the legal profession, called Scientific Policymakers by Ackerman, interpret this clause to correspond to the taking of legal property (as defined above), including intangible benefits such as air rights or future potentiality for profit. Those holding the alternative perspective are called Ordinary Observers and interpret the taking of property as the transfer of control of things whose possession is legitimized by everyday understandings and practices related to possession, and to proper and nonharmful use, such as are presumed to be shared by well-socialized middle-class Americans. For example, the diminution in value of property from the air force's regular incursion into a property owner's airspace would not be considered to require compensation in the Ordinary Observer's view.

The two views of property we have just described correspond to Ackerman's terms "Scientific" and "Ordinary," respectively. But the further distinction between a Policymaker and an Observer implies that the former is more disposed to intervene and reinterpret the law, judging the merits of competing rules in terms of a "Comprehensive view he has imputed to the legal system." An Observer's judgments, in contrast, will be based on an effort "to identify the norms that in fact govern proper conduct within the existing structure of social institutions."[3]

The judge in a case involving compensation may thus take more than one view of his task. He may see himself as an instrument for some larger purpose or valuative principle that he believes to be embodied in the legal system, such as the economic principle of efficiency or a principle of equity or justice. He may see the Constitution, or the bench, as a proper instrument for correcting the actions of other decision-making agencies such as legislatures or bureaucracies, or even for seeking social goals that are only implicit in the Constitution. Such are the views that Ackerman attributes to some[4] Scientific Policymakers; though he notes that these views are not shared by most judges, who remain Ordinary Observers, closer to the perspective of the well-socialized citizen.

Ackerman seeks to resolve this disparity by stimulating a debate including the legal profession and laymen. The result of such a debate might be to modify the accepted principles underlying the law of property by making them more consistent. From a sociological perspective, this is an effort to shape social norms; we shall ask later whether there are rational and justifiable ways for a Scientific Policymaker to do so. The debate Ackerman proposes chiefly involves elites but is conducted in public.

The disparity between these two understandings creates a problem for the legal profession and the courts, and this is the problem Ackerman analyzes. But because this problem could be dealt with elsewhere than in the courts, it ramifies into questions about the proper role of the courts in the political system. These questions resemble questions, increasingly raised today, concerning popular or representative control over professions and experts.

The nature of the proposed debate, and our view of the problem, will be influenced by the particular comprehensive view that we take. If the central choices considered are those of American judges, this view is likely to recognize the existence of property and of rights to it. Any changes considered are likely to be incremental. American economists as a group, though they may subordinate compensation to efficiency, also tend to support the institution of property; it is the basis of exchange. They may want to subdivide it further, as a cluster of rights, than does the Ordinary Observer. But they are not socialists. They favor a perfect market — finely tuned because finely subdivided.

Our symposium has brought out the point, however, that the institution of property may be questioned more deeply than this, particularly if justice and equity are major values in our comprehensive view. Such a comprehensive view may be drawn from sources other than the law, and used to criticize the law. Insofar as the debate that Ackerman proposes extends beyond the legal profession — and includes philosophers and social scientists as our symposium does — it is likely to raise these broader questions. One of my principal concerns here will be to ask what these sources of criticism might be.

ALTERNATIVE VIEWS OF COMPENSATION

The two views of property that we have described correspond approximately to two views of compensation. But if we examine these views of compensation more closely, we shall see that each leads to complexities requiring external standards for judgment — not simply the standard of legal principles on the one hand, or of the views of the ordinary citizen, on the other.

The Scientific Policymaker's view of compensation, insofar as we may represent it by an economic view, derives from welfare economics. One of the bases of contemporary benefit-cost analyses is the Kaldor criterion,[5] whereby a transition from one state of affairs to another is justifiable if all the losers in the transition could be compensated by the gainers. The result, if such compensation occurred, would be a Pareto improvement; and even if it is not, the result has been called a "potential Pareto improvement."[6] If an actual Pareto improvement is required, all losers must be actually compensated;[7] if only its potentiality is required, the standard being applied is nearer to that of benefit-cost analysis.

The case in which compensation is actually required may appear to resemble the provision of the takings clause, but this similarity is limited to the case in which *property* is taken. The Pareto principle would require citizens to be compensated for the taking of *money* by the government in the form of taxes, this compensation taking the form of benefits from government action. The takings clause would thus represent a very conservative principle, were it not restricted in application to a certain set of rights called "property." What comprehensive principle could give rise to this clause? Conceivably it could be the horizontal *inequity* associated with taking one person's property and not another's, that requires compensation; the takings clause would appear to carry with it the assumption that taxation can be done fairly, but the taking of property cannot. The task of compensation in this sense would then be to insure the legitimacy of government action against the possible disaffection that would result from taking things from citizens in a *horizontally inequitable* way.

The problem is actually more complicated that this, however — a complexity that I shall illustrate and then try to avoid in my further argument. I have distinguished between money and property on the presumed ground that the taking of nonmonetary property is more likely to be inequitable. But consider the possibility of an effluent charge (a monetary tax) on persons or organizations that emit a specified type of effluent, recently discovered to be harmful, into a body of water. The degree of equity of such a public policy is similar to that of a nonmonetary regulation prohibiting the emission of more than a certain amount of that effluent. Either of these policies would cause disadvantages for emitters relative to other producers who competed with them without generating these emissions. In either case, the emitters might claim that the establishment of a more finely tuned system, imposing on them some of the costs of their external effects, would be inequitable to them when established. Under a finely divided scientific concept of property, either emitter (whether taxed or regulated) might claim compensation for the diminution of his property. In the case of the effluent charge, the emitter would then sustain no net loss from the imposition of the charge but would immediately have an incentive to reduce the charge by reducing effluents.

This example shows that the distinction between taking monetary and nonmonetary holdings is not in general a distinction between equity and inequity, since a tax conditional on not exercising a certain property right is very similar to a deprivation of that right. Moreover, taxes on certain types of persons or industries are likely to produce initial inequities relative to other types of persons; thus, the degree of inequity of taking property as against money is a matter of degree rather than one of kind. But if finely tuned compensation were extended to the taking of money, Scientific Policymaking would be brought back to the extremely conservative Pareto principle.

This example also illustrates the problems in searching for principles underlying a legal rule such as the takings clause. In the end, it seems to me more important for citizens to decide, through the political process, what the law *ought* to say than for judges to consult an ambiguous body of constitutional law in the manner of the Delphic oracle.

From outside the legal profession we thus ask not only what the law *is* (or what principles it contains), but what it *should* be. Rawls, writing on rule utilitarianism, once pointed out that "one distinguishes two offices, that of the judge and that of the legislator."[8] To ask the larger question as to what the law should be releases us from some of the constraints of Ackerman's argument, but opens up additional problems including that of the role of the legislature, discussed below.

The Scientific Policymaker would give compensation for a "taking" of particular rights, such as air rights, that constitute part of the ownership of something. The Ordinary Observer, in contrast, refuses to compensate for loss of such particular rights unless they are recognized as separable in day-to-day transactions. He is thus more likely to regard an item of property as an inseparable bundle of rights. He requires as compensation "payment . . . sufficient to permit Layman to buy a thing as good as the one he lost." From a sociological perspective, this interpretation of "social property" involves compensation in terms of expectations viewed as legitimate within the society's system of informal norms.[9] If we wished to ascertain these expectations more systematically, we might ask questions of representative samples of the public, examine market prices, or make use of juries or appraisers. The results of these inquiries would help us to define "thing," "as good as," and "sufficient" in the case at hand.

These judgments rest on what members of the society consider legitimate. But in a fundamental inquiry, we need not simply take society's norms as given; we may consider whether society would be better off if they were (and could be) changed. To consider such changes is part of the task of a *genuinely* Scientific Policymaker. Indeed, Ackerman envisages Scientific Policymakers as "(a) translating indigenous doctrine into Scientific sense and (b) teaching the natives how to think like Policymakers," while neglecting "to make sense of the Ordinary Observing tradition in its own terms."[10] In parallel to education these efforts at change of norms might involve the sort of reformulations by elite groups that Ackerman is encouraging by his book. For all these sorts of change, we must ask whether they are desirable (in terms of a particular set of ethical standards), and under what conditions we may properly try to persuade others of their desirability.

If we had an Archimedean point outside these norms themselves—a suitable comprehensive view—we might judge the desirability of changing them. Such an external criterion appears to be proposed by economists and others who teach the scientific view of property in law schools and who may well hope that the layman's view of property will change in this direction. But if such a criterion is proposed for the modification of norms and laws, we must ask by what token it claims to be superior; and we must ask the same question for standards imputed to the law.

We are thus led to two larger questions that we shall consider in the remainder of this paper: (1) How can the notion of a Scientific Policymaker be extended to include the possibility of policies that change the norms of a society? (2) What might be the bases of the comprehensive ethical views underlying such policy judgments?

SCIENTIFIC POLICYMAKING AND
CHANGE OF NORMS

We first consider the restricted question whether, given a comprehensive ethical system, policymakers can make judgments concerning possible changes in the ordinary perspective—changes in the property-related informal norms of the society. This question will lead us repeatedly to the larger question as to how such a comprehensive view can properly be derived, a question that we treat in more detail in the following section.

In Ackerman's analysis, the two external value systems vying for influence on the law are those of economists and those of ordinary citizens. Welfare economics is a rational ethical system, developed in part from some of our widespread convictions about rightness and in part from concepts and procedures of the discipline of economics.[11] The expectations and values of ordinary citizens constitute the informal norms of society as they concern property. They are based on the categories into which things are commonly placed, and the legitimate expectations (in a social, not legal, sense) as to who shall be entitled to do what and to hold what things.

If a comprehensive view such as that of economics is invoked to reform the law, it need not stop short at the informal norms of the society but may consider reforming them as well. Perhaps the economy would function more efficiently if the ordinary citizen viewed property as a divisible cluster of rights. Possibly the economic education now being provided in the law schools will eventually influence the public mind and can be supplemented through further training in public schools and colleges. This possibility can be considered for a variety of comprehensive ethical systems, and not merely for that of economics; I wish to stress here only the fineness of the distinctions made by citizens in their everyday transactions.

The informal norms of society, even more than the formal norms of Anglo-Saxon law, are likely to take the form of disparate, concrete, well-understood rules. Examples are the Ten Commandments, and the Bill of Rights as understood in popular rather than legal discourse. These rules, in order to be understood and supported by citizens themselves, must state in concrete terms what sorts of acts are allowed and forbidden. Their ordinary application does not require elaborate analysis, data collection, measurement, or prediction. If they were not usable in this immediate way, many of our ordinary transactions would be impossible; informal social control would fail;

and people would be far more dependent on lawyers and other professionals than they now are.

These norms may be expressions of underlying values in a society—such as individualism and freedom, on the one hand, or collectivism and consensus, on the other. Sociologists analyzing normative systems may seek to discover such values and may interpret the norms of one social system as more coherent in this sense than those of another. But sociologists' effort to trace all such norms to a single source is less prevalent than similar efforts by legal scholars, presumably because these norms are less coherently organized than the law.

It is unreasonable, therefore, to consider an infinite subdivision of the categories used in everyday transactions. Perhaps some subdivision could be undertaken by way of reform, but it would be limited in degree. As economists recognize, information costs or transactions costs could well increase so as to nullify any advantage gained from the efficiency of finer categories.

To acknowledge this limitation, however, is not to jettison Scientific Policymaking. A Scientific principle valuing efficiency or the satisfaction of preferences must weigh in the balance the cost of public confusion, in both the long and the short run.[12] Ackerman's Scientific Policymaker suffers from an abundance of categories that are presently unintelligible to the public and to the judges. He may be seen as trying to be utilitarian, yet failing for this reason. But a common argument between utilitarians and nonutilitarians takes the following form. A critic accuses the utilitarian of failing to foster happiness or efficiency or whatever the utilitarian goal may be. The utilitarian may capitulate and admit self-contradiction; or he may point out that the critic is in fact making a utilitarian argument, appealing to consequences, and that the critic's argument may well be subsumable in a larger utilitarian framework. If we have not maximized happiness or efficiency or social order (itself a possible source of happiness), perhaps it is not our goal but our means that is at fault. The problem is, then, not whether scientific policymaking in general is a tenable position but what particular version is desirable and on what grounds it might be justified.

To take account of the perspective of the Ordinary Observer, especially in the short run, is thus not inconsistent with guidance by scientific policymaking. Any applied science leads to rules of thumb interpretable in daily transactions. These rules of thumb coexist with the general principles from which they are derived. Specialized disciplines and professions deal with the general principles, which must then be interpreted for the general public. Just how disparate the public view and the expert view must be we need not say. But the necessity of such a disparity is not an argument against the existence of an expert view, even of one that makes recommendations as to the rules of thumb. Judges' interpretation of the takings clause may well be based on considerations of efficiency, even though the litigants have no notion of them. The particular provisions of the law can be spelled out clearly for those who are affected; but the interpretive arguments in judicial decisions and the legal literature can deal with comprehensive justifications. For the two systems of discourse to be mutually consistent, it is necessary only that the comprehensive view take the layman's view into account.

THE ROLE OF THE JUDICIARY IN THE POLITICAL SYSTEM

I have argued that a scientific view can take laymen's views of the law into account and can try to change these views. I have even suggested that a Scientific view might propose more precise definitions to clarify ambiguous constitutional clauses. Such claims, when expressed so blatantly, may well seem presumptuous; for who is this Scientist to claim authority over the citizenry and the Constitution? Even if the Scientist is a judge, he may well draw back from making such claims, either through self-restraint or through knowledge that others will object. The question of presumptuousness leads us to the role of the judiciary—which we shall review as Ackerman treats it—and then to the relation of experts and professionals to citizens in general.

Ackerman situates his problem in the judge's choice and in the recommendations that the legal profession will make. The judge is assumed to be seeking to do right. He must choose among several perspectives, but all are seen as motivated by concern for right action or the general welfare.

As the judge who is an activist Scientific Policymaker looks out at other decision centers, however, he views them less favorably. The legislative or executive, for whatever reason, may fall short of maximizing the general welfare. Bureaucrats may be moved by self-aggrandizement, front-line decision makers by bribes;[13] in such cases the judge feels justified in overturning their decisions and (at least) awarding compensation. The tension, here as in democracy, is between two aspects of our nature—ethical man and self-interested man. In democracy we may be able to play these two roles separately on different occasions, though I should like to hope that public officials play the former. The viewpoint of Scientific Policymakers, as described by Ackerman, is that these problems should be remedied by the courts, and the takings clause is an instrument for this purpose.

But this comparison of an ideal judge with a fallible legislator or bureaucrat is asymmetrical. It is like the comparison of real capitalism with ideal socialism, or vice versa. It also resembles the contrast between our own presumed concern for the general welfare in policy analysis, and our attribution of narrower motives to those who influence the feasibility of our chosen policies.[14] The same problem arose for atomic scientists after World War II who sought to fulfill their "social responsiblity," assuming that their motives were pure and that they were to seek this responsibility within their predefined role.

Such a viewpoint characterizes any profession that views the world from within its own confines.[15] Conceivably some professions are entitled to this claim to virtue, and perhaps the claim encourages virtues; but in general it seems safer to let the claim depend in part on some outside judgment, less contaminated by the interests of the profession in question. That judgment might perhaps derive from other professions, were it not for the possibility of a self-interested coalition *among* professions. It might derive from representative democracy, were it not that representatives (like bureaucrats) can effectively combine to serve their own narrow career interests. I can only propose that mutual criticism among such institutions, together with public participation, will provide better solutions than unchecked decisions made by one institution, or one profession, alone. In particular, the judiciary and the legal profession seem in Ackerman's argument to enjoy a special status that citizens are nowadays reluctant to grant to other professions—and perhaps to lawyers themselves.

We may indeed ask whether the Supreme Court might renounce some of the rights as constitutional arbiter that it assumed early in its history. It, too, may conceivably engage in self-aggrandizement; its members' political skill over the years may have partly served that goal in addition to the general welfare. A major task of political scientists' policy analysis is to examine the propriety of institutional arrangements; and the powers of the courts, deriving from interpretation of the Constitution, should thus not be beyond analysis. There also remains the question whether the courts are the most appropriate instrument for making, enforcing, and modifying policy.[16] That the legal profession might have motives of its own was well known to W. S. Gilbert, who put in the mouth of the Lord Chancellor in *Iolanthe* the words:

> The law is the true embodiment
> Of everything that's excellent.
> It has no kind of fault or flaw;
> And I, my Lords, embody the law.

The compensatory, Paretian function that Ackerman attributes to the courts is in fact attributed to the legislatures by Hochman, who writes that "A variety of mechanisms contained in the political process itself, reduce transitional inequities. These political mechanisms are, in a sense, imperfect substitutes for compensation and when it is not feasible, perform a part of its function.[17] Other economic analyses of the legislative process have also seen logrolling as a means to reduce the deprivation felt by intense minorities.[18]

The alternative I wish to propose is that we transfer some of the power of constitutional interpretation from the courts to the legislatures. Such a transfer may make it possible to codify and clarify the ambiguous phrases of the Constitution in ways that derive their legitimacy and support directly from processes of representation. Although legislatures do not always choose to decide issues in terms of clear principles, we may at least imagine that a widespread debate about questions of property, such as Ackerman proposes, might culminate in the legislature rather than in the courts.

The assumptions underlying this proposal are that legal systems should derive from clear principles, and that these principles should, as far as possible, be enunciated through representative processes. I thus favor judicial restraint on the ground that the codification of law should, if possible, have legitimacy based on representation. Ackerman characterizes one type of restraint by the contention "that the correction of injustice is a proper task for the political branches rather than the antidemocratic judiciary."[19] But I am saying something slightly different. I do not expect direct democracy, or even the legislature alone, to produce clear and principled law; I simply wish the judiciary to be more fully restrained, in its interpretation of the Constitution, by involvement in a system of checks and balances. I hope that this will encourage responsible discussion and adoption of principled law.

I thus favor public debate centered on consistent ethical systems.[20]

Existing Anglo-Saxon law may or may not constitute such a system. Continental law apparently does so to a greater degree. Thus, even though Ackerman warns of the elitism in the continental system with its move away from juries, it is possible that continental law is better understood by the public subject to it than is Anglo-Saxon law by its public, and thus has equal or greater claims to being consistent with democracy.[21] To change gradually in the direction of continental law may be uncomfortable — like the problems of adopting the metric system or simplified spelling, greatly magnified — but future generations might be better off as a result. Whether democracy, as the rule of those now living, can produce such a result is a difficult question; but it will have a better chance to do so if it can rise above the selfish interests of the moment, that is of those now living.

CONCLUSION

Ackerman has proposed a broad discussion through which the divergent perspectives of Scientific Policymakers and Ordinary Observers may be reconciled. In entering into that discussion, I have suggested that an inclusive notion of Scientific Policymaking can itself provide a synthesis, taking into account the categories and norms guiding the Ordinary Observer and suggesting changes in them. This suggestion does not imply that we should propose such changes lightly, because they involve costs in uncertainty, inconvenience, decreased consensus, and possibly even the destruction of useful myths, as well as sheer difficulties of feasibility. But it does mean that we need not regard the categories of the Ordinary Observer as immutable facts, or as results of a process of social evolution that human volition is powerless to change.[22] A genuinely Scientific Policymaker can consider policies that change social norms, even while he recognizes the costs and difficulties of making such changes.

I have also suggested that a genuinely Scientific Policymaker should be concerned not merely with discovering principles in the law and the Constitution, but with legislation, with specifying definitions for ambiguous constitutional clauses, with amending the Constitution if his comprehensive view requires it when the costs are taken into account — and with choosing the comprehensive view that is to be the basis of these changes. This approach clearly transcends the role of the judge who claims merely to be discovering principles already embodied in the law.

Both these activities—changing the norms and the law—require some authority to justify them, as well as to bring them within the realm of feasibility. My suggestion as to where to find the justification is a negative, incremental, pluralistic one: do not seek it in any one institution—not the courts, nor the legal profession, nor the discipline of economics, nor the legislature, nor direct democracy.[23] We are greatly concerned today with the corruption of power, whether it is in the executive branch, the legislative branch, or the professions. We may even consider whether the courts sometimes act in self-interest. But the remedy is not necessarily in greater public participation alone; mass participation alone cannot always assure us of a long view, a comprehensive view, or even the consideration of the general welfare. The disciplined discourse of experts, and mutual criticism among expert groups, can benefit the public if they are also subjected to public scrutiny. The debate that Ackerman proposes can be a step in that direction.

NOTES

1. This paper is a commentary on Ackerman's symposium paper, but also on his larger argument presented in *Private Property and the Constitution* (New Haven: Yale Univ. Press, 1977). Page references to this book will be given below by citation of *PPC*.
2. *PPC*, pp. 116–18. The diversity of definitions of social property, among various societies, is emphasized by the anthropological data cited in Lawrence Becker's paper in this symposium; but our present discussion is centered largely on the United States.
3. *PPC*, pp. 11, 12.
4. We set aside for the present the case of the "restrained" judge who judges other social and political institutions to be functioning well in terms of his comprehensive standards.
5. Nicholas Kaldor, "Welfare Propositions of Economics and Interpersonal Comparisons of Utility," *Economic Journal* 49 (September 1939), pp. 549–52.
6. E. J. Mishan, *Cost-Benefit Analysis: An Introduction* (New York: Praeger, 1971), p. 316.
7. The Pareto condition resembles Ackerman's "Kantian adjudication"; see *PPC*, pp. 73, 222.
8. John Rawls, "Two Concepts of Rules," *The Philosophical Review* 64 (January 1955), p. 7.
9. *PPC*, p. 103, 179; MacRae, *The Social Function of Social Science* (New Haven: Yale Univ. Press, 1976), chap. 8; cited below as *SFSS*.
10. MacRae, "Utilitarian Ethics and Social Change," *Ethics* 78 (April

1968), pp. 188–98; *PPC*, p. 170. This role of the Scientific Policy-maker is similar to the contribution suggested in Edward A. Shils, "Social Science as Public Opinion," *Minerva* 15 (Autumn–Winter 1977), pp. 273–85.

11. *SFSS*, chap. 5.

12. On the cost of deciding each case on its merits, as against deciding in terms of categories, see *PPC*, pp. 45–46.

13. *PPC*, pp. 50–52.

14. Duncan MacRae, Jr., and James A. Wilde, *Policy Analysis for Public Decisions* (North Scituate, Mass.: Duxbury, 1979) chap. 6. The concept of "personal feasibility" is particularly relevant.

15. *SFSS*, pp. 27–28; MacRae, "Professions and Social Sciences as Sources of Public Values," *Soundings* 60 (March 1978), pp. 3–21.

16. Donald Horowitz, *The Courts and Social Policy* (Washington, D.C.: The Brookings Institution, 1977).

17. Harold M. Hochman, "Rule Change and Transitional Equity," in H. M. Hochman and George E. Peterson, eds., *Redistribution Through Public Choice* (New York: Columbia Univ. Press, 1974), p. 330.

18. James S. Coleman, "Political Money," *American Political Science Review* 64 (December 1970), pp. 1074–87. Note, however, that a logrolling legislature is not engaging in the principled codification of laws that we consider below.

19. *PPC*, p. 35.

20. This is the central argument of *SFSS*.

21. *PPC*, p. 186. See also MacRae, *Parliament, Parties and Society in France 1946–1958* (New York: St. Martin's, 1967), pp. 328–30. The question of which public better understands its system of law is ultimately, of course, an empirical one.

22. *PPC*, p. 179.

23. The inelegant and incomplete character of this suggestion is not inconsistent with my advocacy of scientific policymaking; we can be *more* scientific or comprehensive without attempting to resolve the largest political questions definitively in these terms.

14

COMMENTS ON ACKERMAN'S PRIVATE PROPERTY AND THE CONSTITUTION

T. M. SCANLON

Our commonsense judgments are unsystematic and, in some cases, even inconsistent. The desire for consistency and explanatory coherence drives us toward the construction of theories. But theories, insofar as they meet these goals, are apt to conflict sharply with common sense at certain points. *Private Property and the Constitution* identifies a version of this conflict between the drive toward theory and the pull of common sense as an important feature of contemporary legal thought. Ackerman skillfully analyzes this tension as it arises in the law. As he points out, however, the problem is not peculiar to law, though his version may have distinctively legal features. In its general form the conflict arises in philosophy as well.

In introductory lectures in moral philosophy, utilitarianism is commonly said to have great appeal as a moral theory because of its great explanatory power and because it appears to offer an independent vantage point from which prevailing moral beliefs and social institutions can be appraised. In the following lecture it is commonly observed that its radical clashes with ordinary moral intuition constitute a grave problem for utilitarianism. If they do not refute it outright, these clashes at least make the task of defending utilitarianism an uphill struggle.

There are a number of utilitarian responses to this problem. One is to claim for the utilitarian principle a self-evident character that other moral intuitions manifestly lack.[1] Another is to argue that although ordinary moral opinions sometimes conflict sharply with utilitarianism, the arguments offered for these opinions are in fact utilitarian in character; thus, utilitarianism is presupposed in ordinary moral thinking as the true standard of correctness even where ordinary thinking goes astray. A more complete reconciliation may be sought by showing that there are good utilitarian reasons why, in appraising individual actions, we should appeal to ordinary moral precepts rather than directly to the utilitarian principle itself (and do so even if these two methods of reasoning yield different results). This line of defense leads, in the extreme, to what is called rule utilitarianism, in which direct appeal to utilitarian reasoning is reserved for the defense of secondary principles, and these alone are used to judge particular cases.

With one important difference, a central thesis of Ackerman's book is that the difficulties I have just mentioned for utilitarianism infect any view that tries to isolate a few general principles from which all other judgments are supposed to follow. Such a set of principles he calls a Comprehensive View. The strategy of reaching decisions in particular cases by applying such a view he calls Policymaking. This strategy he contrasts with that of the Observer, who reaches decisions by asking which course of action is most consonant with the expectations embodied in the dominant institutions of his society. Ackerman magnifies the contrast between Policymaking and Observing by compounding this distinction with a second one, that between Scientific decision making, in which decisions are made and justified with the help of an esoteric technical language, and Ordinary decision making, which employs only the terms of ordinary language. The contrast he actually discusses is that between Ordinary Observing and Scientific Policymaking.

The problem of choosing between these rival styles of decision making is like the dilemma of utilitarianism I presented at the outset. Scientific Policymaking has the advantages of consistency, completeness, and at least the promise of critical independence. A Comprehensive View can apply to a wide range of cases—the unfamiliar as well as the familiar—and bring them all under a single consistent scheme. But it can yield results, even in some familiar cases, that are wildly implausible by the standards of ordinary thought.

The important difference between Ackerman's dilemma and that posed by utilitarianism is that his contrasting positions are not types of moral theory but methods of legal adjudication. This difference of focus has the effect of increasing the appeal of the intuitive, or Ordinary Observing, position. It does so, for Ackerman, because he is seeking an account of adjudication that describes what judges in the United States actually have done or are doing, and most judges have not been Scientific Policymakers. But, beyond this question of descriptive accuracy, Ackerman seems to feel, and here I think many of us would agree with him, that it is a good thing for judges to reach their decisions and defend them using terminology and methods of argument that are continuous with the ordinary thought and reasoning of those to whom these decisions apply. This is not the only consideration in choosing among different methods of adjudication, but represents one class of significant values.

It is not Ackerman's purpose to argue for Ordinary Observing. The central claims of his book are descriptive. First, that the two conflicting methods he describes are in fact the most important forms of adjudication for contemporary American law. Second, that Scientific Policymaking, not even a contender a generation ago, is now in the ascendancy, although no single Comprehensive View has emerged that can establish itself. I have no quarrel with these claims. Professor Ackerman is far better qualified than I am to tell us what is happening in American law. But Ackerman's descriptive claims are of little interest unless his contrast is a real one and unless there is some reason to care which of these methods judges employ. My concern, then, will be with the soundness of the contrast and with the reasons it gives us to prefer one of the two methods to the other.

Ackerman's contrast between Ordinary Observing and Scientific Policymaking seems to me overdrawn in several respects. First, the drive toward a comprehensive view is already present in ordinary expectations. For these include, on Ackerman's own account, not only (in the case at hand) *norms* of property, but also a conception of the legitimate purposes these norms are to facilitate. A conception of these purposes is essential to the common understanding of these norms, and in particular to the understanding of how the liberty they allow is limited.[2] The need for interpretation, the need to deal with new cases, and the desire to be able to give some account of why the norms of property take one form rather than another (otherwise they would seem quite arbitrary) all press us to articulate the relation between the content of the norms as we understand them and the purposes they are intended to serve. Thus there is always pressure, within the most ordinary understanding of property, toward more consistent and comprehensive formulations. Ordinary property talk is neither static nor untheoretical.

Second, it seems to me plausible to suppose that this ordinary argument and controversy is just where most Comprehensive Views originate and where all of them find their justifications. (See the second utilitarian defense presented above.)

Third, it must be granted that this ordinary theorizing is not eso-teric. But there seems to me no good reason to take esoteric doctrines as typical of Comprehensive Views for the purposes of an argument like Ackerman's. Certainly Kant's theory was esoteric (though he thought that he was giving precise form to the basic mode of ordinary moral reasoning), and so is that of contemporary economic theorists of law. But Mill's nonesoteric theory is no less a Comprehensive View in Ackerman's sense and may be more typical of what most moral theorists are likely to offer.

Fourth, there seems no reason to choose between "a few principles" and none. One could decline to stick with the observation of ordinary expectations while yet admitting a wider range of considerations than either Kant or Bentham would allow.

Finally, there is no reason to think that the only alternative to Or-dinary Observing is to approach every question by a direct applica-tion of one's fundamental principles. Certainly there is no reason for this when something like the Takings Clause is at issue. One of the ef-fects of the shift from moral theory to adjudication is to render a two-tier approach more inviting. A moral theory of the rule utilitarian sort must face with some embarrassment the question: Why should one ever go by rules other than those that are ultimately correct? But the corresponding question in the theory of adjudication is relatively easy to answer. No one expects the ultimate principles of justice (or the theory of the social optimum) to be also a legal code or a constitu-tion. Laws have different purposes: they are addressed to specific problems. And they have standards of validity that do not derive sim-ply from moral principles: they are enacted. The role of principles of justice, or a conception of the social optimum, may be in the extreme to set the limits and objectives of morally acceptable legislation, but their main role in adjudication is to guide the interpretation of law, particularly in novel or unclear cases. I believe that this is all that would be claimed for what Ackerman calls Comprehensive Views by those who advocate them.[3] It seems to me, however, that some of the implausibility Ackerman finds in the Comprehensive Views he con-siders flows from the fact that he assigns them a much broader role than the one I have just described.

I will return to this point in a moment, but first I must mention how Ackerman sees his two modes of adjudication as applied to the Takings Clause. An Ordinary Observing judge approaches a takings issue by asking four questions:

1. Was it his property?
2. Was he deprived of it?
3. Was it state action?
4. Was there justification?

In each case, the question is to be answered by reflecting on the ordinary meanings of the terms involved. By contrast, Ackerman sees the Scientific Policymaking judge as approaching a takings question by direct application of his Comprehensive View. A "Kantian"[4] judge, for example, is said to decide whether owners of marshland must be compensated when environmental protection legislation forbids development of their land by asking whether it would be possible to carry out such compensation in a way that would leave everyone better off. Is the difference between the benefits of this legislation to the society at large and its costs to the marsh owners great enough to cover the procedural costs of carrying out a scheme of compensation? A Utilitarian judge, on the other hand, is described as settling the same question by asking whether the procedural costs of compensation are or are not greater than the contributions compensation would make to the general welfare. Its chief contributions are conceived of as avoidance of the inefficiency that would result if people were discouraged from investing in marsh property due to the risk of uncompensated restrictions on its use and avoidance of disaffection felt by those who have suffered such uncompensated losses.

Ackerman argues that both these approaches lead to results that are quite at variance with the way we ordinarily think. For example, neither of his Scientific Policymaking judges would distinguish between a monetary loss suffered as the result of restrictions on my use of a thing (such as the decrease in the value of my Ferrari when speed limits are lowered to 45 miles per hour) and an equal monetary loss suffered when a thing I own is removed or destroyed. Other things (process costs, inefficiencies due to the incentive not to invest in things whose value may drop without compensation, etc.) being equal, these actions could both count as takings or both fail to do so.

To be sure, this seems odd as an interpretation of the notion of a "taking." But it seems doubtful as to whether it can be considered an *interpretation* at all. Such an interpretation must be based on some specified notion of property—a notion singling out, among the various actions that affect my well-being, those actions that violate my property rights. Any such conception of property rights will always be vague in spots and incomplete. Therefore there will remain a need for some further conception of the purposes a system of property rights is to serve and the moral constraints an acceptable system must satisfy, these serving as guides when the current conception of property rights must be clarified or extended. (Not that these notions in turn can be fully and unambiguiously specified.)

What is surprising about Ackerman's two Policymaking judges is that they seem to proceed without reference to any determinate conception of property rights. They appear to reduce the question whether property has been taken to the question whether the case is of a kind in which compensation is called for by their Comprehensive View. But these questions need not be the same. Even the upholder of a Comprehensive View may think that compensation is sometimes called for even though no property has been taken (perhaps Ackerman's example of the lowered speed limit is such a case). And it is at least conceivable under the two Comprehensive Views to which Ackerman devotes most attention that the reverse could occur, that is, that the Comprehensive View might call for no compensation even though property rights that it generally supports have been abrogated.

This failure to give property rights separate consideration is particularly strange in the case of what Ackerman calls "perfectly restrained" judges who believe, among other things, that the prevailing distribution of property rights in their society is in accord with their respective Comprehensive Views. Given their apparent failure to refer to any such property rights in defending their takings decisions, one wonders what this belief consists in. Perhaps a Utilitarian judge, though he may think the prevailing distribution of benefits satisfactory, cannot, as a Utilitarian, take property rights seriously, since he must decide each case on its own merits by appeal to the standard of maximum utility. If this is so, then obviously the takings clause will make no literal sense for such a judge, who can use it only as an opportunity to pursue his own distinct purpose. But one may doubt whether it *is* so. The restrained Utilitarian judge might be a legal rule utilitarian, who takes seriously the legal definition of property, which he regards as, in the main, productive of maximum utility. Assuming that the takings clause is part of this legal definition, it seems that the restrained Utilitarian judge would normally interpret it by appeal to a standing conception of property rights. Only when this failed to give clear guidance as to whether the given action was a taking would the judge need to refer to the utilitarian rationale for property rights in general and for the takings clause in particular. Only when these in turn fail to give any clear answer, or give a manifestly unsatisfactory one, will the judge go all the way back to the utilitarian principle itself. If the judge is a truly restrained utilitarian, presumably the last of these three cases will almost never arise.

The notions of uncertainty and disaffection that Ackerman refers to sound to me like attempts to construct a rationale of the kind just mentioned; that is, to explain what purposes a requirement of compensation might serve from a utilitarian point of view.[5] But since a restrained Utilitarian judge will need to consult even this rationale only when the reigning legal definition of property rights is quite unclear, it seems unlikely that his use of it would yield results that are startlingly at variance with ordinary expectations. If a case would truly be an easy one for an Ordinary Observing judge, then I would expect it also to be easy for a restrained rule utilitarian. The latter would, I think, have no trouble agreeing with the Ordinary Observing judge in the automobile cases Ackerman cites. The two will diverge only in cases in which (1) the standing legal definition of property rights gives no clear guide, but (2) the ordinary understanding of property rights embodied in the dominant nonlegal institutions of the society do give a clear answer, and (3) this answer is at odds with the one obtained by interpreting and extending the current legal notion in the light of the rationale for the takings clause provided by the dominant Comprehensive View. (By the "dominant" Comprehensive View I mean the one with respect to which the restrained judge takes existing legal institutions and the existing distribution of property rights to be well ordered.)

I do not deny that such cases can arise. But I may differ with Ackerman over how central a problem they present. It would seem to me that there is a strong tendency, particularly in any society that a reasonable Policymaking judge could take to be well ordered, for legal and nonlegal conceptions of property rights to agree in those cases in which both yield clear answers. Legal notions of property become technical and quite independent of ordinary notions chiefly when they deal with problems that do not commonly arise in ordinary life (air rights and subsurface rights, for example), and these are just the cases in which "ordinary understanding" is weak and unlikely to give any clear guide.

I have so far argued that Ackerman exaggerates the clash between Scientific Policymaking and Ordinary Observing by assuming that the Policymaker will handle takings questions by direct reference to his Comprehensive View. Against this I have suggested that a plausible Comprehensive View is likely to support a substantive derived notion of property rights. If it does so then the Policymaker will approach a takings question by asking the same four questions that an Ordinary Observer would ask, although he may produce different answers and will certainly arrive at his answers differently.

This removes that part of the oddity of the Policymaker's method that consisted in the fact that he appeared to ignore property rights altogether in determining whether compensation should be paid. Whether a Policymaker would generally arrive at the same conclusions as an Ordinary Observing judge of the same judicial persuasion would of course depend on how the ordinary expectations of the latter's society fit with the former's Comprehensive View. Since Ackerman is concerned with contemporary American law, the crucial question for him is whether the notion of property supported by a Scientific Comprehensive View would ever be in accord with *our* ordinary expectations. If the Comprehensive View is Utilitariansim or what Ackerman calls Kantianism, this seems unlikely; the dominant institutions of our society are manifestly not well ordered by either of these standards. And these are, Ackerman says,[6] the only Comprehensive Views with enough currency in contemporary American legal thought to make them worth considering.

However this may be, it seems to me that Ackerman's way of presenting the matter understates the appeal of Policymaking as a method of adjudication. For the bulk of his examples are ones in which, when there is a clash between ordinary expectations and the dictates of a Comprehensive View, the ordinary expectations strike us as intuitively plausible and morally acceptable. But this will not always be the case, or at least we should not assume that it will be. A major advantage of approaching a difficult question by attempting to construct an acceptable Comprehensive View rather than by looking for an answer implicit in our ordinary expectations is that, insofar as these methods are genuinely different, the former gives us at least a measure of independence from particular prevailing notions of rights and forces us to adopt a more critical perspective on them or, at the least, to defend them systematically.

Ackerman gives relatively little attention to cases in which the existing distribution of property rights is seriously at variance with the Comprehensive View that a Policymaking judge takes to hold. He generally avoids questions of redistrubtion, either on grounds that available Comprehensive Views give no clear directives, or on grounds that the takings caluse is not a suitable vehicle for a judge's redistributive ambitions. This seems to me unfortunate. It is true that the clause has a conservative character in its obvious reverence for property rights, but there is obviously an important critical role open to the judge in determining which rights are indeed real property rights whose abrogation calls for compensation. The most natural case, and one that Ackerman does mention, arises when a legislature abrogates formerly established property rights in order to effect a redistribution. Here, in order to *deny* compensation that would nullify the legislator's efforts, a judge must be able to invoke some principle going beyond ordinary expectations.

Of course pure deference could enable the court to reach the desired conclusion in such a case, but it would not do so in other cases that, from a critical point of view, would present the same issue. Surely there are cases in which we would say that those who are severely disadvantaged by a state action are entitled to compensation even though their loss is not covered by current notions of property. I admit, however, that it is hard to describe such a case. The difficulty appears to flow from the fact that we can imagine a judge making such a decision only where there is some plausible link between the loss in question and the idea of property. Many losses should be compensated, but only some of these are plausibly handled by a judical redefinition of property rights. Perhaps this shows the importance of ordinary observing, but it does not restrict us to finding answers implicit in ordinary expectations. Among the many plausible extensions or contractions of what could be still called property rights, some may be required by justice, others quite incompatible with it. A jurisprudence that failed to look for such a standard of justice would be impoverished indeed. This leads me again toward the conclusion that the alternatives Ackerman describes, insofar as they are plausible, cannot be as separate as he suggests.

The suggestion that Ackerman understates the appeal of Policymaking may seem surprising given that he has often been taken as a partisan of this approach. Why should Ackerman exaggerate the unattractive features of a viewpoint to which he is at the least quite sympathetic? One reason might be this: the form of Scientific Policymaking that most appeals to Ackerman is the application to law of modern economics. As might be expected from a lineal descendant of utilitarianism, this view does have the extreme qualities Ackerman ascribes to Scientific Policymaking in general. To the degree that the ascendancy of this particular Scientific View within the law is the main object of Ackerman's attention, it is natural that his general category should preserve this view's leading features. Moreover, one reason why economic rationality, despite its bizarre aspects, might seem acceptable as a method of legal reasoning is just that it is seen as the best of a general class of methods (Comprehensive Views), all of which share its unattractive features but which, taken together, represent the only alternative to enshrining as law the piecemeal and incoherent intuitions of your Aunt Sally. I have tried to suggest, on the contrary, that not all alternatives to Ordinary Observing need have such counterintuitive consequences as the Comprehensive Views Ackerman considers.

NOTES

*I am grateful to Sanford Levinson for helpful comments on an earlier version of this paper.

1. As Sidgwick does in *Methods of Ethics*. See Peter Singer, "Sidgwick and Reflective Equilibrium," *The Monist* (1970).

2. This point is illustrated by an example Ackerman considers (pp. 118–20): Do a farmer's property rights extend to the air space above his land? I am more inclined than Ackerman to think that an "ordinary" farmer might answer affirmatively. Moreover, it seems to me that his answer (in so far as it is not an attempt to answer the question of *legal* property rights) would be arrived at more by considering his idea of the normal purposes for which land is owned than by recalling what claims have in the past been substantiated. Those uses of airspace that clearly conflict with normal uses of the land (e.g., flying over it repeatedly at 15 feet) will seem to violate property rights in the airspace while those uses that seem to have no effect on normal use will seem irrelevant to the farmer's rights. This is not to say that "social property" here coincides with "legal property," but only to point out that the internal structure of the ordinary notion of property is less a crude relation between a person and a thing, and more like the sophisticated lawyer's bundle of uses, than Ackerman suggests.

3. See, e.g., Mill's remarks on the principle of utility and "secondary principles" in "On Bentham" and in *Utilitariansim*, chap. 11.

4. Ackerman's Kantianism is closer to welfare economics than most Kantians would find comfortable. He interprets Kant's requirement that all should be treated as ends, not merely as means, in such a way as to make it a requirement that whenever compensation could yield a Pareto superior solution it should be carried out.

5. Surprisingly, the "Kantian" judge's calculations seem more concerned with the consequences in the particular case at hand while the Utilitarian's concerns are more plausibly linked to the effects of general policies of compensation.

6. Ackerman, p. 86.

15

FOUR QUESTIONS FOR LEGAL THEORY
BRUCE A. ACKERMAN*

It was Wittgenstein who led me to *Private Property and the Constitution.*[1] My reading of the *Investigations* had warned me of the perils of premature abstraction. Rather than begin a jurisprudential study of property by asking "What is law?" or "What is property?" I wanted to ask how people *used* property talk. From the start, however, I was concerned with the linguistic practices of a special group of conversationalists—people who, like myself, were trained as lawyers. Not only did my background give me a comparative advantage in exploring the strands of legal conversation, but I was confident that a sound Wittgensteinian analysis would cast light beyond narrow professional boundaries. Although all Americans talk property some of the time, the conversation typically takes a legalistic turn whenever it threatens to get out of control. Even petty property disputes are often "resolved" through a process in which the original disputants glare silently at one another from opposite sides of a courtroom—while their lawyers argue the matter to a conclusion. And from the time of slavery to the moment of environmental crisis,[2] every important redefinition of property has been subjected to a judicial test under one or another constitutional provision—notably the Takings Clause of the Fifth Amendment that prohibits the "taking" of "property" without "just compensation." Since I was interested in describing how the present generation of lawyers constructed their property arguments, I took the question of environmental regulation as the substantive vehicle for my exploration. Here was an area in which property owners have been subjected to massive state control during the past decade—regulation that, predictably, they challenged as unconstitutional under the Takings Clause. The way lawyers, judges, and legal scholars argued these claims would, I hoped, reveal a great deal about the way the profession used property talk.

I found, however, that I could not make much progress in this enterprise without raising larger questions. Legal property talk turned out to be very confused—so chaotic, in fact, that sophisticated lawyers took a perverse pride in asserting that "reasoning" under the Takings Clause was entirely arbitrary. Before I could establish that there was *some* order in the chaos of law talk, I was obliged to account for the extraordinary willingness of the profession to confess its intellectual bankruptcy. It was this task that led me to develop the ideas of Scientific Policymaking and Ordinary Observing that have attracted the attention of Professors MacRae and Scanlon. My initial aim, however, was not to interest political scientists or philosophers in my distinction; instead, it was to convince lawyers that their sophisticated Realist wisdom about the "arbitrary" character of Takings talk was wrong. The confusion, I became convinced, had its source in the fact that different bits and pieces of property talk presupposed different understandings of the nature and object of legal discourse. To "prove" this contention, I invited the members of my primary audience—sophisticated lawyers of the present day—to sort familiar fragments of Takings talk into two groupings—one labeled Scientific Policymaking, the other Ordinary Observing. Once the armory of legal argument had been organized in this way, I sought to persuade my hypothetical lawyer that he could readily transcend the conventional confusion and construct a variety of cogent interpretations of the Takings Clause. Of course, the particular interpretation he ultimately selected would depend upon the particular way he chose to mix Scientific Policymaking and Ordinary Observing into a convincing pattern of takings talk. All these patterns, however, represented familiar strands of contemporary legal argument; none could be excluded as something alien to the present legal culture. It followed that the conventional wisdom about the arbitrariness of takings law represented a superficial diagnosis of the American legal culture. Rather than a random concatenation of text and utterance, the Takings Clause was the locus of convergence for two very different strands of property talk—each of which indulged very different presuppositions concerning the nature and object of legal discourse. Once a sophisticated lawyer had clarified his position about the relative merits of Scientific Policymaking and Ordinary Observing, he would have little difficulty talking about particular property problems. In contrast, a lawyer could not hope to deal with doctrine in a convincing way while remaining oblivious to the philosophical issues that lurked just beneath the surface.

My principal goal in writing *Private Property and the Constitution*, then, was to shadowbox with a phantom that haunts all those who give their lives to the study of legal philosophy. To our dismay, most practicing lawyers are perfectly happy with—indeed prefer—a jurisprudence that does little or nothing to illuminate their practical concerns. Unless the need for serious reflection is demonstrated beyond all reasonable doubt, the brethren are happy to go on talking in familiar professional ways without undue anxiety about conceptual foundations. My task was to meet this heavy burden of proof by showing that only professional confusion awaits those who fail to look before they leap.

But this admonition—even if it were accepted—is only the first step to a resolution of the philosophical perplexities generated every time an American lawyer opens his mouth. To bring a lawyer to recognize that his professional competence depends on whether he argues like a Scientific Policymaker or an Ordinary Observer is one thing; to tell him how to resolve his predicament is quite another. And although I hope some day to present my own conclusions on this subject, *Private Property* was only intended to raise the question for more general discussion. I am, then, very glad that Professors MacRae and Scanlon have taken the invitation seriously; what is more, their thoughtful remarks have helped me gain a clearer sense of the different things we must think about before we can grasp the constitutional foundations of property in our society. And so, without coming to full or final answers, I shall respond to Professors MacRae and Scanlon by distinguishing four different questions—the conceptual, the descriptive, the normative, and the causal—that must be answered in a fully satisfactory account.

I. CONCEPTUAL QUESTIONS

Lawyers talk. Do they talk differently from most people?

This is an empirical question. Before attempting an empirical answer, however, reflect upon the terms in which such an answer might be given. At one extreme, the answer might be an easy and unequivocal no. Here there is a perfect concordance between the language of the law and the talk of ordinary life. Any competent person can walk into a law court[3] and have no difficulty understanding what the lawyers are talking about. In contrast to such Ordinary law talk, I shall define an extra-Ordinary legal conversation as one that requires a special course of instruction before it can be understood. Here, the mere fact that a layman is capable of dealing with the everyday affairs of life is no guarantee that he can grasp the meaning of a legal conversation. Without a special professional education, he will continually misapprehend the significance of the extra-Ordinary symbols that are the lawyers' stock-in-trade.

Not that this first distinction — between Ordinary and extra-Ordinary conversation — is entirely free of difficulty. It is easy, for example, to imagine cases where the "course of instruction" required to make an utterance intelligible is so short and superficial as to make the proper classification a doubtful matter.[4] Nonetheless, I do not think anything very important hinges on whether an occasional whispered explanation constitutes a "special course of instruction." It takes more than a passsing whisper to explain a sentence like "The objective of property law is to internalize externalities." Indeed, it takes many American law students an entire semester to understand what such an expression might mean, let alone make an intelligent judgment as to its legal value. If a layman heard the sentence uttered in a law court, he would lose the thread of the ongoing legal conversation in the time it took for me to provide even a rudimentary explanation. This is the central point that my distinction is trying to capture.

Yet it is not enough to draw attention to the possibility of extra-Ordinary discourse. It is equally important to recognize that legal discourse can become extra-Ordinary by a variety of linguistic means. Thus, imagine that a tribe of French speakers captured England; in ordinary dealing with natives, the invaders are generally content to speak English; so far as lawsuits are concerned, however, they insist that all transactions be discussed in French. On this scenario, I want to say law-French would be an extra-Ordinary language in England even if it passed for perfectly ordinary language in France. In settings like modern-day America, however, it is not an alien natural language that restricts public access to legal discourse. Instead, American legal language can become esoteric either because it employs a raft of jargon or because it authorizes the use of special syntactic conventions — for example, those mathematical operations required for computer modeling — that are unnecessary in coping with the everyday problems of American life. To signal such possibilities, I shall call a stream of legal discourse Scientific when it contains "a set of technical concepts whose meanings are set in relation to one another by clear definitions without continuing reliance upon the way similar sounding concepts are deployed in nonlegal talk."[5]

Legal language, then, may be Ordinary or extra-Ordinary, Scientific or un-Scientific; moreover, it will be a rare legal culture where all conversations can be characterized in the same way. Instead, practitioners may quickly move from the most Ordinary expressions to extra-Ordinary flights of Scientific virtuosity—all without the slightest sense of professional impropriety. But this only shows that I am not making empirical claims about particular facts but proposing a conceptual scheme for classifying possible facts. My proposal, moreover, has a feature that is desirable, if not necessary, for such schemes: universal domain. That is, given the universe of all possible legal cultures, it is, in principle,[6] possible to classify each and every utterance[7] as Ordinary or extra-Ordinary, Scientific or un-Scientific. No legal conversation will escape these classifications.

Now, I have labored these points because I think they help locate important areas of agreement between Professor Scanlon and myself which might otherwise remain unnoticed. Although Scanlon may disagree on other matters, I do not think he questions any of the conceptual distinctions I have developed thus far. Similarly, I do not detect anything that endangers the basic argument centering on my final dichotomy—between Policymaking and Observing. The aim here is to classify legal cultures, not by the language they use, but by the general form of the argument that participants may legitimately deploy in support of their claims. In a Policymaking argument, the claimant justifies his position by linking it to a Comprehensive View said to embody the ideals governing the legal system. In an Observing argument, the claimant justifies his position on the ground that it protects an expectation legitimated by an ongoing social practice. This distinction is important only in worlds that fall short of a utopia where all existing institutions are already neatly organized around a particular Comprehensive View. If, for example, we lived in an ongoing Benthamite paradise, it wouldn't much matter whether lawyers argued like Observers or Policymakers—either way, they would choose the rule generally considered to maximize utility. But I take it that such a perfect congruence between collective ideals and institutional practice will forever be beyond our grasp.

And in nonutopian societies, the distinction between Observing and Policymaking can be of decisive importance. Since there is, by definition, a breach between collective ideals and ongoing institutional practice, at least some conflicts will arise where A's claim is better supported by institutionalized expectations while B's is better supported by collective ideals. Legal victory will then be determined

by the character of the legal culture. If only Observing arguments
are given legal weight, B will be ruled out of order when he tries to
speak about collective ideals and A will win on the merits. If, however, Policymaking is the dominant form of argument, the situation
will be more complicated. B will be allowed to support his claim by
appealing to a Comprehensive View and try to convince the decision
maker that it best expresses the abstract ideals the legal system is trying to further. It does not follow from this, however, that B will inevitably emerge victorious from the Policymaking arena. As Professor
MacRae explains,[8] the Comprehensive View dominant in a particular Policymaking culture will often place a high value on protecting
reliance interests generated by existing institutional expectations. In
contrast to Observing, however, reliance on preexisting expectations
will not invariably have decisive weight; even though A has relied on
an ongoing practice, it is always open to B to argue that the practice
is so unfair or inefficient or what have you that it should be denied
legal support. Consequently, A must expect to keep talking in a Policymaking culture past the point where he has constructed a winning
argument in the Ordinary analogue. He must parry B's claim by arguing that the ideals recognized in the legal system's Comprehensive
View are, on balance, better fulfilled by protecting A's reliance interest rather than B's attempt to invoke collective ideals on his own behalf. A's success in this regard will depend on the particular Comprehensive View recognized as dominant within a given legal culture.
Although it is possible to imagine a "conservative" Policymaking culture where A would win almost all of the time, it is equally possible to
imagine Policymaking cultures in which the prevailing Comprehensive View gives absolutely *no* weight to the preexisting institutionalized expectations recognized in the broader society. In such "revolutionary" Policymaking systems, A's claim would be condemned to
failure.[9]

As a conceptual matter, then, it would seem possible to arrange
Policymaking cultures on a continuum depending on the degree of
their deference to institutionalized expectations: conservative, on one
end; revolutionary on the other; and different kinds of reformist between. Moreover, as a descriptive matter, I have little doubt that Policymaking by American lawyers varies from center-left to center-
right. Nonetheless, the fact that American Scientific Policymakers
take the reliance interest into account does not imply that they do so
in the same way as Ordinary Observers.

Once again, I do not understand Professor Scanlon to dispute this central conceptual point. Instead, most of his arguments deal with descriptive, normative, and causal questions I shall consider shortly. Several of his remarks, however, are helpful in putting my basic argument in perspective. First, Professor Scanlon points out that "the only alternative to Ordinary Observing is [not] to approach every question by a direct application of one's fundamental principles."[10] I entirely agree; moreover, I did not intend to define Policymaking as narrowly as he suggests. Indeed, all familiar forms of Policymaking are acutely aware of the costs[11] involved in case-by-case decision from first principles and often insist upon imposing rules to govern large classes of cases. So long as such rules are justified by reference to a Comprehensive View, however, the pattern of argument does not cease to qualify as Policymaking. Moreover, the Policymaking analyses of the Takings Clause presented in *Private Property* do not contemplate a direct application of Comprehensive Views to concrete facts of particular cases; instead, they try to show that the presently existing *rules* of Takings law would require drastic revision if legal argument about property shifted from Ordinary Observing to Scientific Policymaking.

But Professor Scanlon makes a second point that probes deeper. Let me introduce it by considering the range of legal cultures to which the Observing/Policymaking distinction can meaningfully be applied. As I suggested earlier, questions involving the Ordinariness and Scientificity of legal language have a *universal* domain: each and every conversation in each and every legal culture can be classified as Ordinary or extra-Ordinary, Scientific or un-Scientific. In contrast, the Observing/Policymaking distinction may be usefully deployed over a *restricted* domain. I can think of at least two kinds of legal conversation that elude these categories. To define the first exception, consider that both Observing and Policymaking contemplate conversationalists speaking in terms of some source of legitimacy beyond their personal predilections. It follows that any statement like "X should win simply because *I* say so" fails to fall in either category.

It is, however, a second restriction on the domain that gains Professor Scanlon's attention. Noting that a Comprehensive View is defined to include only a "few" principles, he asks why we should be forced "to choose between a few principles and none."[12] Now, there are in fact many reasons why the effort to move beyond Observing forces lawyers to frame their Comprehensive Views in terms of a relatively few principles.[13] Most obvious is the pressure generated by the sheer number of disputes processed by any modern legal system. The mo-

ment a single B wins his lawsuit by means of an argument that challenges institutionalized expectations, a line of lawyers will form to exploit B's victory for the benefit of their own clients. (This is, after all,
just the kind of thing lawyers are paid to do.) As a consequence, decision makers will be increasingly called upon to explain how one or
another X's case is different from B's. And although decision makers
may sometimes refuse to come forward with an explanation, such a
move is not much favored in legal cultures — since it suggests an indifference to the basic principle of formal justice that requires treating
X like B if he can show his case is identical in all relevant respects.

It is this concern with consistency that motivated me to suggest that
Comprehensive Views would contain a "relatively few" principles:

> My insistence upon a relatively small number of principles is not
> motivated by an aesthetic impulse but rather by a fear that the
> limitless enumeration of principles will make Policymaking an
> untenable professional activity. . . . In order for a Policymak-
> ing system to be functioning coherently, there must be some oc-
> casions upon which at least some professional people attempt to
> appraise the extent to which the various principles said to consti-
> tute the Comprehensive View in fact comprise a self-consistent
> whole worthy of state support. Yet as principles become more nu-
> merous (and less abstract and general), it will become increas-
> ingly difficult to perform this function with any credibility. [14]

Given this (ultimately) pragmatic justification, it might be better
to say that a Comprehensive View cannot be *unduly complex* if it is
to assure the participants that they are involved in a legal culture
that, in principle, is committed to treating like cases alike. Even with
this elaboration, however, Professor Scanlon still has a valuable
point. For surely it *is* possible to imagine a legal culture in which participants were not so tremendously concerned with formal justice —
where lawyers explicitly say that consistency is but a hobgoblin that
can be kept safely in the closet. [15]

Indeed, there is a persistent strand in American legal thought that
both tries to escape from Ordinary Observation *and* explicitly denies
the need for articulating a consistent Comprehensive View. Some of
the Legal Realists — notably Jerome Frank[16] and Thurman Arnold[17] —
held such a position. More recently Guido Calabresi and Philip Bobbitt advanced a similar — if far narrower — argument in their book on
Tragic Choices.[18] According to them, lawyers with a generally Pol-

icymaking orientation should nonetheless recognize that there are certain sensitive issues that force to the surface troubling inconsistencies in the structure of collective ideals. It is such issues, they say, that give rise to "tragic" choices. Rather than using law to resolve all such conflicts by a suitable "clarification" of the system's Comprehensive View, Calabresi and Bobbitt suggest that legal discourse may sometimes be justifiably used to *obscure* the underlying value conflict. While this is not the place to comment on their thesis, such a position cannot, without a good deal of pushing and shoving, be forced into the Policymaking box; yet it does not fit comfortably within the Observing category either.

II. DESCRIPTIVE QUESTIONS

So much for concepts; the next question is whether they actually illuminate the on-going flow of property talk in the American legal culture. Begin with a garden-variety case. Imagine that, in response to the next Arab oil embargo, Congress passes a package of laws designed to decrease fuel consumption by 50 percent. One of the new laws forbids driving at speeds greater than 30 miles an hour. While this statute does save gas, it is nothing less than a disaster for Hertz Rent-A-Car, which finds that many of its regular customers have taken to the train. As a consequence, Hertz is obliged to clear its clogged parking lots by selling fifty thousand cars at bargain-basement prices. It then turns to its lawyers to see whether the government owes it compensation for the losses it has suffered as a result of the new statute.

In response, Hertz's lawyers turn to the constitutional text: "nor shall private property be taken . . . without just compensation." Quite plainly the text requires Hertz to make out two points before it can get some money: first, that its "property" was "taken"; and second, that payment is demanded by the constitutionally appropriate conception of "just compensation." My thesis is that the interpretation of these formulas will depend critically on the kind of legal culture within which Hertz's lawyers understand themselves to be operating. For Scientific Policymakers, the key to the first of the two questions is to be found in their earliest days of law school. It was in "Property I" that they were repeatedly warned against the vulgar mistake involved when somebody calls himself "the" owner of his car or house. Even though I may say the Ford is "mine," I must recognize that my interest in the car is restricted in countless different ways: it is likely that the bank holds "title" on it until I pay my loan; that I can't drive it through a red light; and so forth. In general, a good lawyer should not think of "property" as if it defined the relationship between a person and "his" things. Instead, he should be taught to think Scientifically about property as a relationship *between people* that arises with respect to the *use* of things. On this view, each person is conceived as holding a bundle of user rights vis-a-vis other potential users; and it is probably never true that *all* rights relating to the use of a particular thing are held by the same person. Indeed, the distinctive thing about the law of property is the infinite variety of ways it allows user rights to be legally packaged and distributed in different bundles held by different people. Each of these bundles contains valuable property rights; and many times, a bundle containing only a few strategic user rights is far more valuable than another bundle containing many trivial uses.

Given this conception of property as a *bundle of legally protected uses,* the Scientific lawyer will have very little trouble helping Hertz over the first obstacle it encounters in its effort at recovery. From the Scientific point of view, it is *obvious* that the new statute has "taken" one of Hertz's most valuable property rights — the right to have it cars driven at 55 miles an hour. More generally, the Scientific Policymaker will have no trouble finding that "property" has been "taken" *whenever* the state changes the preexisting pattern of user rights. For him, the really difficult exegetical problem arises only at the second stage — with the recognition that the Constitution does not guarantee payment in *all* cases but only forbids a "tak[ing] . . . without just compensation." These last two words invite the Policymaker to assess Hertz's claim by articulating a convincing set of principles about justice in compensation. The hard work, in short, is to elaborate the implications of the legal system's Comprehensive View in a way that will generate sensible rules for deciding how the cost of legal change is to be justly allocated. Since this *is* very hard work, my book spends a great deal of energy showing how important doctrinal shifts will sometimes depend on subtle changes in the way a judge defines either his role or his understanding of the substantive ideals that best express the aspirations of the American legal system. For present purposes, however, it will suffice to report that an American Scientific Policymaker will find it very *easy* to say that Hertz's "property" has been "taken" by the speeding law but quite *hard* to say that payment is required by the appropriate notion of "just compensation."

In contrast, the Ordinary Observer will look upon Hertz's misfortune with a very different set of conceptual lenses. To fix the meaning of a "taking" of property," the Ordinary Observer tries to recapture his linguistic habits as they prevailed *before* the rite of passage called "Property I." The critical question is now how a competent but professionally untrained American would describe Hertz's misfortune: Would he say that the new law had "taken" Hertz's "property" from the company?

But if this is the question, then the Scientific yes must be transformed into an emphatically Ordinary no. Even though cars must now be driven slowly, it would be silly to say, as a matter of Ordinary English, that they had been "taken" from Hertz—for aren't they still in Hertz's parking lots under the control of Hertz employees? Can't a Hertz employee still drive any of the cars whenever and wherever the company wants him to? When asked to describe what is going on, the unprofessional American would say: "While Hertz is certainly inconvenienced by the speeding statute, the law hasn't taken Hertz's cars away from it." And so long as this is the way a layman would describe the event, the Ordinary Observer would deny that a "taking" of "property" had occurred. For him, there is a difference of constitutional dimension between a statute that "merely" deprives Hertz of an *opportunity* to use its things and a statute that deprives the Company of *the thing itself.*

But this, for the Scientific lawyer, is a distinction without difference. For him, property is not a thing but a bundle of legally authorized uses. Taking a legally authorized use out of a person's[19] property bundle is the only kind of "taking" that the lawyer is trained to recognize. This is not to say that the layman's habit of reifying property into a thing is without legal interest. Such forms of property fetishism[20] may well be supported by institutionalized practice. And since American Policymakers are hardly revolutionary, they may well give this reliance interest considerable weight in their interpretation of "just compensation." Yet they will hardly join the Ordinary Observer in making it the only decisive factor in constitutional analysis. Instead, if a Scientific Policymaker is convinced that the ideals of the legal system require compensation, he will insist that it be paid even if a layman would not say that the "state has taken Hertz's thing away from it"; similarly, analysis may reveal that the appropriate Comprehensive View requires the denial of compensation in some situations where a reifying manner of talk would make it easy for the Ordinary Observer to say that "property" had been "taken."

The coexistence of Scientific and Ordinary conceptions of property,

then, makes it possible for American lawyers to view familiar disputes of the Hertz variety in very different ways. Equally important,
the Scientific side of the legal culture will suggest to lawyers the propriety of applying the constitutional idea of "just compensation" to
settings that seem quite unfamiliar to the Ordinary eye. Professor
MacRae, for example, raises the question whether an effluent charge
on polluters may ever be subjected to a serious Takings inquiry. As
he points out,[21] a high tax on pollution may deprive a marshland
owner of his development rights just as effectively as a decision to
make the land into a National Park. While an Ordinary Observer
will have trouble finding a "taking" in the tax case, the Scientist will
deny that the state can somehow insulate its action from constitutional scrutiny by adopting an innovative form of regulation. For the
Scientific Policymaker, an effluent charge, no less than a more traditional act of confiscation, represents a state effort to revise the preexisting distribution of "property" rights. The change in regulatory
form does not change the substantive decision to shift the development right from the marsh owner to the general public. Indeed, the
ease with which the Scientific Policymaker can pierce such regulatory
innovations gives him confidence in the validity of his general approach to constitutional law—for is it not a virtue of an interpretation that it preserves the meaning of basic constitutional norms in the
face of a changing reality?

This does not imply, of course, that a Policymaking analysis of an
effluent charge should, in all respects, be identical to that appropriate for a case of direct regulation.[22] The point is simply that a Scientist would refuse to shield a taxation scheme from inquiry under the
"just compensation" clause on the ground that a "taking" of "property" was not involved.

A similar Scientific ambition will be obvious when the subject
turns to the way the state goes about spending its tax revenues. Thus,
imagine that Congress—in response to a balance-of-payments crisis—passes a statute requiring all recipients of social security to live in
the United States if they hope to keep receiving their monthly checks.
The Scientific Policymaker will look with undisguised disdain upon
his Ordinary counterpart's question whether social security represents some lesser form of interest that fails to rise to the constitutional
dignity of "property" for Takings Clause analysis.[23] Nor will he view
welfare recipients as if they were merely the beneficiaries of a charity
who, unlike owners of "real" property, have no right to complain
about sudden changes in the terms upon which they can demand fi-

nancial support. While such welfare rights may have a problematic status on the Ordinary Observer's understanding of "property," the Scientist will have no trouble finding that these forms of entitlement fall within the ambit of Takings Clause concern.

Once again, this is not to say that the Scientist, having satisfied himself that "property" rights have been "taken," will inevitably proceed to award compensation to those disadvantaged by the legal change. Instead, he will assess the merit of the welfare claimant's case in the same way he will test the claims advanced by Hertz or the marshowner. As before, the task will be to elaborate the guiding ideals of the legal system in an effort to establish a sensitive set of rules of "just compensation" for those who lose by changes in the legal status quo.

In making such an analysis, an effort must be made to take into account the distinctive features of the kind of property interests subject to legislative alteration. A Utilitarian Policymaker, for example, may be impressed by the fact that poor people depending on welfare suffer abnormally high losses in utility if they are deprived of their entitlements; or he may fear that most people will experience high uncertainty costs[24] if they know that they cannot depend on social security payments when they reach age sixty-five. Professor Scanlon, however, makes a very fair criticism when he remarks on my failure to treat the distinctive Policymaking problems posed by the taking of these forms of "new" property with anything like the care I lavish on the "older" forms. This is a very real deficiency and represents the most pressing item on the Policymaker's analytic agenda.[25] Before reaching this issue, however, I thought a prior task even more important. Thanks to the work of Charles Reich[26] and others, the present generation of lawyers has been sensitized to the usefulness of property talk in providing a cogent legal analyses of welfare law. Nonetheless, there remains a widespread sense that when lawyers speak about "new" property they are talking in a way that is different in kind from lawyerly talk about "older" varieties. My aim in *Private Property* was to demonstrate that the idea of "new" property could not be dismissed as some more chitchat from the leftist fringe of the profession; instead, it represents a straightforward application of a form of property talk with which the profession is entirely familiar. While this recognition represents only the beginning of a reconceptualization of the reach of the Takings Clause, it is a necessary first step. And revolutions in legal thought often proceed one step at a time.

The picture, then, I wish to draw is of a profession torn between two legal cultures. On the one hand, the present-day rules of takings doctrine remain faithful to the categories of the Ordinary Observer. Thus, efforts to apply the Takings Clause to "new" forms of property like welfare payments or social security have met with a complex, but generally negative, reception;[27] the relevance of just compensation law to tax cases is only dimly perceived;[28] and garden-variety cases, like the one involving Hertz Rent-A-Car, are handled in a way that tracks Ordinary ideas of a "taking" of "property."[29] On the other hand, if one looks beyond the black letter to the legal conversation in which it is embedded, Ordinary Observation seems far more vulnerable. Although lawyers can still recite their Ordinary lines, they have (at least for the moment) lost conviction — indeed, they are so embarrassed with prevailing doctrine that there is comfort in calling it "arbitrary." Moreover, if we lift our eyes from the island of doctrine called takings law to other legal areas in which property talk is relevant, say taxation or antitrust, Scientific Policymaking has already made a profound mark on the letter, as well as the spirit, of the law.[30]

Now, it would appear that my two reviewers have different attitudes to this sketch. Professor MacRae not only accepts my description of Scientific Policymaking in the law but tries to link this tendency to intellectual patterns he described in his thoughtful book on *The Social Function of Social Science*.[31] Professor Scanlon is more ambivalent. Although he recognizes that legal discourse may sometimes be distinctive, he cannot really believe that Scientific property talk is what I say it is. Indeed, he altogether misses the fact that all important streams of Policymaking talk adopt the Scientific conception of property when he says: "What is surprising about Ackerman's two Policymaking judges is that they seem to proceed without reference to any determinate conception of property rights."[32] Professor Scanlon's "surprise" is best understood as evidence of the gap between the property talk indulged by Scientific lawyers and the Ordinary property talk current among philosophers. Indeed, his reliance upon Ordinary conceptions of property is made even clearer when he explains that any interpretation of the takings clause "must be based on some specified notion of property — a notion singling out, among the various actions that affect my well-being, those actions that violate my property rights. Any such conception of property rights will always be vague in spots and incomplete."[33] Yet this description of the takings problem will only meet the approval of an Ordinary Observer. So far as a Scientific Policymaker is concerned, conceptions of property rights need not "always" be vague and incomplete. Under the Scientific conception of property as legally authorized use, there will be no deep difficulties involved in deciding whether the right to welfare or marsh development are "really" property rights. Indeed, it should *always* be possible, in principle, to write out a *complete* specification of the pattern of user rights obtaining at a particular time. While such a Scientific description of property rights might well reveal that some user conflicts have not been clearly resolved, these areas will be far smaller than the Ordinary notion of property will suggest and can be eliminated by statutory clarification if the costs of further specification seem smaller than the benefits.

Even more important, the Scientific Policymaker will reject Professor Scanlon's assumption that it is the job of the concept of *property* to carry the entire burden of interpretation of the takings clause. Instead, it is the theory of *just compensation* that plays the main role in singling out those changes in the status quo that warrant compensation. But this is not because Scientific Policymakers have an "indeterminate" conception of property; instead, it is the very determinacy of the Scientific notion of property as legally authorized use that makes the theory of just compensation so necessary. Without such a theory, the Scientific Policymaker would have no choice but to interpret the Takings Clause as one of the most ringing endorsements of the status quo in the history of the human race—protecting *all* uses once they have been legally authorized. But the text does not impose such an absurd command. Instead, whenever the legislature changes the prevailing pattern of property rights, the Scientific Policymaker understands the clause to require him to assess the merits of the inevitable claims by elaborating the concept of "just compensation" that is most consistent with the aspirations of the American legal system. If this Comprehensive View suggests that it is unfair for Hertz or the welfare recipient to bear the cost involved in their loss of property rights, then the victory is theirs; if not, not.

I cannot, then, share Professor Scanlon's doubt as to whether the Scientific Policymaker's approach to the text "can be considered an interpretation at all,"[34] by virtue of its failure to specify a "determinate" conception of "property." Though the Scientific interpretation is not the only one available to American lawyers, it is my central descriptive claim that it *is* an interpretation that has an important cultural reality in the professional talk of lawyers. Although I can well understand that others find this surprising, this fact—in a paradoxical way—confirms the utility of my enterprise. To put the point broadly, my aim has been to suggest the fruitfulness of using Wittgenstein in a new way in the philosophy of law. Instead of confirming our "ordinary" habits of talking, a careful investigation of specialist talk will reveal that these ordinary habits can be radically called into question by a professional subcommunity. It follows that the thoroughgoing use of Wittgensteinian methods reveals the inadequacy of ordinary language philosophy.[35] Rather than dissolving abstract jurisprudential questions in the acid of everyday speech, Wittgensteinian methods instead force us back to old-fashioned puzzlements about the relationship of law to the larger society.

III. NORMATIVE QUESTIONS

Yet we have not simply rediscovered familiar jurisprudential ground. Rather than declaiming abstractly about the "nature" of private property, the descriptive exercise prepares us for asking a different normative question: How should constitutional lawyers talk about takings? This new way of asking the question permits us to place the particular dispute about property in a new normative perspective. After all, lawyers talk about lots of things other than takings. And perhaps there are some very general normative arguments on behalf of Scientific Policymaking or Ordinary Observing that apply *whenever* lawyers try to talk about *anything*. If such arguments can be developed, they may suggest that the dispute between Scientific and Ordinary conceptions of "property" is but a special case of a more general question about the best way to organize a legal culture. Once we adopt even a tentative position on this larger issue, the particular interpretative problems surrounding the takings clause may seem easy—or at least more tractable.

A similar if less cosmic exercise is suggested by the fact that lawyers view their Takings talk as more closely related to some areas of legal discourse than others. In particular, professional adepts recognize the Takings problem as embedded within a larger pattern of discourse conventionally called constitutional law—where the legal culture claims for itself the right to judge the legitimacy of the nation's political output. Given the particular location of the Takings problem in the web of legal culture,[36] we may generate some useful insights by viewing the arguments for Scientific Policymaking and Ordinary Observing from the general vantage point of constitutional theory: Are lawyers committed to reading the Constitution like Ordinary Observers or like Scientific Policymakers once they have accepted certain very general principles of constitutional law?

Not that an answer to such broader questions would *necessarily* resolve the problematic interpretation of "property" as it arises in the Takings Clause. Even if, say, there were powerful reasons for *usually* reading the Constitution like a Scientific Policymaker, there may well be *special* reasons for indulging a different kind of interpretation when it comes to "private property." Nonetheless, we may see our way more clearly to a conclusion on this particular question if we try to take a broader view.

Begin, then, with the most abstract formulation of the normative question: How, in general, should a legal culture be organized? Should lawyers be generally required to talk in the way described by the Ordinary Observer or the way described by the Scientific Policymaker, or should some particular mix of these modes be generally approved? The first step in my argument tries to frame an answer by forging a link between this question of legal philosophy and the normative theory of the state. To do this, I shall require a new distinction that differentiates two large families of normative political theories. On the one hand, I want to define a large class of "activist" theories to include any political doctrine that conceives the state as normatively justified in sometimes changing the underlying distribution of power prevailing in society at large in the name of some value—justice, efficiency, or what have you. On the other hand, I want to define an "invisible hand" theory as one that denies that the state may legitimately challenge the legitimacy of the prevailing societal power structure. For present purposes, it is not important how any particular invisible hand theory tries to validate the status quo—it may legitimate power by extolling the virtues of a free market or a benevolent deity or an inscrutable destiny. The critical point is that the state is *not* seen as an appropriate vehicle for criticizing the expectations generated by the existing institutional matrix.

Now, I trust the relation between these two kinds of political theory and the Scientific Policymaker/Ordinary Observer dichotomy is not hard to see. For an invisible hand theorist, it would be a fundamental mistake to approve a legal culture organized on Scientific Policymaking lines. Such a legal culture commits lawyers to a pattern of talk that assumes state officials are entitled to criticize preexisting expectations and use state power to alter the power structure that generates them—a position the invisible hand proponent denies (by definition). In contrast, the "activist" takes a different view. Although Ordinary Observing may play a valuable subordinate role in adjudication, the activist will deny that it can ever appropriately provide a complete description of the legal culture. At least at certain times and places, authoritative decision makers must be authorized to inquire whether the legal protection of existing expectations is inconsistent with the Comprehensive View affirmed by the "activist" state. Otherwise the legal system would seem committed to a normative political theory of a kind to which the activist is (by definition) opposed. Similarly, the activist cannot reject the notion of a Scientific legal language out of hand. Using law to reform the power structure thrown up by the invisible hand is a tricky business at best. Although steps should, of course, be taken to control the abuse of esoteric discourse, the notion that the activist state can entirely do without specialized analysis will typically be dismissed as naive.

So much for the first stage in the argument, which can be schematized in two lines:

(1) If A, then S-P with O-O playing at best a subordinate role.
(2) If I, then not S-P.

where A = activist state, I = invisible hand, S-P = Scientific Policymaking and O-O = Ordinary Observing. The second stage in the argument explores the significance of these normative relationships on the level of constitutional law. Although this is a very complex matter, I shall content myself here with a narrow claim about the legal significance of a single event in our recent constitutional history. I have in mind the constitutional confrontation between the Old Court and the New Deal that ended with the "switch in time" that validated the bulk of Roosevelt's political program. Now, although the precise meaning of this constitutional revolution remains a hotly contested matter, my argument requires a claim that does not, I think, involve serious controversy:

(3) The defeat of the Old Court by the New Deal established the constitutional legitimacy of some forms of activist state.

Yet if this is so, it follows from (1) that:

(4) Lawyers should read the constitutional text in a way that does not deny the legitimacy of S-P.

Even if this is so, however, it does not follow that the *takings clause* should be read in an S-P way. Perhaps the clause should mark one of the islands of O-O discourse in an S-P sea. This leads to a new meta-question: How are constitutional lawyers generally committed to Scientific Policymaking to talk about the special occasions on which Ordinary Observing represents a suitable way of talking?

Despite the perils of infinite regress, I do not think this a silly question; nor do I think it unanswerable. To frame an answer, however, the Scientific Policymaker must descend to particulars and elaborate the substantive Comprehensive View that he thinks best captures the ideals of the American constitutional system. Thus, a lawyer who interprets the Constitution from a utilitarian viewpoint may well define the supplemental role of O-O'ing in a way different from those who take a view that I have called Kantian.[37] This is not the place, though, to give these more detailed issues the extended treatment they deserve. All I can say is that *if* there is a principled case for the use of O-O in the interpretation of the Takings Clause, I suspect that it must be generated as an exception to the normative presumption in favor of S-P as the standard technique of constitutional interpretation.

The tentative character of this claim should be emphasized. I offer it only as an example of the kinds of argument, and types of conclusion, that are possible once legal theory takes a genuinely Wittgensteinian turn. Further exploration may yield other arguments that will shift the balance toward an acceptance of O-O as the generally applicable mode of constitutional discourse while limiting S-P to special circumstances. I do not imagine that I have fully explored even the tip of this iceberg.[38]

Professor MacRae's commentary suggests a second direction in which normative investigation must be extended. Making normative sense of the legal culture is only part of the larger enterprise of making sense of the political system of which it is a part. Moreover, even in so legalistic a culture as America, it would be wrong to exaggerate the judicial place in the constitutional structure. Although courts decide concrete cases, the Constitution is not what the judges say it is. Instead, legal formulations are simply a part of a larger process by which the ideals of the American polity are shaped and reshaped over time. Nonetheless, while I suspect that MacRae is right in thinking that, as a legal academic, I tend to idealize the role of courts, there is something of an equal and opposite defect in his proposal for a shift in the present balance of power to the political branches: "Although legislatures do not always choose to decide issues in terms of clear principles, we may at least imagine that a widespread debate about questions of property . . . might culminate by action in the legislature rather than the courts."[39] Rather than imagining a "final" solution by either courts or legislatures, it is best to imagine an ongoing dialogic process in which both agencies, as well as many others, play a part in constitutional decision and in which none has the "last say."

Within this more dynamic picture, I do not think I exaggerate the role that courts may properly play in the ongoing development of American political culture. On the contrary, the rise of the activist state creates an even greater need for institutions — like the courts — to engage the political process in ways that generate an ongoing discussion of the ideals that justify this ceaseless activity. Moreover, there is reason to believe that a legal culture organized on S-P lines is peculiarly well suited for carrying on this larger political dialogue. As S-P lawyers engage in their daily task of applying abstract ideals to concrete situations, they will constantly uncover cases where their understanding of the requirements of the Comprehensive View is cloudy at best. Although judges will doubtless resolve these "hard" cases by one or another expedient well known to the trade, these difficulties will not go away until the received understanding of the Comprehensive View is clarified. Within a setting of democratic norms, this means that principled Policymaking judges will be constantly attempting to prod the political branches into a clearer statement of the polity's basic principles — for it is only by legislative clarification of the Comprehensive View that "hard" cases may be transformed into "easy" ones. In contrast, the O-O judge will conceive the character of a "hard" case in a different way. For him, legal difficulty does not arise from *political* uncertainty about collective ideals but from the open-textured character of *institutionalized expectations.* This diagnosis will make it seem far less likely that a dialogue with the political branches will resolve the judiciary's sense of legal difficulty. For even if a degree of *political* clarity is attained by this process, *social* practice may remain just as confused as it ever was. And it is fidelity to the latter, and not the former, that defines the O-O judge. It follows that the principled O-O judge will respond to "hard" cases quite differently from his S-P counterpart. Rather than placing much stock in dialogue with the political branches, he will tend to a stoic fatalism when confronted with clear cases of indeterminacy in the structure of social expectation. Since he is paid to resolve conflict, he will come down with a decision in one way or another; yet, until a dominant pattern of social expectation somehow crystallizes, there is little he can do to enhance the legitimacy of his particular decision.

IV. CAUSAL QUESTIONS

Although legal philosophers should talk about the way lawyers should talk, we should not fool ourselves into thinking that the fate of a legal culture depends only on normative argument. As an empirical matter, there are many forces that affect the shape of the legal culture—economic, social, political, as well as ideological and philosophical. Thus, it is possible for every single reader of this volume to conclude unanimously, say, that lawyers ought to argue like O-O's and yet also unanimously predict—after elaborating one's favored causal theory—that in fifty years lawyers will be speaking with one voice like S-P's with a Kantian point of view. Or vice versa.

Unfortunately, when I look around for plausible causal theories, the situation seems nothing short of desparate. Legal scholars themselves must take a goodly share of the blame. We have been too indiscriminating in our reception of the genuine insights of our Realist forefathers. It is one thing to say that legal doctrine is not the *only* factor in an adequate causal account of legal decision; it is quite another thing to say that it is not an important factor. Moreover, a healthy Realist skepticism about the impact of legal rules should not blind us to the fact that the legal culture is much more than a collection of rules; it is also a pattern of conversational conventions that, as I hope my study of private property suggests, condition the way lawyers go about analyzing problems. Even those who disparage the impact of formal *rules* should think again before they minimize the causal importance of legal *culture*. Nonetheless, the Realist climate has not invited deep exploration of the way this professional culture is being shaped by larger social forces.

Nor has the most recent wave of post-Realist work in law and economics helped matters one bit. Although the rise of this movement *is* a very important sign of a more general tendency toward Scientific Policymaking, many of its leading practitioners share the Realist tendency to belittle legal culture as an important variable in causal explanation. Indeed, the Chicago branch of the movement has tried to show that, regardless of the way lawyers and judges may talk, the common law system has in fact generated a pattern of rules that they find "efficient."[40] Speaking personally, I am entirely unpersuaded by these studies. More important here, however, is that scholars committed to such reductionist work are hardly disposed to serious efforts at providing a causal account of the way legal cultures themselves change over time.

Worse yet, when one looks beyond legal scholarship to other potentially relevant fields, the harvest is not a rich one. The sociology of knowledge still is more programmatic statement than serious theory;[41] as are European efforts to merge Marxism and structuralism.[42] While I have found the work of Mary Douglas[43] and Jurgen Habermas[44] genuinely helpful for my own thinking, I suspect that Weber still contains more that is useful than anybody else.

Allow me, then, a crude Weberian sketch: The legal profession finds itself in an increasingly bureaucratic world — where power goes to those who claim possession of special analytic techniques that permit the "rational" solution of complex problems. While these new professions have many names — policy analysts, computer scientists, business school managers, economists — they all argue in a way that is isomorphic, if not identical, to the forms of Scientific Policymaking on the ascendant in American law.[45] Moreover, these professions increasingly challenge the dominion of the traditional American caste of public policymakers — called lawyers. In response to this challenge, it would not be surprising if the traditional caste tries to dominate its new competitors by assimilating a good deal of their culture — hence the gradual legal shift from Ordinary Observing to Scientific Policymaking.

But this is too simple a story. All that is clear is that the power struggle among elites will have a profound impact on the way all of us come to talk about power — hence property — in the years ahead.

NOTES

*I would like to thank Ruth Gavison, Tony Kronman, and Arthur Leff for their thoughtful comments on an earlier draft of this chapter.

1. New Haven: Yale Univ. Press; 1977. Henceforth cited as *Private Property*.
2. See, e.g., Dred Scott v. Sanford, 19 Howard 393, 450 (1856); Penn Central Transportation Company v. City of New York 98 S. Ct. 2646 (1978).
3. Or any other forum for authoritative dispute resolution.
4. And there are other line drawing problems as well — notably those involved in filling out the phrase "socially competent person."
5. *Private Property*, pp. 10–11.
6. Resolving all line-drawing problems of the kinds suggested by n. 4 and

accompanying text.

7. There is a problem here involving the unit of discourse that is to count as an "utterance." Given the possibility of whispered simultaneous translation noted in the text, at p. 354, a single unfamiliar word or usage will not necessarily preclude a sentence from qualifying as Ordinary. Instead, the status of an individual sentence will depend upon the frequency of esoteric usage over a longer conversational interval. Similarly, it may sometimes be difficult to tell whether a sentence is Scientific or un-Scientific without looking at the larger conversational context in which it is embedded.

8. See pp. 333–35 in this volume, as well as *Private Property*, p. 198, n. 22.

9. It may be objected that a *purely* "revolutionary" Policymaking culture is fated to become more "conservative" over time if the revolutionary regime succeeds in transforming social institutions into its favored image. Although this may be true as an empirical matter, it does not damage the conceptual point made in the text.

10. See p. 344 above.

11. Financial and otherwise. See, e.g., discussion and sources cited at *Private Property*, p. 205, n.3.

12. See p. 344 above.

13. See *Private Property*, pp. 197–98, for some of them.

14. Ibid.

15. Recall that I am here talking about the way lawyers *talk*, not about what is "really" going on. Lawyers often say one thing and do another. The empirical relationship between legal talk and legal decision is a part of my fourth—causal—question. We are concerned here, however, with a characterization of the varieties of legal culture, not the relation between culture and outcomes.

16. I discuss Frank's *Law and the Modern Mind* in *Daedalus* (Fall, 1974), pp. 119–30.

17. See e.g., *Symbols of Government* (New Haven: Yale Univ. Press, 1935); *The Folklore of Capitalism* (New Haven: Yale Univ. Press, 1937).

18. New York: Norton, 1977.

19. I shall not consider whether Hertz and other corporations should be treated as "persons" for purposes of constitutional law. While this is a fundamental issue deserving serious thought, American lawyers at present have no trouble answering in the affirmative. See First National Bank v. Bellotti, 98 S. Ct. 1407 (1978).

20. I mean to use this loaded term in a descriptive rather than normative sense (as a cultural anthropologist might).

21. See p. 330–31, above.

22. See *Private Property*, pp. 59, 211–12, n. 34.

23. See, Flemming v. Nestor, 363 U.S. 603 (1960). Cf. Califano v. Aznavorian, 47 U.S. Law Week 4037 (U.S. Sup. Ct. 1978).

24. The concept of uncertainty cost is elaborated at *Private Property*, pp. 44–46.

25. Indeed, I believe that such work would not only clarify issues central to social welfare law but would also go a long way toward placing even more vexed issues of just compensation—like those raised by the *Bakke* case—in a broader and more nuanced perspective.

26. See Reich's classic article, "The New Property," 73 *Yale Law Journal* 733 (1964).

27. See Califano v. Aznavorian and Flemming v. Nestor, n.23 above, as well as the cases discussed in *Private Property* pp. 268–69.

28. It is an important sign of the times, however, that the U.S. Supreme Court was recently obliged to reverse a Scientific Policymaking opinion of the Pennsylvania Supreme Court that invalidated a tax scheme under the takings clause. See Alco Parking Corporation v. Pittsburgh, 453 Pa. 245, 307 A. 2d 851 (1973), rev'd 417 U.S. 369 (1974).

29. Although this is not the place to defend such a controversial judgment, I think that the Supreme Court's recent decision upholding the effort by New York to declare Grand Central Station an historic landmark, Penn Central Transportation v. City of New York, 98 S. Ct. 2646 (June 26, 1978), once again shows the dominion of Ordinary Observing concepts in takings law. To see the extent to which other forms of discourse challenge O-O-ing, however, it is only necessary to compare *Penn Central* with other (isomorphic?) cases decided under different doctrinal rubrics during the very same week in which Penn Central was decided. E.g., Duke Power Company v. Carolina Environmental Study Group, Inc., 98 S. Ct. 2620 (June 26, 1978); Allied Structural Steel Company v. Spannaus, 98 S. Ct. 2716 (June 28, 1978); Regents of University of California v. Bakke, 98 S. Ct. 2733 (June 28, 1978).

30. See sources cited in *Private Property* pp. 214–15, nn. 39–43.

31. New Haven: Yale University Press, 1976.

32. See p. 346 above.

33. See p. 345, above.

34. See p. 345, above.

35. Not to say that people like Austin imagined that ordinary language was the last word as well as the first. See his "A Plea for Excuses," *Proceedings of the Aristotelian Society*, 57 (1956), p. 11.

36. For some more general reflections on the possibility of drawing a "contextual map" of the legal culture, see my essay on "The Substructure of Subchapter C: An Anthropological Comment," 87 *Yale Law Journal* 436 (1978). For a seminal essay relevant to these purposes, see C. Geertz, *The Interpretation of Cultures* (1973), pp. 3–33.

37. See *Private Property*, chap. 4.

38. See *Private Property*, chap. 7, for a preliminary overview of the complex tangle of argument that seems relevant.

39. See p. 337, above.

40. See Paul Rubin, "Why Is the Common Law Efficient?" 6 *Journal of Legal Studies* 51 (1977); George Priest, "The Common Law Process and the Selection of Efficient Rules," 6 *Journal of Legal Studies* (1977); and sources cited therein.

41. The most useful books I have found in this field are Peter Berger and Thomas Luckmann, *The Social Construction of Reality* (New York: Anchor, 1967); and Magali Larson, *The Rise of Professionalism* (Berkeley: Univ. of California Press, 1977).

42. Though it is hard work piercing the theology, both Althuser's book, *Reading Capital* (New York: Pantheon, 1970) esp. pp. 94–105, and Poulantzas' work, e.g., *Political Power and Social Classes* (New York: Sheed & Ward, 1973), may be worth the effort.

43. *Purity and Danger* (Praeger, 1966); *Natural Symbols* (New York: Vintage, 1973); *Cultural Bias* (London Royal Anthropological Institute, 1978).

44. *Legitimation Crisis* (Boston: Beacon, 1975).

45. For a revealing textbook, see Edith Stokey and Richard Zeckhauser, *A Primer for Policy Analysis* (New York: Norton, 1978).

16

PROPERTY RIGHTS AND THE CONSTITUTION

LAWRENCE G. SAGER

I

These comments originated as a critique addressed to a paper on "property rights and the human personality." As events have transpired, that paper is not being published in this volume, and my remarks have lost the edifice against which they once leaned. It thus becomes necessary to re-create, if only by way of *trompe l'oeil*, the facade of the argument to which I am responding.

The argument begins with a remarkable passage from Madison's *Federalist* No. 10:

The diversity in the faculties of men, from which the rights of property originate, is . . . an insuperable obstacle to a uniformity of interests. The protection of these faculties is the first object of government. From the protection of different and unequal faculties of acquiring property, the possession of different degrees and kinds of property immediately result.[1]

It then proceeds on a literal and contemporary reading of the phrase "rights of property" and finds in Madison's attribution of such rights to the "diversity in the faculties of men" a theory of property. Madison is understood to advance a claim that the fulfillment of the human personality requires that property rights—in the narrow and now orthodox sense of property—be respected and that their protection should thus be "the first object of government."

The argument then takes another turn. Madison's vision, it is claimed, has prevailed, and those whose personal faculties drive them to seek fulfillment through the acquisition and retention of property enjoy the paramount respect of our society, our legal system, and especially our Constitution. In this sense, it is argued, Madison and his colleagues were consciously shaping a Constitution for capitalism and succeeded in this venture. Finally, it is suggested that our contemporary constitutional tradition perpetuates this aspect of the Madisonian design.

It is with this last proposition that I want to take issue here. I will argue that our contemporary constitutional tradition does not reflect a predisposition toward the nurturing of the human personality through the protection of property. To the contrary, it is rather strikingly bereft of the ingredients of such a predisposition.

It must be stressed, however, that my observations are ahistorical in two senses. First, it is not clear that the line of argument that serves as my foil is correctly pended to the Madisonian dictum in *Federalist* 10. There is, for example, substantial support for the proposition that Madison's concept of "property" encompassed a broad range of personal claims of right; and thus that the *Federalist* passage is more appropriately understood as a general claim for the respect of human liberties than a special pleading on the rights of private property.[2] Second, in assessing the complexion of our constitutional tradition, my concern is with its modern form. At certain times — most notably in the decades that bracketed the turn of the century — that tradition better served the security of private property and any aspects of the human personality that might thereby flourish. Although each of these historical questions is surely of considerable interest, neither is my central object here, though I will make passing reference to the evolution of our constitutional tradition.

I will proceed by considering several different senses in which a legal system might undertake to protect the opportunity of individuals to fulfill themselves through the acquisition and enjoyment of property and, in turn, by assessing the extent to which our constitutional tradition in fact reflects such an undertaking. Ultimately, I will argue that even those aspects of our constitutional tradition that are explicitly property based are presently applied in pursuit of values other than the protection of private property as such and bear on such protection only in an indirect and diminished fashion.

II

The most obvious way in which a legal system could undertake to protect the institution and prerogatives of private property in the service of individual fulfillment would be to protect the relationship between individuals and specific parcels of land or other personally valued objects of property. The homestead presents the claim for a linkage between the institution of private property and the enrichment of the human personality in what is perhaps its most compelling and appealing form; and a legal system that was sensitive to this linkage might well undertake to secure the bond between individuals and specific property resources of this sort.

In fact, however, our own constitutional tradition is quite barren in this regard. Protection of the personal relationship of an individual to a particular property resource would necessitate a restriction of some substance on the power of governmental entities to interrupt this relationship. At a minimum, this would entail the imposition of a substantial burden on the state to justify any taking of property against the will of its owner. An appropriate refinement of this burden might further recognize a loose hierarchy of individual property concerns pursuant to which the state was obliged, for example, to prefer where possible the forced acquisition of undeveloped land held for purposes of investment or speculation over personally owned and actively used residential property.

While exercises of the power of eminent domain nominally depend for their legitimacy upon the existence of "a public purpose," that requirement has passed beyond the pale of serious judicial enforcement. In practice, eminent domain may be employed for any scheme a governing body that has not utterly taken leave of its corporate senses might choose to undertake.[3] And we have not erected a legal hierarchy of individual property; we are, in fact, quite callous in our legal response to an act of government that severs an individual from his homestead.

The only inhibition that our constitutional tradition effectively places upon the power of eminent domain is the requirement of compensation. To be sure, this requirement deters the public acquisition of property generally. But it does not differentiate in its impact between voluntary and involuntary transfers of land into the public domain, or between personally cherished individual property and property of indifferent personal attraction. Although governmental entities must pay for land they acquire, once a decision to undertake the expense is made the compensation requirement does not provide even marginal deterrence to the use of eminent domain to sever an individual from his property. The compensation requirement is thus only indirectly and insubstantially promotive of the relationship between individuals and particular pieces of property.

III

A legal system could undertake to provide for individual fulfillment in the use and ownership of property in quite a different sense. It might seek to insure that a plentiful supply of property remains in the private sector in order to make the personal rewards of owning, developing, and trading property broadly available. Although failing to guarantee the lasting bond of an individual to a particular piece of property, this approach would still serve to protect the opportunity of private ownership generally.

A constitutional tradition that reflected this concern would presumably erect some barrier to the public acquisition of property — probably in the form of a substantial burden of justification for any such acquisition — or it would place a limitation on the amount of specific property resources, like land, that could be diverted from the private to the public sector. Here, too, our own constitutional tradition is bereft of any such restrictions. Our previous observation of the vapidity of the "public purpose" requirement applies with equal force in this context: no direct restraint of any substance checks the impulse of a governmental entity to acquire property. Nor is there any legal restriction on the amount of property that can be absorbed into the public sector; indeed, in some regions of the country a quite remarkable proportion of the land is held by the state or federal government. Further, well-sanctioned regimes of taxation and government enterprise have served to draw a substantial share of the capital wealth of our country under the aegis of government.

Again, of course, the compensation requirement operates as a check on the acquisition of property by the state. But that check operates only to the extent that either (a) constitutional provisions limit the power to tax, which for these purposes they do not,[4] or (b) political forces effectively restrain the imposition of tax measures, which they surely do. In effect, therefore, the role of the compensation requirement in this context is to insure political and economic responsibility. But once taxpayers and voters endorse the absorption of property into the private sector, the Constitution asserts no bar to the effectuation of the public will.

IV

Perhaps, however, we should shift our focus from the protection of private property as such to the protection of private wealth. In an earlier era, it may have been possible to treat property and wealth as nearly synonymous, but the two are now quite distinct. A legal system that was quite careless about property might nevertheless exhibit great solicitude for wealth; and the claim that links the Constitution, the human personality, and property rights can easily be transposed to one in which the trailing term is wealth rather than property. Under these conditions, the question becomes whether our constitutional tradition can be understood as protecting a state of affairs pursuant to which individuals are for the most part unfettered in the pursuit of wealth by the means of their choosing, and further, for the most part able to retain the fruits of their acquisitive efforts.

On the face of the matter, our constitutional tradition seems more promising here. While quite ill suited to the protection of property, the compensation requirement seems nicely tailored for the protection of wealth; its effect, after all, is to frustrate the redistributions of wealth that would inevitably be the consequence of uncompensated governmental takings of property.

But this superficial promise of the constitutional protection of wealth does not survive close consideration. Reasoning from the compensation requirement to the conclusion that rights to wealth are secured by the Constitution is like encountering an impermeable part of the walls of a sieve and concluding thereby that the vessel in question holds water. As presently enforced by the judiciary, our Constitution appears to leave with the state the capacity to redistribute wealth drastically through the mechanisms of taxation and regulation. This was not always so, of course. Early limitations placed by the judiciary in the name of the Constitution on the power of the states and the federal government to tax[5] and on governmental regulatory authority[6] can be read with conviction as responding at least in part to an underlying resistance to efforts by the state to redistribute wealth and the opportunity to acquire it. But each of the legal traditions that can be so interpreted has been interred by the federal judiciary. With extraordinary generality and finality, the federal courts have ceased to find in the Constitution any basis for intervening in the decisions of governmental entities to tax or to regulate economic affairs.[7] Indeed, the repudiation of the earlier tradition of resisting the redistribution of wealth and economic opportunity is far more dramatic, pervasive, and conclusive than was the earlier tradition itself.

In an environment where the state is constitutionally free to tax and spend differentially and to exert the power of eminent domain and to regulate the economy with redistributive consequences, it is difficult to find in the requirement of compensation for takings of property any solace for those who seek the protection of wealth in our constitutional tradition. This raises the question, tangential to our discussion, of what ends the compensation requirement ought to be understood as serving. Without wanting to back carelessly into a subject that has enjoyed the close and illuminating scrutiny of others,[8] I will proffer my own view. The compensation requirement, I believe, should be understood as promoting two values. First, by requiring politically accountable bodies to expend public monies to compensate persons whose property has been taken, it allows the political process to operate as a check on ill considered or unpopular decisions to consume property resources. Second, and more significantly, it functions as a barrier to the drastic inequities that would result if individual property owners were made to bear the costs of governmental projects by sacrificing their property to these projects. In this respect, uncompensated takings of property would be like taxation measures that on arbitrary grounds singled out a handful of persons for assessment. While we comfortably tolerate redistributional measures that are visited on a class of persons defined by their resources, or other plausible criteria, and indeed are extraordinarily deferential to legislatve delineations of such classes, we would not tolerate the arbitrary visitation of such economic deprivations. At root, I think, the compensation requirement responds to this impulse of equity.

V

A final refuge of the argument that seeks the protection of property rights in our constitutional tradition might be in what Charles Reich termed the "new property."[9] On this view, the link between property rights and the human personality consists of the role of property as a buffer between the individual and the state. At least in a materialistic society, to control one's own wealth is to have a degree of personal autonomy, and to forfeit such control is to forfeit autonomy. Thus, precisely because so large a portion of our national wealth has been absorbed by the state, the new property must consist of legally secured claims against the largesse of the state. Accordingly, the argument could run, it is for the protection of "property" claims of this sort that our constitutional tradition should be canvased.

Our constitutional tradition, although far from vigorous in this respect, does show some signs of respecting procedural claims against the largesse of the state.[10] But to seek in decisions of this sort comfort for the proposition that our Constitution embodies a respect for private property in the name of human individuality would be to miss the point of our inquiry. The new property, such that it is, is a strand of legal analysis that takes as its point of departure the demise of the old property. Even in its most elaborated conception, the new property is a recipe for securing some medium of personal autonomy in the age of the welfare state; it is not a means of resisting the advent of that age.

VI

The case I have tried to construct reduces to a simple proposition: our constitutional tradition plainly tolerates an economy in which private property and private wealth figure prominently, but it by no means guarantees or even seriously inclines toward such an economy.

NOTES

1. *The Federalist Papers*, No. 78, ed. C. Rossiter (1961).
2. Madison wrote of his conception of property in the *National Gazette* of March 29, 1792:

> This term [property] in its particular application means "that domination which one man claims and exercises over the external things of the world, in exclusion of every other individual."
>
> In its larger and juster meaning, it embraces every thing to which a man may attach a value and have a right; and *which leaves to every one else the like advantage* [italics mine].
>
> In the former sense, a man's land, or merchandize, or money is called his property.
>
> In the latter sense, a man has property in his opinions and the free communication of them.
>
> He has a property of peculiar value in his religious opinions, and in the profession and practice dictated by them.
>
> He has property very dear to him in the safety and liberty of his person.
>
> He has an equal property in the free use of his faculties and free choice of the objects on which to employ them.
>
> In a word, as a man is said to have a right to his property, he may be equally said to have a property in his rights.

* * *

Conscience is the most sacred of all property; other property depending in part on positive law, the exercise of that, being a natural and inalienable right. To guard a man's house as his castle, to pay public and enforce private debts with the most exact faith can give no title to invade a man's conscience which is more sacred than his castle, or to withhold from it that debt of protection, for which the public faith is pledged, by the very nature and original conditions of the social pact.

* * *

If the United States mean to obtain or deserve the full praise due to wise and just governments, they will equally respect the rights of property, and the property in rights: they will rival the government that most sacredly guards the former; and by repelling its example in violating the latter, will make themselves a pattern to that and all other governments.

6 *The Writings of James Madison,* ed. G. Hunt (1906), pp. 101–3.

3. "We think that it is the function of Congress to decide what type of taking is for a public use. . . . [T]his Court has said that when Congress has spoken on this subject 'Its decision is entitled to a deference until it is shown to involve an impossibility.' " United States *ex rel* Tennessee Valley Authority v. Welch, 327 U.S. 546, 551–52 (1946).

Courts have suggested that if the ultimate purpose behind the taking is a matter subject to legislative control, the finding of a public use is almost inevitable, if not automatic. See, e.g., Berman v. Parker, 348 U.S. 26, 34 (1954); Barnridge v. United States, 101 F.2d 295, 298 (8th Cir. 1939). See generally, Comment, "The Public Use Limitation on Eminent Domain: An Advance Requiem," 58 *Yale Law Journal* 599, 611–13 (1949). The fact that private individuals, and not the government or the general public, may ultimately be utilizing the land has not daunted the judiciary in the modern era. See Berman v. Parker, supra (slum clearance project contemplated development by and for private persons); Courtesy Sandwich Shop, Inc. v. Port of New York Authority, 12 N.Y.2d 379, 190 N.E.2d 402, 240 N.Y.S.2d 1, *appeal dismissed*, 375 U.S. 78 (1963) (proposed World Trade Center to be leased by private individuals engaged in business relating to "world trade"). Moreover, the *Courtesy Sandwich Shop* court made it clear that the use of a portion of the property need not even allegedly have anything to do with a public purpose if it serves as a means of raising revenue for the rest of the project. See 12 N.Y.2d at 389–91, 190 N.E.2d at 405–6, 240 N.Y.S.2d at 6–7. Indeed, despite the prevalence of forceful public purpose dicta in early cases, actual invalidation of exercises of eminent domain was rare and confined to instances of direct benefit to private parties. See, e.g., Taylor v. Porter, 4 Hill 140 (N.Y. Sup. Ct. 1843) (private roads); Matter of The Split Rock Cable Road Company, 128 N.Y. 408, 28 N.E. 506 (1891) (benefit to private business).

4. See n. 7, infra.
5. See, e.g., Loan Association v. Topeka, 87 U.S. (20 Wall.) 655 (1875);
    Pollock v. Farmers' Loan and Trust Company, 157 U.S. 429 (1895);
    Quaker City Cab Co. v. Pennsylvania, 277 U.S. 389 (1928). In his ar-
    gument to the Court in the *Pollock* case, Hoseph H. Choate assailed
    the federal tax:

    > Now, if you approve this law, with this iniquitous exemption of
    > $4000, and this communistic march goes on and five years hence
    > a statute comes to you with an exemption of $20,000 and a tax of
    > 20 per cent upon all having incomes in excess of that amount,
    > how can you meet it in view of the decision which my opponents
    > ask you now to render?

    *   *   *

    > One of the fundamental objects of all civilized government was
    > the preservation of the rights of private property.

    *   *   *

    > One thing is certain, absolutely certain, that although the power
    > was given Congress to tax, no power was given it to confiscate.

    39 L. Ed. at 799.

    > [Attacking the attorney general's suggestion that the law in ques-
    > tion is designed to bring about an approximation of equality of
    > taxation:] This is a doctrine worthy of a Jacobin Club that pro-
    > posed to govern France; it is worthy of a Czar of Russia propos-
    > ing to reign with undisputed and absolute power; but it cannot
    > be done under this Constitution. Id. at 807.

6. See, e.g., Lochner v. New York, 198 U.S. 45 (1905).
7. As to taxation, compare Lehnhausen v. Lake Shore Auto Parts Co.,
    410 U.S. 356 (1973), with Quaker City Cab Co. v. Pennsylvania, 227
    U.S. 389 (1928); See City of Pittsburgh v. Alco Parking Corp. 417
    U.S. 369 (1974). As to regulation, see generally, McCloskey, *Economic
    Due Process and the Supreme Court: An Exhumation and Reburial,*
    1962 *Supreme Court Review* 34.
8. See Michelman, "Property, Utility and Fairness: Comments on the
    Ethical Foundations of 'Just Compensation' Law," 80 *Harvard Law
    Review* 1165 (1967); Sax, "Takings, Private Property and Public
    Rights," 81 *Yale Law Journal* 149 (1971); and B. Ackerman, *Private
    Property and the Constitution* (1977).
9. See Reich, "The New Property," 73 *Yale Law Journal* 733 (1964).
10. See, e.g., Board of Regents v. Roth, 408 U.S. 564 (1972); Perry v.
    Sinderman, 408 U.S. 593 (1973). Compare Bishop v. Wood, 426 U.S.
    341 (1976).

PROPERTY AND JUSTICE:
A SELECT BIBLIOGRAPHY
GERALD F. GAUS

My premise in compiling this bibliography is that, at least for the political or social philosopher, the study of property naturally leads to questions concerning economic justice. And that, in turn, leads to issues involving the economic basis of property rights, the nature of the distribution of wealth and income, the relation between property, individualism and liberty, and the like. Therefore, although I have concentrated on works dealing directly with property and property rights, I have also attempted to provide some departure points for the researcher in these other areas. It also ought to be noted that owing to space considerations I barely touch here on the huge body of literature dealing with Marxist critiques of private property and capitalism.

I. HISTORICAL PERSPECTIVES

A. General

Aron, Raymond. *Progress and Disillusion.* New York: Praeger, 1968.

Barbu, Zevedei. *Problems of Historical Psychology.* London: Routledge & Kegan Paul, 1968.

Blum, Jerome. *The End of the Old Order in Rural Europe.* Princeton: Princeton University Press, 1979.

Goldman, Lucien. *The Philosophy of the Enlightenment: The Christian Burgess and the Enlightenment.* Henry Moss, translator. Cambridge: MIT Press, 1968, Chapter 1.

Halevy, Elie. *The Era of Tyrannies.* R. K. Webb, translator. Garden City, N.Y.: Anchor Books, 1968.

Harrington, Michael. *The Accidental Century.* London: Macmillan, 1965.

Hartz, Louis. *The Liberal Tradition in America.* New York: Harcourt, Brace & World, 1955.

— — —. ed. *The Founding of New Societies*. New York: Harcourt, Brace & World, 1964.

Jouvenel, Bertrand de. *Power: The Natural History of Its Growth*. J.F. Huntington, translator. London: Batchworth Press, 1952.

Laski, Harold J. *The Rise of European Liberalism*. London: George Allen & Unwin, 1936.

Lloyd-Jones, Hugh. *The Justice of Zeus*. Berkeley: University of California Press, 1971.

McNeil, William H. *The Rise of the West*. Chicago: The University of Chicago Press, 1963.

— — —. *The Shape of European History*. Oxford: Oxford University Press, 1974.

— — —. *A World History*, 2nd ed. Oxford: Oxford University Press, 1971.

Moore, Barrington. *Social Origins of Dictatorship and Democracy*. Boston: Beacon Pres, 1966.

Pocock, J. G. A. *The Machiavellian Moment*. Princeton: Princeton University Press, 1975.

Polanyi, Karl L. *The Great Transformation*. Boston: Beacon Press, 1957.

— — —. *The Livelihood of Man*. New York: Academic Press, 1977.

Quinton, Anthony. *The Politics of Imperfection*. London: Faber and Faber, 1978.

Schochet, Gordon J. *Patriarchialism in Political Thought*. New York: Basic Books, 1975.

Sidorsky, David, ed. *The Liberal Tradition in European Thought*. New York: Putnam, 1970.

Sigmund, P. E. *Natural Law in Political Thought*. Cambridge: Winthrop, 1971.

Skinner, Quentin. *The Foundations of Modern Political Thought*, 2 vols., Cambridge: Cambridge University Press, 1978.

Trevor-Roper, Hugh. *The Rise of Christian Europe*. New York: Harcourt, Brace & World, 1965.

Walzer, Michael. *The Revolution of the Saints*. Cambridge: Harvard University Press, 1965.

Woodhouse, A. S. P., ed. *Puritanism and Liberty*. Chicago: University of Chicago Press, 1951.

B. Economic History

Anderson, Perry. *Passages from Antiquity to Feudalism*. London: New Left Books, 1978.

Appleby, Joyce Oldham. *Economic Thought and Ideology in Seventeenth-Century England*. Princeton: Princeton University Press, 1978.

Ashton, T. S. *An Economic History of England: The 18th Century*. New York: Barnes and Noble, 1955.

———. *The Industrial Revolution*. Oxford: Oxford University Press, 1970.

Baechler, Jean. *The Origins of Capitalism*. Barry Cooper, translator. Oxford: Basil Blackwell, 1975.

Bois, Guy. *Crise du feodalisme*. Paris: Presses de la Foundation national de sciences Politiques, 1976.

Braudel, F. *Afterthoughts on Material Civilization and Capitalism*. Baltimore: The John Hopkins University Press, 1977.

———. *Capitalism and Material Life*. Miriam Kochan, translator. New York: Harper & Row, 1973.

Clarke, Peter. *Liberals and Social Democrats*. Cambridge: Cambridge University Press, 1978.

Dorfman, Joseph. *The Economic Mind in American Civilization*. New York: Viking Press, 1946.

Finley, M. I. *The Ancient Economy*. Berkeley: University of California Press, 1973.

Freeden, Michael. *The New Liberalism: An Ideology of Social Reform*. Oxford: Clarendon Press, 1978.

Gordon, Barry. *Political Economy in Parliament, 1819–1823*. New York: Barnes and Noble, 1977.

Hampshire-Monk, F. "Political Theory of the Levellers: Putney, Property and Professor Macpherson." 24 *Political Studies* (December 1976), 397–422.

Hicks, John R. *A Theory of Economic History*. Oxford: Clarendon Press, 1969.

Hirshman, A. O. *The Passions and the Interests: Political Arguments for Capitalism Before Its Triumph*. Princeton: Princeton University Press, 1977.

Holmes, Graham. *Britain and America: A Comparative Economic History*. New York: Barnes and Noble, 1976.

Horne, Thomas, A. *The Social Thought of Bernard Mandeville: Virtue and Commerce in Early Eighteenth Century England*. London: Macmillan, 1978.

Kamenka, Eugene and R. S. Neale, eds. *Feudalism, Capitalism and Beyond*. New York: St. Martin's Press, 1974.

Lowry, Todd S. "Recent Literature on Ancient Greek Economic

Thought." 17 *Journal of Economic Literature* (March 1979), 65–86.

Macfarlane, Alan. *The Origins of English Individualism: The Family, Property and Social Transition*. Oxford: Basil Blackwell, 1978.

Macpherson, C. B. *The Political Theory of Possessive Individualism*. Oxford: Clarendon Press, 1962.

North, Douglas C. and Robert Paul Thomas. *The Rise of the West: A New Economic History*. Cambridge: Cambridge University Press, 1973.

O'Brien, George A. *Essay on Medieval Economic Teaching*. Fairfield, N.J.: Kelley, reprint of 1920 edition.

Pirenne, Henri. *Economic and Social History of Medieval Europe*. I. E. Clegg, translator. New York: Harcourt, Brace & World, 1937.

Postan, M. M. *An Economic History of Western Europe: 1945–1964*. London: Methuen, 1967.

——— and H. J. Habakkuk, general eds. *The Cambridge Economic History of Europe*, 2d edition. Cambridge: Cambridge University Press, 1966.

Pryor, Frederic L. *The Origins of the Economy: A Comparative Study of Distribution in Primitive and Peasant Economies*. New York: Academic Press, 1977.

Robbins, Caroline. *The Eighteenth Century Commonwealthman*. Cambridge: Harvard University Press, 1959.

Robbins, Lionel. *The Evolution of Modern Economic Theory*. Chicago: Aldine, 1970.

———. *The Theory of Economic Development in the History of Economic Thought*. New York: St. Martin's Press, 1968.

Roll, Eric. *A History of Economic Thought*, 4th edition. London: Faber and Faber, 1974.

Vries, Jan De. *The Economy of Europe in an Age of Crisis, 1600–1750*. Cambridge: Cambridge University Press, 1976.

Weber, Max. *The Protestant Ethic and the Spirit of Capitalism*. Talcott Parsons, translator. New York: Charles Scribner's Sons, 1958.

C. The History of Property

Anderson, Terry and P. J. Hill. "Evolution of Property Rights: A Study of the American West." 10 *Journal of Law and Economics* (April 1975), 163–79.

Barker, Ernest. *Greek Political Theory*. London: Methuen, 1952.

Cunliffe, Marcus. *The Right to Property: A Theme in American History*. Atlantic Highlands, N.J.: Humanities Press, 1974.

Dickenson, H. J. *Liberty and Property: Political Ideology in Eighteenth Century Britain*. New York: Holmes and Meier, 1978.

Diosdi, Gyorgy. *Ownership in Ancient and Preclassical Roman Law*. New York: International Publishers, 1970.

Engels, Friedrich. *The Origin of the Family, Private Property and the State*. New York: International Publishers, 1972.

Engerman, Stanley L. "Some Considerations Relating to Property Rights in Man." 33 *Journal of Economic History* (March 1973), 43–65.

Finley, M. I., ed. *Studies in Roman Property*. Cambridge: Cambridge University Press, 1976.

Germino, Dante. *Modern Western Political Thought: Machiavelli to Marx*. Chicago: Rand McNally, 1972.

Grace, Frank. *The Concept of Property in Modern Christian Thought*. Urbana: University of Illinois Press, 1953.

Greed, John Anthony, ed. *Property Law in the Stagecoach Days*. Bristol: St. Trillo, 1976.

Harding, Richard W. "Evolution of Roman Catholic Views of Private Property as a Natural Right." 2 *Solicitor Quarterly* (April 1963), 124–37.

Hengel, Martin. *Property and Riches in the Early Church*. John Bowden, translator. Philadelphia: Fortress Press, 1974.

Hobhouse, L. T. "The Historical Evolution of Property, in Fact and in Idea." In his *Sociology and Philosophy*. London: G. Bell and Sons, 1966, 81–106.

Holt, J. C. "Politics and Property in Early Medieval England." 57 *Past and Present* (1972), 3–52.

Hunt, Emery Kay. *Property and Prophets: Evolution of Economic Institutions and Ideologies*. New York: Harper & Row, 1975.

Katz, Stanley N. "Thomas Jefferson and the Right to Property in Revolutionary America." 19 *Journal of Law and Economics* (October 1976), 467–88.

Larkin, P. *Property in the Eighteenth Century*. New York: Howard Fertig, 1969.

Levy, Ernst. *West Roman Vulgar Law, the Law of Property*. Philadelphia: American Philosophical Society, 1951.

Mosca, Gaetano. *A Short History of Political Philosophy*. Sondra Z. Koff, translator. New York: Thomas Y. Crowell, 1972.

North, Douglas. "The Creation of Property Rights in Western Europe, 900–1700 AD." In Svetozar Pejovich, ed. *The Codetermination Movement in the West*. Lexington, Mass.: Lexington Books,

1978.

Schlatter, Richard Bulger. *Private Property: The History of an Idea.* Brunswick, N.J.: Rutgers University Press, 1957.

Schochet, Gordon J., ed. *Life, Liberty and Property: Essays on John Locke's Political Ideas.* Belmont, Calif.: Wadsworth, 1971.

Scott, William B. *In Pursuit of Happiness: American Conceptions of Property from the Seventeenth to the Twentieth Century.* Bloomington: Indiana University Press, 1977.

Silbey, Mulford Q. *Political Ideas and Ideologies.* New York: Harper & Row, 1970.

Simcou, E. J. *Primitive Civilizations or Outlines of the History of Ownership in Archaic Communities,* 2 vols. New York: Gordon & Breach, 1977.

Strauss, Leo and Joseph Cropsey. *History of Political Philosophy,* 2d edition. Chicago: Rand McNally, 1972.

Watson, Alan. *The Law of Property in the Later Roman Republic.* Oxford: Clarendon Press, 1968.

———. *Rome of the XII Tables: Persons and Property.* Princeton: Princeton University Press, 1975.

II. PROPERTY AND PROPERTY RIGHTS

A. Philosophic Treatment

Aron, Raymond. "Sociology and the Philosophy of Human Rights." In Miriam Bernheim Conant, ed., translator. *Politics and History: Selected Essays of Raymond Aron.* New York: The Free Press, 1978, Chapter 7.

Becker, Lawrence. "Labor Theory of Property Acquisition." (with reply by J. J. Thompson). 73 *Journal of Philosophy* (October 21, 1976), 533–66.

———. *Property Rights.* London: Routledge & Kegan Paul, 1977.

Benn, Stanley I. "Property." In *The Encyclopedia of Philosophy.* New York: Collier Macmillan, 1967.

——— and R. S. Peters. *Social Principles and the Democratic State.* London: George Allen & Unwin, 1959, Chapter 7.

Bhardwaj, K. K. "The Right to Property." 6 *Journal of Political Studies* (February 1973), 54–63.

Braybrooke, David. *Three Tests for Democracy.* New York: Random House, 1968, Chapter 2.

Flathman, Richard. *The Practice of Rights.* Cambridge: Cambridge University Press, 1976, Appendix.

Helm, Paul. "Professor Hart on Action and Property." 80 *Mind* (July 1971), 422–31.

Hodgskin, Thomas. *Natural and Artificial Right of Property Contrasted.* Fairfield, N.J.: Kelley, 1978.

Hoffman, Frank Sargent. "The Right to Property." 19 *International Journal of Ethics* (1909), 477–87.

LeFeure, Robert. *The Philosophy of Ownership.* Larkspur, Colo.: Rampart College, n.d.

Lehing, Percy B. "Social Contract and Property Rights." In Pierre Birnbaum, Jack Lively, and Geraint Parry, eds. *Democracy, Consensus and Social Contract.* Beverly Hills: Sage, 1971, 279–94.

Lopata, B. B. "Property Theory in Hobbes." 1 *Political Theory* (May 1973), 203–18.

Machan, T. R. "Justification of Private Property." 55 *Personalist* (Winter 1974), 61–63. Reply: G. I. Mavrodes. 55 *Personalist* (Spring 1974), 186–88. Machan's Rejoinder: 56 *Personalist* (Winter 1975), 75–76.

Macpherson, C. B. "Human Rights as Property Rights." 24 *Dissent* (Winter 1977), 72–77.

——— ed. *Property: Mainstream and Critical Positions.* Toronto: Toronto University Press, 1978.

Melden, A. I. *Rights and Persons.* Oxford: Basil Blackwell, 1977, Chapters 6 and 7.

Milne, A. J. M. *Freedom and Rights.* New York: Humanities Press, 1968, Chapter 10.

Minogue, Kenneth R. "Natural Rights, Ideology and the Game of Life." In Eugene Kamenka and Alice Ehr-Soon Tay, eds. *Human Rights.* New York: St. Martin's Press, 1978, 13–35.

Moore, James. "Hume's Theory of Justice and Property." 24 *Political Studies* (June 1976), 103–19.

Overstreet, Harry Allen. "The Changing Conception of Property." 25 *International Journal of Ethics* (1915), 165–78.

Sheldon, W. L. "What Justifies Private Property?" 4 *International Journal of Ethics* (1894), 17–40.

Steiner, Hillel. "The Natural Right to the Means of Production." 27 *Philosophical Quarterly* (January 1977), 41–49.

———. "The Structure of a Set of Compossible Rights." 74 *Journal of Philosophy* (1977), 767–75.

Tay, Alice Erh-Soon. "Law, the Citizen and the State." In Eugene Kamenka, Robert Brown, and Alice Erh-Soon Tay, eds. *Law and Society.* London: Edward Arnold, 1978, 1–17.

Teichgraeber, R. "Hegel on Property and Poverty." 38 *Journal of the History of Ideas* (January 1977), 47–64.

Williams, Howard. "Kant's Concept of Property." 27 *Philosophical Quarterly* (January 1977), 32–40.

B. Legal Considerations

Abraham, H.J. " 'Human' Rights vs. 'Property' Rights: A Comment on the 'Double Standard.' " 90 *Political Science Quarterly* (Summer 1975), 288–92.

Ackerman, Bruce. *Private Property and the Constitution.* New Haven: Yale University Press, 1977.

———, ed. *Economic Foundations of Property Law.* Boston: Little, Brown, 1975.

Baldwin, Fletcher N., Jr. "Concept of Property from a Jurisprudential Viewpoint." 23 *Georgia Bar Journal* (November 1960), 171–90.

Bastiat, Frederic. *The Law.* Dean Russell, translator. Irving-on-the-Hudson, N.Y.: Foundation for Economic Education, 1950.

Buchanan, James M. "Politics, Property and the Law: An Alternative Interpretation of Miller et al. v. Schoene." 15 *Journal of Law and Economics* (October 1972), 439–52.

Commons, John R. *Legal Foundations of Capitalism.* Madison: University of Wisconsin Press, 1957.

Dolzer, Rudolf. "Welfare Benefits as Property Interests." 29 *Administrative Law Review* (Fall 1977), 525–75.

Friedman, W. *Law in a Changing Society.* Berkeley: University of California Press, 1959.

Funston, R. "The Double Standard of Constitutional Protection in the Era of the Welfare State." 90 *Political Science Quarterly* (Summer 1975), 261–87.

Glennon, Robert Jerome. "Constitutional Liberty and Property." 51 *Southern California Law Review* (March 1978), 355–98.

Henely, Bernard D. "Property Rights and First Amendment Rights: Balance and Conflict." 62 *American Bar Association Journal* (January 1976), 77–83.

Hickenlooper, Bourke B. "International Rights of Property: Some Observations" 2 *The International Lawyer* (October 1967), 51–59.

Honore, A. M. "Ownership." In A. G. Guest, ed. *Oxford Essays in Jurisprudence.* Oxford University Press, 1961, 108–47.

Horowitz, Morton J. "Transformation in the Conception of Property in American Law, 1780–1860." 40 *University of Chicago Law Re-*

view (Winter 1973), 248–90.

Jones, Alfred Winslow. *Life, Liberty and Property: A Study of Conflict and a Measurement of Conflicting Rights.* New York: Octagon Books, 1964.

Kruse, Frederik Vinding. *The Right of Property,* 2 vols. P. T. Federspiel and David Philip, translators. Oxford: Oxford University Press, 1939, 1953.

Levine, Philip J. "Towards a Property Right in Employment." 22 *Buffalo Law Review* (Spring 1973), 1081–1110.

Libling, D. F. "The Concept of Property: Property in Intangibles." 94 *Law Quarterly Review* (January 1978), 103–19.

Polinsky, A. M. "Controlling Externalities and Protecting Entitlements." 8 *Journal of Legal Studies* (January 1979), 1–48.

Powell, Richard B. "Relationship Between Property Rights and Civil Rights." 15 *Hastings Law Journal* (November 1963), 135–52.

Sathe, S. P. "Supreme Court, Parliament and Constitution." 35 *Economic and Political Weekly* (August 21, 1971), 1821–28 (August 28, 1971), 1873–80.

Scott, William B. *In Pursuit of Happiness: American Conceptions of Property from the Seventeenth to the Twentieth Century.* Bloomington: Indiana University Press, 1977.

Sparks, Bertel. "Changing Concepts of Private Property." *Oklahoma Bar Association Journal Quarterly Supplement (June 1972),* 355–63.

"Statutory Entitlement and the Concept of Property." 86 *Yale Law Journal* (March 1977), 695–714.

Stone, Alan A. "Law, Property and Liberty: A Polemic That Fails." 42 *American Journal of Orthopsychiatry* (July 1972), 627–31.

Stone, Julius. *Human Law and Human Justice.* Stanford: Stanford University Press, 1965.

Tay, Alice Erh-Soon. "Property and Law in the Society of Mass Production, Mass Consumption and Mass Allocation." 10 *Archives for Philosophy of Law and Social Philosophy* (1978), 87–106.

Tigar, Michael E. and M. R. Levy. *Law and the Rise of Capitalism.* New York: Monthly Review Press, 1977.

Yannacone, Victor John, Jr. "Property and Stewardship: Private Property Plus Public Interest Equals Social Property." 23 *South Dakota Law Review* (Winter 1978), 71–148.

Yiannopoulos, W. N. *Civil Law and Property.* Saint Paul: West Publishing, 1965.

C. Economic Approaches

Alchian, Armen A. *Economic Forces at Work*. Indianapolis: Liberty Fund, 1977.

———. *Some Economics of Property*. Santa Monica: Rand, 1961.

——— and H. Demsetz. "Property Right Paradigm." 33 *Journal of Economic History* (March 1973), 16–27.

Bettelheim, Charles. *Economic Calculations and Forms of Property*. New York: Monthly Review Press, 1976.

Cheung, S. N. S. "Private Property Rights and Sharecropping." 76 *Journal of Political Economy* (November 1968), 1107–22.

Demsetz, Harold. "Some Aspects of Property Rights." 9 *Journal of Law and Economy* (October 1966), 61–70.

———. "Toward a Theory of Property Rights." 57 *American Economic Review* (May 1976), 347–59.

Furubotn, Erik and Svetozar Pejovich. "Property Rights and Economic Theory: A Survey of Recent Literature." 10 *Journal of Economic Literature* (December 1972), 1137–63.

——— eds. *The Economics of Property Rights*. Cambridge: Ballinger, 1974.

Gonce, R. A. "The New Property Rights Approach and Commons's *Legal Foundations of Capitalism*." 10 *Journal of Economic Issues* (December 1976), 765–98.

Manne, Henry G. *The Economics of Legal Relationships: Readings in the Theory of Property Rights*. Saint Paul: West Publishing, 1975.

North, Douglas C. and Robert P. Thomas. *The Rise of the West: A New Economic History*. Cambridge: Cambridge University Press, 1973.

Telly, Charles S. "Classical Economic Model and the Nature of Property in the Eighteenth and Nineteenth Centuries." 13 *Tulsa Law Journal* (1978), 406–507.

D. Politics, Society, and Property

Beaglehole, Ernest. *Property*. New York: Arno Press, 1974.

Bendix, Ranhard. *Max Weber*. Garden City, N.Y.: Doubleday, 1960.

Binns, David. *Beyond the Sociology of Conflict*. New York: St. Martins Press, 1977.

Blumenfeld, S., ed. *Property in a Humane Economy*. La Salle, Ill.: Open Court, 1977.

Bruce, Andrew Alexander. *Property and Society*. Chicago: A. C.

McClung & Son, 1916.

Burns, Tom and S. B. Saul, eds. *Social Theory and Economic Change.* New York: Tavistock, 1967.

Chaudhuri, Joyotpaul. "Toward a Democratic Theory of Property and the Modern Corporation." 81 *Ethics* (July 1971), 271–86.

Coleman, James S. *Power and the Structure of Society.* New York: W. W. Norton, 1974, Chapter 2.

Cropsey, Joseph. "Conservativism and Liberalism." In his *Political Philosophy and the Issues of Politics.* Chicago: University of Chicago Press, 1977, 116–30.

Dietz, Gottfried. *In Defense of Property.* Chicago: Henry Regnery, 1963.

Dworkin, Ronald. "Liberalism." In Stuart Hampshire, ed. *Public and Private Morality.* Cambridge: Cambridge Universtiy Press, 1978.

Eddy, Arthur James. *Property.* Chicago: A. C. McClung & Son, 1921.

Field, Oliver P. "Property and Authority." 3 *Journal of Politics* (1941), 253–75.

Friedrich, C. J. *An Introduction to Political Theory.* New York: Harper & Row, 1967, Lecture 1.

Giddens, Anthony. *The Class Structure of Advanced Societies.* London: Hutchinson University Press, 1973.

Goldberg, Victor P. "Public Choice — Property Rights." 8 *Journal of Economic Issues* (September 1974), 555–80.

Hobhouse, L. T. *Liberalism.* New York: Oxford University Press, 1964, Chapters 4 and 8.

Jouvenel, Bertrand de. *Sovereignty.* T. F. Huntington, translator. Cambridge: Cambridge University Press, 1957.

Kent, Edward. "Property, Power and Authority." 41 *Brooklyn Law Review* (Winter 1975), 541–58.

Kouatly, Youssef I. "Issues in Private Property and Nationalization." 42 *Insurance Counsel Journal* (July 1975), 386–98.

MacIver, R. M. *The Web of Government.* New York: Macmillan, 1947, Chapter 6.

Macpherson, C. B., ed. *Property: Mainstream and Critical Positions.* Toronto: University of Toronto Press, 1978.

Mansfield, Harvey C. "Liberal Democracy as a Mixed Regime." In his *The Spirit of Liberalism.* Cambridge: Harvard University Press, 1978, 1–15.

Mill, John Stuart. *Principles of Political Economy.* Sir William Ashley, ed. Fairfield, N.J.: Kelley, 1976, Book II, Chapter i.

Moorhouse, H. F. and C. W. Chamberlin. "Lower Class Attitudes Towards Property." 8 *Sociology* (September 1974), 307–405.

Myrdal, G. *The Political Element in the Development of Economic Theory.* Cambridge: Harvard University Press, 1965.

Noyes, Charles Renold. *The Institution of Property.* New York: Longmans, Green and Co., 1936.

Parsons, Talcott and Neil J. Smelser. *Economy and Society.* Glencoe, Ill.: The Free Press, 1956.

Rose, David, Peter Saunders, Howard Newby, and Colin Bell. "Ideologies of Property: A Case Study." 24 *Sociological Review* (November 1976), 699–730.

Samuels, Warren J. "The Physiocratic Theory of Property and the State." 75 *Quarterly Journal of Economics* (February 1968), 96–111.

Sennholz, H. "On Private Property and Economic Power." 11 *Freeman* (January 1961), 11–14.

Shaffer, Thomas L. "Men and Things: The Liberal Bias Against Property." 57 *American Bar Association Journal* (February 1971), 123–26.

Skinner, A. S. and T. Wilson, eds. *The Market and the State: Essays in Honour of Adam Smith.* Oxford: Clarendon Press, 1976.

Thambyahpillai, T. "The Right to Private Property and Problems of Land Reform." 18 *International Social Science Journal* (1966), 69–80.

Tricker, R. I., ed *The Individual, the Enterprise and the State.* New York: John Wiley & Sons, 1977.

Tufte, Edward R. *Political Control of the Economy.* Princeton: Princeton University Press, 1978, Chapter 4.

Weber, Max. *Economy and Society.* Ephraim Fischoff et al., translators. New York: Bedminster Press, 1968.

Wunderlich, G. "Property Rights and Information." 412 *Annals of the American Academy of Political and Social Science* (March, 1944), 80–90.

III. THE DISTRIBUTION OF WEALTH AND INCOME

Amin, Samir. *Accumulation on a World Scale.* Hassocks: Harvester Press, 1978.

Atkinson, Anthony Barnes. *The Economics of Inequality.* Oxford:

Oxford University Press, 1975.

———, ed. *The Personal Distribution of Income.* Boulder, Colo.: Westview Press, 1976.

——— and A. J. Harrison. *Distribution of Personal Wealth in Britain.* Cambridge: Cambridge University Press, 1978.

Blinder, Alan S. *Toward an Economic Theory of Income Distribution.* Cambridge: MIT Press, 1974.

Bronfenbrenner, Martin. *Income Distribution Theory.* Chicago: Aldine-Atherton, 1971.

Brown, Henry Phelps. *The Inequality of Pay.* Oxford: Oxford University Press, 1971.

Champeroune, D. G. *The Distribution of Income Between Persons.* Cambridge: Cambridge University Press, 1975.

Dunlop, John T., ed. *The Theory of Wage Determination.* New York: St. Martin's Press, 1957.

Ely, Richard T. *Property and Contract and Their Relations to the Distribution of Wealth.* Port Washington, N.Y.: Kennikat Press, 1971.

Fogarty, Michael. *The Just Wage.* London: G. Chapman, 1961.

Forsyth, Murray. *Property and Property Distribution Policy.* London: Policy Studies Institute, 1977.

Frey, Bruno S. *Modern Political Economy.* New York: John Wiley & Sons, 1978.

Harris, Donald J. *Capital Accumulation and Income Distribution.* Stanford: Stanford University Press, 1978.

Hicks, John R. *The Theory of Wages.* New York: St. Martin's Press, 1964.

Horowitz, Irving C. *Equity, Income and Policy.* New York: Praeger, 1977.

Lydall, H. *The Structure of Earnings.* Oxford: Oxford University Press, 1968.

Meagher, Robert F. *Toward an International Redistribution of Wealth and Power.* Elmsford, N.Y.: Pergamon Press, 1978.

Pen, Jan. *Income Distribution.* Trevor S. Priston, translator. Harmondsworth: Penguin, 1971.

Rothbard, Murry W. *Man, Economy and the State.* Los Angeles: Nash, 1970.

Sahota, Gian Singh. "Theories of Personal Income Distribution: A Survey." 16 *Journal of Economic Literature* (March 1978), 1–56.

Schnitzer, Martin. *Income Distribution: A Comparative Study.* New York: Praeger, 1973.

Smith, Bruce L. P., ed. *The New Political Economy*. New York: John Wiley & Sons, 1977.

Thurow, Lester C. *Generating Inequality: Mechanisms of Distribution in the U.S. Economy*. New York: Basic Books, 1975.

Tinbergen, Jan. *Income Distribution: Analysis and Policies*. Amsterdam: North-Holland, 1975.

———, ed. *Income Differences: Recent Research*. Amsterdam: North-Holland, 1975.

Wood, Adrian. *A Theory of Pay*. Cambridge: Cambridge University Press, 1978.

IV. COMPARATIVE SYSTEMS

A. General

Arrow, K. *The Limits of Organization*. New York: W. W. Norton, 1974.

Batra, Raveendron. *The Downfall of Capitalism and Communism*. London: Macmillan, 1978.

Cameron, David R. "The Expansion of the Public Economy: A Comparative Analysis." 72 *The American Political Science Review* (December 1978), 1243–61.

Clecak, Peter. *Crooked Paths: Reflections on Socialism, Conservatism, and the Welfare State*. New York: Harper & Row, 1977.

Eckstein, Alexander, ed. *Comparison of Economic Systems*. Berkeley: University of California Press, 1971.

Grossman, Gregory. *Economic Systems*. Englewood Cliffs, N. J.: Prentice-Hall, 1967.

Hirschman, A. O. *The Strategy of Economic Development*. New Haven: Yale University Press, 1958.

Ilchman, Warren F. and Norman T. Uphoff. *The Political Economy of Change*. Berkeley: University of California Press, 1969.

Kaye, Roger. "Capitalism and Communism: Property in a Divergent World." 3 *Kingston Law Review* (1971–72), 13–24.

Lindblom, Charles E. *Politics and Markets: The World's Political-Economic Systems*. New York: Basic Books, 1977.

Lipson, E. *A Planned Economy or Free Enterprise: The Lessons of History*. London: A. & C. Black, 1944.

Montias, John Michael. *The Structure of Economic Systems*. New Haven: Yale University Press, 1976.

Pryor, Frederic L. *Property and Industrial Organization in Communist and Capitalist Nations*. Bloomington: Indiana University

Press, 1973.

Robbins, Lionel. *Political Economy: Past and Present.* New York: Columbia University Press, 1976.

Schumpeter, Joseph A. *Capitalism, Socialism and Democracy,* 3d edition. New York: Harper, 1950.

Stretton, Hugh. *Capitalism, Socialism and the Environment.* Cambridge: Cambridge University Press, 1976.

Van Doren, John W. "Ownership of Yugoslav Social Property and United States Industrial Democracy: A Comparison." 26 *Rutgers University Law Review* (Fall 1973), 73–108.

Wiles, P. J. D. *Distribution of Income: East and West.* New York: American Elsevier, 1974.

———. *Economic Institutions Compared.* New York: Halsted Press, 1977.

B. Capitalism and the Welfare State

Berle, Adolf and Gardiner Means. *The Modern Corporation and Private Property.* New York: Harcourt, Brace & World, 1968.

Brenner, Philip, Robert Borosage, and Benthany Weidner. *Exploring Contradictions: Political Economy in the Corporate State.* New York: Longmans, 1974.

Furniss, Norman. "Property Rights and Democratic Socialism." 26 *Political Studies* (December 1978), 450–61.

Galbraith, John Kenneth. *The New Industrial State,* 2d edition, revised. Boston: Houghton Mifflin, 1971.

Giddens, Anthony. *Capitalism and Modern Social Theory.* Cambridge: Cambridge University Press, 1971.

Goldfrank, Walter L., ed. *The World System of Capitalism: Past and Present.* Beverly Hills: Sage, 1974.

Harbrecht, Paul P. *Toward the Paraproprietal Society.* New York: Twentieth Century Fund, 1960.

Harrington, Michael. *The Twilight of Capitalism.* New York: Simon and Schuster, 1976.

Heilbroner, Robert L. *Business Civilization in Decline.* New York: W. W. Norton, 1976.

———. *The Limits of American Capitalism.* New York: Harper & Row, 1966.

Hirsch, Fred. *Social Limits to Growth.* Cambridge: Harvard University Press, 1976.

Jones, Alfred W. *Life, Liberty and Property.* New York: Octagon Books, 1964.

Kalecki, Michael. *Selected Essays on the Dynamics of the Capitalist Economy, 1933–70.* Cambridge: Cambridge University Press, 1971.

Kanter, Rosabeth Moss. *Men and Women of the Corporation.* New York: Basic Books, 1977.

Kaplan, Barbara Hockey. *Social Change in the World Capitalist Economy.* Beverly Hills: Sage, 1979.

Mandel, Ernest. *Late Capitalism,* revised edition. Joris De Bres, translator. London: New Left Books, 1975.

Mason, Edward S., ed. *The Corporation in Modern Society.* New York: Atheneum, 1966.

Miliband, Ralph. *The State in Capitalist Society.* New York: Basic Books, 1969.

O'Connor, James. *The Corporations and the State.* New York: Harper & Row, 1974.

Parkinson, C. Northcote. *Big Business.* Boston: Little, Brown, 1974.

Robson, William A. *Welfare State and Welfare Society: Illusion and Reality.* London: George Allen & Unwin, 1976.

Shonfield, Andrew. *Modern Capitalism.* Oxford: Oxford University Press, 1965.

Silk, Leonard et al. *Capitalism: The Moving Target.* New York: Quadrangle, 1974.

Wilensky, Harold L. *The Welfare State and Equality.* Berkeley: University of California Press, 1975.

C. Socialism and Communism

Anderson, Perry and Robin Blackburn, eds. *Towards Socialism.* Ithaca: Cornell University Press, 1966.

Bornstein, Morris, ed. *Plan and Market: Economic Reform in Eastern Europe.* New Haven: Yale University Press, 1973.

Brus, Wlodzimierz. *The Economics and Politics of Socialism.* London: Routledge & Kegan Paul, 1973.

Chevigny, Paul G. "Reflection on Civil Liberties Under Socialism." 2 *Civil Liberties Review* (Winter 1975), 53–66.

Crosland, Anthony. *The Future of Socialism.* London: Cape, 1956.

Holland, Stuart. *The Socialist Challenge.* London: Quartet, 1976.

Howard, Michael and J. E. King. *The Political Economy of Marx.* Harlow: Longman, 1975.

Kolakowski, L. and Stuart Hampshire, eds. *The Socialist Idea: A Reappraisal.* London: Weidenfeld and Nicolson, 1974.

Lane, D. *The End of Inequality? Stratification Under State Socialism.* London: Penguin, 1971.

————. *The Socialist Industrial State.* Boulder, Colo.: Westview Press, 1976.

Markovic, M. *From Affluence to Praxis.* Ann-Arbor: University of Michigan Press, 1974.

Martyn, Sloman. *Socializing Public Ownership.* London: Macmillan, 1978.

Minogue, Kenneth. "The Uncertainties of Socialism." *Times Literary Supplement* (March 21, 1975).

Nove, Alec. *Economic Rationality and Soviet Politics.* New York: Praeger, 1964.

Stojanovic, Svetozar. *Between Ideals and Reality: A Critique of Socialism and Its Future.* Oxford: Oxford University Press, 1973.

Wilczynski, J. *The Economics of Socialism.* Chicago: Aldine, 1971.

Wiles, P. J. D. *The Political Economy of Communism.* Cambridge: Harvard University Press, 1962.

D. Country Studies

Blackwell, William C. *Russian Economic Development from Peter the Great to Stalin.* New York: New Viewpoints, 1974.

Brown, Richard P., Jr. "Soviet Law and Procedure Concerning Property and Inheritance." 3 *The International Lawyer* (July 1969), 187–96.

Cameron, George D., III. "Development of Individual Property Rights Under Soviet Law." 14 *American Business Law Journal* (Winter 1977), 333–55.

Cohen, Stephen S. *Modern Capitalist Planning: The French Model.* Cambridge: Harvard University Press, 1969.

Currie, Robert. *Industrial Politics.* Oxford: Clarendon Press, 1979.

Curtin, Richard T. *Income Equity Among U.S. Workers.* New York: Praeger, 1977.

Deleyne, Jan. *The Chinese Economy.* New York: Harper, 1974.

Drucker, Peter F. *The Unseen Revolution: How Pension Fund Socialism Came to America.* New York: Harper & Row, 1976.

Fleisher, F. *The New Sweden.* New York: David McKay, 1967.

Granick, David. *Enterprise Guidance in Eastern Europe.* Princeton: Princeton University Press, 1975.

Harrod, Roy. *The British Economy.* Westport, Conn.: Greenwood, 1977.

Hunter, Holland. *The Future of the Soviet Economy, 1978–1985.* Boulder, Colo.: Westview Press, 1978.

Koviebrodzki, Leopold B. "Administrative and Civil Law in the Regulation of Property Rights in Present-Day Poland." 15 *American Journal of Comparative Law* (1966–67), 772–81.

Lipset, Seymour Martin. *Agrarian Socialism*. Berkeley: University of California Press, 1971.

Maggs, Peter B. "Security of Individually-Owned Property Under Soviet Law." 10 *Duke Law Journal* (Fall 1961), 525–37.

Montias, John Michael. *Economic Development in Communist Rumania*. Camridge: MIT Press, 1967.

Nakane, C. *Japanese Society*. Berkeley: University of California Press, 1976.

Narian, Jagat. "Indian Supreme Court on Property Rights and the Economic Objectives of the Indian Constitution." 3 *Journal of International Law and Economics* (Fall 1968), 147–80.

Newby, Howard, Colin Bell et al. *Property, Paternalism and Power*. London: Hutchinson University Press, 1978.

Pipes, Richard. *Russia Under the Old Regime*. London: Weidenfeld and Nicolson, 1974.

Rusinow, Dennison. *The Yugoslav Experiment, 1848–1974*. Berkeley: University of California Press, 1977.

Singh, D. "Socialism, Right to Property and Judicial Review in India." 7 *Journal of Political Studies* (February 1974), 50–64.

Stolper, Wolfgang F. *The Structure of the East German Economy*. Cambridge: Harvard University Press, 1960.

Vanek, Jaroslav. *The Participatory Economy*. Ithaca: Cornell University Press, 1971.

V. PROPERTY AND JUSTICE

A. Liberty, Equality, and Property

Bayes, William, W. "What Is Property?" 20 *Freeman* (1970), 392–400.

Brenkert, George C. "Freedom and Private Property in Marx." 8 *Philosophy & Public Affairs* (Winter 1979), 122–47.

Chapman, John W. "Hayek's *The Mirage of Social Justice*." 16 *Journal of Economic Literature* (March 1978), 96–98.

Dickinson, H. J. *Liberty and Property: Political Ideology in Eighteenth Century Britain*. New York: Holmes and Meier, 1978.

87 *Ethics* (January 1977).

Friedman, Milton. *Capitalism and Freedom*. Chicago: University of Chicago Press, 1962.

Gottfried, Dietz. *In Defense of Property*. Chicago: Henry Regnery,

1963.

Greenleaf, W. H. *Oakeshott's Philosophical Politics.* London: Longmans, 1966.

Hayek, F. A. *The Constitution of Liberty.* London: Routledge & Kegan Paul, 1960.

————. *New Studies in Philosophy, Politics, Economics and the History of Ideas.* London: Routledge & Kegan Paul, 1978.

Jencks, Christopher. *Inequality.* New York: Basic Books, 1972.

Johnson, E. A. J. *The Foundations of American Economic Freedom.* Minneapolis: University of Minnesota Press, 1973.

Koerner, K. F. *Liberalism and Its Critics.* Ph.D. dissertation, University of Toronto, 1975.

Lakoff, Sanford. *Equality in Political Philosophy.* Cambridge: Harvard University Press, 1964.

Lauterbach, Albert. *Economic Security and Individual Freedom.* Ithaca: Cornell University Press, 1948.

Loevinsohn, Ernest. "Liberty and the Redistribution of Property." 6 *Philosophy & Public Affairs* (Spring 1977), 226–39.

Lukes, Steven. *Individualism.* New York: Harper & Row, 1973.

Macpherson, C. B. "Liberalism and the Political Theory of Property." In A. Kantos, ed. *Domination.* Toronto: University of Toronto Press, 1975.

——— ed. *Property: Mainstream and Critical Positions.* Toronto: University of Toronto Press, 1978.

Malchulup, Fritz. *Essays on Hayek.* New York: New York University Press, 1976.

Meade, J. E. *Efficiency, Equality and the Ownership of Property.* Cambridge: Harvard University Press, 1966.

Minogue, Kenneth. *The Liberal Mind.* London: Methuen, 1963.

Okun, Arthur M. *Equality and Efficiency.* Washington: The Brookings Institution, 1975.

Pennock, J. Roland and John W. Chapman, eds. *NOMOS XIX: Anarchism.* New York: New York University Press, 1978.

———, eds. *NOMOS IX: Equality.* New York: Atherton Press, 1967.

Plamenatz, John. "Liberalism." In Phillip Paul Wiener, ed. *Dictionary of the History of Ideas.* New York: Charles Scribner's Sons, 1973, Vol. 3.

Proudhon, Pierre Joseph. *What Is Property?* Benjamin R. Tucker, translator. New York: H. Fertig, 1966.

Robbins, Lord. *Liberty and Equality.* London: The Institute of Economic Affairs, 1977.

Ryan, Cheyney C. "Yours, Mine and Ours: Property Rights and Individual Liberty." 87 *Ethics* (January 1977), 126–41.

Sen, A. K. *On Economic Inequality.* New York: W. W. Norton, 1973.

Shklar, Judith. *Freedom and Independence.* Cambridge: Harvard University Press, 1976, Chapter 3.

Stone, Alan A. "Law, Property and Liberty: A Polemic That Fails." 42 *American Journal of Orthopsychiatry* (July 1972), 627–31.

Tawney, R. H. *Equality,* revised edition. London: George Allen & Unwin, 1951.

Tolischus, William. *"Private Property and Freedom."* 11 *Freeman* (February 1961), 46–49.

van der Veen, Robert J. "Property, Exploitation, Justice." 784 *Acta Politica,* 433–65.

Wilson, Bryan, ed. *Education, Equality and Society.* New York: Barnes and Noble, 1975.

Wolff, Robert Paul. *The Poverty of Liberalism.* Boston: Beacon Press, 1968.

Wollheim, Richard. "Equality and Equal Rights." In Frederick A. Olafson, ed. *Justice and Social Policy.* Englewood Cliffs, N.J.: Prentice-Hall, 1961, 111–27.

B. Theories of Justice and Economic Morality

Acton, H. B. *The Morals of Markets: An Ethical Exploration.* London: Longman, 1971.

Barry, Brian. *The Liberal Theory of Justice.* Oxford: Clarendon Press, 1973.

Bedau, H. A., ed. *Justice and Equality.* Englewood Cliffs, N.J.: Prentice-Hall, 1971.

Brandt, R. B., ed. *Social Justice.* Englewood Cliffs, N.J.: Prentice-Hall, 1962.

Chapman, John W. "Justice and Fairness." In Carl J. Friedrich and John W. Chapman, eds. *NOMOS VI: Justice.* New York: Atherton Press, 1963, 147–69.

———. "Natural Rights and Justice in Liberalism." In D. D. Raphael, ed. *Political Theory and the Rights of Man.* Bloomington: University of Indiana Press, 1967.

Clark, Barry and Herbert Gentis. "Rawlsian Justice and Economic Systems." *Philosophy & Public Affairs* (Summer 1978), 302–25.

del Vecchio, Giorgio. *Justice: An Historical and Philosophical Essay.*

Lady Guthrie, translator. Edinburgh: Edinburgh University Press, 1952.

Dick, James C. "How to Justify a Distribution of Earnings." 4 *Philosophy & Public Affairs,* (Spring 1975), 248–72.

Durkheim, Emile. *Professional Ethics and Civil Morals.* Cornelia Brookfield, ed. London: Routledge & Kegan Paul, 1951.

Dworkin, Gerald, Gordon Bermant, and Peter G. Brown, eds. *Markets and Morals.* New York: John Wiley & Sons, 1977.

Eccles, David. *About Property Owning Democracy.* London: Conservative Political Centre, 1948.

Feinberg, Joel. "Justice and Personal Desert." In his *Doing and Deserving: Essays in the Theory of Responsibility.* Princeton: Princeton University Press, 1970, 55–94.

———. *Social Philosophy.* Englewood Cliffs, N.J.: Prentice Hall, 1973.

Hayek, F. A. *Law, Legislation and Liberty,* 3 vols. Chicago: University of Chicago Press, 1973, 1976, 1979.

Hook, Sidney, ed. *Human Values and Economic Policy.* New York: New York University Press, 1967.

Husami, Ziyad I. "Marx on Distributive Justice." 8 *Philosophy & Public Affairs* (Fall 1978), 27–64.

Jacoby, Neil H. *Corporate Power and Social Responsibility.* London: Macmillan, 1973.

Jouvenel, Bertrand de. *The Ethics of Redistribution.* Cambridge: Cambridge University Press, 1951.

Kaplan, Morton A. *Justice, Human Nature, and Political Obligation.* New York: The Free Press, 1970.

Kelsen, Hans. *What Is Justice?* Berkeley: University of California Press, 1971.

Macpherson, C. B. *Democratic Theory: Essays in Retrieval.* Oxford: Clarendon Press, 1973.

———. *The Life and Times of Liberal Democracy.* Oxford: Oxford University Press, 1977.

Meade, J. E. *The Intelligent Radical's Guide to Economic Policy.* New York: Crane Russak, 1975.

———. *The Just Economy.* London: George Allen & Unwin, 1976.

Meade, J. E. et al. *The Structure and Reform of Direct Taxation.* London: George Allen & Unwin, 1978.

Miller, David. *Social Justice.* Oxford: Clarendon Press, 1976.

Nathan, N. M. C. *The Concept of Justice.* London: Macmillan, 1971.

Nozick, Robert. *Anarchy, State and Utopia*. New York: Basic Books, 1974.

Olafson, Frederick A., ed. *Justice and Social Policy*. Englewood Cliffs, N.J.: Prentice-Hall, 1961.

Perelman, Chiam. *The Idea of Justice and the Problem of Argument*. John Petrie, ed. New York: Humanities Press, 1963.

Phelps, Edmund S. "Taxation of Wage Income for Economic Justice." 87 *Quarterly Journal of Economics* (August 1973), 331–54.

Pitkin, Hanna. *Wittgenstein and Justice*. Berkeley: University of California Press, 1972.

Plattner, Marc F. "The Welfare State vs. the Redistributive State." 55 *The Public Interest* (Spring 1979), 28–48.

Raphael, D. D. *Problems of Political Philosophy*. New York: Praeger, 1970, Chapter 7.

Rawls, John. *A Theory of Justice*. Cambridge: Belknap Press of Harvard University Press, 1971.

Rescher, Nicholas. *Distributive Justice*. Indianapolis: Bobbs-Merrill, 1966.

Runciman, W. G. *Relative Deprivation and Social Justice*. Berkeley: University of California Press, 1966.

Tucker, R. C. "Marx and Distributive Justice." In Carl J. Friedrich and John W. Chapman, eds. *NOMOS VI: Justice*. New York: Atherton Press, 1963, 306–24.

Unger, R. M. *Knowledge and Politics*. New York: The Free Press, 1975.

———. *Law in Modern Society*. New York: The Free Press, 1976.

Varian, Hal R. "Distributive Justice, Welfare Economics and the Theory of Fairness." 4 *Philosophy & Public Affairs* (Spring 1975), 223–47.

Wright, William K. "Private Property and Social Justice." 25 *International Journal of Ethics* (1915), 498–513.

INDEX

Abrams, Howard, 28
"Abstract Right" (Hegel), 132–33, 134
Accession, 110, 112–13
Ackerman, Bruce A., 327–39, 341–50, 351–75
Acquisitiveness, 200–201
Action(s): in externality, 134, 135, 142, 162, 163; law of, 33, 37; rejection of determinate, 135; rights and, 247, 248
Adorno, T. W., 163
Agglomerative tendency, 32–48, 55–56, 57, 58
Alchian, A., 301
Alienation: of labor, 97, 141–42, 151–55; for public purposes, 119–20 (*see also* Property, governmental takings of); rights, 117, 120, 125, 191, 192, 207, 209, 226 (*see also* Transfers; Transmissibility)
Altruistic collaboration, 291, 304–5, 312
Anglo-American law, 34, 44, 57, 206
Anglo-Saxon law, *See* English law
Anthropology, 198, 225, 226
Antiproperty arguments, 194–96, 204, 213, 222, 223, 229, 231, 233–35, 237, 240
Appellate court cases, 48–55

Appropriation, 12; rightful, 252–53
Aquinas, St. Thomas, 17
Arendt, Hannah, 163
Aristotle, 4, 6, 209, 277
Arnold, Thurman, 358
Aron, Raymond, 303
Arrow, Kenneth J., 303
Artifice, 120, 121, 122, 124–25
Artificial virtues, 105, 108–9, 110, 113, 114
Asiatic mode of production, 21, 23–24
Autonomous centers of decision, 270, 272, 280, 287

Baechler, Jean, 269–88, 299
Barry, Brian, 304–5, 306, 312,
Beaglehole, Ernest, 209
Becker, Lawrence C., 20, 172, 183, 187–220, 222–41
Bell, Daniel, 6
Bentham, Jeremy, 114, 126, 177, 237
Bequest, 125, 251, 256
Berle, Adolf A., 162
Berlin, Sir Isaiah, 245, 290
Berry, Christopher J., 89–100
Blackstone, Sir William, 4, 34, 41, 43, 73, 74, 101–3, 104, 114–26, 127, 133, 177, 221, 222
Blau, Peter, 203–4
Bobbitt, Philip, 358–59
Bourgeoisie, 81

Bracton, Henry de, 39
Brandt, Richard, 237
Braudel, Fernand, 298, 299
Bundle of rights, 69, 76, 79, 81, 82, 102, 104, 127, 172–73, 182, 183, 190, 192, 313; and governmental takings, 327–28, 331–32, 360, 361
Burke, Edmund, 8, 222, 223, 224
Byron, Lord, 12

Calabresi, Guido, 358–59
Cameron, David R., 297
Capital, 10, 16, 160–61; Hegel's view of, 147–48
Capital (Marx), 152, 153
Capitalism, 70, 74–80, 82, 131, 150–55, 163, 200, 299, 300, 301, 302–4; democratic, 273, 276–77, 280
Capitalist societies, 297
Carlyle, A. J. and R. W., 176–77
Causation, 91–93, 94, 98–99
Centennial (Michener), 174
Chain generalized exchange, 203
Chapman, John W., 289–324
Christianity, 139–40
Churchill, Lady, 16
Citizenship, 5–6
Civil community, 6–7, 9, 16, 20, 21
Civil law, 111
Civil rights, 28–29, 47, 120
Civil society, 117, 119, 126, 131; vs. civil community, 6, 7, 9, 16, 18, 21; Hegel's view of, 132, 134–35, 136, 137, 144–45, 147–48, 160
Class, 81, 136, 145, 147–48, 155
Clausewitz, Karl von, 299

Codere, Helen, 208
Coercion, 270, 305, 312
Collingwood, R. G., 98
Commentaries (Blackstone), 115, 123
Commercial society, 124, 125, 126
Common law, 115–16, 119, 121, 123, 126
Communist Manifesto, The (Marx), 153
Communist society, Marx's view of, 155–57, 161
Communist states, 15. *See also* Marxist states
Compatibility requirement, 193, 195–96, 214
Compensation: just, 173, 181, 328–32, 337, 345, 347, 348–49, 359, 360, 362, 363, 364, 365, 378–79, 380, 381; for natural resources, 252–53. *See also* Reciprocity, compensatory
Comprehensive View, 342, 343–44, 345, 346, 347–50, 355, 356, 357–59, 360, 361, 369
Condemnation cases, 50, 52, 54
Condillac, Étienne Bonnot de, 17
Constitutional cases, 49–50, 51, 52, 53, 54. *See also* U.S. Constitution
Consumption and destruction rights, 191, 192
Continental law, 33, 34, 41, 44, 338
Contract, 29, 105, 161; property as basis for, 131, 132, 143–46
Contrived property dispersal principle, 296

Conveyance(s), 33-34, 37, 38, 40, 42, 43, 48, 50, 54
Coordination problem, 193, 194-95, 196, 229-30
Copyholder, 37
Copyrights, 75, 103, 122, 301
Coquillette, Daniel, 28
Corporations, 75, 80, 162, 277, 298, 300-303, 313; Hegel's view of, 132, 136, 144, 145, 147, 149, 154
Covenants, 38, 43
Cranston, Maurice, 246
Creative solidarity, 291
Creditor's rights cases, 50, 51
Criminal cases, 48, 49, 51, 52, 53

Dahl, Robert A., 303
Damage cases, 49
Day, Patrick, 244
Democracy, 22, 272, 273, 278-81, 299, 302-4, 309-10, 338; capitalist, 273, 276-77, 280; neolithic or agrarian, 273, 275-76, 279, 280; paleolithic, 273, 274, 279; participatory, 306-7, 308; procedural, 303-4; segmentary, 273, 274-75, 279
Demsetz, H., 301-2
Deontological justification, 179, 183, 230
Desert, 179
Despotism, 5, 18, 19, 21-23
Destructibility of contingent remainders, doctrine of, 38
Determinate action or determinacy, 134, 135-36, 142, 151, 159
Devise, 124, 125
Difference principle, 295-98, 303, 312, 315, 316
Digest, 176

Disjustificatory theory, 221-41
Dissertation on the Passions, (Hume), 91-92
Distribution, 3-4, 20, 21, 134, 144, 181, 182, 250, 306. *See also* Redistribution
Distribution branch, 295-96, 297
Dominance solutions, 195, 232
Donahue, Charles, Jr., 28-68
Douglas, Mary, 372
Durkheim, Émile, 203, 240
Dworkin, Ronald, 221, 296, 305-6, 312-13

Easements, 41, 43
Economic authority, 302, 303, 307, 308, 310, 311, 312, 313-14
Economic efficiency, 114, 304, 305, 310, 313
Economic exchange, 208-9
Economic rationality, 296-98, 300-301, 310, 312, 350
Economist, The, 297
Economists, 71
Economy: command, 306-7; market, 208, 209, 293, 311-12; mixed, 79; planned, 312; political, 208, 209; social, 208, 209
Edel, Abraham, 187
Egalitarianism, 285-86, 291, 293, 304-5, 306-13, 315. *See also* Equality
Egalitarian teleocratic gradient, 290-91, 310-11
Egoism, 200-202
"1844 Manuscripts" (Marx), 153
Ekeh, Peter, 203, 241
Eminent domain, 38-39, 181, 378-79
Enclosure, 174
Engels, Friedrich, 77-78

England, 299, 305. *See also* Great Britain

English law, 37-40, 43, 55-56, 58, 115, 118, 120, 123, 338. *See also* Anglo-American law

English Settled Land Acts, 41

Entitlements, 71, 72; intangible, 75, 77, 78, 80, 82; original, 250-59

Environmental issue, 29, 30, 46, 53, 56, 162-63, 207, 351

Epicurus, 189

Equal concern and respect, 291, 305-6, 312

Equality, 14, 15, 24, 183, 269, 277-79, 285-86, 290, 292, 296-98, 305-13; of exchange, 152; of opportunity, 293, 294, 295, 302, 304, 305-6, 307, 310, 312, 316, 317; party of, 284; of power, 278. *See also* Egalitarianism; Liberty, equal

Equitable servitude, 41-42, 43

Equities, 33

Equity, concept of, 277, 278, 284, 285, 286, 287

Essay Concerning Human Understanding (Hume), 95

Estates, 43

"Estranged Labour" (Marx), 153

Estrangement. *See* Alienation

Ethical life, 144, 148, 160

Ethology, 200, 201-2

Exchange value, 155

Expropriation, 163, 285-86. *See also* Eminent domain; Property, governmental takings of

Extra-Ordinary language, 353-54, 355

Family, 146, 148, 154

Federalist No. 10, 376, 377

Feudalism, 11, 73-74, 124, 125, 126, 200, 207, 283

Fichte, J. G., 96

Filmer, Sir Robert, 89, 97

Finley, M. I., 298, 308

Flathman, Richard E., 173, 187, 221-43

Florentinus, 177

Forfeiture, 119

France, 299

Frank, Jerome, 358

Freedom, 97, 163, 289-317; Hegel's view of, 132, 135, 137-38, 139-40, 141, 142, 146; Marx's view of, 152, 153; and well-being, 290, 294-95, 310, 316. *See also* Liberty

Freeholders, 39-40, 55

Free-market system, 114

French Civil Code, 73, 74

French Declaration of the Rights of Man and of Citizens (1789), 177

Fuller, Lon, 175

Funds, 122

Generalized exchange, 203

General justification(s), 187-188, 189, 192-96, 222-23, 240; plurality of, 228-41

German Ideology, The (Marx), 291

Gewirth, Alan, 290, 294, 295, 296, 310, 316

Glanvill, Joseph, 39

Governmental property cases, rise in, 52-53, 54, 56

Grand Central Station case, 72

Gray, John, 244

Great Britain, 7, 8, 297, 298. *See also* England; English law

Greece, 4, 5, 139, 275, 282, 298

Grey, Thomas C., 69-85, 173, 187

Grotius, Hugo, 89, 97

Grundisse (Marx), 153

Habermas, Jurgen, 372

Hallowell, Irving, 199, 227-28, 241

Hardin, Garrett, 174

Harrington, James, 3

"Harrison Bergeron" (Vonnegut), 14

Hart, H. L. A., 246

Hayek, F. A., 290, 292, 293, 295, 296, 310, 314-15, 316

Hegel, G. W., 74, 90, 96-99, 130-52, 154, 158-64, 209-10, 311

Henry VIII, King of England, 38

History of England (Hume), 125

Hobbes, Thomas, 18-19, 225

Hochman, Harold M., 337

Hocking, William Ernest, 179

Hohfeld, Wesley N., 30, 127, 233, 235

Honore, A. M., 172, 190, 206, 224, 226

Horwitz, Morton, 28

Household, 4; public, 6

Human condition, 189, 196, 197, 238, 253, 257

Human dignity, 181, 182

Human nature, 95, 107, 113, 305, 308, 309, 312

Human rights, 162-63, 171, 176

Hume, David, 90-93, 94, 95, 98-99, 101-3, 104-14, 115, 120-21, 122, 124, 125-26, 127, 193, 229, 230, 231, 232, 236, 237

Hunting and gathering societies, 199-200, 274

Idealists, 74, 139

Income, right to, 190, 192, 207

Incorporeal hereditaments, 121-22

Independence, 7-8

Individual distance or spacing, 201, 210

Individualism, 90, 93-94, 99; possessive, 39, 40-41, 44, 58

Individuality, 130-64; morality of, 290, 291-94, 309. *See also* Personality

Industrialization, 163, 200, 299

Inequality, 279-82, 284, 286, 293, 294, 303, 309, 311, 312, 316-17. *See also* Egalitarianism; Equality

Inequality of Pay, The (Phelps Brown), 296

Inheritance, 104, 110, 120, 125, 207, 295

In personum rights, 71

Inquiry Concerning Morals (Hume), 104-5, 114

In rem rights, 71

Institutions, 159-60; as actualizations of will, 137

Intersubjectivity, 131, 142-43, 144, 152-53, 164

Investigations (Wittgenstein), 351

James II, King of England, 19

Jefferson, Thomas, 74

Jouvenel, Bertrand de, 289, 290

Judges, 328-29, 335-39, 342-49, 360, 369-71, 380

Jus gentium, 176

Jus naturale, 176-77

Justice, 4, 5, 24, 289-317; as

artificial convention, 90-91, 93, 98, 105-15, 124; distributive, 249-50; economic, 81, 290; Hegel's view of, 132, 135, 144, 154; procedural, 293, 310, 314; as proportional equality, 277, 278, 280, 284, 286, 287; social, 289-90, 292-93, 315; in transfer, 104

Kaldor criterion, 330
Kant, Immanuel, 73, 74, 139, 141, 248, 250, 251, 252, 344
Kantian view, 345, 348, 369, 371
Kennedy, Duncan, 28
Kojève, 95
Krauss, Melvyn B., 297
Kula exchange, 202

Labeo, 176
Labor, 9-10, 147-48, 156, 158-60; alienation or estrangement of, 97, 141-42, 151-55; division of, 136, 145, 153, 155, 161; and self-ownership, 249-50, 255-58, 260. *See also* Wage labor
Labor principle, 204-5, 213, 239
Labor theory of property, 19-20, 77, 95, 188, 195, 209, 224-30, 232; labor-desert, 193-94, 233-34; Lockean, 103-4, 110, 122, 193-94, 233
Labor theory of value, 18, 20
Laissez-faire theories, 248, 249, 250, 251, 252, 253
Land, 3, 37-40, 199-200, 250-51; use, 36, 37, 42, 43, 46-47, 71, 207

Landlord-tenant law, 29, 35, 47
Lange, Oskar, 290
Laslett, P., 89
Laws (Plato), 17
Legislature, 331, 337, 338, 349, 365, 369-70
Levellers, 7, 8
Leviathan (Hobbes), 18-19
Liability rules, 29, 46, 72, 191
Liberalism, 44, 47, 58, 305; classical, 73-74, 77, 101, 102, 104, 105, 115, 124, 246, 248, 250, 257, 290, 291, 294, 310, 314-16; welfare, 290, 295-96, 297, 298, 305, 314-15, 316
Liberty, 8, 17, 24, 171, 182, 188; argument, 114, 123, 193-94, 195, 209, 229-32, 234-36; and capitalism, 78-79; distribution of, 281-82; empirical theory of, 22-23; equal, 246-51, 253, 255-61; minimization and maximization of, 245-46; negative vs. positive, 270; vs. property, 182; property as basis of, 130-31, 133-35, 140-42, 163-64; and slavery issue, 244-45. *See also* Freedom
Life, 130-31, 133-34, 140, 141, 163, 171, 173, 182
Lindblom, Charles E., 290-91, 298, 300, 301, 302, 303, 304, 314
Lochner Case, 171, 172
Locke, John, 9-10, 11, 12, 17, 19-21, 74, 89-90, 93-95, 96, 97, 98, 99, 101, 102-3, 107, 109, 115, 116, 120, 122, 124, 125, 133, 140-141, 146, 172, 229, 230, 231, 232, 248, 250, 251, 252, 257, 259, 292, 303

Long, Theodore E., 187

Macpherson, C. B., 290, 291, 292, 306-8, 310, 312
MacRae, Duncan, Jr., 326-40, 352, 353, 356, 362, 364, 369
Madison, James, 376-77
Magna Carta, 38
Maitland, Frederic W., 39
Malcolm, Norman, 240
Malinowski, Bronislaw, 198, 202
Management, 190, 192, 227
Marital property cases, 50, 54

Market exchange, 207, 208, 209, 214, 252. *See also* Economy, market
Market socialism, 290-91, 298-300, 302, 307, 314, 315
Married Women's Property Acts, 41
Martineau, Harriet, 253
Marx, Karl, 4, 8, 21, 23-24, 77-78, 130, 131, 149-61, 163-64, 222, 229, 231, 232, 234, 291, 302, 306, 308
Marxism, 79-80, 81
Marxist states, 131, 161, 163. *See also* Communist states
Maslow, Abraham, 205, 241
Meade, J. E., 294, 296, 298, 312
Melden, A. I., 240
Metaphysics of Morals (Kant), 73
Michener, James A., 174
Middle Ages, 5, 6, 37-40, 43, 55-56, 282
Mill, John Stuart, 21, 130, 135, 229, 231, 232, 237, 301, 344
Minogue, Kenneth R., 3-27
Modification right, 191, 192
Monopoly, 23

Moore, G. E., 237
More, 222, 229

National debt, shares in, 122
Native title, 187
Natural resources, original entitlements to, 250-55, 257-58
Natural rights, 74, 89-90, 103-4, 107, 120, 124, 126-27, 172, 176-77, 223, 237, 250, 251, 255. *See also* State of nature
Natural virtues, 105, 108
Nature, domination of, 130, 137-38, 139, 151, 156, 162-63
Necessity thesis, 225-26, 227-28
Nerva Filius, 176
Netherlands, 297, 299
New Deal, 368
"New man," 285-86
Nonfreeholders, 39-40
Nonproperty view, 31. *See also* Antiproperty arguments
Non-Western societies, 31
Norms, 333-34, 343
North, Douglass C., 299, 300
Nozick, Robert, 104, 223, 235, 248-49, 250, 251, 252-53, 290, 310
Nuisance, 46, 119
Nye, William P., 187

Original position, 316
Ownership, 13, 16, 24, 75, 102, 104, 189-92, 212, 226-27, 228, 231; absolute, 104; division of, in Rome, 35; elements of, 190-91, 224; fragmentation of, 69-70, 80; full, 119, 190, 191, 192, 198, 206-7; full exclusive, 192,

213; vs. management in corporations, 162; partial, 198-99; vs. possession, 33, 39; pride in, 178; private vs. public, 188; of self or body, 140-41, 249, 253-54, 258; shared, 257-58; simple, 73-74; variety of, 172-73

Paine, Thomas, 17
Pandectists, 41
Pareto principle, 330, 331
Parliament, 115
Particular justification, 187, 188, 193, 196
Passmore, John, 308
Patents, 75, 103, 301
Peace and order, 123-24
Pennock, J. Roland, 171-86
Perpetuities, 41, 43, 124
Personality, 77, 132-33, 140, 141, 209-10, 211, 287, 376-77, 378, 380, 381. See also Individualism; Individuality
Persons, law of, 32-33, 35
Petty industry, 249-50
Phelps Brown, Sir Henry, 294, 296, 300, 312
Philosophy of Right (Hegel), 97, 130, 132, 140, 146
Plamenatz, John, 317
Plato, 17, 24-25, 132, 222
Polanyi, Karl, 207-8, 209
Policymaking, 355-56, 357, 359. See also Scientific Policymaking
Political authority, 302, 308
Political development, 210-11
Positive law, 116, 119, 122, 124, 126
Poskocil, Art, 187
Posner, Richard, 174
Possession, 91, 92, 93, 97, 98, 125, 174, 190, 192, 226;
adverse, 187; vs. ownership, 33; vs. property, 90, 93, 98, 133-34; "stability of," 105, 106, 111-12
Potlach, 202
Poverty, 131, 147-48, 154, 163
Power: balancing, 272-73; distribution of, 281-82; equality of, 278. See also Economic authority; Political authority
Prescription, 110, 112, 187
Primitive communism, 190, 196
Primitive societies, 198, 202, 204, 205, 207, 208, 209, 224, 231-32. See also Democracy, paleolithic
Private law, 38, 78, 79
"Private Property and Communism" (Marx), 153
Private Property and the Constitution (Ackerman), 341, 351, 353, 357, 363
Profit-sharing, 301
Proletariat, 87
Promise keeping, 105, 113
Property: abolition of, 17, 77-78; absolute right to, 119, 120, 126, 180-81; active vs. passive, 13, 14; as artifice, 101-27; capitalist private, 150-54; as civil right, 120; and Constitution, 341-50, 376-82; contemporary significance of, 3-25; "content" of, 273; definition of, 30-34, 118-19, 122, 172-73; disintegration of, 69-82; disjustificatory theory of, 221-41; etymology of term, 11-12, 31, 39; freedom, individuality and, 130-64; governmental takings of, 72, 119-20, 173, 181, 206, 327-39, 241-

52, 259-67, 369, 378-82 (*see also* Eminent domain; Expropriation); history of, 30-58; intangible, 104, 121-22, 125, 180; as internal relation, 91, 93, 98; justice, freedom and, 289-317; legal vs. social, 328; liberty, equality and, 269-87; moral basis of, 187-214, 238-41; "new," 53, 72, 162, 363, 381-82; personal, 12-15, 19-20, 115-16; and possession, 88-99; present usages of term, 71-72; productive, 10, 12-15, 16, 18, 20, 56; public, 175, 273; real, 115, 116; right to private, 171-83; slavery, socialism and, 244-61; social, 328, 332; socialized, 131, 161, 163; "substitutes," 22; universality of, 198-200, 224-25, 226-27

Property Rights (Becker), 193, 233

Proprietarius, 35

Proprietas, 31, 35

Proudhon, Pierre-Joseph, 174, 229, 234

Psychological justification, 177-79, 180

Public authorities, 132, 154

Public interest, 108, 112

Public law, 46

Pufendorf, 89, 91, 97

Raphael, D. D., 94-95

Rawls, John, 3, 4, 23, 81, 259-60, 290, 295-96, 298, 305-6, 308, 309, 311, 313, 314, 315, 316, 331

Realists, 139; Legal, 358-59

Reason, 138, 145, 159-60

Reciprocity, 202-4, 208, 213-14; compensatory, 290, 295-96, 309, 310, 316; cooperative, 311

Redistribution, 208, 285, 292, 303, 349, 380-81

Regulation, 43, 44, 81, 362, 380; Locke's view of, 103, 104

Reich, Charles, 29, 162, 363, 381

Reilly, Wayne, G., 187

Renner, Karl, 78

Republic (Plato), 132

Residuary rules, 191

Responsible judgement, 8

Reyburn, Hugh A., 146

Richard II, King of England, 38

Right(s), 22, 108, 221-22, 236, 247; to a body, 248-49 (*see also* Self-ownership); Great, 172, 173, 179; personal vs. property, 171-72, 182; procedural, 259; property as basis of, 140-41, 163-64; property as human, 171-83; vs. relations, 106-7; and remedies, 118; set of, 247-48, 251, 253; substantive, 259. *See also* specific rights

Ritchie, David G., 172

Ritter, Joachim, 138

Rivers, W. H. R., 198

Rome, 4, 5, 6, 34, 35-36, 39, 41, 44-46, 55, 57, 58, 111, 139, 251, 275, 298

Rousseau, Jean-Jacques, 146, 172

Sager, Lawrence G., 376-84

Sartorious, Rolf, 237

Scanlon, T. M., 237, 341-50, 352, 353, 355, 356-57, 363, 364, 365

Scientific language, 354-55, 357. *See also* Scientific Policymaking

Scientific Policymaking, 327, 328-39, 342-44, 345, 347-48, 349, 352-53, 356, 359-60, 361-72. *See also* Policymaking

Search-and-seizure cases, 53

Security, 191, 192, 271

Self, 177-78; -objectification, 136-37; -ownership, 12, 140-41, 249, 253-54, 258. *See also* Personality

Seneca, 176

Shareholders, 257-59, 260, 301

Shelley's Case, 38

Shils, Edward, 290

Sidgwick, Henry, 237

Simple circulation, 151-52

Skinner, B. F., 162

Slavery, 244-46, 249, 250, 254, 255, 257, 260; Hegel's view of, 139-40, 142, 160

Social attraction, 203

Social exchange theory, 202-4

Social Function of Social Science, The (MacRae), 364

Socialism, 9, 16, 24, 77-78, 79, 81, 130, 163, 204, 260, 293, 304, 307; transition to, 79-80

Socialists, 21

Social order, 109, 112

Sociobiology, 200, 202

Sovereignty, absolute, vs. despotism, 18-19

Soviet Union, 200, 314

Spain, 299

Specific justification, 187, 188, 193, 196, 209, 211, 214

Spencer, Herbert, 248, 250, 251-52, 257-58

Spendthrift trust, 42

Spera, George, 28

State, 4, 6, 16, 36, 38-39, 43-44, 53, 56, 79; activist, 367-68, 370; Hegel's view of, 131-32, 146, 148, 154; invisible hand, 367, 368; normative theory of, 367; welfare, 81, 162, 260, 297, 309

State of nature, 17, 18, 98, 104, 107, 116, 117, 176

Statutory law, 115, 116

Steedman, Ian, 244

Steiner, Hillel, 244-65

Stewart, Justice, 171

Stillman, Peter G., 130-67

Stoics, 96

Succession, 110, 114, 117, 120

Suffrage, property qualifications for, 7-8

Sutherland, Graham, 16

Sweden, 297-98, 305

Sympathy, morality of, 309-10

System of needs, 132, 135, 136, 146, 162

Takings clause, 329, 330, 331, 335, 336, 344-45, 346, 349, 351-53, 357, 362, 363-64, 365, 366, 369

Taxes and taxation, 43-44, 49, 54, 180-81, 191, 207, 293, 295, 296, 297, 379, 380, 381; as taking, 330-31, 362, 364

Taylorism, 162

Ten Commandments, 176

Term, absence of, 191

Territoriality, 200-201, 210

Theory of Justice, A (Rawls), 4, 81

Thing(s): "-in-itself," 139; intangible, 104, 122, 125; "invisible," 121-22; -ownership, 73-74, 76-81; rights in, 69,

70, 102; will and, 97, 136, 140

Third Reform Act (1884), 7

Thomas, Robert Paul, 299, 300

Thurow, Lester C., 296

Title, 113. *See also* Native title

Tito, 290

Tocqueville, Alexis de, 21, 132

"Tragedy of the Commons, The" (Hardin), 174

Tragic Choices (Calabresi and Bobbitt), 358

Transfers, 104, 105, 125, 207–9, 251; by consent, 105, 110, 111, 113, 120–21, 125

Transmissibility, 191, 192, 209, 211, 226

Treatises of Government (Locke), 9, 19–20, 89, 104

Trespass, 119

Tribe, Laurence, 171–72

Trusts, 50, 51, 56, 70, 191. *See also* Spendthrift trust

Unger, Roberto Mangabeira, 291, 309–10, 312

United States, 7, 46, 126, 297; state constitutions, 73

U.S. Constitution, 21, 43–44, 181, 337, 338, 360, 366–67, 369, 377, 379–80, 382; Fifth Amendment, 43, 44, 328, 251 (*see also* Takings clause); Fourteenth Amendment, 43; Fourth Amendment, 43, 44

U.S. Supreme Court, 72, 171, 336

"Universal Declaration of Human Rights," 171, 172, 176, 177

Universality thesis, 198–200, 224–25, 226–27

Un-Scientific language, 355

Use, 97–99, 117, 125, 190, 192; innocent, 206; prohibition of harmful, 191, 206; vulnerability of, 205–7, 213. *See also* Land use

Usufructuary property, 117

Utilitarianism, 176, 179–80, 182, 183, 223, 229–33, 236–38, 244, 250, 334, 341–42, 345, 346–47, 348, 363; evolutionary, 293–94, 315; rule, 342, 344, 347

Utilitarianism (Mill), 237

Utility, 108–9, 111–14, 123, 125, 193, 194

Utopian communities, 222

Van der Veen, Robert, 244

Virginia Declaration of Rights, 177

Vocation, 136, 145, 146

Vogel, Ursula, 244

Vonnegut, Kurt, 14

Wage labor, 142, 147, 152, 155, 161

Walden Two (Skinner), 162

Waste law, 41

Wealth, 131, 147, 148, 154, 163, 313, 317, 380–81; of communist society, 157–58

Weber, 372

Welfare rights, 171, 362–63, 364

Western society, 31, 32, 45, 58, 131, 140, 161–62, 163, 200, 207, 275, 282, 283, 300, 307–8

Whelan, Frederick G., 101–29

Wiles, Peter, 300, 302, 308

Will, 15, 160; collective, 16;

dissolving of, 16; expression
or objectification of, 96–97,
98, 132–45
Winch, Peter, 240
Wittfogel, Karl, 21
Wittgenstein, Ludwig, 187,
226, 227, 231, 239–40, 351,
365

Yugoslavia, 298, 300, 301, 302,
307, 314

Zoning and planning, 42, 44,
50, 52, 54